Erik Durschmied

Erik Durschmied was born in Vienna in 1930. After the Second World War he emigrated to Canada. A television war correspondent for the BBC and CBS, he covered every major crisis, from Vietnam, Iran, Iraq, Belfast, Beirut, Chile, to Cuba and Afghanistan. Winner of numerous awards, *Newsweek* wrote 'Durschmied is a supremely gifted reporter who has transformed the media he works in', and *Le Monde* said, 'He's survived more battles than any living general'. He has recently been appointed Professor of Military History at the Military Academy of Austria. Erik Durschmied's previous books are: *The Hinge Factor*, *The Weather Factor* and *Whisper of the Blade*. He lives in Paris and Provence with his family.

Also by Erik Durschmied

The Hinge Factor
The Weather Factor
Whisper of the Blade

The Hinges of Battle

How Chance and Incompetence Have Changed the Face of History

Erik Durschmied

CORONET BOOKS
Hodder & Stoughton

First published in Great Britain in 2002 by Hodder and Stoughton
First published in paperback in 2002 by Hodder and Stoughton
A division of Hodder Headline

A Coronet paperback

3 5 7 9 10 8 6 4 2

A CIP catalogue record for this title is available
from the British Library

ISBN 0 340 81978 2

Typeset in Sabon by Palimpsest Book Production Limited,
Polmont, Stirlingshire
Printed and bound in Great Britain by
Clays Ltd, St Ives plc

Hodder and Stoughton
A division of Hodder Headline
338 Euston Road
London NW1 3BH

For Annelise

Contents

Acknowledgements

The editorial team and military experts who helped me on my first two books in the series, *The Hinge Factor* and *The Weather Factor*, have assisted me once again in taking a further look at battles which have influenced world history. I have travelled afar to visit the places described in the book, spoken to the survivors of Stalingrad and Diên Biên Phu, checked the archives in libraries from London to Moscow, Istanbul, Stalingrad, Hanoi, Dublin, Vienna, Paris and West Point.

The earliest accounts of Attila's *chevauchée* were kept by the Church, amended to portray the deeds of its heroic bishops, and thus paid little or no attention to tactical details. Constantinople was easier to research, since it took place a thousand years later and military reporting had already become an art. There was no shortage of Napoleonic literature. The 'last stand scenario' of Custer's cavalry, of British regiments at Isandhlwana and Rorke's Drift, were well documented at the time. The Rising at Dublin was almost contemporary. And as for Gleiwitz, Stalingrad and Diên Biên Phu, there are still some survivors able to tell their stories.

In the winter of 1983, I received a surprise invitation from the Communist regime in Afghanistan to cover the ongoing war from their side (and that of their Soviet allies). After eight weeks 'in-country' with Afghans and Russians, it left me with a general impression of a war that couldn't be won by sophisticated modern means. The confrontation was never one of two armies, but a struggle of two worlds separated in time and space by a thousand years. After the dramatic events of September 2001 and its military response, we added a chapter at the end of this book concerning Afghanistan and a frightful blunder that took place there 150 years ago. During my stay in 1983 I discovered the full story of the disastrous British retreat from Kabul in 1842.

I owe much gratitude to the many who have offered me strategic advice or personal accounts, and the librarians in state and private libraries who helped me find historic archival material and ancient manuscripts. I've talked to participants and survivors, independent observers and geostrategists. Everyone gave much of their valuable time to fill in gaps, tell their stories or offer good counsel. They supplied unsurpassed experience and cool historic judgment. I am also deeply indebted to all those who applied their renowned historical, military or editorial skills and shared so much in the preparation of this book: Roland Philipps and Luigi Bonomi for their advice in planning the book; General Pierre Gallois (Diên Biên Phu and modern armament); Colonel Ken Hamburger (American military history); Robert Kee (Ireland); and Ailie Geddes, whose criticism has been pertinent. To them, and all the many who helped make this book possible, go my special thanks.

As for historical errors, I accept all responsibility. I wasn't present when Attila turned left; I've only read about it. In the final analysis, it didn't matter which way he turned. What did matter was that he lost the battle.

E.D.
Domaine de Valensole, France
Summer 2001

Prologue

The Truth, and Nothing but the Truth

'He is come to open
The purple testament of bleeding war . . .'
William Shakespeare, *King Richard II*

On 14 October 1973, a week into the Arab–Israeli War, we heard rumours – it should be stated that wars and rumours are like mustard and hot dogs; they always go together – about a significant clash between Israeli and Egyptian tank forces in the Sinai desert. We headed south in our rental car and had just passed a number of convoys when we arrived at a major crossroads. There were no signs such as would be expected in a war, like 'Military Traffic Only' – not even a 'Danger – minefield!' Just a lonely military policeman directing traffic. We thought it quite normal when he stopped us. After all, his country was at war and we were running around armed with nothing more lethal than a press pass. He asked politely: 'Where to?'

'The tank battle.'

'Ah, yes. The tank battle,' said he. 'Well, if you want to see burning tanks, take this road,' and he directed us on to the road leading off to the left. He was absolutely right. Within an hour we stumbled upon an amazing sight – a desert floor littered with the shells of burning Egyptian tanks.

Ten years later, in another part of the world during another war, I had a drink with an Israeli colleague who, at the time of the Yom Kippur War, was in Israeli intelligence, looking after the foreign press. We talked about 1973 and I told him the story of the policeman at the intersection who had pointed us in the direction of the burning Egyptian tanks. My journalist friend smiled before he admitted: 'I know all about it. We put him there.'

'You did?'

'You see, had you driven straight on, you would have seen more burning tanks – only these were ours.'

This only goes to show what cleverly applied 'psychological warfare' can achieve with the media. The fact is, we did get our scoop and reported on it, but we missed the real story.

So what is the real story? How much is hidden behind the thin screen of 'whose bread I eat, his song I sing'? If we cannot perceive a war's truth, standing right in front of it, how can we possibly tell what really took place in the days when most bards believed in war as a glorious adventure and memorialised events with romantic conceit? We eagerly read their accounts on granite steles, on yellowed parchment, or watch events on inflammable rolls of nitrate film – and we believe that we are actually standing next to them in battle. Despite the horrors of war, their reports were often incorrigibly optimistic; observing the worst that men could do to one another, they wrote about heroism and valour, and believed in the best of humanity. They were not naïve, but they were certainly hopeful.

For three millennia, the course of recorded history was shaped by epic conflicts, sometimes small but decisive, sometimes with the pounding step of mighty forces as they marched against each other to the drumbeat of warlords. Battles were fought and battles were won. Some by brilliance, many by minor but significant quirks of fate. Many will argue that mere chance alone does not direct the flow of human destiny, but few will deny that warfare has never been an exact science, and its outcome depended frequently on a series of coincidences, bad luck or outright blunders. Everything is simple in war, but then suddenly the simplest thing becomes difficult. War is one of the great tests that separate planning from execution. Courage or cowardice, energy or weakness, strength or impotence, intellect or imbecility – all play a vital role. Then there is always something called 'the chance factor' – the proverbial racing car that runs out of fuel yards before it crosses the finishing line. So it was with mortal combat. Too often the reason why wars were lost was that someone bungled his chance when he thought the battle won.

The concept of absolute war is the concept of absolute violence. 'War is the province of danger, and therefore courage above all things is the first quality of a warrior . . .' wrote Clausewitz, the father of modern strategy. His method was to define the real nature of war and then compare it with warfare as soldiers practised it. French colonel Ardant du Picq stated: 'The human heart is the starting point in all matters pertaining to war. Centuries have not changed human nature. Passion, instincts, among the most powerful one of self-preservation, may be manifested in various ways . . . Fear! There are soldiers who do not know it, but they are rare. The mass shudders – because you cannot suppress the flesh.' He ended with a key phrase: 'Let us then study man in battle – for it is he who really fights!'[1]

It is true that all men are afraid on the battlefield, but most, despite their fear, remain products of their culture and their value system.[2] It is equally true that it is the individual who decides the issue and that courage, imagination, will and energy are vital ingredients in doing battle, but not always the decisive factor in achieving victory. Because if something unexpected intervenes, a general is suddenly plagued by

1 A. Du Picq, *Battle Studies*, New York 1921.
2 General S.L.A. Marshall, *Men against Fire*, New York 1947.

doubts. And when uncertainty enters the equation it will invariably lead to disaster. That moment is the 'Hinge of Battle'.

1

Flagellum Dei – the Scourge of God

7 September, AD 451 – Attila the Hun

'Put, oh Lord, a fear onto them
so the barbarians will know that they are human!'
Bishop St Nicaise of Rheims, beheaded by Attila in AD 451

'Praecipuus Hunnorum Rex Attila
Patre genitus Mundzuco
Fortissimorum gentium dominus!'
(Thou, greatest of Huns, King Attila
Son of Mundzuc
Master of the mightiest people!)
Eulogy by Attila's warriors during his funeral, AD 453

'I've heard it being said . . .' is how one of the great epic poems begins. The *Hildebrandlied*, which fathered the *Nibelungensaga*, was written four hundred years after the event. The setting of this blood-dripping drama is Frankenland (France). The main cast consists of heroes and villains – the good, the bad, and the beastly. The epic sings of pure maidens and jilted love, treachery and betrayal, shining heroism and dark villainy. There is Siegfried, young, blond, handsome and utterly naïve. A buxom blonde in body-fitting armour, Brunnhilde, who is actually Siegfried's aunt, is so impressed by his valour that she falls madly in love and makes his life miserable with tantrums of jealousy once she discovers that her hero is in love with the fair Kriemhild, sister of the Burgundian king. The jilted Brunnhilde marries this king, then seduces his knight Hagen, a sinister character lurking in the shadows, and persuades him to murder Siegfried. End of part one – but fear not, there is always a second part. It comes in the form of retribution, as hell hath no fury like a woman in pain. Siegfried's widow Kriemhild is willing to go to any lengths in order to achieve vengeance for the brutal murder of her beloved. She consents to marry King Etzel, a brutal overlord, assassin and tyrant, and conspires to have her own tribe, the Nibelungen (Burgundians), brutally done to death by an act of treachery. She invites them to partake in her wedding feast. That's when the dark Hagen appears back on the scene. At last, the sinister man turns into a great Germanic hero and gives his life in the defence of his tribe and his king. Finally, Kriemhild kills King Etzel on their wedding night, and the curtain comes down.

'I've heard it being said . . .' – every drama has its true origin, every tale is based on a cast of real characters and events. It is the only source which we have at our disposal in order to reconstruct the events of a distant past.

There did indeed exist a Brunichilde (Brunnhilde), a Sigibert (Sigmund) and a Gundicarius, King of the Burgundians (King Gunther); all were somehow involved in a terrible blood feud that broke out among the Frankish tribes. There was a King Theodoric (Dietrich von Bern). And most assuredly was there a King Etzel, only he wasn't called Etzel. His real name, one that instilled terror and fear, was Attila the Hun, Flagellum Dei, the Scourge of God.

The Huns and their cruel master, Attila, are more fully represented in the memory of the Western world than any other tribe of nomads. 'The Huns!' – a name that still evokes with force the terrors which have haunted the spirit of man since ancient days; a wild, brutal tribe which has left to history a name that has gone down in infamy. Nothing is known about their origin, or their name, 'Hun', which could have originated from *Hiong-nu*, Chinese for 'common slave'. They may have been part of the Turanian warrior tribes from the Altai mountains of central Asia that Emperor Hwang-te tried to stop when he ordered the Great Wall to be built (258 BC).

When Rome was at its zenith, their emperors came and went; all were powerful, greedy, brutal, lecherous or sanctimonious, and all were masters of the Roman universe, which they ruled with the help of auxiliary armies. Augustus, Tiberius, Claudius, Trajan, Hadrian, Marcus Aurelius, Diocletian – all were 'heathens' until Constantine, following his victory over his rival Maxentius at Saxa Rubra (27 October, AD 312), created an historic watershed by establishing Catholicism as the state religion, and thereby made it into the world religion. The split between East Rome and West Rome became a political reality and a new rivalry was born. Soon East Rome took the sun away from the West.

While the West Roman Empire was involved in bloody internal conflicts to regain its former glory and power, a new threat loomed from the East – the nomadic tribe of the Huns. Soon their herds grazed on the land between the Baltic and the Black Sea. Inside the boundaries of this rapidly extending empire security reigned, but this did not extend to the peripheral nations, forever under the shadow of yet another sudden advance by the brutal rider hordes. Surprise, cunning and mobility were the Huns' major assets. Their combat superiority lay in their incredible mobility and their hit-and-run tactics. They never offered a set battle, never went for man-to-man fighting, but circled their enemy and buried him under a shower of arrows from bows made mainly of horn, as their steppes were treeless. For this form of attack they depended entirely on their small ponies, agile and manoeuvrable. Faced by the much heavier horses of Western riders, good only for straight-line formation charges, the Huns wheeled their ponies at will and dashed off to sting once more from the flanks. In whirlwind advances and tactical retreats they wore down their cumbersome enemies time and time again.

But their strength was also their problem. Ponies needed grass to feed on, and that was not always easily available. Therefore they had constantly to keep on the move. The 'Hun Plague' began in 395, when the first hordes devastated the lands of the Fertile Crescent along the Euphrates, and from there advanced into Syria and Armenia. 'The whole East trembled, for swarms of Huns had broken forth from the far distant Sea of Azov, the icy Don River and from behind the mountains of the Caucasus,' wrote St Jerome. 'They filled the whole earth with slaughter and panic alike as they flitted hither and thither on their swift horses. By their speed they outstripped rumour, and they took pity neither upon religion nor rank nor age nor wailing childhood.'[1]

It was at this time that a message reached Rome that the Burgundians, a Germanic warrior tribe of the Rhine region near Worms, had invaded Rome's Northern Provinces and were warring with the Belgians. The Roman commander, Aetius, pressed for reinforcements, dispatched an urgent plea for military assistance to the King of the Huns, Oktar, to which the Hun agreed in exchange for copious land grants. Under Roman command, the Huns took up arms against the Burgundians. 'At this time, Aetius marched against Gundicarius, King of the Burgundians, who pleaded for peace, but was not granted it and he and his people were slaughtered by the Huns.'[2] The Burgundians were massacred and the survivors fled into the wooded hills of what today is

1 F.A. Thompson, *A History of Attila and the Huns*, London 1948.
2 Prosperus Titus, papal scribe of Pope Leo I, writing around AD 435.

Burgundy. With the help of the Huns, Legate Flavius Aetius had managed to drown the rebellion in Burgundian blood. But in doing so he committed a fatal blunder when in 435 he led the Hunnish host across the Rhine and showed them the splendours and treasures of the West.

The Burgundians, few as they were, would not forget the massacre; they trained and armed themselves to avenge their people. This was to lead to an incident in which history and legend interweave. 'As one night the King of the Huns Uptaros [Oktar] ate and drank so much that he died, the Burgundians set upon the leaderless Huns, slaughtered a great number, and, being only 3,000, achieved a great victory.'[3] This bloody event was immortalised in the Nibelungenlied, the great Germanic epic.

Strengthened by an influx of auxiliary legions formed from Huns under Roman centurions, all went relatively well under the Roman Emperor Theodosius. The tribes provided warriors for Rome, and in exchange their king received his yearly ransom of gold. But then an accident occurred that changed the entire scenario. On 26 July 450, while on a hunt, Theodosius was thrown from his horse and killed. General Markianos (428–78), who made his way to the throne via the bed of Theodosius's daughter Pulcheria, succeeded him. Rather foolishly, Markianos stopped paying the yearly tribute to the Hun king.

During a thunderstorm in 433, Hun King Rugila had been killed by lightning and replaced by his two nephews, Bleda and Attila. In 445, Attila murdered his brother Bleda and usurped the crown as the Huns' undisputed leader. A born warrior, short of stature, with a thick neck and eyes that sent out flashes of lightning, he was not only cruel but also extremely smart. He nurtured ambitions other than to serve as a mercenary surrogate for Rome's armies. His opportunity came when Empress Placida's daughter Honoria,

[3] Socrates Scolasticus, a papal scribe, only tells us what happened, not why.

a nubile seventeen-year-old, got herself pregnant by one of the servant boys in her household. To avoid the royal scandal, she was expelled from court. In her fury, she offered a ring and her portrait to Attila, begging him to marry her. Attila had no desire to bed the daughter of a Roman emperor, but he could see the advantage in her proposal. He claimed Honoria as his bride, and with her the dowry – nothing small, just half of the Western Empire! Quite understandably, the emperor told him to go and ride his horse somewhere else.

In 450, the Ripuarian Frankish King Chlodion died and a quarrel over the succession broke out between his two sons, Merovée and Gundebaud. Merovée was quicker off the mark and turned to Rome, which left Gundebaud no choice other than to ask Attila for his military assistance. This demand from Gaul, plus his claim for Honoria's dowry and the emperor's refusal to pay the yearly ransom, gave Attila reason to invade the Gallo-Roman territories. And so it came to be that in 450 the Huns saddled up and went upstream along the Danube, headed for the heart of Europe. Nothing stood between Attila's hordes and the Rhine; the thinly manned Roman garrisons at the gateway of the Danube, Carnuntuum and Vindobona (Vienna), fled behind the river. Because of the Huns' threat to the culture of the Occident, a strange coalition was formed. This was no simple matter, nor was the man who undertook to put it into place a simple ambassador. He was the *de facto* master of a puppet emperor and he was the empire's final hope. Flavius Aetius, 'the last of the Romans', was called upon to turn the tide and change the course of the inevitable.

Flavius Aetius was born in Silistria. His father, a Roman officer on garrison duty, was murdered by his own troops during a rebellion. Young Aetius achieved the rank of a *comes domesticorum et cura palatii* (imperial secretary), and was dispatched to the court of King Alarich of the Visigoth as a Roman hostage (407–10).[4] In 410 an event took place which left a permanent mark, not only on Aetius but also on all of Western civilisation. Alarich's Visigoth went on a rampage, which ended in Rome. Bereft of all defences, Rome fell and the Visigoth devastated the city. After plundering its treasures, they took off. Aetius swore to himself that the Visigoth would never again be allowed to get near Rome, a promise he was to remember forty years later. By 423, at a time when the Eastern and the Western Empires were fighting over control of Europe, Flavius Aetius, now back in Italy, was put in command of Emperor Johannes' Imperial Guard, a key position on the way to the top. His rapid rise was due to his good relationship with the Huns, indispensable as allies for the Western Empire in safeguarding its predominant role. The armies of East Roman General Ardas had overrun upper Italy, captured Emperor Johannes in Ravenna and then cut off his head. With an army of Hunnish auxiliaries, Aetius defeated the Eastern troops and put a child emperor, Placidus Valentinianus, on Rome's throne. Aetius followed this up with a palace revolt (446) and took supreme power as 'consul for life'. He used the Hun auxiliaries to usurp and suppress. But the price he had to pay for this help was heavy; Rome ceded Savia Pannonia, the lands between the Save and Danube (today's Yugoslavia and Hungary), as a permanent homestead for the Huns. With this single step, Aetius had opened for Attila the way into the heart of Europe. When Attila marched in 450, Aetius found himself stripped of his auxiliary help and too weak to put up any resistance. He switched from the role of conqueror to that of intriguer, a role he was to maintain for all the years of his reign as dictator of Rome.

The danger for Rome had always come from the north. At that time there existed several belligerent Alemanic tribes,

[4] Hostages were not exchange prisoners, but more a kind of high-ranking official safeguard against hostilities.

some of which had supplied Rome with mercenaries for centuries – for example, the Vandals of King Gaiseric. Wherever he went, Gaiseric acted without pity, leaving to humanity the word 'vandalism'. But the main danger was always the Goths, a huge mass of tall, blond warriors from the northern part of Russia and Scandinavia. Moving from their original Gotland, they had split up into two distinct factions, the Ostrogoth (Eastern Goths) and the Visigoth (Western Goths). Rome, in their endeavour to 'divide and rule', had managed for a long time to keep these two groups at loggerheads, like quarrelling brothers. Both their great warrior masses were hovering dangerously close to Rome's vital water barriers, the Ostrogoth north of the Danube and the Visigoth along the Loire. The Ostrogoth, under their Prince Walamir, settled in those eastern parts of Germany that had established contact with the Huns. As allies to the Hun, they now presented the greatest danger. That left the Visigoth under King Theodoric, whose kingdom of Gothia (today Aquitaine) bordered Roman Gaul and would be endangered should the Huns cross the Rhine.

When Attila's immense host reached the impassable Black Forest, he split his forces in two. The faster Gepids, another nomadic tribe, crossed the Rhine near Basle and moved from there in a south-westerly direction towards Besançon, while the much larger northern wing, made up mostly of Huns under Attila himself, crossed the Rhine unopposed at Trier and from there took the Roman road towards Mettis (Metz). While the Roman garrisons folded their tents and silently stole away, the Huns crossed the hapless countryside, leaving in their wake a swath of fire, destruction and death. Cologne, Mainz, Trier, Strasbourg, Amiens and Tournai were sacked. Metz was left without defences but for a bishop and his monks. The Huns entered the town on Easter Saturday, 7 April, AD 451.[5] 'They threw fire upon the city, killed one

[5] This is the first and only confirmed date of the Hun invasion of Gaul, related to a noted religious holiday. It was from this date that all subsequent dates were worked out.

and all with the tip of their swords and even murdered the priest on the holy altar.'[6]

After the sack of Metz, the Hunnish hordes set out on the road to Lutetia Parisiorum (Paris). On their way they had to pass the major city of Rheims, a sacred place for all Catholic Gauls. The town was undefended but for a heroic and courageous bishop, Nicaise (St Nicaise). He had received a note from Consul Aetius instructing him to bar the doors to the Hun, but Nicaise knew that such an action was hopeless. His few hundred armed citizens would achieve nothing but a massacre of the town's people in the face of half a million approaching Huns. When Attila rode through the open gate, he was met by Bishop Nicaise, barring his way with a cross.

'What message was it that Aetius did send to you, Bishop?' demanded Attila.

'If I have burned his letter so was this not to inform you of its content,' replied a defiant Bishop Nicaise.

'You shall pay for this.'

'He who lives under the claw of a tiger can only ask for the animal's leniency. But hear me, Attila, I'm not asking for clemency because only my God can grant it.'

'This we shall see,' responded Attila, and promptly ordered the bishop's head cut off.

'Put, oh Lord, a fear on to them so the barbarians will know that they are human!' said the holy man who was soon declared a saint, before his head rolled down the gutter. In the end, it was up to a pious and exquisitely beautiful woman, Eutropia, to stand up to the Huns. 'By her purity she stopped the Huns from their murderous ways and they fled from the city in great panic.'[7] Before the host reached Paris they sacked another important town, Durocortorum Catalaunum (Châlons-sur-Marne). After several thousand of its citizens were slaughtered, Attila ordered the establishment

[6] Gregoire de Tours, Bishop of Tours, a contemporary monk and scribe, in his *Histoire des Francs*.
[7] Ibid.

The Catalaunian Fields
7 September, AD 451

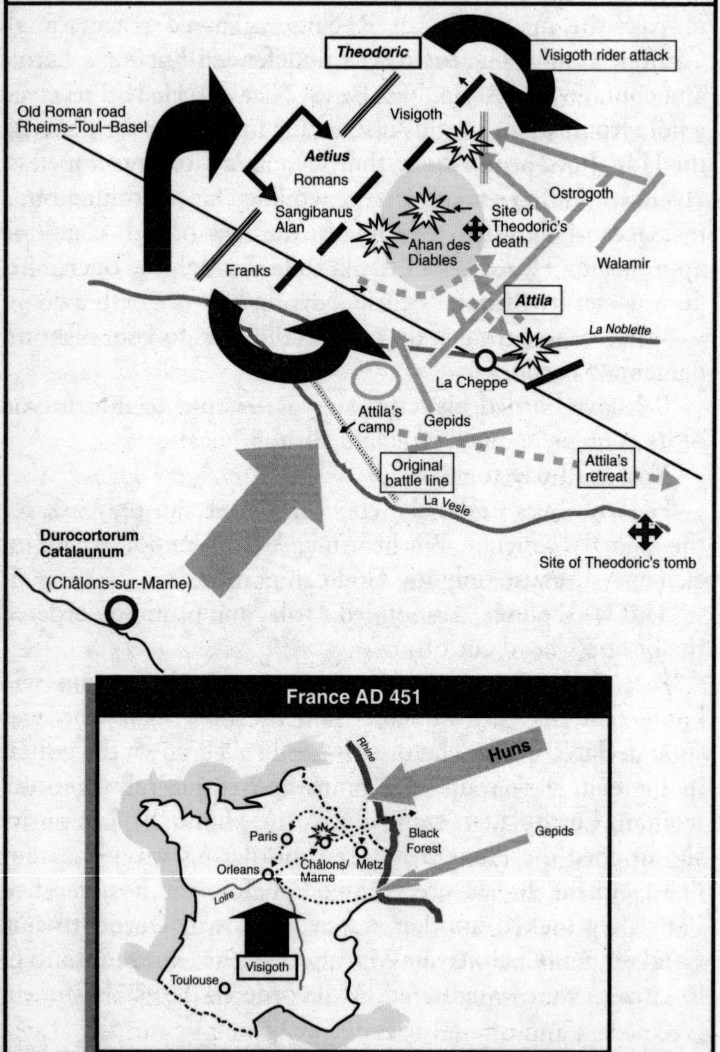

Theodoric
Visigoth rider attack
Old Roman road
Rheims–Toul–Basel
Visigoth
Aetius
Romans
Ostrogoth
Sangibanus
Alan
Site of
Theodoric's
death
Ahan des
Diables
Walamir
Franks
Attila
La Noblette
La Cheppe
Attila's
camp
Gepids
Original
battle line
Attila's
retreat
La Vesle
Durocortorum
Catalaunum
(Châlons-sur-Marne)
Site of Theodoric's tomb

France AD 451

Rhine
Huns
Paris
Black
Forest
Gepids
Orleans
Châlons/
Marne
Metz
Loire
Visigoth
Toulouse

of a permanent supply camp there. This town, controlling the Marne crossings, was to play a vital role in the months to come. From there, the Huns bypassed Troyes and Sens without attacking them and moved on Paris.

Before Paris they faced another encounter with a saintly woman. Sainte Geneviève was a maiden of seventeen from the neighbouring village of Nanterre who roused the women of the city to shame their men, ready to take to their boats and flee before the terrible 'Scourge of God', into burning the bridges to the island from the mainland and then taking up arms in defence of the town. Great quantities of food were stored inside the walled city and all ferry-boats were sunk. The siege of Paris, an island in the midst of the wide Seine, would have been too long and costly, and therefore Attila abandoned the attempt. 'By the faith of a maiden the city was saved . . .' (Sainte Geneviève is still the patron saint of Paris).

Attila's army was headed for the Loire. Its advance was slow, the speed of the whole force dictated by the slowest ox wagon. The troops dragged their feet; discipline was lax. There were sporadic attacks on the rearguard. It is astounding that up to this point there was no sign of Aetius or his legions, nor any indication that he really intended to put a stop to the Hunnish juggernaut. Attila must certainly no longer have counted on serious Roman resistance; it should have come much earlier, on the wild waters of the Lech, on the wide Rhine, or in the narrow defiles of the Ardennes mountains. Safe in this belief, he set out from Paris for France's key to its interior, Orleans, the town bridging the Loire. For a moment it looked as if the town would be handed to him without a fight. The King of the Alan, Sangibanus, had migrated with his people from his native Valence to settle around Orleans. Faced with the threat of annihilation from Attila's hordes, he panicked and offered to hand over the town to the Huns without resistance, but this was prevented by men loyal to their warrior bishop. 'The King of the Alan, Sangibanus, had spoken from fear when he offered Attila to open for him the doors of the town of Orleans, in which he and his men were at the time. When Aetius and Theodoric heard of this, they ordered a high wall built around the town and put the Alan under the observation of others.'[8]

Attila knew that the gates would be closed against him, and that in the town was a bishop who promised to make life difficult for him – the Bishop of Orleans, Anianus (St Aignan), a born Alan from Vienne (Rhone), 'a pious and clever man who put his trust in God'.[9] Attila couldn't bypass the town as he had done Paris. He needed the bridge to lead his army across the wide Loire. Also, Orleans would present a permanent threat to his rearguard in case a strategic retreat was called for. Unlike Paris, Aureliana (Orleans) was vital. Attila reached the town in the first week of June 451.[10] Negotiations to allow the Huns to cross the bridges came to naught and Attila laid siege to the town. For five weeks, his rams pounded the walls; his arrows killed hundreds of defenders. Bishop Anianus walked around the crumbling walls carrying holy relics. Just like the maiden Joan one thousand years later, speaking from the very same ramparts, he kept up the townspeople's spirits. 'We fight because we must hold until the Lord send us help in this great hour of need. It will come, I know, the Lord has so promised. We sit astride the only good road south. Until we fall, Attila can take no great force in search of our friends. They will gather and defeat the evil the Hun has brought about our land. We must buy that time for them.'

But this time was running out fast.

* * *

8 Ibid.

9 Ibid. And in the *Vita Aniani*, the life of Bishop Anianus.

10 Earlier estimates gave the date for the decisive battle at the Catalaunian Fields as 20 June. This is virtually impossible, since the distance between Orleans and Châlons is too great and no host, travelling by ox cart, could have covered the distance in time.

What had happened to the Roman armies the bishop so fervently believed in during all this time? Why did Aetius leave his Gaul provinces undefended? His legions were not just some slapdash put-together force, but made up from veterans of the Roman Army. There had been ample possibilities to defend Gaul from the invasion – along the Rhine, in the narrow valleys of the Ardennes – and yet Aetius did nothing. That is the great historic mystery, and the only explanation is that Aetius had planned it that way. He was counting on the fact that somewhere in the depths of Gaul the two masses of barbarians, Hun and Goth, would meet and pulverise each other, thereby leaving the road open for Rome's continued world supremacy. The Goth were just as much of a menace to Rome as the barbarous Hun. It was a devilish plan, but one absolutely within the strategic grasp of someone like Aetius: to lure the Huns towards the kingdom of the Visigoth, those blond, bearded giants of a warrior nation, and an eternal threat to Rome's borders. By betraying both sides, first his erstwhile allies, the Huns, and thereafter the Visigoth, Aetius hoped to re-establish Rome's supremacy. And that can be the only valid reason why he did not act sooner. Only once the direction of the Hun's advance became clear – Orleans, on the very doorstep of the land of the Visigoth – did he set his scheme in motion.

Attila had played beautifully into his hands. Since the Huns had appeared on the scene, Gaul had known no peace. His hordes had ravaged the lands, burned the crops, killed the people and plundered the cities. Its women were raped, its girls sold into slavery. Its villagers were dead, of hunger, by the sword or from the plague. The Huns has so enslaved the provinces that survivors from villages had come with their scythes and sickles to join the Roman Army and to have a go at the enemy, though they knew that they would die in the attempt. Until now Aetius had offered no great battle because with what he had at his disposal he couldn't expect to win. But finally he was ready to catch Attila in an unfavourable position and destroy him in one great battle. But for that he needed the Visigoth's mighty force.

Aetius knew that he was faced with a most difficult mission; the Goths had grave suspicions about the true intentions of the Romans, who governed the world by proxy and let their *feoderati* (auxiliaries) take the casualties and do their fighting for them. But now, with the Huns at the Loire border of the Visigoth kingdom, the situation had changed. Now each needed the other. Roman Consul Aetius, accompanied by Senator Avitus (who became Western Emperor from 454 to 456), went to Tolosa (Toulouse) to meet with the wisest of the Visigoth, King Theodoric, a giant in his seventies with a flowing white beard. It took a silver-tongued approach to convince the Goth.

> Common sense orders you, oh noble king, to come to an alliance with Rome and face up to the tyrant of the Earth. He doesn't even look for a reason to start a war, he just does anything he likes. He satisfies his ambition with brutality, his arrogance with licentious unrestraint, he shows a total disregard for right and law, he is even the enemy of nature. He, who has sinned against all of humanity, deserves only the hatred of us all. Recall your own setbacks against these Huns, they all came about by treachery. Can you bear that shame any longer? You command a mighty nation in arms. Therefore consider a way to escape another duplicity and ally yourself with Rome's legions. Rush to the help of those who depend on you and your might. How much we seek such a union you can see by the evil scheme of our common enemy.

The vote by the king's nobles was divided; some of his advisers were in favour, while Theodoric's eldest son, Thorismund, was against. Having listened to their counsel, Theodoric thought matters over for a long time before he finally gave Aetius his answer:

> Your wish must be our wish. The Goths have no choice. The animosity of our people with the men of Attila carries deep and proud warriors cannot forget the shame. Now we will chase him wherever he turns. May he show off with his overbearing claim for victory over other mighty tribes, the Goth nation will know how to stand up to the one with the evil spirit. A war is not difficult to lead if it is based on honourable grounds. Nothing can faze the warrior who is sure of the favour of the One and Divine Majesty.[11]

Only after Aetius had departed with an assurance of mutual assistance did Thorismund ask his father: 'What about this Roman Aetius? Can you trust him?'

Theodoric slapped his sword. 'Yes, the length of this blade.'[12]

At Orleans, Bishop Anianus once again climbed the wall to assess the situation. Great chunks had been knocked from the enclosure protecting the bridges. Their situation was hopeless. 'And it was the third time he climbed the wall and decided on their final stand, when they saw a great cloud of dust in the far distance. It was the Visigoth King Theodoric with his son Thorismund in company of Aetius – and in a short but bloody battle they threw the Huns back and delivered the town of Aureliana. And Attila and his hordes fled the field and raced to the fields of Campus Mauriacus and there prepared for battle.'[13]

The Huns weren't expecting, and therefore were not prepared to fight, a defensive battle; nothing can be more decisive

11 H. Homeyer, *Attila der Hunnenkönig von seine Zeitgenossen dargestellt*, Berlin 1951.

12 By far the best source for anything on Goths is Jordanes, an autodidact Christian Goth, who wrote two monumental works, *De originae actibusque Getarum*, or *The Origins and Deeds of the Goths*, around AD 551.

13 Ibid.

than a siege army suddenly finding itself under attack from the open rear.[14] It is like the bite of a hungry dog into a mighty lion's neck. 'Driven from street to street, beaten down by stones hurled at them from the roofs of the dwellings, the Huns didn't know what was to become of them before Attila sounded the retreat. Such took place on 14 June 451 and the civilisation of the West was saved from total destruction.'[15]

After his defeat at Orleans, Attila was left with three options: a planned retreat using his hit-and-run tactics to offer delaying measures, running fast and disappearing into the Hungarian steppes before the enemy had time to follow up on their victory, or facing Aetius and Theodoric in a great, final battle to avenge his shameful setback at Orleans. Attila chose to stand and fight. 'At this point, Attila considered a fast retreat, but this was more shameful than death itself. So he decided to inquire with his seers . . .'

Attila, like all barbaric rulers, never undertook a combat without first consulting his seers (Hitler was somewhat similar). The Hun shamans slaughtered an animal, studied its innards stretched out over a heated thighbone, and came to the conclusion that a confrontation would bring about the death of his enemy. Attila took this to be Aetius. 'And his seers told him that, although he might face possible defeat, it would bring about the death of his enemy's leader . . . he chose to begin battle at the ninth hour [after sunrise] to benefit, should the battle end in defeat of the darkness of night . . .'[16]

Attila's reasoning was based on consideration of his principal goal; in order to achieve global hegemony he had to kill the man who stood between him and his rule over the Antique world, Aetius, the Dictator of Rome. Without its charismatic leader, Rome ceased to be a power. Therefore,

14 In 1683, a relatively small force of 50,000 Imperials defeated the Turkish siege army of 200,000 at Vienna.
15 A. Thierry, *L'histoire d'Attila*, Paris 1856.
16 Jordanes.

allowing for possible defeat – and for this reason he would hold off giving battle until late in the day so that he would have the option of escaping in darkness – by killing his adversary he would eventually end up the victor. Gathered around his mainstay, his Huns, were the breakaway Ripuarian Franks of Gundebaud, the Gepids of Ardarich, and the Ostrogoth of Walamir. As battlefield he chose the Campus Mauriacus in the Roman province of Campania (Champagne), a flat plain across the Marne on the Campi Catalaunici[17] – the site that was to go down in the history books as the Catalaunian Fields.

The army Attila was about to face was mighty: Theodoric at the head of his Visigoth host, well armed, well trained and disciplined; Aetius with two and a half Roman legions brought in forced marches from Provincia (Provence) and Upper Italy; and young Prince Merovée, son of King Chlodion, with his Salisian Franks, arch-enemy of his brother Gundebaud's Ripuarian Franks; plus a smattering of allied tribes – Burgundians (who hadn't forgotten their tribe's massacre by the Huns), a large group of Helvetian footguards, and the doubtful Alan contingent under their King Sangibanus. Only months before at Orleans, when Sangibanus had seen the changing tide, he had quickly switched sides. Theodoric didn't trust him and Attila hated him.

When Sangibanus met Aetius, he tried to make the Roman believe that it was strictly due to his non-intervention that Orleans had not been taken. Aetius frowned. 'You had no more power to change the issue after Bishop Anianus shut the gates. With your treachery you've betrayed Attila. He will not easily forget. So you'd better stand and fight for your life.' In fact Sangibanus was more of a liability than an ally, but put in front of reliable troops he and his men would be unable to retreat and would be forced to fight.

17 This is today near the village of La Cheppe, not far from Châlons-sur-Marne.

While the Western coalition partners were gathering their forces between the Loire and the Marne, and showed no great hurry to pursue their enemy, Attila was left with plenty of time to prepare his defences. Near Brolium (today Saint Mesmin, in memory of Deacon Memorius) a minor incident occurred King Ardarich of the Gepids, riding as Attila's vanguard, had reached the small River Aube, when he was met by a delegation of seven Catholic priests and monks. Marching at the head, Châlons' *diacon* (deacon), Memorius, carried a silver cross. As he held it up, a ray of sunshine reflected from it, blinding the king's horse, which reared and threw the king. The Gepids saw only their king's distress and the priests confronting him. Without a moment's hesitation, they hacked down six priests; only one managed to escape to relate the story. According to Church annals, this took place on 7 September 451, and thereby the date is known for what was to become a much larger action.

There can be nothing more lethal than the meeting of two hostile brothers. On the morning of the main battle a vanguard of Gundebaud's Ripuarian Franks spied a small contingent of Merovée's Salisian Franks across a brook and splashed across to attack. The initial skirmishers were quickly reinforced by both Frankish hosts. Now Gundebaud committed a fatal blunder. He told his riders to dismount and form a solid line in the face of charging heavy cavalry. With a mighty blast from a war horn, Merovée's cavalry trotted forward, preparing to meet their brothers head on. With a hundred paces to build up momentum, they struck the leading elements of Gundebaud's riders, simply rode over them and drove their enemy back, wheeling away as yet another wave charged through to strike. When that battle was over, the screams of pain from the fallen mingled with shouts of triumph from the victors. The losses were great; at least 15,000 Franks lay dead on the field, including Prince Gundebaud. With him, Attila had lost one of his key participants for the forthcoming confrontation.

In the camp of the victorious Franks there was great rejoicing; everywhere Merovée went, his men cheered him. He could feel a certain pride in that. He had won a battle and it had been worth winning. Because with victory assured, Merovée went on to unite the quarrelling Frankish factions into one great nation. That day on the field of blood he founded a dynasty, the Merovinger, which ruled over the Kingdom of the Franks (France) until the eighth century.[18]

But the two main protagonists still hadn't met. Because of the earlier battle, Aetius and Theodoric had now decided on a crossing of the Noblette higher up, and thereby upset Attila's battle plan, which was to intercept them at the crossing near his entrenched camp. Attila had to shift his contingent to confront the new situation. He refused to give battle; his plan was still to wait for late afternoon. By the early afternoon of 7 September, the opposing forces were lined up and the battle lines set. They were now formed across the Roman road which led from Rheims via Toul to Basel. On the Aetius/Visigoth left wing were the giants of Theodoric; the centre was Sangibanus and his Alan a little to the front of Aetius and his Roman legions. On the right were the Burgundians and the Helvetians, strengthened by the recently victorious Salisian Franks. Behind the line was one Roman legion which Aetius held as a final reserve.

On the opposite side of the plain, Attila set Walamir and the Ostrogoth to face the Visigoth, assuring himself that the two enemy brothers would clash with violence and without pity. There were more Ostrogoth, but the Visigoth were better armed and probably better disciplined. There was another good reason for this disposition: compared with his small, bow-legged Huns, the Goths were true giants, and their heavy chargers, once in full cry, would ride over his lightly mounted Mongol warriors. His fast Gepid rider hordes he planned to send in a flanking attack against the foot-soldiers of the

[18] The Merovingers were supplanted in 751 by the Carolingians.

Roman legions. For his Huns he reserved the special pleasure of going up against the centre of the traitor Sangibanus; this also meant that they would attack the Roman phalanx of shields and spears head on.

Hectic activity erupted around the tent of the Roman commander. He assembled all the leaders around him. 'King Gundicarius, upon the signal of Prefect Ferreolus, pull from the centre and strengthen the left wing . . . King Merovée, do not strengthen the Alan centre, I will do this with my legions, but move your riders also to the left wing and wait for the signal from Legate Maecilius to swing around the Huns . . . The Helvetian will move from the centre towards the right wing, they will then hold the line and while the Visigoth pull out their cavalry . . . King Theodoric, my friend, tonight we shall taste victory together . . .'

Attila was also surrounded by his commanders. He had studied the enemy's battle line. They had their flanks covered by their heavy cavalry, Visigoth and Franks, and there his light Hun riders could not attack. The best place was right in the centre; Sangibanus and his Alan were the least reliable and certainly the weak link. Attila decided to drive his cutting wedge straight at the enemy centre.

> Ha, the Roman has set his line . . . see there, the Alan in the centre . . . Ellak my son, you will go against Sangibanus, he is the weakest and most unreliable ally of the Roman, he shall be the first to die, the traitor and his Alan dogs . . . then we shall tear wide open the centre and roll up the enemy lines . . . King Ardarich, take your riders around the flank of the Franks, harass them enough so they will not attack towards the centre . . . Prince Walamir, ride on my right flank, attack Theodoric . . . drive him against the hammer of my centre, do not lose contact with me . . . now patience, my friends, we shall wait now . . . and then unleash hell!

In the centre of the plain was a rise, not much higher than the surrounding terrain but high enough to offer some advantage for a down-slope rider attack. It was the fight for possession of this hill which started the battle – a rather useless waste of men for a rather meaningless hill. But that was also where Sangibanus held his position. And Attila had sworn that this traitor would be the first to die. Hun cavalry and their accompanying foot-soldiers had formed up in a wedge – riders in first, then the foot-soldiers would fan out and roll up the enemy from the rear.

The sun was past the zenith when Attila raised his battle flag. All along his line the commanders raised theirs. The flag came down. 'Unleash hell!' the commanders cried, repeating their leader's command. A blast from the horn, and the quiet of a moment before was shattered by battle cries. A great mass of horses raced up the gentle slope, heading for the dismounted Alan in the centre. Despite the flights of arrows that created havoc among horses and riders, the Huns drove their ponies in utter frenzy and managed to close in with the Alan's first rank. The impact was terrible; the Alan lost half their men in the initial contact. They put up a desperate struggle, yet the weight of the attackers soon proved decisive. They isolated the Alan into a pocket from which there was only one escape lane, already piled high with bodies and slippery with blood. 'Aetius, help us,' Sangibanus cried out in panic. 'Back! Back!' But they couldn't go back and they couldn't advance. The Alan king saw Attila on his horse, and what he saw was death. Sangibanus was cut off and surrounded. 'Peace,' he yelled, 'I give in . . . back from me . . . pity, Attila . . .' Up on the hill sat a solitary leather-clad rider, staring down on him. 'Pity . . .' was Sangibanus' last word; an arrow pierced his throat and the King of the Alan fell from the saddle. That took the fight out of the Alan, which gave the Huns the opportunity to push their wedge towards the Roman phalanx.

By the time Aetius finally moved one of his legions into

battle, the Huns had taken possession of the summit ridge. With the Alan auxiliaries lying dead before them, his Roman centre took on the full weight of Attila's attack. Still, the Roman legion stood as one man, shield to shield; behind heaps of corpses they faced the renewed onslaught. The Huns attacked from all sides, mounted archers with their short bows maintaining continuous fire on the Roman legions piled up in the centre. Aetius brought up his reserve legion to plug the many holes that appeared in his centre, caused by the ceaseless shower of arrows. Attila now threw everything he had into the fray. A simply overwhelming mass of Huns soon pressed the legionnaires so close together that they could no longer use their lances. They were tiring, fighting on bravely until the centre of their shield wall buckled and they were driven back in great confusion. The Huns drove their massed wedge deeper and deeper into the Roman phalanx until the legions' centre shattered. Aetius waved his hand vigorously and the legions' trumpets sounded a frantic retreat, but for many there was no retreat possible. Now victory was within Attila's grasp.

While this singular slaughter continued in the centre, another fierce battle had erupted on Attila's right wing, where the Ostrogoth had crashed into the Visigoth. Both sides fought like lions and the slaughter was fearsome. For a while the outcome hung in the balance, before the Ostrogoth gained the upper hand. But this pulled them away from Attila's centre and opened a dangerous gap between the right wing and the centre. Attila had backed up his initial wedge by throwing nearly all his remaining Huns against what amounted to hardly a legion and a half of Romans. He was certain that this would decide the outcome, and now he could no longer extricate them to plug the gaping hole between his centre and the Ostrogoth wing. He cursed himself; while that traitor Sangibanus had distracted his attention, he had overlooked the ruse of old Theodoric. It was a trap! While his Huns advanced in the centre, a wall of riders gathered on his flank – Theodoric and his Visigoth giants.

Theodoric saw confusion reigning in the Roman centre. Unless he acted immediately, the battle was surely lost. He issued an order to give way slowly to the onrushing Ostrogoth, to lure them away from Attila.

Walamir, fighting like the god of war, and his Ostrogoth pursued the retreating Visigoth farther and farther. It was a matter of kill or be killed. Attila dispatched a messenger to stop him: 'No more advance, make a slow retreat to get in contact with the centre.' Before Attila's dispatch rider could deliver the urgent message, he was struck down by an arrow. Every minute counted now; every minute the distance between Attila's centre and his right flank widened dangerously. To complicate matters it was getting dark, and in the diffused light fighters could no longer be clearly identified. That's when it happened.

It was at this moment of greatest peril, with both the Romans and the Visigoth in retreat, that the likely outcome of the battle was reversed. While Walamir the Ostrogoth battled on, in the belief that he had the entire Visigoth force before him, Theodoric planned a daring manoeuvre; for this he had to operate a flanking movement around the Ostrogoth, in order to get his heavily armed Visigoth into the press of the Huns' centre. He left a covering screen of Helvetians and dismounted fighters behind and then raced ahead of his massed riders towards Attila's vulnerable flank.

Aetius was conspicuous among his Roman legionnaires in his crimson coat, desperately trying to rebuild the shattered centre in order to stem the flood of Huns pouring through it. For the moment the Huns had pulled back and were milling around the centre, slaughtering his Romans. Shortly they would form up for another charge against his wings. He turned for an instant from his own battle to look for Theodoric, just in time to see the Visigoth lead his heavy cavalry off to the left.

On a series of horn signals the Visigoth riders spread first to a hundred then to five hundred abreast. They spurred their heavy mounts on. The ground shook under the mad charge by the savage Visigoth. The leading horsemen drove on harder as arrows flew at them with a deadly sound. In a moment the air was thick with them. As one flight struck, another arched out. Horses reared and crashed into each other, men fell, the next line stumbled over fallen horses to be themselves brought down. More came on; nothing could stop their charge.

For a long while Attila had sat grimly astride his horse atop a small knoll, watching the battle develop and dispatching orders. His mouth was set in a hard line. Below him were a mass of fighting, screaming and dying men, slashing with hooks and axes, swords and scythes into living flesh. The slope was soon filled with the sounds of pain and terror. The light was getting bad; darkness began to settle over the field. What worried him was looming in the distance, on his right wing – the advancing Ostrogoth still moving away from his centre. Attila cursed himself – why hadn't he kept back a reserve to fill the gap? With a reserve one could always exploit the enemy's mistakes, and victory generally went to the side that made the fewest errors. Suddenly he noticed a change in the distant battle between the enemy tribes of Goths. He breathed a sigh of relief; at last, Walamir had received his order to make his slow retreat towards his centre. The Ostrogoth riders were finally pulling back – but why so fast? Now the unbelievable happened right in front of his eyes. Thousands of Huns raced off towards the distant river, raising a cloud of dust as they whipped their ponies to greater speed. Fool that he had been – what he had thought to be withdrawing Ostrogoth were in fact Theodoric's heavy Visigoth cavalry! And they were about to annihilate his centre.

To the Huns, the sheer weight of the rapidly advancing Goths was overpowering; blond, tall and muscular, with their caps of iron they resembled a horde of extraterrestrial devils. Already the sight of them had put the fear of God into the Huns. With a spine-chilling war cry from thousands of throats, Theodoric's Visigoth massed riders raced straight for the Huns. There were screams and shouts and the Huns faced about, bewildered. For an instant they didn't know whether to stand and fight or to run – and then it was too late. The impact came in a tremendous head-on collision, and it was entirely one-sided as the much heavier European chargers rode over the light ponies of the steppe. The mass of chargers formed an irresistible battering ram as they pressed onward, catching the Huns from the side and from behind. Within seconds the Huns had become totally disorganised; thousands were trampled under the hoofs of the mighty Goth mounts, while long Teutonic swords hacked swaths through the confused enemy, cutting down everything in their way. The Huns turned, but the pressure from behind was too strong. With Theodoric in the van, his barbarous fighters scythed through the Mongol hordes. Much better armed than their enemy, they bashed in heads with their fearsome battleaxes while their heavy-bladed swords sliced off limbs, and they speared dozens with their iron-tipped pikes. It wasn't a contest, it wasn't even a battle – it was slaughter. Nobody could withstand such onslaught by the blond giants, certainly not the Huns. The whole brawl lasted probably not more than fifteen minutes, but they were fifteen minutes that changed history.

'The Huns flee,' came triumphant shouts. And so it was. The Huns, who had found an escape lane and had abandoned the field in utter panic, were hacked down on the bank of the Noblette by Franks waiting for them, or simply drowned in the river. 'The stream between two shallow riverbanks was coloured red from the blood of the fallen; it was not like after a heavy shower, swollen by the rains, but the blood had turned it into a raging river. And those, whose wounds forced them to still their thirst, did so with blood reddened water. Thus the poor souls had to drink the very blood their wounds had flown into the gully.'[19]

Thus ended one of the fiercest battles of ancient time.[20]

The victors fell to their knees. A Christian God had shown himself in all his glory. But he showed no signs of favour. He had chosen the most valiant to be slain. Night laid its dark mantle over the field. Only then did the slaughter stop. Most of the leaders were dead. For hours after darkness, the Catalaunian Fields resounded with the screams of the dying. But nobody was fighting any longer, not even the ghosts of the many lying there. A few torches sent out circles of light. What were they looking for? For survivors? Or to slaughter the wounded enemy? Who could tell.

Having seen that all was lost, Attila had withdrawn inside his earthen-walled fortress. The Hun cursed his own foolishness – his dream of a kingdom for the Huns lay out there, with broken limbs and severed heads. All for nothing, because his shamans had been wrong in their predictions: that cursed enemy leader was not dead, he was very much alive, and surely as the sun rises each day he would lead his legions to destroy what was left of the decimated Huns. The dawn would see his end – but he would never allow himself to be taken alive. He was ready to die a fiery death rather than be captured by Visigoth and Romans.[21] He ordered his men to use their wooden saddles and pile them into a huge pyramid, his own funeral pyre. Slowly, downhearted, they dragged their saddles to the middle of the camp, reciting their age-old prayer of death to their god Loki. In the darkness a monumental mountain of saddles

[19] Ibid.

[20] Jordanes gives 150,000 Huns as casualty figures. That seems exaggerated, but 50,000 to 60,000 is a reasonable estimate.

[21] E. Creasey, *The Fifteen Decisive Battles of the World*, London 1851.

grew.[22] The survivors begged their leader to lead them in a breakout in the coming dawn. Perhaps their god would be lenient and grant them a miracle. But Attila knew that the God of Huns had outlawed miracles. In this hour of despair, he wasn't aware of a momentous incident that had taken place earlier, one that was to spare him and his Huns.

As darkness had settled over the battlefield, and the horns of the Visigoth had finally called the warriors to end the combat, among those who failed to answer the call was one whose absence was felt the most: an old man with a flowing white beard – Theodoric the king. 'During the fierce battle, Theodoric King of the Visigoth was thrown from his horse and was trampled to death under the hoofs of the horses of his own, advancing mass of riders.'[23]

While his men went out to look for him, a centurion in his crimson robe arrived at the tent of Flavius Aetius. He tore off his helmet and put a fist to his chest. 'Hail, Consul, be it known but to you that Theodoric is slain,' he pronounced, out of breath.

The Roman consul was stunned. 'How be it?'

'He was thrown in the final charge. I saw it myself.'

With the king dead, the warriors would elect a new king: Thorismund, his son – and Thorismund was the avowed enemy of Rome. That changed everything. For three hours, while chaos reigned in every camp, while survivors bandaged their wounds or simply fell asleep from battle exhaustion, Aetius disappeared from his camp. In the darkness, no one saw him and no one ever discovered what really went on in these decisive hours before dawn. Chances are he went for a secret meeting with Attila.

22 Attila's camp is today a military proving ground. In 1793, during excavations, a large hole, measuring some twenty feet in diameter, was discovered, which contained remains of wood not normally found in France. This, therefore, was the site of Attila's intended funeral pyre. There were also some coins, all predating AD 451.

23 Jordanes.

Logic dictated it. The death of King Theodoric had eliminated the only man who could have seen through the schemes of the Roman. Aetius acted immediately; with the Visigoth menace out of the way, and a young, inexperienced new ruler, the weak West Roman Empire could continue to play the leading role on the continent. But for this he now needed once again the Huns as his *feoderati*. He would use the tribe to checkmate the Eastern Emperor Markianos and, at the same time, to stop the Visigoth from moving on Italy. He knew that he could reach an agreement with Attila; therefore, it was vital to let the Huns get away, and in fairly good order. How he passed this message to Attila is one of the enigmas of history. But it could only have happened during these hours of darkness.

King Theodoric's body was found under a pile of dead warriors; the great hero of legend fell where the fight had raged the fiercest. In his funeral procession, followed by every single one of his victorious Visigoth, the king was carried in plain sight of Attila's camp and placed on a magnificent funeral pyre, erected from the saddles of his slain foe.[24] His courage and energy were the stuff legends are made of . . . and his spirit lives on in the greatest epic of the blood-soaked fields of central Europe, the Nibelungenlied.

As predicted, his warriors on the battlefield elected Thorismund as their new king; he sought counsel from his Roman ally. Aetius offered it with great cunning; he pointed out to the new Visigoth king the danger he might have to face from his five brothers in Tolosa (Toulouse), who would vie for Theodoric's inheritance – unless he were to return home immediately and make known his right to the throne.

> After all was finished, Thorismund, shaken by the death of his father sought counsel from the Patrician Aetius

[24] It is believed that his ashes were buried near the battlefield, at Poix, near today's Route Nationale 394.

how to avenge the death of his father. What to undertake in the morning. Aetius, vastly superior in wisdom and age to the young king, advised the Goth to round up his survivors and speedily to return to their homelands to forestall other claims for the throne. Or his brothers might just take the crown away from him. Thorismund failed to see the treachery, considered Aetius' advice as nothing but that of a well-meaning friend, and returned into the interior of Gaul. Thus can human weakness, especially when furthered by baneful advice and influenced by suspicion, become the reason to forgo the opportunity for great historic feats.[25]

This great feat would have been the complete annihilation of Attila and his Huns, and it is significant that it was actually a Roman who stopped the extinction of the Huns. Within the year Aetius was to regret his act. Thorismund failed to see the treachery. While Aetius looked on as his Visigoth ally rode off towards the west, Legate Maecilius reached for his hand and fell to his knee. 'Attila is beaten, Gaul is free and now we must use our victory well. Great Aetius, you have saved Rome!' Aetius looked to the west, where the first rays of the morning sun touched the walls of the city of Catalaunium. He didn't see salvation, only danger.

'Gaul has been saved for Rome – but for how long?'

A fine prophecy. Within the year, Gaul was forever lost to Rome.

The facts

From what took place in the days that followed victory, it becomes obvious that Jordanes' description of the

25 Jordanes.

monumental betrayal was accurate. The powerful Visigoth had to be put aside to save Attila for Aetius' future designs. The Roman consul could easily have decimated the Huns, still encircled in their Camp d'Attila, a hastily put-up field fortification that was protected only by water-filled ditches and earthen walls not much higher than a man.[26] At this stage, even the reduced Roman legions would have sufficed to finish off the Hun; instead the legionnaires remained impassively in camp while Attila's hordes were allowed to move off without hindrance. For Rome's *raison d'état*, a young and naïve Visigoth had been persuaded to take his men from the field in order to save Attila's Huns. Once this act of political juggling was accomplished, and the Visigoth had disappeared over the horizon, the veterans of Aetius' Gallo-Roman legions were only too happy to sit by and watch the Huns vanish across the Rhine. At Châlons, it wasn't the Romans who had supplied the cutting edge. Only two and a half of Rome's legions had fought, a mere 25,000 out of many hundreds of thousands. Who, then, held history in the balance? The Germans, Visigoth and Frankish warrior nations that served the will of Rome.

Aetius' equation didn't succeed; he had sown dragon's teeth. By ridding himself of his bothersome Germanic allies and stripping Italy of its Roman legions to lead them against the Huns, he left Rome without defences. Within ten months, Attila had rallied his tribes around his overpowering personality. This time he invaded the heartland of Rome (452), the fertile Upper Italian plains. Attila's *chevauchée* was terrible, his fury unbridled, his brutality without restraint; his hordes burned, raped and murdered. He descended across the Julian Alps on Aquileia, whose citizens fled to an offshore island and thereby founded Venice. One city after another was

[26] Today, the visitor will find a road sign at La Cheppe, indicating: *Enceinte préhistorique, dit Camp d'Attila.*

put to the sack: Padua, Vincenza, Verona, Brescia, Bergamo, Milan and Pavia. To give his hordes a rest he halted on the Mincio. There he was met by Pope Leo I, 'and the awe of Christianity was upon him . . .' It wasn't the thundering of the Church but the huge ransom the Pope paid Attila out of Church funds which helped Pope Leo – who for his daring endeavour achieved sainthood and was thereafter known as Pope Leo the Great – to rid Italy of the Huns.

Attila's sudden death, shortly after meeting Pope Leo I, was interpeted by the Christian nations as a holy miracle in which the representative of God on Earth subdued the Flagellum Dei, Satan incarnate, son of Nimrod, the Antichrist. This belief in holy relics as political ammunition for papal authority, backed up by the pious maiden Geneviève, who had saved Paris with her prayers, and the 'miracle of Orleans' performed by Bishop Avianus, added to the mystical belief in the ultimate power of the Christian Church. 'Thus it can be truly said that indirectly the King of the Huns contributed more perhaps than any other historical figure towards the creation of that mighty factor in the politics of medieval Italy, the Pope-King of Rome.'[27]

Attila died in 453 in Pechelarn (Pöchlarn in Lower Austria), his demise said to have been caused by a nosebleed brought on by drink and exhaustion during his wedding night with the fair Ildico (Kriemhild, Siegfried's widow). As he lay on his bed and the blood flowed down his throat, it drowned him. Another account represented a more Teutonic version: having avenged Siegfried, the noble Kriemhild would not give herself to the vile Asian and cut his throat. Whatever the case, Attila was dead, and with the death of their 'little father' – Attila was actually a diminutive of *atta* for father, while the Goths called him Godegisel for *Gottesgeisel* or, in Roman, *Flagellum Dei* – the Hun kingdom fell apart. King Ardarich of the Gepids, who had been Attila's lieutenant at Châlons

27 T. Hodgkin, *Italy and Her Invaders*, London 1880.

and had miraculously survived the battle, joined with the Ostrogoth in revolt. In the ensuing battle at the Netad river in Pannonia (454), Ellak, son of Attila, was killed. The Gepid took Dacia and the Ostrogoth Pannonia. With Ellak's defeat, the Huns vanished altogether.

In 454, the 'last of the Romans', Consul-for-Life Flavius Aetius, demanded Emperor Valentinianus' daughter for his own son. The emperor invited Aetius to a banquet during which he stabbed him, jealous of his consul's power. One of Aetius' lieutenants, Petronius Maximus, took terrible revenge; at the head of the imperial cohort, he marched on the imperial palace, where he had the entire court put to the sword, murdered Valentinianus and forced the emperor's widow, Eudoxia, to marry him. In her distress, she sent a message to the ruthless Gaiseric, King of the Vandals, to come to her rescue. Gaiseric, who had already devastated most of North Africa, responded to her call, met Eudoxia, stripped her of her jewels, and then put Rome to the sack. In an act of 'vandalism' at its purest, he butchered most of Rome's patrician population during two weeks in June 455.

Aetius wanted to defend Rome and Attila wanted to destroy it. Both succeeded, and yet Attila and Aetius were the losers. A Goth king died at the moment of his greatest victory, and a Roman dictator thought he could save Rome. His betrayal didn't spare the Western Roman Empire from obliteration. Aetius did nothing but open the way to others – to the hordes of Attila in 452, to the Vandals in 455, and in 472 to the Burgundians and Suevi. The end of a thousand-year-old Rome came on the morning of 4 September 476, when Odoaker, a barbarian partly Goth and partly Hun, deposed Rome's last emperor, Romulus Augustus.

With Rome's demise, Visigoth and Franks expanded throughout western Europe. Both nations formed mighty empires. In the final outcome, King Theodoric's heirs were the winners. The Battle of Châlons was one of the decisive battles of history. A victory by Attila would have brought about the collapse of Western civilisation, the end of Christianity, and possible domination of Europe by Asian masters. It brought about the end of Rome. In its stead, a new world power emerged, the Catholic Church. Its spiritual leader, the Pope, replaced Imperial Rome as the only valid authority throughout the Middle Ages.

Theodoric's death had removed the linchpin that could have saved Rome. It is possible that he, and only he, could have maintained a conciliatory position that would have saved the empire, and the great Greco-Roman culture it represented. Instead, one man's death signalled the beginning of the Dark Ages.

The Hinge of Battle on the Catalaunian Fields was the death of a valiant king whose wisdom would have subverted the plans of a dictator who was indeed 'the last of the Romans'.

The Catalaunian Fields brought about the fall of Rome.

2

Through a Gate Wide Open

29 May 1453 – The Fall of Constantinople

'Wa lillahi el maschreq wa el maghreb.'
(Allah is the Orient, Allah is the Occident.)
Call of the muezzin to prayer (from the Koran, Surate 2/115)

'Bear yourself bravely for God's sake! If God wills, ours shall be victory!'

The emperor's captain, Giustiniani,
before the Turks' final assault, 29 May 1453

The fall of Constantinople to the Turkish armies of Sultan Mahomet II,[1] greatly assisted in his victory by the genius of a Hungarian cannon-maker, was a strategic event that changed Europe, set new religious boundaries, marked a watershed in military history, and brought about the end of existing structures of armoured hosts. It was at Istanbul that cannons and firearms spelled *finis* to the chivalrous Middle Ages.

Medieval battles of close-in fighting with cutting weapons left behind battlefields more typical of a slaughterhouse. But once the cannon was added to hand-to-hand knightly combat, the results were truly horrific. Gunpowder revolutionised

[1] Mahomet or, as in some accounts, Mehmet.

history as much as the printing press, and at roughly the same period – the middle of the fifteenth century. It was the age of discovery: Gutenberg invented the printing press, Columbus was about to travel the seas, the teaching of Johann Hus rocked the Catholic Church to its foundation, and an obscure German monk, Berthold Schwarz, invented *Schwarzpulver* (black powder). It was a time when progress moved with lightning speed. The most dramatic confirmation of the effectiveness of gunpowder and shot as the new ultimate weapon is the story of the fall of Constantinople. Its walls, though certainly in decay, had withstood attacks over many centuries. But the highly effective siege artillery of the Turkish Sultan battered down these walls in a mere fifty-five days.

It began when a Hungarian bell-maker tried out the German monk's magic powder in an overturned bronze bell. He mixed the Schwarz formula, and lit it with a length of hemp. It didn't give much of a bang, just a searing flame. Next he added a stone and pushed some rags around it. Then he lit the fuse – and vroooom! Chickens, cows and farmhands fled; the stone landed in a field and made a large hole. Master Janos Urban, the Hungarian, improved on the bell shape by sculpting a lengthy tube of clay to fit a round stone, after which he poured bronze into the form. A cannon! Urban said farewell to his beloved ones, climbed on a horse and travelled with only a drawing to Constantinople, to offer his invention to the East Roman Emperor, Constantine XI Dragases. He never got to see the emperor because court officials showed him and his invention the door. Understandably, Master Urban was furious about this personal affront and the lack of faith in his brainchild. He looked for other prospective customers and found a wealthy client, Mahomet II, Sultan of the Ottoman Turks, who was about to embark on the conquest of the very emperor who had so shabbily treated Master Urban and his newfangled contraption.

* * *

The East Roman Empire was founded in 324, when Emperor Constantine I chose Byzantium as his capital. Soon new dangers appeared *ante portas* in the person of Hugalu, grandson of Genghis Khan, who quickly subdued Byzantium's bordering tribes and set up Ertughril from a nomadic tribe, the Turkomans, as his provincial governor. While the Serbs and Bulgars diverted the attention of the Byzantine emperor, Ertughril's son, Othman, took his Turks on a rampage that left the surrounding lands piled high with corpses. In 1281 he founded the kingdom of the Ottoman Turk. His successor reorganised the Turkish Army by adding an élite formation of Christians, aptly called 'the new troops' or janissaries. When John V, Emperor of Constantinople, was defeated by the Serbs, he offered his daughter's hand in marriage to the Sultan, in exchange for military assistance, and the Turks set foot in Europe. Of the sultans that followed Othman, the mightiest was Murad I, who decisively defeated the Serbs in 1387 on the plains of Kosovo. When a Serb posing as a deserter assassinated Murad, Murad's brother, the ferocious 'Thunderbolt' Bayazid, launched a war of extermination during which he ordered that every captured Serb be put to death. This again forced Byzantine Emperor Manuel II to cry for help from his mortal enemy, the Catholic Church and its Pope, Boniface IX, who called for a 'Holy Crusade against the murderous Turk'. In 1396, 100,000 Hungarians under King Sigismund marched against the infidel Turk and were routed by Bayazid, who then marched on Constantinople, which he besieged in 1402. That he failed to conquer the city was due not to its defences but the danger to his realm from an even more brutal killer, the Mongol overlord Tamerlane, whose trademark was to slaughter every soul in the cities he conquered and then pile their skulls in giant pyramids before the city gate. Bayazid rushed with his army to face the Mongol threat, by which time Tamerlane had already retired to his capital of Samarkand.

Next came Murad II, who moved against the Catholic Hungarians and won a two-day battle in October 1448 that left 8,000 Hungarian knights dead on Kosovo's fields. His victory spelled the end for Constantinople. Other than by sea, the city was cut off from the rest of Europe and its potential allies. Murad II died in 1451 and was succeeded by his son, Mahomet II, who was soon to acquire the title of 'The Conqueror'.

The middle of the fifteenth century was the time of the Black Death, when life lost all its meaning. It was also the time of some of the most notorious butcheries committed by ruthless despots whose names have erected a monument to cruelty: the Mongol Timus the Lame (Tamerlane), Prince Dracul of Valachia (Dracula), and the equally ruthless Albanian Scanderbeg. The English and French fought for supremacy in western Europe; the Pope of Rome, one week in bed with the Milanese, the next with the Venetians or Florentines, struggled for supremacy in Italy. The Holy Roman Emperor of Germany had a hard time getting rid of religious zealots, the Hussites. The longevity of a Byzantine emperor depended entirely on avoiding an assassin's dagger or the poison of a jealous courtier. And Sultan Murad II drowned the Balkans in a deluge of blood.

Mahomet II (1451–81), the son of Sultan Murad II and the beautiful Albanian slave Mara Brankovich, the dominant personality in the Sultan's harem, was a product of this period. Other than his mother, he had not much use for female companionship. On his father's death, Mahomet was twenty-one, and from that moment on his overpowering mother pushed him to excesses. They began when he usurped the Sultan's throne by the simple expediency of having his half-brother assassinated (as had Attila the Hun), after which he himself beheaded the assassin. Again on his mother's counsel, he sent his father's younger concubine, the mother of his dead half-brother, into a whorehouse in central Anatolia. He was of slight build, with a sensual face, highly cultured and spoke five languages. Furthermore, he seemed anxious to add to his universal wisdom, especially in the field of military technology. This thirst for knowledge brought him into contact with a Hungarian bell-maker, destined to play a vital role in the Sultan's plans for conquest – Constantinople. As a young boy, when he first saw the gilded spires of the Christian capital from across the water, he swore that one day he would make it his. From then on, every one of his actions was guided by one central thought – to bring about the fall of the pearl of Byzance. But his ambition went further than that. 'He wished to conquer not only Constantinople, but the world, to see more than Alexander and Caesar or any other valiant man who has ever lived.'[2] He was a conqueror who knew no pity, neither towards the enemy nor his own troops, who called him 'Hunkar', or 'the Drinker of Blood'. His favourite form of punishment was to nail a turban to a man's head, and then cut the head off and impale it on a pike outside his tent. It was a clever psychological move that he had copied from the similarly bloodthirsty Count Dracula, and it kept his generals and courtiers in constant fear for their lives, and thereby willing to obey his every command. 'Of a master who never forgives, the orders are seldom disobeyed.'[3]

The stage for a Muslim takeover of the Byzantine capital had been set centuries before (1073) by Pope Gregory VII when he pronounced: 'It is far better for a country to remain under the rule of Islam, than being governed by Christians who refuse to acknowledge the rights of the Catholic Church.' If confirmation was needed of the hatred between the Catholic Church of Rome and the Orthodox Church of Constantinople it was reaffirmed by the Byzantine Grand Duke Lucas Notaras: 'It is better to see the city in the

[2] G. Finlay, *A History of Greece*, London 1877.
[3] E. Gibbon, *The Decline and Fall of the Roman Empire*, Dent, 1960–62.

power of the Turkish turban than that of the Latin tiara.' The Great Turk knew that he had a clear road and nothing to fear from Rome. All he needed now was a way to breach the massive walls of Constantinople.

At this propitious junction in time, a new character entered the scene: Master Urban, the wizard bell-maker from Hungary, who now outlined his invention to the Sultan.

'Will it work?' asked the Sultan.

'Your Magnificence, I will do my very best to make sure that it will.'

'Master Urban,' replied Mahomet with a sardonic smile, pointing at the forest of poles with its crop of heads planted outside the tent, 'I'm certain that you will do better than that.'

A shaky Urban knew that he must do better than try. He made several cannons, one of them a true monster, which, in honour of the Sultan, he called 'Mahometta'. It was a huge *bombard*, weighed 20 tons, and – according a recent calculation – could fire a 1,450lb stone ball over a mile. Because of its uncontrolled recoil, the cannon had to be carefully aligned after each shot. Also, its muzzle-loading barrel, built up from bars encased with hoops, had to cool sufficiently before it could be safely reloaded. This limited its rate of fire to about six to seven rounds a day. The ground over which this monster gun moved was levelled to provide smooth passage for the sixty oxen that were needed to pull it. To prove the cannon's worth, Urban lined it up on the shore, aimed carefully and then fired a single round at a Venetian galley anchored in the Bosphorus. With a mighty bang the galley cracked open like an eggshell. The Sultan jumped with joy and pounded his cannon master's back before he showered him with honours and jewels. To keep Urban happy, he even provided him with nubile slave girls who soon had the cannon genius forgetting the dumpy wife he had left behind on the Hungarian *puzsta* (plain).

* * *

By the time of the death of Byzantine Emperor John III in 1448, the once mighty empire of Constantine I, which had encompassed the Balkans, Asia Minor, Syria, Palestine and Egypt, was little more than a few churches surrounded by the walls of a city. The only vestige of former greatness was the monumental gilded dome crowning the Church of St Sophia. The cupola of this white stone cathedral, built from hand-hewn blocks and decorated with an ornamental carved stone girdle, looked like the helmet of a divine warrior. Dotted along the seafront were the splendid palaces of the rich; but the rest of the city was beset by wretchedness and misery in overcrowded, dirty lanes, where a sometimes barbarous and thieving populace vegetated in meaningless unhappiness. For them, life was but a long disease under a permanent sentence of death. The idiot children and the discarded old were left to die in their excrement, completing a picture of hopeless degradation. For centuries, the ruling classes had encouraged the grossest laxity and unheard-of corruption. Scenes of the vilest debauchery were the rule. 'A nation that had become an inert mass, without initiative, without will. Before Emperor and Church the population grovelled in the dust; behind them it rose up to spit at them and shake their fists. Tyranny and exploitation above, hatred and cowardice beneath; cruelty frequently, hypocrisy always. Political and social bodies were rotten. Selfishness placed itself on the throne of public interest and tried to cover its hideousness with a mantle of false patriotism.'[4]

The city was girdled by two eight-metre-high walls; the walls had 112 towers twenty metres high. The towers were thrust forward, powerful bastions which overhung a deep, moatlike ravine, as if giving warning of certain doom awaiting any who tried to take this capital of eastern Christianity by

[4] C. Mijatovich, *Constantine, the Last Emperor of the Greeks*, London 1892.

force of arms. Many had tried it and few had succeeded. More towers on the interior wall awaited those who were bold enough to overcome the defensive fire or the hot oil poured down on them from the outpost bastions. For those who came to the city as guests, the way in was through a number of heavy cast-iron gates, guarded day and night by sentries. At every gate stood a priest in a black cassock who greeted the arrivals with reserved bows or dispensed absolution to thieves and sinners, on their way out to the gallows on the glacis.

The wall had been built a thousand years earlier, by Emperor Theodosius II, and it was in a shocking state of repair. Towers had crumbled; wide cracks from earthquakes and natural erosion had dissected the brickwork. Still, the wall was formidable, and never since the sack of Constantinople by a crusader army in July 1203 had it been breached; despite repeated attempts in the previous centuries, it had withstood all Turkish attempts to storm the city. The length of the land wall was thirteen miles; it stretched from the Sea of Marmara to the Golden Horn. The vital entrance into the Bosphorus was blocked off with a heavy chain. Behind the safety of this chain lay the imperial fleet of twenty-six vessels at anchor, manned by Venetian and Genoese and captained by Gabriele Trevisano. Faced with the looming danger, Emperor Constantine XI Dragases put out a call for fighters. As proof of their abject cowardice, a mere 4,900 of the 100,000 available male population of the city responded to his call. From Italy he hired a Genoese band of mercenaries under the Condottiere Giovanni Giustiniani, who came '*per honor de Dio et la Christianitade*'. That brought Constantine's effective force to 8,000. Giustiniani, perhaps the outstanding soldier of his time, audacious and skilful, was nominated Captain-General with dictatorial powers. He was a charismatic figure, battle hardened and a man of decision when under pressure. The cowardly citizenry offered no help; they

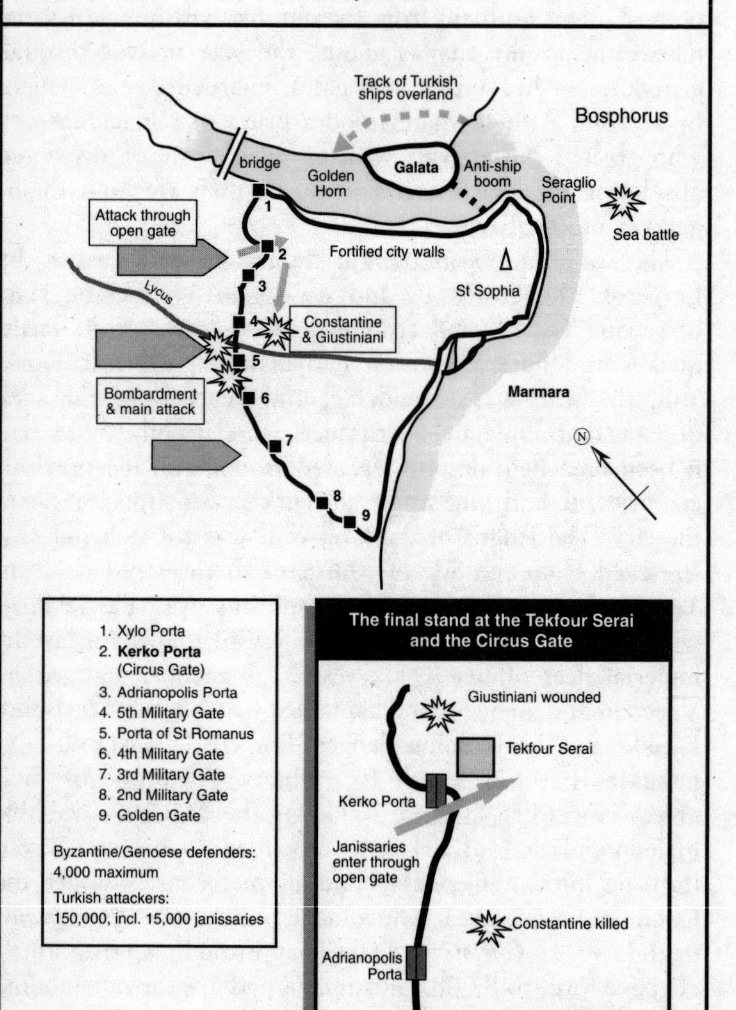
Constantinople
29 May 1453
Track of Turkish ships overland
Bosphorus
bridge
Golden Horn
Galata
Anti-ship boom
Seraglio Point
Sea battle
Attack through open gate
Fortified city walls
St Sophia
Lycus
Constantine & Giustiniani
Bombardment & main attack
Marmara
N
1
2
3
4
5
6
7
8
9
1. Xylo Porta
2. Kerko Porta (Circus Gate)
3. Adrianopolis Porta
4. 5th Military Gate
5. Porta of St Romanus
6. 4th Military Gate
7. 3rd Military Gate
8. 2nd Military Gate
9. Golden Gate
Byzantine/Genoese defenders: 4,000 maximum
Turkish attackers: 150,000, incl. 15,000 janissaries
The final stand at the Tekfour Serai and the Circus Gate
Giustiniani wounded
Tekfour Serai
Kerko Porta
Janissaries enter through open gate
Constantine killed
Adrianopolis Porta
300 metres

flocked into St Sophia to pray for their wellbeing and that they might escape the coming storm unscathed. Other than light a few candles they did nothing, leaving the handling of their defence to the 700 mercenaries, spread so thin on the walls that most defensive towers were manned by three guards only.

Across the ditch, the Sultan's force numbered 150,000, a lot of it soldiery but the rest 'thieves, plunderers and others following the army for gain and booty'.[5] The fighting force was mainly undisciplined rabble, called the *bashi-bazouk*, plus the provincial levies; both these contingents were to provide the cannon fodder for the initial assault. They were expected to accept heavy casualties. The real assault was to be undertaken by the Sultan's élite, the janissaries. Their units were formed of men with a Christian background, forcibly converted to Mohammedanism between the ages of eight and twelve; they then underwent a harsh and thorough training in all the military arts and were forbidden to marry. They could achieve great fame and were in fact a cast of warrior monks. Their obeisance to their superior was exemplary. They wore a coat of mail reaching to their knees, a white peaked cap ornamented with plates of silver, and were armed with sword, bow or mace. Some carried a flintlock pistol. For an attack they relied on lightning-fast Arab stallions. Their technique was often based on trickery, pretending to abandon the field in panic until their pursuing enemy was so stretched out in his pursuit that he became easy prey for their sudden turnabout. They numbered 15,000, and no Christian army had anything comparable in assault cavalry to put up against them.

Finally, but most vital, was Mahomet's artillery, operated entirely by Christians who were helped in their task by hordes of slaves and oxen trains. Now that Mahomet had observed

[5] According to Niccolo Barbaro.

proof of the efficiency of his super-weapon, he began planning the assault.

Mahomet's plan of attack was divided into four sections as follows:

1. Zagan Pasha from Galata and the Golden Horn to attack the Xylo Porta.
2. Caraja Pasha in the centre to attack the Adrianopolis Porta.
3. Isaac Pasha between the St Romanus Porta and the Sea of Marmara.
4. Halil Pasha providing the fatal thrust in the depression of the Lycus Valley, where the walls promised to be most vulnerable.

The Sultan based his entire siege strategy on an unproven siege weapon, Urban's formidable cannons. Master Urban was provided with foundry facilities in Adrianopolis; a lot of the necessary bronze and iron came from melting down Greek and Roman statues and many valuable artefacts fell victim to Master Urban's smelting pits. Workers slaved day and night on clay forms in order to cast the muzzle-loaders. Many died from noxious fumes, heat or burns. To save the ritual of a burial, the dead were dumped unceremoniously into the pits of molten bronze, which added vastly to the impurities in the casting process, and cannons with bubbles in their cast would frequently burst after a few rounds. Altogether Urban was ordered to produce one hundred pieces, of which twelve were true monsters. Mahomet's four main batteries were made up of four *bombards* each, capable of firing stone balls of one ton. To operate one of these giant guns took 400 men and 60 oxen.

By the spring of 1453, everything was in place to begin the siege. Mahomet started his attack by conquering two minor outposts at Therapia and Studium. To show Constantinople's defenders what was in store for them unless they surrendered, he had his captives lined up outside the walls and then impaled. It had the opposite psychological effect to the one the Sultan had hoped to achieve; his brutal demonstration showed that the defenders could expect nothing but a painful death, and therefore it would make them fight much harder. One of the condottieri captains was Niccolo Barbaro, who survived, and whose account of the siege provides the best account of the days to follow.[6]

On 5 April 1453, the entire force of Sultan Mahomet II gathered on the glacis before the land wall of Constantinople. It was a most impressive sight – thousands of green pennants of the Prophet, with blaring trumpets and tubas, crashing cymbals and drums, regiment after regiment in all their oriental splendour. At last came the janissaries, trotting along the walls like an armoured flood, professional soldiers confident in their abilities. Condottieri Giustiniani climbed to the top of a tower. He thought it better for the morale of his troops to be seen in the forefront with the ranks.

A few days after this display, the Sultan's artillery was rolled up for what was to become the first major siege bombardment in history.[7] To the accompaniment of cymbals and trumpets, a giant flame shot from the monstrous 'Mahometta'. 'Since the creation of the world nothing like it had been heard.'[8] Yet the damage to the wall was negligible, and Mahomet watched in silent fury while his cannons peppered away, until Master Urban advised him not to disperse his shot all over the outer walls, but to concentrate all his guns on one single spot. Almost immediately the situation changed and the bombardment began to show results. Cracks appeared and top sections tumbled. But the lower portion of

[6] N. Barbaro, *Giornale dell' assedia di Constantinopoli*, (repr.) Venice 1856.

[7] There were some previous minor bombardments, such as at Zara (1346) and Cyprus (1373). The huge Mons Meg of Edinburgh was made after the siege of Constantinople, in 1455.

[8] Mijatovich.

the wall held. The first breach, some twenty feet wide, was hammered through the outer wall near the Adrianopolis Porta. Impatiently, and although the breach wasn't nearly wide enough to use his vast superiority in a massive attack, Mahomet ordered an all-out attempt for the morning of 18 April. The first waves of Turks rushed for the breach with their battle cry: '*Yagma!*' A fearful noise and slaughter began, with swords, maces, crossbows, and 'the ringing of bells, the clashing of arms, the cries of fighting men, the shrieks of women and the wailing of children, produced such a noise that it seemed as if the earth trembled. Clouds of rancid smoke fell over city and camp, until the combatants could no longer see each other.'[9] This hand-to-hand struggle lasted until Captain-General Giovanni Giustiniani's men, using mainly handguns loaded with several lead pellets (like a modern shotgun), managed to kill a number of Turks and throw the rest into the outer ditch. The subsequent retreat by his badly mauled troops so infuriated the Sultan that he considered for a while having all the slain bodies of his 'cowardly units' stuffed into Urban's cannons and fired over the city walls.

Mahomet, having had to witness the shameful retreat of his forces before the heroic stand by Giustiniani, retired to his tent to sit down and dictate a letter. His face took on the look of a fox, which put his advisers on guard. 'You will have to learn,' he admonished his generals, 'that victory is not always achieved with cannons and gunpowder.' There were things that could be done with words and gold which weapons couldn't achieve. His letter was to Captain-General Giustiniani, assuring him of a golden handshake as the Sultan's Commander-in-Chief. The letter, affixed with the Sultan's seal for authenticity, was carried by a splendidly garbed rider, accompanied by a mounted trumpeter, to the city walls.

[9] Account from *The Old Slavonic Translation of the Chronicle of Simeona Logothea*, St. Petersburg 1905/London 1971.

'What is it, Turk?' yelled a soldier from a tower.

'A personal missive, if you please, from our exalted Padishah, may Allah protect his soul, to your Captain-General.'

A basket was lowered from the tower. 'Put it in. I'll see that he gets it.'

'I am to await the reply.'

'No, come back when the sun is at the zenith. We will allow you safe passage.'

Giustiniani, overseeing the construction of more defensive machines, was handed the letter within the hour. What he read was full of flowery phrases and elaborate compliments, but the meaning was clear enough. He dictated a brief reply: 'A man can only swear fealty to one lord, and I have already done so.'

While the repulsed land army prepared for a new offensive and the cannonade continued unabated, the action shifted to the open sea. Three Genoese warships, crammed with mercenaries and ammunition, plus a grain ship, were approaching the city when the wind suddenly died, and the warships now lay becalmed at the entrance to the Bosphorus. Mahomet ordered his fleet to stand out and capture the four vessels. With 145 Turkish ships against four Genoese, there could be no doubt about the eventual outcome. The defenders crowded the walls and the Turkish nobles lined the shore to watch the spectacle of the vast fleet of Turkish galleys, captained by the Bulgarian renegade Admiral Baltoglu, in a competitive race to be the first to engage in the battle. Once the first Turks arrived near the Christian ships it became obvious that the Genoese ships had much higher gunwales; this gave them the advantage. Venetian and Genoese sailors used their axes to cut the ropes of the grappling hooks, poured hot oil and Greek fire on to the Turkish galleys and set dozens aflame, while deck-mounted swivel guns blasted holes through paper-thin Turkish warships and sent them to the bottom. After they had been bobbing on the calm sea for an hour a strong breeze came up, and the four great Genoese vessels sailed majestically through the floundering Turkish ships like cruisers through a fleet of sardine fishermen and, to the cheers of the defenders on the battlements, on into the Golden Horn. An outraged Mahomet galloped up and down the beach, cursing and screaming, and only the Grand Vizier stopped his Sultan from having Captain Baltoglu impaled. However, this maritime encounter showed Mahomet the vital importance of gaining control of the Golden Horn anchorage and preventing more reinforcements reaching the beleaguered town. He couldn't get over the walls and he couldn't breach the heavy harbour chain. In what must be one of the masterstrokes of siege warfare, a Greek naval engineer working for the Turks rounded up thousands of slaves, constructed a slipway of grease-covered logs and hauled seventy Turkish warships across land into the Golden Horn. At the same time, the Turks laid a bridge across the Horn; floating on wooden barrels, it was 600 metres long and three metres wide. With this, Constantinople was now completely encircled and condemned to a last-stand situation. Panic ensued. Patricians offered bags of gold to Venetian captains to take them from the city; the mob stormed ships, threw their crews overboard and tried to make a getaway, only to founder within sight of shore.

The emperor remained stout hearted and refused to seek his salvation in flight. 'Never will I leave my children who God has entrusted into my care.' Of the last Emperor Constantine, the eleventh bearer of the illustrious name of the East Roman Empire's founder, it must be said that, in shining contrast to his many predecessors, who had sold off imperial privileges in exchange for a soft life, Constantine XI was neither intriguer nor coward. 'I will die here with you,' he continued, with tears in his eyes, and with him wept the Holy Patriarch and all those who gathered around him. His moral strength instilled in his people new, if false, hope, because from that moment on they counted on his survival to lead them from disaster. Their hopes were dashed when a small brigantine, disguised as a Turkish trader, made a night sortie to look for the Pope's promised relief fleet and lead it into the harbour. The fleet was nowhere in sight, because Rome's Pope had never intended to keep his promise and save Orthodox Christendom from the Turkish yoke.

The artillery bombardment continued unabated, day and night, keeping citizens and defenders from their badly needed sleep. A flash of fire from the muzzles; a crack from the iron mouths; smoke; an echo returning. The noise of the guns blended and rolled into space. Brown mushrooms of smoke rose along the wall. Everything was in uproar; a terrible grinding process was taking place. The walls still withstood the onslaught, but for how much longer?[10] Urban's monsters pounded the city's walls and punched holes into the outer fortification, and every night Giustiniani's men plugged the breaches with makeshift barricades of timber ripped from roofs. On 3 May Sultan Mahomet ordered an attack by 50,000 Turks. The holes in the wall weren't large enough to launch massive attacks, and the gaps were held by an impenetrable barricade of spears, pikes and swords on which Mahomet's men broke themselves again and again, but never got through.

Another attempt, four days later, ended again without noticeable result. The walls held. Mahomet was livid. He ordered every piece of his artillery to shoot at once and a hundred stone balls crashed into a small section of wall. Large cracks appeared, the structure trembled, '. . . and the wall came tumbling down'. Not like in biblical times, by the power of faith and Joshua's trumpet; this time religion was replaced by round, hand-cut stones, some weighing a ton and propelled by a charge of gunpowder from Master Urban's tubes. They

[10] These were of course not explosive shells.

shattered the hard-baked bricks. A breach opened, although not wide enough to allow deployment of massed rider formations. The Sultan seethed with impatience. More shots had to be fired – and faster.

It was on 12 May that a giant explosion shook the city. When the defenders raced to their battlements, they stared at a huge cloud of smoke and dust and a black hole where the monster 'Mahometta' had stood only moments before. It was the Sultan's impatience which had brought disaster – he had ordered Urban to increase the rate of fire and the metal hadn't cooled sufficiently from the previous shot before gunpowder was stuffed down the bronze muzzle. Before the reloading was completed, the monster *bombard* blew up and killed every single one of its crew of two hundred, including Master Urban.

This mishap didn't stop the Sultan, and he ordered the bombardment from his seventy guns to increase. The wall was now so weakened that whole sections came crashing down, especially near the Adrianopolis Porta. This concentration of gunfire frequently forced Giustiniani to order his force to take shelter behind the inner wall.

The Sultan's impatience increased with his nervousness. Throughout entire nights he sat before his tent and observed the wall, looming defiantly in the darkness. He was pressed for time; should he fail to storm the wall by the end of May, he knew that he would have to abandon the siege, because the more troops rushed to his assistance, the more difficult became his supply problems. On 18 May, another attempt was launched. Under the cover of a mobile wooden siege tower, a *helepolis*, waves of Turks crept up to the walls. Hundreds of men strained on ropes to pull the tall monster up the gentle slope that led to the wall. Sergeants whipped the rope-slaves and shouted out the cadence; boys poured melted fat on the axles. At that speed, they would reach the wall by early afternoon; this allowed ample time for Giustiniani to plan a countermeasure. He prepared several barrels of gunpowder, attached fuses and had these rolled down the slope. A spark, a flame, a bang, and the tower, and with it thousands of Turks, blew up, their bodies spread over a wide area. For once, Mahomet was not in his usual bad temper; he admired Giustiniani for his inventiveness: 'What would I not give to win this man over to my side.'

Next the Turks dug a tunnel to undermine the wall with an explosive charge (it was history's first recorded use of gunpowder in a mining operation). On 25 May, one of the defenders, a certain Johann Grant, heard strange subterranean noises near the outer wall. He ordered a bucket with water put on the ground, and by monitoring the water's increased vibration detected the exact location of the shaft. During the night, his men drilled a counter-shaft, and just before dawn the Byzantines were exposed to yet another awesome spectacle. 'It was as if lightning had struck the place, for the earth shook and with a great crash and greenish whirlwind carried the Turks into the air. Fragments of men and timber fell into the city. The besieged ran away from the wall and the besiegers fled back from the ditch.'[11]

The time had come for Mahomet to make a final decision. Spies had brought news about a relief army under the Hungarian Catholics on its approach from Valachia. The Sultan called for his generals' council. The Grand Vizier, Halil Pasha, opted for abandoning the field. Another military leader, Zagan Pasha, vociferously contradicted him: 'O Padishah, thou knowest well the great dissensions that are raging in Italy, and in all Frankistan generally. The Infidels are incapable of united action against us . . . they always stand in fear of each other, they think much, speak much and explain much, but after that do very little . . . O

[11] From *The Old Slavonic Translation of the Chronicle of Simeona Logothea*, op. cit.

Padishah, do not lose hope but give us the order to storm the city!'[12]

Caraja Pasha, the youngest and most brave of his captains, burst out: 'Honour demands that we fight.'

The audience room fell into stunned silence. A young general had dared to challenge the honour of the great Sultan. Mahomet smiled before he replied: 'I have never been one to fight merely for honour. But so be it then, in two days' time we shall climb the walls and smash the Infidel.'

To assure success, he came to a tactical decision that had no precedent: 'You will engage, successively and without halt, one body of fresh troops after the other, *without giving thought to casualties*, until harassed and worn out the enemy will be unable to further resist!' On his command, 150,000 fresh troops were to be thrown against 4,000 exhausted, starving defenders. In order to draw out the already thin wall defence, the Turks would assault the entire length of the land wall. For this, they built 2,000 scaling ladders, practically one for every defender! Without let-up, day and night, the cannons of the Great Turk pounded away at a precise spot in the wall. It had been the late Master Urban's discovery that firing two projectiles in short order at the same target caused the most damage. The first made the wall vibrate and the second caused it to crumple. With this technique, great portions of the outer wall in the Lycus Valley and around the Adrianopolis Porta were reduced to rubble.

Giustiniani climbed to the top of the cracked battlements; the Turkish camp was lit by campfire, drums pounding out a rhythmic beat. He felt that the crisis would come that morning. Unless some unforeseeable luck intervened, it would be their *dies irae*. The defence of Constantinople, the survival of an empire, had been fated from the outset to be but a bloody spasm of mystical hope, a courageous if

12 Ibid.

blind expression of spiritualism on the part of its emperor in the face of corruption and cowardice. Giustiniani felt infinite desolation. Words reeled through his mind, repeating themselves over and over again: 'Must I tell them it's hopeless . . . there's no help to come . . . my men will be slaughtered . . .' He stared down at the thousands of tents – one stood out, one with a giant green banner in honour of the Prophet – before he raised his eyes to the star-speckled night sky: 'Not by my will, oh Lord, but Thine.'

The emperor was alone in his palace, a dark and empty place that night. The unlit crown hall was so familiar that he had no trouble crossing it in the darkness. The massacre outside his walls had raged on for fifty-five days. The Sultan's artillery shook the earth; countless thousands of rounds had crashed like the ocean's waves against the wall, trying to penetrate the breach caused by gunpowder and shot. Nobody tried to relieve the pain of the screaming wounded, crying out for help until their cries became weaker and then stopped altogether. This was madness; more, it was obscene. A wave of sadness for which he was not prepared swept over Constantine. Was the prophecy concerning the end of the Eastern Empire about to be played out? He shook the thought off. If his heart failed him now, then the vile Turk would assuredly win. He straightened his shoulders and stepped outside for the short walk towards the cathedral.

On that night of 28 May 1453, a throng of sobbing and wailing citizens congregated around their emperor in St Sophia for what was to be the last Christian service in this magnificent church. In this high citadel of the faith, this most beautiful of all Christian structures, locals and mercenaries, wives and warriors mingled to celebrate the undefiled and divine mysteries of the One and Holy Saviour. The young monks, standing on the steps of the main entrance, bowed deeply as the emperor mounted the stairs in company of his captain-general. The sound of matins could be heard from inside, but the liturgy was one of approaching death.

The mood was bleak; everyone knew that dawn would be decisive.

The high arches, stretching upwards to the dome of the cupola, were hardly visible through the fog of myrrh and the smoke from a thousand candles. The ancient murals, the icons in gold and silver with the stern eyes of Jesus Christ and the Mother of God, flashed with Scythian fire. The altar was heavy with chased silver. The Patriarch of Constantinople, in a robe embroidered with gold and jewels, raised his arms: 'To Him we pray for us all forever . . .'

'Glory to God in the highest,' sang the chorus, 'and on Earth peace to all men . . .' There was little chance of that.

'Let us fight or die for our Holy Faith and our Fatherland,' intoned the emperor in a voice filled with genuine religious agitation and ecstasy. The patriarch raised his hand and blessed the emperor and his captain-general. Every emperor, or heir to the throne, had always made his pilgrimage to receive the blessing from the patriarch of St Sophia before going to war.

'Let us remain stout hearted for the Church of God and for Thee, our Emperor,' hailed the handful of defenders, before the patriarch celebrated a final *Kyrie eleison.* It was the most dramatic service ever held in this ancient church, which had represented Christianity for well over one thousand years.

Unknown to the heroic defenders, the dice had been thrown. This came about by a curious coincidence. The previous morning, a scavenger from the city's slums had managed to sneak outside the wall to loot the bodies of the fallen. He was caught by a Turkish sentry, who was about to cut off his head when the thief screamed for mercy and offered in exchange a valuable secret: he claimed he could lead the attackers into the city without their having to breach the walls. The sentry dragged him to the tent of Halil Pasha, whose face remained as impassive as ever; only a light whitening of the skin above the cheekbones indicated a reaction. He thought matters over for a moment and considered it was worth a try. Chances were that this scum of the earth was not bluffing because he was much too scared; this filthy little man, cowering on the ground and peeing in his frock, was a slum weasel, and weasels often did slide through holes in walls and fences to accomplish their dirty deeds. He threw the Greek a cunning smile: 'If such is as you say, you shall be well rewarded.' With that, he threw him a bag of Judas gold. He ordered a captain of his janissaries to put the thief's claim to the test under cover of night, and added that, whatever the result, the scoundrel's head should be chopped off. He nodded disgustedly in the grovelling man's direction: 'Take him out of my sight.'

In the pitch-black period around midnight, the rear of Theodosius Wall was a ghostly sight. Giustiniani's mercenaries were leaning tiredly against the battlements or playing dice around small fires. Nobody tried to sleep; they knew what awaited them at sunrise. Priests walked about, dispensing sacraments and encouragement to those in need. As good Catholics, some felt that kneeling down before an Orthodox priest was unworthy; perhaps it was nearness to death and a need to rid themselves of their sins which made them change their minds. Few shared a common language with the Greek priests as they confessed. On the wall's catwalk were dark silhouettes, sentries outlined in the sheet-lightning flashes of the Sultan's cannons. The final nightmare was about to begin.

Emperor Constantine moved down the line of his own valiant troops, admiring their stoic courage. They had been abandoned by the population they were prepared to defend to the death, those cowardly patricians shivering behind the locked doors of their comfortable palaces. If only he could have raised another thousand, two thousand. He turned his thoughts to an immediate problem and ordered every one of the military gates of the inner wall to be kept shut, and not to be opened whatever the reason. This would safeguard the inner wall as the city's ultimate barrier: at the same time it would prevent the defenders abandoning their positions on the outer wall – they would stop the attack or die doing so.

Shortly after midnight on 29 May 1453, accompanied by the crash of cannons, the blaring of tubas and the roll of drums, waves of Turks formed on the glacis. Giustiniani passed along the order to stand to arms; the defenders donned their helmets and uncomplainingly took up their positions with heroic forbearance. Then they waited. Maybe they'd get out of this and maybe they wouldn't.

During his career as a warlord, Giustiniani had seen a lot of men die. The ones who talked in life usually died quietly. And the quiet ones wanted to make up for lost time in their final moments. Their time was now.

Urban's terrible weapons had done their job only too well; huge gaps had been punched through the outer wall. The waves of Turks began to move with the blood-curdling shout of '*Yagma!*' Waves of the dispensable *bashi-bazouk* ran and screamed and died. Ladders were pushed against the wall. Though numbering in the thousands, the attackers stood no chance against the unbreached portion of the tall wall, where a mere handful of defenders held them off by pouring down pots of boiling oil and firing bolts and arrows. The wall held.

The main attack was aimed at the sector near the Adrianopolis Gate, at the gaping hole several hundred feet wide. The badly armed, badly trained *bashi-bazouk* couldn't break through the cordon of heavily armed Genoese encased in steel mail, guarding the breach. Time and again, they repulsed the Turk's howling cannon fodder. More came on and more died. As the pressure began to build up, many were hemmed in by the steel-clad Genoese, who pushed them into a killing cauldron. Pouring more men into the pocket was worse than useless; there wasn't enough room to take advantage of their numerical superiority. When the *bashi-bazouk* tried to retreat, they were driven back by their own *chaoushes* (military police), placed behind with chain whips or maces with which they simply bashed in their heads. Thus ended the first charge, and the men of Giustiniani raised cheers.

While arrows were recovered from the field and redistributed among the archers manning the wall, the next wave of attackers formed up. This time it was made up of provincial levies, the Anatolians, ferocious but undisciplined. Their fate was no different from that of the *bashi-bazouk*. They stumbled over bodies and dashed around the rubbled abatis, towards the archers lined up on top of the wall, who stood resolutely and in silence, before they began to fire volley after point-blank volley into the seething masses below them. The Anatolians were decimated and driven back with horrendous losses. But the number of defenders was also shrinking dangerously, and the survivors were close to total exhaustion. Some got hurt when they ventured outside the wall to undertake some personal fighting rather than let the archers do the work. With the second attack stopped, the emperor rode along the line of defenders, shouting at the top of his voice: 'Bear yourselves bravely for the Lord's sake! I see the enemy retires in disorder! God willing, ours shall be the victory!' But he knew and they knew that the Turk was still dangerous.

Then came the 15,000 élite janissaries. 'They didn't run to the walls like the Turks, but like lions.' Their line swept forward, a thick column, aimed like an arrow at the wide breach in the wall. Several flights of arrows struck among them before they reached the opening. They continued to press forward, heedless of losses, walking their horses over bodies and into the breach. Ahead rode the 'Sultan's giant' Hassan. He was not only huge, but exceedingly brave. He wallowed among the defenders; dozens fell to his Saracen blade before the broadsword of a Genoese hacked him down. Giustiniani was prepared for the janissaries inside the peribolos (the space between the outer and inner wall); on his signal his archers, placed on both walls, let go with a terrific hail of bolts and bullets from handguns, crossbows and catapults.

Their splendid silk tunics, over which they wore only a protective mail breastplate, offered little protection against the bows, arquebuses and crossbows of the Italian archers and grenadier companies. This was followed up by the advance of a solid line of steel-clad warriors, which managed to sweep the janissaries from the peribolos and through the breach into the water ditch outside the wall. This furious shower of arrows, bolts and balls, plus Hassan's death, brought about an unexpected retreat by a number of janissaries. They halted their horses on the glacis and re-formed for a renewed attack. Then they wheeled and came on again. In close hand-to-hand combat, Giustiniani's steel-clad men were fighting like tigers, and, just as a tiger's claw is superior to a lion's jaw, they managed to repel three consecutive assaults. Every man was on his own, an island encased in steel wallowing in a sea of attackers. Fires broke out, until the breach looked like the pit of hell, a tangle of smoke and fire, shouting men, riders unhorsed, dying fighters and riderless mounts, maddened by fire and plunging into everyone. Through it all, the bolts and arrows flew with their deadly bite. The defenders struck out without being aware of the destruction around them, as do most men lost in the act of battle, until a shortness of breath and increasing tiredness slowed up their sword arms. Still they stood steadfast in the breach, and there was little doubt that they would have managed to repel another assault. But a series of incredible circumstances were to lead to their loss.

But now an incident occurred for which the defenders had no countermeasure. The captured Byzantine grave-robber had indeed betrayed a deadly secret. There was one weak point in the double wall: only a single wall surrounded the Palace of the Porphyrogenitus (later called the Tekfour Serai). Next to the palace and hidden from view, located in a bend in the double Theodosius Wall, was a small gate, the Kerko Porta or Circus Gate. A quarter of a millennium before, following the sack of Constantinople by the French Crusaders of Thibaud de Champagne (1204), this door had been walled up and then forgotten – except by beggars and thieves who squatted in hovels against the wall. Their shanties were so foul and putrid that no wall guard ever ventured near them; to get through the wall and commit their thievery without drawing undue attention at the gates they had removed some bricks from the walled-up gate, which created a space just big enough for a man to slip through. On the wall's inside it was hidden behind a shanty, and dense undergrowth prevented it being detected from the outside. The hole was a 'secret amongst thieves' and thereby left undefended. The present slaughter suited the thieves, as the many corpses provided them with a golden opportunity to rob the dead. Before they cut off the head of their captive, fifty janissaries slipped through the Theodosius Wall. Without light, they moved stealthily through the filth, deposited over the years around the gate by the army of beggars. The stink made many retch. They headed towards the sound of battle from the St Romanus Porta, where they caught the defenders from the rear in the narrow confines between the outer and inner walls. The surprise was total. A scream went up: 'The Turk is in!'

Captain-General Giustiniani rounded up two dozen men and led an immediate counter-attack. His Genoese milled about in the smoke and the flame, galled by a ceaseless shower of arrows; the dismounted line was more than able to kill the dozen janissaries who stormed out of the smoke. His furious counter-charge had almost brought the situation under control when a ball from a janissary's handgun struck him between body armour and helmet. The projectile pierced his neck and Giustiniani fell to the ground. Despite the pain, he managed to stagger towards a locked military gate in the inner wall; ignoring the emperor's strict order, the guards opened the gate to let their commander pass into the sanctuary of the city. That instant, a Turkish flag appeared over the tower of the Adrianopolis Porta. 'The Turk has taken the gate!' yelled one of the guards. They stared at the flag in panic and their attention was momentarily diverted. Before they were able to act and bar their inner-wall gate, a dozen janissaries had cut their way through the military gate. More followed and fanned out into the streets of a defenceless city.

Emperor Constantine had heard the cry: 'The Turk is in!' while he led the defence at the hard-pressed Adrianopolis Porta; he wheeled his horse and raced to help. Don Francis de Toledo and Captain Theophilus Palaeologus joined him. Constantine yelled to his companions: 'God forbid that I should live an Emperor without an Empire! As my city falls, so will I fall with it!' They were in sight of the open military gate with the Turks rushing through when they found themselves surrounded by a great number of janissaries. In the ensuing mêlée, Don Francis and Theophilus were the first to be cut down by the Saracens; Genoese mercenaries pushed their way through the mass of janissaries to rush to the assistance of the emperor. One of them even managed to use his body to shield the sovereign before he was felled. And then, in full view of the defenders, the unimaginable happened: Emperor Constantine XI was hacked from his horse. Those who were near him thought to hear him cry the words of Jesus Christ on the Cross: '*Eloi! Eloi! Lama Sabactani?* – My Lord! My Lord! Why hast Thou forsaken me?'

The news raced along the walls and towers and from there spread through town. 'Our emperor is dead!' – the wail created such distress among the leaderless defenders that they put down their arms and waited for the end.

With the death of the last ruler of the Eastern Empire, the battle was over. The Turks invaded the city unopposed and carried out an indiscriminate massacre. Nothing could stop them, not even the sanctity of the Church of St Sophia; its venerable patriarch was beheaded at the altar. For three terrible days, houses were ransacked, books burned, women defiled and churches plundered. Four thousand Byzantine were slaughtered before Sultan Mahomet managed to gain control over his rampaging *bashi-bazouk* by ordering his disciplined monk cast of janissaries to kill without pity all looters and rapists. More of the Sultan's 'scum from the steppes of Asia' died within the next few hours, executed by the janissary monks, than were killed during the entire assault on the city. Victory turned to carnage, bodies heaped in Constantinople's streets and lanes, those of foe and friend, civilians and soldiers, nobles and slum dwellers, Christians, Jews and Muslims.

St Sophia, the greatest church in Christendom, became a mosque. It still is one to this day.

Nothing is known about the whereabouts of the remains of Emperor Constantine XI. Some said that the Turks took his body, naked and covered in blood, and threw it into the sea. The wounded Giustiniani was carried on to a Genoese ship and taken to Chios, where he died two days later. He was buried in the Church of St Domenico, and a present-day visitor may read the inscription: 'Here lies Giovanni Giustiniani of illustrious fame, who, in the war against Mahomet the Turk, as Generalissimo of His Serene Highness Constantine, last Emperor of Eastern Christians, died of a mortal wound.'

And what about the nimble Hungarian gunsmith, the one who helped bring down the walls of Christendom's stoutest fortress? Master Janos Urban was never buried because not much of him was ever found. But he was certainly not forgotten. Sultan Mahomet was so thrilled by the efficiency of his artillery that he ordered – as do most conquerors – a monument erected to his own glory. Only it wasn't a triumphant arch, but a palace with a giant courtyard. And in the courtyard were displayed Master Urban's remaining sixty-eight bronze cannon. There they stood for 354 years, bearing silent witness to the greatness of a victorious Sultan.

In 1807, at the height of the Napoleonic Wars, and fresh from their tremendous victory at Trafalgar, an English fleet sailed up the Dardanelles. In the face of Britannia's gunboat policy, backed up by its maritime might, London believed the Turks could put up no defence. The Sultan of all Islam and Ruler of the Faithful ordered his antique museum pieces lined up along Istanbul's sea wall. Two of the original Urban monsters of 1453, each weighing seventeen tons, were wheeled from the courtyard, dragged to the shore and stuffed with powder and 350kg cannon balls (their size and weight almost those of a modern battleship gun!). Then the flower of Islam's soldiery kneeled on their prayer rugs to ask Allah to give them strength – and most of all that the 350-year-old bronze cannons wouldn't blow up in their faces. As the vessels of the British fleet entered the Dardanelles narrows, buntings and all, the Turks aligned the two monster cannons by eye on the leading British man-of-war. They lit the fuses, put the mesh against the firing holes, and – carrrooom!!! The city shook, its ancient walls cracked – while out at sea the mighty battleship shuddered. One moment she was there, the next she was gone. The pride of English sea power blew apart with a mighty flame, and within seconds she went down, drowning sixty good and true English sailors.

In 1867, Sultan Abdul Aziz came on an official state visit to England. Londoners stared in wonder at the gift the Sultan presented to Queen Victoria. They can still do so today in the Tower of London. There she stands, all of seventeen tons and five hundred years old, the 'Dardanelles Gun'.

The facts

Despite the heroic last stand by a small number of men, the Islamic crescent replaced the Christian cross over Constantinople. The spoils of victory were shared out among the Sultan's viziers and the noble janissaries; 50,000 citizens of the conquered city were dragged into slavery to serve their new masters. Many of them had to sweep the floors in the very palaces of which they had been masters. Greek princesses were stuffed into harems to produce mixed offspring. Grand Duke Notaras and his sons were dragged before the Sultan, who had their heads cut off in his presence. With Notaras died the last heir to the Byzantine throne. After a thousand years of existence, the Great Eastern Empire was demolished, its vestiges burned, its once thriving commerce, culture and literature buried under Turkish ignorance and utter brutality.

The fall of Constantinople – quickly rebaptised Istanbul – led to repercussions way beyond the actual storming of the walls of a city. It opened wide the eastern door to Europe and bequeathed it with a new religious problem. Islam established itself as a religion on the European continent, and its rise in south-eastern Europe became only a matter of time.

The shock of the brutal sack of Constantinople reverberated through Christendom. 'How might one persuade the numberless Christian rulers to take up arms? Look at Christianity,' despaired the future Pope Pius II in 1458. The role Rome played in the demise of the Eastern Empire created an irrevocable schism between the Eastern Orthodox and Western Catholic churches and ended for many parts of Europe its Christian autonomy. Rome's failure to rush to the succour of its Christian brothers and the Pope's duplicity were among the many reasons for the upheaval of the Reformation. After 1,500 years of boisterous unity, Christendom was shattered and spiritually divided, and its leaders challenged, criticised and abandoned.

Europe was at its most vulnerable. Epidemics and wars decimated its population; kings and popes had to worry about palace revolts by princes and priests. Aragon fought with Genoa, Genoa fought with Venice, and the Pope fought with everybody. Spain, with its many Christian rulers, had its focus on the problem of the Moors of Granada, and the Holy Roman Emperor had his own troubles with the warring Hussites. The King of France had finally expelled the English, but had to worry about a new invasion, as the English were thinking about taking revenge for their defeat. As for the Germans, their country was truncated into principalities and dukedoms where every city had a king of its own. Western Europe had nothing to unite it behind an anti-Islamic banner.

The Mediterranean was turned into a Turkish lake, and this again put an end to the naval predominance of Venice and Genoa. It gave rise to new maritime powers, Portugal and Spain, Holland and England, as maritime trade shifted from the Mediterranean centres to the Atlantic coast and the Channel ports. In the wealthy Italian Renaissance towns that had come by their wealth through the spoils of the Crusades during centuries of the rape of the Orient, all trade dried up.

That was before the Great Plague invaded Europe and swept away millions.

In the years to come, the armies of the sultans overran all the Balkan countries. Their conquest destroyed all vestiges of Western civilisation; the conquered lands were degraded, ethnic cleansing reduced entire nations to the status of cattle, morality was emasculated and the once prosperous commerce along the Danube foundered. The new masters gave their subjugated Christian population a choice of becoming Muslims or being put to death.

The expansion of Islam was finally brought to a halt at the gates of Vienna in 1529, when Count Salm and his 16,000 Viennese held out for a month against Sultan Suleiman the Magnificent and 120,000 Turks. After an all-out assault on 14 October 1529, and repelled by the Viennese with great loss to the Turks, Suleiman lifted the siege.

On 7 October 1571, a mighty Christian fleet of 250 sail-powered vessels of war under Don Juan of Austria, ably assisted by Admiral Andrea Doria, smashed the Turkish fleet at Lepanto. In a master-stroke, Don Juan ordered all iron rams removed from his battle fleet. In a manoeuvre that was to revolutionise naval warfare, he then led his flotilla at an angle across the Turkish fleet, using only his firepower.[13] Don Juan's victory was complete – 230 Turkish ships were

[13] In 1805, Nelson applied the same oblique approach at Trafalgar.

captured or sent to the bottom. He re-established Christian predominance over the seas in a battle that proved costly to both sides: 15,000 Christians and almost 40,000 Turks died. But Don Juan's victory did liberate 15,000 Christian galley slaves. Lepanto not only broke the Turkish stranglehold on Mediterranean sea power, it marked the end of the classical sea battles of head-on attack; oar and metal ram were replaced by sail and broadside firepower.

The Turks invaded central Europe one last time. Having entered an alliance with King Louis XIV of France, who more than anything wanted to put the Habsburg Empire into a vice, Kara Mustapha Pasha and 140,000 Turks attempted to storm the imperial capital of Vienna. On 12 September 1683, following a three-months siege by the Turkish host, a Christian army of 70,000, paid for by the Pope and under the command of the Polish Warrior King Jan Sobieski III,[14] came to the relief of the besieged city. The Christians stormed down from the heights surrounding Vienna, and in a bloody encounter managed to push the Turkish host into the Danube. With his six Pashas killed and the battle lost, Kara Mustapha jumped on his horse and rode away into the night.

Gunpowder was once more to play a decisive role in a Turkish war, but not in the manner orginally intended. The Austrian emperor's field marshal, Prince Eugène de Savoie, confronted the Turks at the gates of Belgrade (16 August 1717). In a brilliantly executed tactical night manoeuvre, he led 40,000 Austrians against his enemy's 180,000 and decisively defeated them in an enveloping attack that dislodged the armies of Ibrahim Pasha from their defensive position. Part of it was luck. A cocky Polish gunner, claimed to be the finest shot in Prince Eugène's army, fired a carefully aimed mortar bomb – for a wager! The first shot missed and so did the second. But the third shot struck the Turks' main

[14] This outstanding military commander had been offered a substantial sum by Louis XIV, enemy to the Habsburg and ally to the Turks, to stay out of the conflict – but for once, the Pope paid more.

powder magazine, which exploded with unbelievable force. The falling deluge of timber and rocks from this man-made volcano buried or killed thousands of the Pasha's defenders. It also knocked down the tall, slender minarets of the city mosques. Seeing their sacred minarets break and tumble suggested to the superstitious Turks that Allah had cast the evil eye on them. In the confusion, Austrian hussars raced through the breach and did the rest. This brought the end of Turkish power in Serbia.

The Balkans, with its religious differences, has remained the powder keg of Europe. To this day, the religious strife between its indigenous populations has not abated, as recent conflicts between Orthodox Serbian and Islamic Bosnian, and Kosovite, Muslim Albanians and Christian Macedonians, with all their acts of barbarism, bear witness.

The Hinge of Battle at Constantinople was gunpowder and the cannon, a weapon destined to revolutionise future warfare. And a gate left wide open.

Constantinople opened the door into Europe for Islam.

3

A Confederacy of Dunces

20 October 1805 – Napoleon, or the Unequal Contest at Ulm

'Mit der Dummheit kämpfen Götter selbst vergebens.'
(Against stupidity the gods themselves struggle in vain.)
Friedrich von Schiller

'Unsere Soldaten können deren Soldaten schlagen, aber deren Generäle schlagen die unseren.'
(Our soldiers can beat their soldiers, but their generals beat ours.)
Austrian officer at Ulm, October 1805

On the night before the Battle of Austerlitz, a *grognard*, a veteran of the Revolutionary Wars, stepped up to his emperor as he was visiting his troops' camp: '*Sire, tu n'auras pas besoin de t'exposer* . . . Sire, you don't have to expose yourself. I promise you in the name of all your *grenadiers de l'armée* that you will have to fight with your eyes only. On the morning we shall present you with the Austrian banners and the Russian artillery to celebrate the anniversary of your coronation.' Napoleon was touched by this show of allegiance and trust in his genius; he knew he could count on his Vieille Garde. But it would still take something more than faith to beat the foe that held superiority in both men and terrain. This something was superior leadership, and in that he was greatly accommodated by the imbecility of some of the generals he fought.

Examples of ineptness, if not outright stupidity, are not unusual in military leadership. The average general is hardly better suited to his task than a mediocre businessman or investment broker, but his mistakes are more costly in terms of human suffering. People don't necessarily die when the market crashes, but a battle lost through sheer imbecility is dear in spilled blood. The absent-mindedness of a single general can cost the lives of hundreds of thousands. It is a fact that such folly seldom costs the general's life, only that of his hapless men. Of all the examples in modern military history, none seems more archetypal than that of a series of generals facing up to the genius of Napoleon in the weeks leading up to his most glorious victory, that of Austerlitz on 2 December 1805.

Following a relatively unsuccessful campaign against Napoleon's marshals in the Swiss mountain regions, Marshal Suvorov's misfortunes were numerous. To the Russian soldier of the wide steppe, having to do combat in narrow mountain gorges was disheartening. Still, Suvorov's main body had recoiled without serious loss before the enthusiastic revolutionary army of a young Napoleon. Now the column was moving slowly through difficult terrain, crossing the Alps to come to the aid of their emperor, who was ready to engage another French army on the Austrian plain. To reach the valley of the Danube, Suvorov had to cross some of the highest mountain passes in Europe. Hampered by his heavy artillery pieces and his supply train, halted by raging mountain streams, with small bands of revolutionaries closing in on his rear, he faced a trial similar to that of Hannibal with his elephants, two thousand years before. Only this time the Russian marshal could count on the assistance of an expert to lead him from the enclosure of the Alps. Russia's allies, the Austrians, had provided the marshal with their great geographical specialist, a man who supposedly knew the region better than anyone else. General Weyrother hatched an intricate plan and drew up a detailed map. The Russian army set off, along a country road that eventually turned into a narrow, steep trail used only by cows, leading up to the St Gotthard pass. The weather conditions were appalling; thunderstorms and deep snow soon made every step sheer hell. Horses and oxen slipped on the ice and guns had to be manhandled up the inclines; when the men lost their footing and the heavy cannon rolled back, legs were crushed beneath the massive wheels of the gun carriages. Valiantly they struggled on, step after painful step, towards the lofty heights – before the trail ended against a sheer rock face! Not to put too fine a point on it, the delicate contours the geographical wizard had drawn on his guide map were nowhere in sight. General Weyrother had sent an entire army into the wrong valley, on to the wrong path and up the wrong mountain! After weeks of delay, Suvorov's army arrived too late to join the battle.

Did this finish the Austrian general's military career? Far from it! He had another go at imbecility. In 1805, intricate timing was required for the two mighty armies of the Russian and Austrian emperors to join up at a precise point in time and place to bar the route to Napoleon's army, coming down the Danube valley. Napoleon knew that speed was of the utmost importance; he had to fall upon the Austrian Army before Kutuzov's Russians could come to its support. Napoleon needn't have worried; he had all the time in the world. Because none other than the same General Weyrother was seconded to Marshal Kutuzov to help plan his march through Austrian-held Polish territory and set a combined timetable for the campaign. Weyrother took his time and worked everything out on paper before presenting his finished plan to Kutuzov. Without intelligence about his enemy's movements

– by this time, Napoleon's force was virtually flying down the valley of the Danube – Weyrother suggested a 'measured approach', ignoring the urgency of the matter. One may well imagine an emperor's distress and a marshal's surprise when both were informed that the French had achieved complete victory at Ulm and had already marched past them on their way to Vienna. While Napoleon walked unopposed into the Austrian capital, Kutuzov's army camped on the River Inn in Tyrol. The imbecile General Weyrother had done it again: in his planning he forgot to factor in the ten-day difference between the Western Gregorian calendar and the Russian Julian calendar! The army of the Russian emperor was of no use in stopping the French, and it was of no use in running after them down the Danube. In fact, it was just being marched around a country with no enemy in sight.

By 1805 Austria had not forgotten its earlier defeats inflicted by the Corsican and was planning to reconquer its lost Italian territories. The key was a political and military coalition between two emperors, those of Russia and Austria, and the King of Prussia. Napoleon engineered a masterstroke when he acted speedily on a suggestion by his brilliant *diable boiteux* Talleyrand: '*Sire, offrez le Prusse un os à ranger* . . . Give the Prussian a bone to chew on.' In order to keep Prussia out of the campaign, he dispatched General Duroc to Berlin to offer King Friedrich Wilhelm title to Hanover, a hereditary part of the British crown, and under French occupation under General Bernadotte. The offer was tempting, but Friedrich Wilhelm couldn't decide; he vacillated between France's offer and the threat of a Russian invasion across his borders. Just to be prepared, he put an army of 80,000 Prussians on a war footing, refusing to burn his boats in case Napoleon did come to a separate peace arrangement with Austria. With this utmost on his mind, the Prussian sent his foreign minister, Graf von Haugwitz, to negotiate either with the Austrian emperor or Napoleon; by the time Haugwitz arrived in

Vienna, both were already on their way to do battle with each other in Moravia. In any case, Napoleon hardly needed Haugwitz to tell him that the danger to his flank came from Berlin; he could take on the Austrians, he could take on the Russians, he could even take on the Prussians, but he couldn't take on all three at the same time. Therefore, it was vital to hoodwink the Austrians into a decisive battle.

On 7 September 1805, Austria sent one of its armies under General Karl Freiherr Mack von Lieberich across the Inn into French-allied Bavaria to surprise Napoleon. One never surprised Napoleon, forever with one eye on England and the other on the Continent. A mathematical genius, whenever he formed one plan he always considered the alternative. 'I shall invade Germany with 200,000 men and will not halt before I crash through the gates of Vienna,' he informed Talleyrand. 'I shall not allow the Russians and Austrians to unite, I shall strike them singly before.' Quickly he laid out his strategy, dispatching his marshals Massena to Italy, Junot to Spain, Gouvion Saint-Cyr to Naples, and Duroc to Berlin. After some hesitation, and with the French pressure building up, the principalities of Baden, Bavaria and Württemberg offered him reinforcements and unhindered passage along the vital Danube valley.

For once, the French population, which had always acclaimed him as their hero and saviour, was not with him; nor were the business community and the banks. War was expensive, the vaults in the Banque de France were empty, and the market bankrupt. What was needed was a thundering victory. 'Before two weeks are out, I shall have the Austrians, the Russians, and then we see to the bankers who let us down,' he promised. 'Right now, I need my people to support my call and follow their *chef*.' Napoleon collected his Grande Armée, 186,000 men and 350 guns, and, to surprise his enemy, divided the force into seven corps under his most able generals: Bernadotte, Marmont, Davout, Soult, Lannes, Ney, Augerau. His 30,000-strong cavalry he put under the command of Murat. Napoleon kept personal charge of his Imperial Guard. On 27 September, his army crossed the Rhine at Strasbourg. He let them march past him, planted in the midst of the bridge. These were battle-tested men from proud regiments; their battle flags carried bloody names: Marengo, Rovereto, Arcola, Rivoli, Bassano, the Pyramids. 'Soldiers, your emperor is in your midst. Never forget that you represent the avant-garde of a *grande nation*. Whatever obstacles the enemy will put in our way, we shall overcome them and plant our eagles on the enemy's lands.' The soldiers threw their hats into the air and cheered as one: '*Vive l'Empereur! Vive Napoléon!*'

General Karl Freiherr Mack von Lieberich was camped with his 80,000 Austrians between Augsburg and Ulm, awaiting the arrival of Kutuzov's Russian reinforcements – which would never make an appearance because some Austrian planning genius had overlooked the difference in dates of two different calendars. Mack expected the French Army to come from the source of the Danube and down the open valley. But Napoleon never did the expected. Instead, he formed a giant flank movement through the Main and Neckar valleys, with another French army which crossed the Rhine at Mainz, then bypassed Frankfurt and Würzburg, to come down straight to the Danube at Elchingen and Donauwörth, in order to cut Mack's army off from a possible retreat to Austria.

But before this happened another one of those incidents occurred which point to a general's utter stupidity. Marshals Murat and Lannes came upon the strategically vital Tabor bridge across the Danube near Spitz. It was defended by a strong Austrian contingent with several batteries of heavy guns lined up at the opposite end of the long wooden span. There seemed no weak point in the Austrian bridge defences – the cannon were well deployed and the Austrian soldiers secure behind the cover of a shore embankment. The French marshals could have attempted to storm the bridge, but by this time the Austrians would have blown it up, and the French couldn't afford the delay of finding another crossing. Only one way was open to them – a ruse. Lannes came up with the idea: bluff the Austrian commander, who they knew to be an old, senile count. General Count von Auersperg was a septuagenarian whose only qualifications for military command were his family's wealth and their connection to the imperial House of Habsburg.

Murat and Lannes left precise instructions with their troops as to how to react, and then the twosome, garbed in their resplendent blue coats and white-plumed hats of Napoleonic marshals, started to march across the bridge, past flabbergasted Austrian engineers ready to light the fuses and blow the vital crossing to smithereens. Unperturbed, the two senior commanders walked towards the gaping mouths of the Austrian artillery. Halfway across they were met by an Austrian colonel, who saluted and demanded to know the reason why two noted marshals were walking unarmed across a bridge in the midst of a war. 'We wish to meet with your commander as we have an urgent message to convey to his Excellency.' Politeness was by far the best approach; in this they had taken a lesson from Talleyrand. While the officer rushed off to see Count von Auersperg, the first French troops sidled on to the wooden structure. Unobserved by the Austrians, French sappers managed to climb hand over hand along the understructure of the wooden span and cut the fuses leading to the barrels of powder.

The two marshals were escorted across the rest of the bridge, where they finally met the elderly Austrian commander; he first offered them a glass of his best wine before he enquired what this was all about. '*Votre Excellence*, be it known to you that Your Imperial Emperor and Our Majesty have come to an armistice, and that only twenty-four hours ago.'

'What did you say?' asked the old man, bad of hearing, and Lannes patiently repeated the well-rehearsed phrase.

'Ah, armistice, you say? Well, that then is a different matter.' And with this, General Count von Auersperg gave the order to remove the cannon from the bridge's end. Within two hours, every single element of two French corps had crossed the Danube without firing a shot. Auersperg was eventually court-martialled and sentenced to death. Yet, in another typical reversal that saved one more imbecile general, the Austrian emperor overturned the sentence. 'We cannot allow a general and aristocrat to be shot like a common criminal.' While Murat and Lannes went on to assure a series of brilliant victories, Auersperg died in military prison.

But what took place next is unique in the annals of the Napoleonic Wars. While Kutuzov was wandering leisurely towards the Danube, and Murat and Lannes were crossing the river without opposition, in a series of strategic brilliant moves and minor encounters Napoleon cut off the main Austrian army at Ulm, the town on the confluence of the Danube and the Iller.

'Hapless Mack', he was called, and hapless he was. In a sense, the débâcle wasn't even his fault – he had been handed a task that was too big for him to handle. Mack was an accomplished planner, but not an officer used to taking action. Where Napoleon could, and did, act decisively, Mack planned, then planned some more, and finally asked the advice of some bureaucrats hovering around him about the availability of practicable roads and sufficient munitions. Put up against someone of the stature of Napoleon, Mack was plainly outmanoeuvred. It began when the Austrian emperor dispatched him to stop the Corsican, without awaiting the reinforcements promised by the Tsar of Russia.

'*Die Armee sucht den Feind auf, er stehe wo er wolle. Wie ein reissender Strom wirft sie alle Dämme nieder die der Feind ihr entgegensetzt* . . . The army confronts the enemy wherever they find him. Like a raging flood they tear down every dam that the enemy puts in their way.' So ran General Mack's inspiring address to his troops. Matters turned out quite differently. Mack marched off, and when he reached the Upper Danube region with his 80,000 troops, and a considerable number of useless camp followers, a friend informed him excitedly that it was all over, that the English had invaded the French coast at Boulogne and that Napoleon was rushing with the bulk of his armies to contain the English threat. How this friend had come by this news he never bothered to reveal. This was five days before Mack was hit by Napoleon at Ansbach.

Napoleon was anxious to annihilate the Austrian threat before taking on the Russians. Again, fate was on his side, as fate always sides with the daring. First, he didn't count on Weyrother's date blunder, which would prevent the Russians from getting there in time; and second, Mack was so inept that he failed to reconnoitre the French advance and was left in the dark concerning Napoleon's disposition. The flaws in Mack's deployment, compounded by the disorganisation in the command and the men's rawness, allowed Napoleon to engage the Austrians in separate actions and drive them back. Mack retired to Günzburg, and while trying to cross the Danube was caught by Napoleon's 6th Corps. The Austrians lost 2,000 men and fled towards Ulm after suffering more defeats during skirmishes at Memmingen and Elchingen. Before Mack fully realised what had hit him, he was caught in Ulm. This was not only a pretty town and medieval trade centre; it was furthermore the key to the Danube valley. Leading out of town was the great bridge. Two roads branched off along the banks of the river, one towards the west and France, the other to Austria.

More of Mack's beaten troops kept arriving by the hour. They received no central direction; positions were taken as individual battalion commanders thought best and safest. Amid scenes of growing panic, the inhabitants packed up to leave the city. This two-way flow on the Danube bridge turned traffic into a jumble of carriages and guns, with people trying to get out and shattered units marching in. Explosions from far off helped add to the general hysteria. Officers ordered the bridge cleared and civilian carriages were simply hoisted up and dumped into the river. The population protested, shots were fired and people died. The confusion and chaos provided a foretaste of things to come.[1]

On 16 October, French corps crossed the Danube where least expected, at Neuberg; they moved ahead at lightning speed and by nightfall had encircled Ulm. Mack and his army were caught like a rat in a trap; all he could do was defend the Danube crossings. Or he could lead his forces in a breakout. For that he had enough guns, ammunition and men. Instead he did nothing and hoped for the arrival of Kutuzov's Russians. They would never come. General Weyrother had made sure of that.

Inside the city a quarrel erupted between Mack and his second-in-command, Archduke Ferdinand, who insisted on striking at least one of the corps and achieving a breakout. Overcome by a feeling of utter despair and hopelessness, Mack couldn't decide or act in any coherent manner. The general supposed to be directing an army was near collapse. For hours he just sat near his window, staring at maps and moving flags representing elements that no longer existed. His only contribution was the decision to draw his troops into the city, where they got in each other's way without doing anyone much good. Even to Napoleon, who had never before come across Mack, the Austrian's lack of aggression and decisiveness came as a surprise.

The French artillery shelled the town – this was not very effective but was decidedly nerve-racking. Archduke Ferdinand screamed and yelled, even called Mack an abysmal coward. The insult did not fire Mack into action; on the contrary, it served to depress him even more. Ferdinand

[1] F. Schlosser, *Geschichte des 18 Jhdts bis zur Schlacht von Austerlitz*, Heidelberg 1864.

acted. He took 25,000 men and attempted a *sortie en force*. Unsupported by artillery, the white-dressed Austrian battalions marched forward, volleyed and forced part of the French screen to move back. Near the village of Haslack the archduke ran into a single division. The 4,000 men of General Dupont turned the tide and gave the Austrian archduke a bloody nose; some units broke and ran. But others stood and fought well, and it was at the moment when Ferdinand had almost broken through the French ring that a dispatch rider appeared with a message from the Austrian supreme commander. In utter panic, Mack recalled Ferdinand's unit to Ulm. Under fire from the French batteries, the Austrians withdrew with remarkable speed and considerable disorder. Ferdinand was livid. Another heated confrontation took place, which ended when Ferdinand took 6,000 riders and left Mack to his fate. The archduke ran out of luck. Marshal Murat's cavalry caught up with him and delivered a three-sided attack; the firefight developed quickly, with the French getting the best of it. It was fire, load and run. The Austrians ran back and the French ran forward. The archduke's men fought well, but Murat's lightning strike was a remarkable tactical feat. The French marshal didn't stop with Archduke Ferdinand's regiments; in his forward rush, his cavalry overrode two more Austrian divisions. That netted Murat 26,000 prisoners altogether, though the archduke got away. It was the final straw for poor General Mack. Kutuzov was nowhere in sight and Mack had to look on while his troops were either captured or decimated by the French bombardment. With his morale at zero, he sent the Prince of Liechtenstein as his envoy into Napoleon's camp. The prince was a diplomat, not a general, and he tried to negotiate the withdrawal of Mack's remaining army to Austria.

'*Quelle raison ai-je de vous accorder cette demande?* What reason have I to grant you such a demand? In eight days you are mine without condition.' Napoleon was right, and Liechtenstein knew it. For Mack there was nothing to do but unconditionally surrender. On 20 October, the gates of Ulm opened, and 30,000 more Austrians marched into captivity, past a French conqueror who looked imperially down on them from his Michelsberg grandstand as they deposited their muskets and flags at his feet. The poor General Mack von Lieberich had only this to add: 'Sire, the hapless General Mack bows before you.' An entire Austrian army had been surrounded and captured without a shot being fired.

The same evening, Napoleon sent a *note d'amour* to Josephine: '*J'ai rempli mon dessein* . . . I have accomplished my design; I have destroyed the Austrian army with simple march manoeuvres, now I will turn on the Russians. They are lost.'

Had the Austrian Army promptly crossed the Danube, they might have stood a fair chance of success. Instead of leading his troops forward, General Mack spent the time composing a demand for surrender. It cost Austria dearly. They lost an entire army of 70,000, plus 200 cannon. The French lost 6,000. For them, Ulm was a cheaply achieved victory.

The following day, 21 October 1805, Nelson sank the French fleet at Trafalgar.

The defeat of the Austrian Army at Ulm had grave consequences; not only did it deprive the allies of an entire army for their forthcoming campaign, it made the Prussian king hesitate to join the Third Coalition of Austria and Russia. Meanwhile, Napoleon rushed to Vienna and entered the city without a fight (13 November 1805). Within two days, he had left again, this time towards the north and Bohemia to keep a rendezvous with destiny at a place called Austerlitz.

It was to be the battle that Napoleon had been waiting for. His overall strategy leading up to it was brilliant. Ney and Marmont blocked Austria's Archduke Charles with 80,000 troops on the Tyrolean mountain passes with a mere 20,000 men. Archduke Ferdinand, who had escaped at Ulm, was held at Prague with 18,000. But most important, his clever diplomatic manoeuvres and a cheaply won victory had kept the Prussian king from joining the Third Coalition.

Austria's Francis II and Russia's Alexander I had finally united their troops and were moving down from Olmütz along the Brünn turnpike towards the village of Austerlitz. To win time, and await the arrival of the army of Archduke Charles (they were unaware of his problems in the Tyrol), they entered into negotiations with Napoleon. Because of a possible threat to his rear from Prussia, the French emperor might just as well have negotiated as fought. But when Prince Dolgorouki negotiated on behalf of Tsar Alexander and demanded that the French abandon Belgium, Napoleon was overheard to ask him in great irony: 'What, also Brussels? We are in Moravia, and even if you were on top of Montmartre, I wouldn't give it. Go and tell your emperor that I will not be thus insulted,' and with this the talks were at their end.

Napoleon resorted to any available stratagem to lure the combined Austro-Russians out of their position. He had only 139 cannon to the enemy's 278 pieces, and 73,000 men against Marshal Kutuzov's 92,000. He deliberately over-extended his right wing in plain view of the allied scouts. He put only one division near Telnitz, a village three kilometres from Austerlitz, and then told them to pull back with a great deal of noise suggesting hysteria on the eve of the battle. He counted that this ruse would pull the combined Austro-Russian forces out of their strong defensive position and on to the open Pratzen plateau. It did. When the allied commanders noticed the manoeuvre, they planned to strike at Napoleon's weak right wing and get between the French army and its communications with Vienna.

'Before tomorrow night, this army is mine,' Napoleon exclaimed as he watched his enemy march into battle position. His trap worked. He gave detailed instructions to his marshals, placed his cannon, and talked to his men. He was simply everywhere, and everywhere he went his men cheered

Napoleon's campaign of Austerlitz
2 December 1805

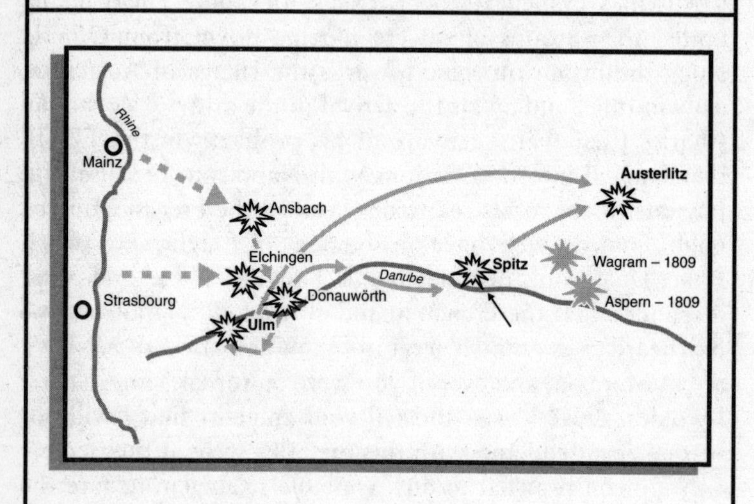

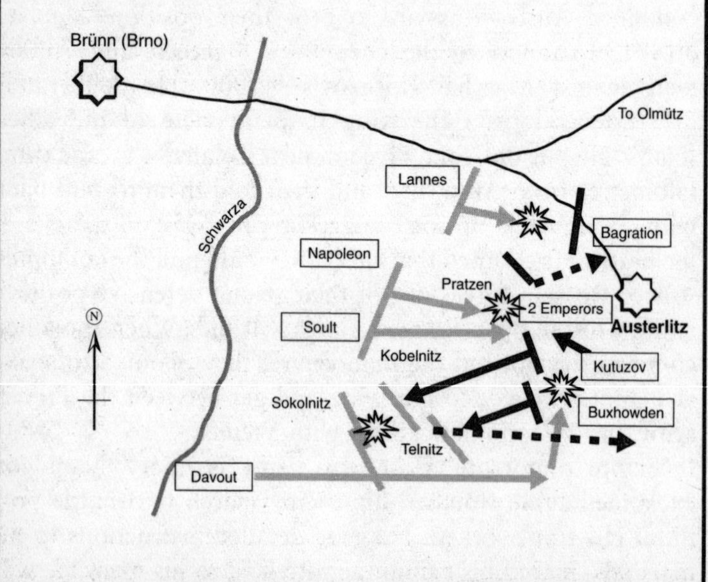

him. 'We have to learn to live and to die,' he said, 'that is the great lesson of modern tragedy.'

The morning of 2 December broke with golden sunshine. '*Le soleil d'Austerlitz*,' mused the emperor. 'A good day to do battle, soldiers. We must end this campaign with a thunder-clap and teach our enemy humility.' The soldiers cheered and waved their hats from the tip of their bayonets.[2]

A spy had provided the French with the allies' secret trumpet signals for attack. While mist still shrouded the low-lying fields, French trumpeters sounded the stolen signals to lure the Austro-Russians into a premature attack on the now heavily reinforced villages of Telnitz and Sokolnitz. Standing on his hill, Napoleon watched with glee as the Russian battalions marched into his trap. His plan was pure genius – he enticed the Austrians into an attempt to turn his right flank while actually marching into the concentrated fire of his *grande batterie* of 130 guns, about to spit out grapeshot and death. Napoleon took full advantage of the manoeuvrability of his artillery – he had made it the most important tool of his warfare. In the mist of the cold winter morning, all French eyes strained as they attempted to pierce the fog lying across the Moravian land. Suddenly a breeze began to lift patches of fog, unmasking the heavy battalions of Russians advancing not more than three hundred yards away. Stretching as far back as the eye could see were allied troops, a sheer mass of Russians and Austrians laid out like a carpet. The French cannon thundered and began to decimate the advancing corps of General Buxhowden. Despite heavy losses from the cannonade, the allied battalions continued to advance bravely until they came within range of the muskets; only then did the French gunnery captains call for a momentary pause, so that the black smoke from the Gribeauval twelve-pounders

[2] L. Frèche, *Dans le sillage de Napoléon, sergent du 24 Reg d'infantrie*, (repr.) Levallois 1994.

with their prefabricated cartridges would not spoil the aim of the grenadiers. They had been ordered to fire chest high, paying special attention to mounted officers. The riflemen fired as one, a sheet of orange flame rippling down the length of the solid line. While the first rank stepped back to reload, the second rank fired, and then the third. This steady fusillade tore apart the advancing columns. By 9 a.m. the French were acting on a new order; they slowly retreated, luring more Russian infantry on to the killing field.[3]

General Bagration's Russian corps moved laterally across the French front, and Napoleon sprung his trap. Lannes's corps hit Bagration's infantry in its flank while Soult's grenadiers stormed up the Pratzen plateau. The allied infantry turned and charged repeatedly across the muddy, snow-flecked fields only to be repulsed with great loss by a fresh French unit, Bernadotte's men, who had now come up from the south. This added to the confusion in the allied lines. The front ranks threw down their haversacks and began to fire wildly and aimlessly, while officers spurred their horses forward, attempting to rally their men. It was of no use, and many officers were killed in their futile effort to save the day. The brown fields around the Brünn–Olmütz highway were now as white as freshly fallen snow with the uniformed bodies of fallen Austrians and Russians, many still living though seriously wounded.

This premature attack on the villages, brought about by the fake trumpet signals and Bagration's lateral move, opened a gap in the allied line, permitting Soult and Vandamme's corps to climb the Pratzen Heights and cut off the Allied left from its centre. Kutuzov ordered one last, desperate counteroffensive to restore the situation, alas in vain. His lines were enfiladed, since the Russians never mounted the fire or gained the momentum their numbers should have permitted. On the Pratzen ensued a terrible, final mêlée of riders, sabres,

[3] Ibid.

guns and bayonets, cannonball and shrapnel tearing into the mingled mass. The Russians, being too disorganised, were thrown in rout from the plateau. Their battalions broke alart when their commanders were killed. They fled while shrapnel scythed thousands down with terrible accuracy. As the remnants of Kutuzov's army tried to escape across the frozen lakes and ponds, French artillery struck the ice and thousands more drowned in the icy waters.[4]

In the Battle of the Three Emperors, two went down to defeat while Napoleon's victory was complete. There can be no doubt that this was his strategic masterpiece.

The facts

'*Il vous suffira de dire: J'étais à Austerlitz, pour que en vous répondre: Voilà un brave!* . . . It is enough for you to say: I was at Austerlitz, and the people will say: Here is a brave man!' Thus Napoleon honoured his valiant troops the morning after the battle.

At Austerlitz, Napoleon's audacity was vindicated by his troops. The French proved themselves exceptionally good at gunnery, whether with musket or cannon. But what made the entire campaign a formidable military task was neither the size of the forces nor their skill in combat, but the speed with which Napoleon moved and took everyone by surprise. Napoleon had reached the apex of his career. With one stroke he abolished the Holy Roman Empire that had been in existence for almost a thousand years. To checkmate any future adventurism by the Habsburgs, he shaped from the pieces of what had been a Germanic empire the Confederation of the Rhine, a weak round table under the tutelage of the French and presided over by Napoleon himself. He was

4 Ibid., and F. Schlosser.

now called: Napoléon, Empereur des Francais, Roi d'Italie et Protecteur de la Confédération du Rhin.

With the Pope, who tried to get into a scrap with him, he dealt in his own way: '*Votre Sainteté* . . . Your Holiness is the sovereign of Rome, but I am the emperor!' Now that he had achieved the defeat of his enemies, he could turn his attention towards internal affairs, and also order a monument to his, and his army's, glory. The 'Sun of Austerlitz' was to shine for ever through a triumphant arch on the Champs-Elysées.

After a year, new thunder struck. The King of Prussia, who had first abstained from interfering during the *affaire d'Austerlitz*, now foolishly decided to go it alone. Napoleon hurried to Germany, where he organised an army. His opponents in the field were the foxy Duke of Brunswick, Prince Hohenlohe and 'Old' Blücher.[5] On 14 October 1806, Napoleon met the Prussians, who had refused to join the Austrians at Austerlitz and now found themselves without an ally, at Jena; on the same day, another encounter took place at Auerstedt. With a cool: '*Que l'affaire commence* . . . Let battle begin', Napoleon sent his army into the attack. Both encounters, though extremely costly in human lives, went to Napoleon's marshals. On 27 October 1806, at the head of his victorious army, the French emperor made his triumphant entry into Berlin.[6]

Though the Austrian and Russian troops possessed great personal bravery and fanatical devotion to their respective emperors, they were sadly let down by their generals. In assessing the causes for the allied fiasco, much was made of their mistakes. Weyrother, Auersperg and Mack were a confederacy of dunces. Poor overall strategy also helped to account for the miserable record of 1805, but the fault that dwarfed all others was poor leadership. The competition was keen, but in sheer folly the hapless General Mack von

5 At Lübeck, 7 November 1806.
6 This show inspired Hitler. In 1940 he wanted to emulate Napoleon's Berlin feat by riding through Paris; however, he was dissuaded 'for personal safety'.

Lieberich outperformed all others. He was intelligent, but in a crisis he panicked and let his fears take over. It can be said, in all fairness, that the mistakes of generals such as Weyrother, Auersperg and Mack led directly to the disaster at Austerlitz.

The blunders and defeats had a sobering effect from which many changes in the handling of military affairs resulted. The lost battles had demonstrated, as had the Revolutionary War before them, the futility of applying an archaic monarchical military system without modification to modern warfare, to France's *attaque à l'outrance* and the superiority of new battlefield techniques, like the deployment of Napoleonic artillery. Mack's ignoble failure to show any kind of leadership qualities was held up as an example and brought about a reorganisation. To the younger officer corps, the experience of Ulm was deeply humiliating. It did much to correct the errors and to form the basis for other improvements. Nothing can be achieved overnight, and so it took more defeats and another eight years, until the Battle of Nations at Leipzig, before this change came to fruition. From the defeat at Austerlitz that led directly to the formation of a young officer cadre came the policy that, in the next forty years, formed the basis for the conquest of Poland, Hungary, Slovakia, the Balkans and the Danube valley for the Austro-Hungarian monarchy.

In 1809, Austria declared yet another war on Napoleon, and it led to several battles. On 21 May 1809, at Aspern on the outskirts of Vienna, Napoleon suffered his first defeat, when Archduke Charles floated sand-laden barges downriver and destroyed the only bridge, cutting Napoleon's forces off from their supply base. The battle raged for eleven hours, and the village of Aspern changed hands nine times. At nightfall, as Marshal Lannes raced from one regiment to the next, a ball shattered his knee. '*Sauvez l'armée* . . . Save the army' were Lannes's dying words to his emperor. Napoleon saved his army and quickly reversed his defeat at Wagram (6 July 1809), but at enormous cost. Though victorious in the end, he lost more men than his enemy. The genius of earlier years had left him. Wagram was not a strategic masterpiece but more a case of each side hammering at the other with cannonballs and grapeshot. Aspern had shown that 'the Corsican ogre' was not invulnerable, and Wagram backed this up. Uprisings broke out throughout the occupied lands, from Tyrol (Andreas Hofer) to Prussia (Major Schill). They were drowned in blood and their leaders executed.

But nothing would ever be the same again after his day of glory on a Moravian field.

Ulm was not a battle – it was a strategic victory so complete and so overwhelming that the real issue was never seriously contested on the field. Ulm opened the most brilliant period in Napoleon's career. Austerlitz was Napoleon's masterpiece and ranks with Alexander's Arbela and Hannibal's Cannae. Afterwards, the absolute superiority he had enjoyed for some years imperceptibly declined. A policy that earlier had helped him – to raise the strongest possible force and concentrate it on the essential objectives – now began to work to his disadvantage. He was driven into wars that were beyond the resources even of the empire, which stimulated his opponents to extraordinary efforts, and which in the end could be won neither tactically, nor strategically, nor politically. His victories became more equivocal; the unity of military and political authority in his person led to disastrous policies. But this was for after Austerlitz, when a great man failed to limit his ambition. Not so at Austerlitz. The harsh truth was that at Ulm and Austerlitz, history had been made. But for all the mistakes and errors, acts of cowardice and bravery, the eventual outcome of the Napoleonic Wars was not altered.

In the end came Waterloo – because there is always a Waterloo.

The Hinge of Battle at Ulm was the speed with which

Napoleon moved his armies. And a timid general, who was afraid of committing a blunder.

Ulm was directly responsible for the end of the thousand-years-old Holy Roman Empire.[7]

[7] It began with Charlemagne in 800 and ended with Francis I in 1806.

4

The Fool Who Rode to His Death

25 June 1876 – Custer's Last Stand

'*Yellow Hair was a great warrior, but a fool who rode to his death.*'
Sitting Bull, Spiritual Chief of the Sioux nation, 1876

'*The only good Indian is a dead Indian.*'
Lt Gen. Philip Sheridan,
Head of Indian Territories, January 1869

On 5 July 1876, as a new superpower, the United States of America, celebrated its hundredth anniversary, having just emerged from a disastrous civil war, and the future seemed bright and without complication, the telegraph clattered in the Ministry of Defence in Washington. The message came from Bismarck, Dakota Territories. Once the duty operator had decoded the dots and dashes, he looked at the message, stunned: 'GENERAL CUSTER ATTACKED THE INDIANS JUNE 25 AND HE WITH EVERY OFFICER AND MAN IN FIVE COMPANIES WAS KILLED . . .'

What would American history be, what would Hollywood be, without the enigmatic tale of 'Custer's Last Stand'? A man with golden hair in a buckskin jacket, pistol in hand, standing bravely against the backdrop of a cobalt-blue sky, ringed by madly howling Indian braves. 'He died with his boots on . . .' In truth, his operation held nothing of the glorious and spectacular, but was a foolish and sadly bungled affair.

Like many otherwise insignificant places that have gained notoriety through ordeal, so it was with a sleepy backwater in the Black Hills of Dakota. Even today, Little Big Horn is redolent of a drama that was played out in a mere forty minutes – forty minutes of history in which, like the actors in a western movie, Indian braves of the Sioux nation confronted the 7th US Cavalry. It was neither the first such encounter, nor even a major battle, rather a 'scrap', involving a few hundred American troopers. But the figure of their leader turned this encounter into a legend of epic proportions.

Lt-Col. George Armstrong Custer,[1] reverently addressed by his men as 'the General' and known to history as 'the American Murat',[2] gained more glory in defeat than he ever had during his colourful military career on the day he sacrificed his 7th Cavalry in a reckless attack to clear his tarnished prestige. His death is wrapped in a mystery that has led to endless controversies – because nobody knows what really happened that afternoon of 25 June 1876 on top of Last Stand Hill. The site has become a holy shrine, marked by the headstones of the fallen at Custer Battlefield National Monument.

George Armstrong Custer is an enduring American enigma – this scion of American nobility with a slim, hard body, just above medium height, with a handsome face and a somewhat sarcastic aura. His military beginnings held no promise. Cadet Custer graduated at the bottom of his West Point class, and nobody would have predicted the glorious career that led him quickly to the rank of major-general during America's Civil War. He was reckless and brave to the point of foolhardiness, a flashy image-seeker, a self-confident

1 After the Civil War, his rank as a major-general of volunteers was converted to a regular army rank of lieutenant-colonel.
2 After Napoleon's most famous marshal.

and undisciplined cavalier soldier. Modesty was never his forte; his problem was that of any prima donna. In 1867 he had already totally disregarded Gen. Hancock's orders so as to pursue his own ends; the episode ended when Custer abandoned two of his men to the cruelty of Indians. The following year, his unit overrode a village and killed 103 Cheyenne, mostly women and children, which earned him the sobriquet of 'squaw-killer'. His leadership and tactical awareness were so bad they defy analysis. All these attributes define a man historians will not leave alone. 'Custer was the central figure in a Greek tragedy, hemmed in by a closing net of adverse circumstances while his every movement to extricate himself served only to hasten the inevitable end.'

Custer nearly missed his rendezvous with destiny. A few months before the outset of the Indian War of 1876, and well aware of the rampant corruption among senior officials of the Indian Bureau, Custer went to Washington to offer unsolicited testimony to the American Congress. The Indian Bureau never bothered to check his allegations. They were more concerned with accommodating the outrageous demands of New York railway barons than with such minor considerations as the wellbeing of the Indian tribes in Nebraska or the Dakotas entrusted into their care. Honest and brash, but not astute in politics, Custer pointed his accusing finger at Orville Grant, brother of US President Ulysses S. Grant, with the dire consequence that the President ordered Col. Custer kicked out of the US Army. It is strange to imagine the scene – this dashing figure of a cavalry commander pleading for reinstatement with his superior, the military commander of the Dakota Territory, Maj.-Gen. Alfred H. Terry (who was appointed when Custer was sacked). In the end it was through the direct intervention of Lt.-Gen. Phil Sheridan, the North's cavalry genius, that Custer was brought back into service. A man whose public image meant more to him than his life, he rejoined his old unit with one thought in mind: to achieve a spectacular coup in order to restore his image as America's heroic icon.

Custer's regiment, the 7th US Cavalry, was the best rider unit in the army and had an outstanding record. Much of it was due to Custer's initiative; from his men he demanded not only unquestioned loyalty but also admiration. At times he could be harsh; once he had ordered twelve deserters – they had taken off on a drunken spree – to be shot in front of his lined-up companies, while he himself frequently abandoned his regiment without permission to visit his beautiful wife. His soldiers feared and respected him; many of his fellow officers vilified him, mainly jealous of his successes. Anyone trying to damage his image had to bear the dire consequences; then he did everything in his power to bring their career to a rapid end. His number two and three were among those who didn't like him; both had been longer in the service and therefore considered that command of the regiment should have been theirs by right of seniority. Maj. Marcus A. Reno was an efficient officer with a service record that was as unspectacular as it was unblemished; but he did not possess the leadership qualities of a Custer. Capt. Frederick W. Benteen came from a wealthy Southern family; all his brothers had served with the Confederates, but young Frederick had chosen to enlist in the Army of the North. He had risen to the rank of colonel of a volunteer regiment, and was reintegrated into the regular US forces with the rank of captain. He was a much better field commander than Reno, and having to serve under the flamboyant Custer made him embittered. Their animosity was made public when the *St Louis Democrat* published an article about Custer's role during the Battle of Washita; in this Indian encounter, Custer rode off the field and supposedly abandoned Maj. Elliott and sixteen troopers to their fate. When the article appeared, Custer ordered his senior officers to find the culprit, so he could horsewhip him. 'All right, General, start your horsewhipping now,' said Benteen, 'it was me.' Custer never forgot the insult and blocked Benteen's deserved promotion to major. Both these men, Maj. Reno and Capt. Benteen, were to play a vital role in the upcoming drama. To counterbalance the anti-Custer faction of company commanders, cleverly imposed on him by the hierarchy in Washington, the colonel picked commissioned officers from his own family; his brother, Capt. Thomas Custer, commanded 'C' troop, and his sister's husband, Lt James Calhoun, 'L' troop.

The Indians hated, but also feared, Custer, who they called Yellow Hair owing to his non-regulation goldilocks. At the beginning of the Indian War, Custer had publicly issued a general order to hang all 'renegade Indians', to drag their wives and children into captivity, to burn down the tribe's tepees and slaughter its pony herds. It must have been obvious to him that he and his men could expect a similar fate, should they be caught – but nobody imagined such an eventuality, certainly not Colonel Yellow Hair.

For his outstanding service record during the American Civil War, Lt-Gen. Philip H. Sheridan had been appointed Head of the Indian Territories of the Missouri. His duty was to ensure that the Indian tribes remained well within their assigned reservations and didn't bother the white settlers, including the gold-diggers penetrating their lands. Sheridan never matched his military skills with tactful diplomacy. He is best remembered for a phrase blurted out during a meeting with fifty Indian chiefs at Fort Cobb (now Oklahoma), where Comanche chief Toch-a-way introduced himself with: 'Me Toch-a-way, me good Indian.' To which the blunt Sheridan replied: 'The only good Indians I ever saw were dead!'[3] His widely reported statement helped to set the stage for the events to come.

* * *

[3] His phrase was eventually turned into: 'The only good Indian is a dead Indian.'

In 1868 the American government had settled territorial rights with the Sioux and Cheyenne by granting them sole possession of a triangle bordered by the Missouri, Little Missouri and the Black Hills as Indian tribal lands. With big financial stakes involved, the Indian Bureau blatantly took sides. The Indians took to the warpath when gold-rushers and the iron horse penetrated into Indian Territory, despite the existing treaty with the American government protecting their lands from encroachment. The tribes began reprisal raids, striking at settlements outside their reservation's boundaries. The Indian Bureau dispatched messengers to the tribes to proclaim that any Indian brave found outside his reserve after 31 January 1876 would be considered a bandit. This edict did not put a stop to Indian raids; wagon trains bringing new settlers to the Far West were ambushed and families massacred.

In March 1876, a punitive expedition under the command of Maj.-Gen. Alfred Terry was mounted. The operational plan called for a three-pronged attack into the heartland of the Sioux nation, the Dakotas. The three units were to form a noose around the Indian territories and bring about the capitulation of the Redskins, or face a bloody end. Col. John Gibbon, with six companies from the 7th Infantry and four from the 2nd Cavalry, 450 men altogether, was ordered to leave Fort Ellis in Montana. The second column, under Brig.-Gen. George Crook, made up of the 2nd and 3rd Cavalry, plus the 4th and 9th Infantry, a thousand men in all, marched from Fort Fetterman. Terry took charge of the third column, comprising the 7th Cavalry (Custer), plus the 17th, 6th and 20th Infantry. Terry had 925 men under his command; from Fort Lincoln he marched westward to the Yellowstone in order to join up with Gibbon's force.

On 10 June, Maj. Reno and six troops of the 7th Cavalry were dispatched on a reconnaissance-in-force up the Powder and Tongue rivers. They didn't find hostiles, so Reno disregarded his specific orders and continued on to the Rosebud river. Bingo! A trail, recently used by a large number of Indians, led across the hillside towards the Little Big Horn river. Even more significant were the traces left by thousands of tepee poles. When Reno asked his Crow scouts to give him an estimate of the number, their eyes opened wide with fright: 'Plenty-plenty, Chief.' What was plenty-plenty? The Crows came up with a rough estimate from the sheer width of the trail, half a mile: three thousand braves!

'That is nonsense, there aren't that many Indians that will ever talk to each other,' stated Terry, when Reno's messenger returned with the news. In a way, Terry was right – the Indian tribes did have a tendency to fight each other. Only this time it was to be different.

Terry was not pleased that Maj. Reno had disobeyed his specific order to scout only the Tongue river region. He was worried about the fate of Crook's column, coming up from Fort Fetterman. In the meantime, Gen. Terry sent a message to Reno, ordering him to stay where he was and wait for the arrival of his own column. But the one who was really angry when Terry told him about the possible presence of a large Indian unit near the Rosebud was Custer. That fool Reno had stumbled across the Indians' main force but then had failed to inform him, his direct superior, first. This could well be the chance Custer had been waiting for, and that was why he was furious.

A foretaste of things to come happened on 17 June, precisely where Reno had discovered the big trail. Near the headwaters of the Rosebud river, Gen. Crook's southern column was ambushed by a vast horde of Indian braves, and his losses were so great that he was forced to retreat to Fort Fetterman. The message relating his premature withdrawal never reached Terry in time. Their victory gave the Sioux braves much reason to celebrate – they had discovered that the terrible US Cavalry was far from invincible. The braves from the Battle of the Rosebud joined forces with Chief Crazy Horse, Chief

Gall and Chief Crow King near the headwaters of the Little Big Horn river. This in itself represented a unique event; for the first time, but also the last, it welded the customary Sioux and Cheyenne rivals into a single fighting force of thousands of braves with at least three hundred rifles. And not just any rifles, but the latest Winchesters and Henry repeaters, which outgunned the single-shot carbines of the US Cavalry. And braves, used to stalking wild animals, were considerably better shots than the average soldier was.

On 21 June 1876, Gen. Terry finally acted upon Reno's information and on reports from agents of the Indian Bureau, who had estimated the number of renegade Indians who roamed outside their reservation as 'a few hundred'. In fact there were two entire warrior tribes, the Sioux and the Cheyenne, more like ten thousand braves than just a few hundred. Terry held a command conference aboard his floating headquarters, the riverboat *Far West*, which had steamed up the Missouri and the Yellowstone before anchoring at the mouth of the Rosebud river. Following a strategy discussion, Terry offered Custer the battalion support of Maj. James Brisbin of the 2nd Cavalry, plus three of the new rapid-fire Gatling guns. Custer refused the offer: nothing would make him share victory with anyone but his own 7th Cavalry. It was decided that the two columns were to move out separately, Col. Gibbon on the north bank of the Yellowstone and Custer's command up the Rosebud river, and from there, should Reno's observation hold up, across to the Little Big Horn. Then the columns were to wait for support. This strategy was based on the (false) premise that Cook's column was moving up from the south to put pressure on the Indians. Nobody gave any consideration to the fact that they were up against a highly mobile enemy who could move at will against any of the convergent forces now widely dispersed all over the hills of Dakota; that they didn't know their enemy's strength, and had to operate in uncharted territory without a viable system of communication to provide support in case of need.

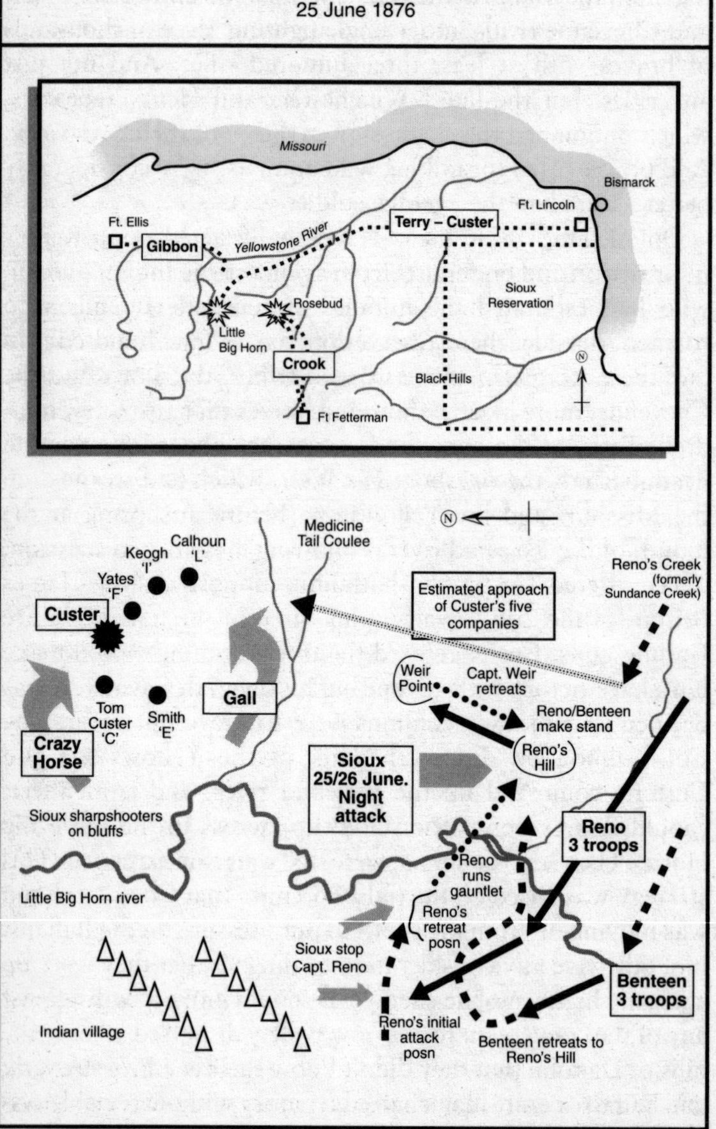
Custer's Last Stand
25 June 1876
Missouri
Bismarck
Ft. Lincoln
Ft. Ellis
Gibbon
Yellowstone River
Terry – Custer
Sioux
Reservation
Rosebud
Little
Big Horn
Crook
Black Hills
Ft Fetterman
N
Medicine
Tail Coulee
Calhoun
'L'
Keogh
'I'
Yates
'F'
Custer
Tom
Custer
'C'
Smith
'E'
Crazy
Horse
Gall
Estimated approach
of Custer's five
companies
Reno's Creek
(formerly
Sundance Creek)
Weir
Point
Capt. Weir
retreats
Reno/Benteen
make stand
Reno's
Hill
Sioux
25/26 June.
Night
attack
Sioux sharpshooters
on bluffs
Reno
3 troops
Reno
runs
gauntlet
Little Big Horn river
Reno's
retreat
posn
Sioux stop
Capt. Reno
Benteen
3 troops
Indian village
Reno's initial
attack
posn
Benteen retreats to
Reno's Hill

Lt-Col. Custer was handed confirmation of his order, dictated by Gen. Terry and written by Terry's ADC, Capt. E.W. Smith. It was worded in such a confusing manner that it became one of the underlying causes of the disaster:

> Camp at the Mouth of Rosebud River, Montana Territory
> 22 June 1876
> To: Lt. Col. Custer, 7th US Cavalry
>
> Colonel,
> The Brigadier General commanding directs that . . . you will proceed up the Rosebud in pursuit of the Indians whose trail was discovered by Maj. Reno a few days since . . . *the Department Commander places too much confidence in your zeal, energy and ability to wish to impose upon you precise orders which might hamper your action when nearly in contact with the enemy* . . . but it is hoped that the Indians, if upon the Little Big Horn, may be so nearly enclosed by these two columns [Terry/Gibbons and Crook] that their escape will be impossible . . .

Such a phrase – 'too much confidence in your zeal . . . to wish to impose upon you precise orders' – if interpreted by someone with an overblown ego like Custer, meant a free hand in his every decision. If confirmation was needed that he would go it alone, he made it clear as the 7th Cavalry rode out of the camp. The regiment passed the reviewing stand and Gen. Terry called out: 'God bless you!'

Col. Gibbon shouted: 'Now, Custer – don't be greedy. Wait for us.'

Custer turned in the saddle and fixed Gibbon with a brief 'No, I will not!'

What did his answer refer to? To the 'Don't be greedy' or the 'Wait for us'? 'No, I will not!' Everything was contained in this single phrase: Custer had no intention of waiting for assistance from anyone. Glory was to be his, and his alone.

His decision became even more obvious once he outlined his plans to his officers, something he had seldom done before. For once he justified his refusal to accept the offered Gatling guns and the contingent from 2nd Cavalry. What he didn't know was that Brig.-Gen. Crook had already retreated behind the stockade of Fort Fetterman; that Gibbon was moving with his men in the wrong direction; and that the 7th Cavalry was headed straight for the main body of two warrior tribes. Custer's only concern was that someone would get there first. Therefore, he pushed his troops to catch up with the Indian braves before anyone else had a go at them. He needn't have worried – the Indians were not about to run away. They were actually waiting for him.

A series of grave mistakes led to the disaster. First error: hardly out of sight of Terry's base camp, Lt-Col. Custer disobeyed his superior's marching orders. By changing direction without advising the general, Custer could no longer count on support from either Terry or Gibbon. Half Yellow Face, Reno's Crow scout, who knew the region, told him about a direct trail leading across the watershed from the Rosebud to the Little Big Horn river; more than ever, Custer was convinced that it was there that the hostiles had pitched their tepees. His two Indian scouts, Mitch Bouyer and Bloody Knife, plus half a dozen Crows who knew the area, were sent ahead of his column. Within hours the Crows came upon a recent trail made by many ponies and tent poles, which led in the direction of the Little Big Horn. Soon another, wider trail joined the original from a southerly direction. (These were the trails made by victors of the encounter with Crook on the Upper Rosebud.)

On the morning of 24 June, the regiment came upon the remains of an Indian camp. It was large and had been arranged in a defensive circle. Custer wasn't impressed either by the telling arrangement or by the great number of fireplaces. George Herendeen, a white scout, suggested reporting their discovery to Gen. Terry, but Custer forbade him to leave the column. As justification he claimed that it was much too risky for a white man to ride back alone. He called for his officers. 'I intend to follow the trail until we get the redskins, even if it takes us to the Missouri or into the Nebraska Agency.' It was now obvious that he intended to allow no one to interfere in what he considered his private war. Lieutenants Wallace, Godfrey and McIntosh walked to their bivouac tent, where Wallace said out of the blue: 'I think our general is going to be killed. I've never heard him talk like this before.'

Scout Mitch Bouyer approached them. 'Half Yellow Face wants to know if any of you have ever fought Sioux before.'

'Why does he want to know?' Lt Godfrey demanded.

'Because he says you have a big fight on your hands, perhaps bigger than this regiment can handle.'

'Does he now? Our boys can deal with anything they have to put up against us.'

And Lt Wallace asked almost as an afterthought: 'What does Half Yellow Face call a big fight?'

Half Yellow Face said something in Crow and held up the spread fingers of one hand.

'Five hundred?' Wallace smiled.

Bouyer shook his head. 'No – five thousand!'

The three lieutenants seemed stunned. 'Does the general know?'

'If you tell him he won't listen. It's his game.'

The regiment had now covered almost sixty miles over rough territory; and at a pace too fast for the packhorses. In a recent economy drive, the US Army used for pack animals such horses as had been decommissioned from active cavalry duty. To enable him to push on at this horse-killing rate, Custer assigned the troop of Capt. Thomas McDougall, in all 130 riders, or a fifth of the regiment's strength, to ensure the safety of the pack train while he moved on with the rest. This decision separated the actual fighting unit from its ammunition store; each soldier carried with him a hundred rifle bullets and twenty-four revolver bullets. While the pack animals were allowed a rest, Custer and his men rode until 2 a.m. Before sunrise on 25 June, Lt Varnum, Mitch Bouyer and three Crow scouts were sent up a nearby hill (Crow's Nest) to spy ahead. They couldn't make out details since everything was blanketed by dense smoke, which could only have come from hundreds of campfires. One of the Crow rode forward and frantically waved his arms. He had spotted 'the biggest pony herd any man ever saw'. Scout Mitch Bouyer put it more succinctly: 'Biggest village ever – a heap too big!'

During their night ride a small incident had occurred, one that was to have a major impact on the drama. One of the few packhorses that had been taken along with provisions for the day had slipped its cargo, and Sgt Curtis was sent back with two men to recover the missing crates. They crested a hill and there, right before them, were six braves, sitting around the biscuit tins and feeding on hardtack. When Curtis charged downhill, the Indians jumped on their ponies and raced off. While his soldiers recovered the cargo, Sgt Curtis galloped ahead to warn his commander. Along the way he saw more Indian braves watching him from the skyline. With Curtis's report, Custer knew that the element of surprise was gone. He had to act, and act fast, because he couldn't permit the Indians to slip away; first, he had wilfully disregarded Terry's order, and second, failure now would mean the end of his military career. Without further reconnaissance, he ordered his regiment to saddle up. This alone proved Custer's contempt for his enemy. He advanced some four miles, then rode up to Crow's Nest to see for himself. By now, the heat made it impossible to distinguish summer haze from wood smoke. 'Where in the hell are your Redskins?' he demanded of Scout Bouyer, who had ridden with him to the top of the hill, and once again warned him: 'General, I's telling you, down there is the largest goddam Indian village you's ever seen on the plains.' As soon as he came down, Custer called his officers: 'We must attack immediately or the Indians will scamper.' Custer's confidence in the invincibility of his boys of the 7th was supreme; no Indian horde could possibly stand up to the charge from the US Cavalry.

Benteen knew him well enough to understand that the regimental commander was working something out in his head – probably just how much he wanted to tell them about the day's business and how much he wanted to leave out. 'You haven't told us anything so far,' Benteen wanted to remind him, but he knew only too well it was hopeless. Whenever Custer talked like that it was no use raising doubts or asking any more questions. He wanted to tell his boss that he was embarking the regiment on a ridiculous, perhaps even reckless, mission. And that he, who insisted on being called 'General', was nothing but a vain and stupid glory-hunter.

'Any questions?' asked Custer. The way he said it made it clear that argument was the last thing he wanted. He wanted cheers, but got none from Reno, Benteen or Weir. Only a junior lieutenant offered some faint praise: 'General, we sure shall ride through them like a knife cuts through butter.'

'We sure will, men. I'm always right,' the general declared. For once he was wrong.

Two of the fiercest warrior tribes of North America, the Sioux and the Cheyenne, had gathered their forces around the great wise man of the Plain Indians, the Hunkpapa Sioux medicine man, Chief Sitting Bull. Only two moons before, he had had a vision of many bluecoats falling upon his people. Though he himself took no part in the actual fight, he called for a pow-wow, during which he pleaded with great wisdom and helped to unite the quarrelling tribal chieftains. 'Braves! *We have everything to fight for – and if we are defeated, we have nothing to live for*. Therefore, let us go out and fight like brave warriors.' With that simple phrase he set in motion an attack which, even to this day, stands out as the prime example of Indian warriors fighting white soldiers.

Before they set out on the final approach, Custer ordered the scouts to sneak up on the Indians' pony herds, kill the guards and stampede the horses. 'Indians are like the Huns, they cannot fight barefoot!' Once again, he was to be proven wrong. But his major error was one of tactics. The 7th had been spotted, that much was now certain, and the element of surprise was gone. More important still, Custer didn't have the answer to the two elementary questions relevant to planning an attack: the enemy's disposition and the enemy's strength. He compounded his mistakes with his next error, perhaps the most fatal of all. The capital sin of a commander in the field is to divide his unit without detailed information about his enemy. But that is precisely what Custer did. He split his regiment's eleven troops into three separate battalions. Rushing blindly into enemy-held territory, without spare ammunition and with a regiment divided into three separate units, made each column vulnerable to annihilation by a superior force. While Custer's plan was to attack simultaneously with two battalions, the Indians could choose their time and place, pick any of three targets and throw everything at it, before turning on the next. Years later, Chief Red Horse admitted: 'Had the soldiers not divided they would have killed many Sioux.'

The die was cast. The regiment moved out in three columns (actually four, allowing for the pack train which was already separated from the main unit).

1. Capt. Benteen with 'D', 'H' and 'K' troops was ordered to protect the left flank, with the order to cut off escapees from the Indian village once Custer had routed them.

2. Maj. Reno with 'A', 'G' and 'M' troops was to move parallel to Custer's unit along the Sundance Creek (soon to be renamed Reno's Creek). He was to make a diversionary attack on the southern extremity of the village, stampede the

pony herds and spread confusion among the tepees to divert the attention of the Indians.

3. Lt-Col. George Armstrong Custer's battalion was coming down from the north to lead the main attack on the village, which he believed to be lying behind the series of bare knolls bordering the Little Big Horn river. Custer's unit was made up of five companies: that of his brother, Thomas Custer, 'C'; Smith's 'E'; Yates's 'F'; Keogh's 'I'; and Calhoun's 'L' troop. Custer's 225 men plus one reporter were headed for an appointment with destiny.

And because destiny so decided, facing the squaw-killer 'Yellow Hair' was one of the most astute Indian braves. Chief Crazy Horse was an Oglala Sioux, who had fought many battles and had learned from the white man's way of fighting. In contrast to Custer, who stumbled blind into Indian territory, Crazy Horse was being kept informed of his enemy's every move. He had no intention of 'slipping away', and was surprised to hear that the regiment had split into four separate forces. He now could hit every column separately, and for this he counted on something between 3,000 and 8,000 braves.

When he was told of the two main parties approaching along the banks of Sundance Creek, he figured that the one coming down the left bank (Reno) would cross the Little Big Horn at the only passable ford and attack the Indian village from the south. His plan had to be basic and simple to execute, because he was only too aware that Indian bands could never be brought to fight in any disciplined manner. They loved to ride circles around the enemy, firing arrows and bullets at them as fast as they could, but often without noticeable results. This he had to change, but first he had to overcome a psychological problem: it was an Indian brave's belief that without his pony he was not a true warrior. It took some persuading, but he managed it. He took his best marksmen and laid ambushes, one in wooded terrain at the southern edge of the village and another behind the cover of bushes atop the river's bluffs. He also organised a large rider unit, which was to prevent the advancing columns, harassed from the front, from retreating to the river. His scouts kept him informed of every move the two columns made, so when he heard about the latest change in direction by Custer's unit, he quickly revised his strategy and formed two mounted parties of several thousand riders each, one under Chief Gall and the other under his own command. He told Gall to hide his braves under the bluffs of Medicine Tail Coulee, a narrow creek which cut through the hills to end in the Little Big Horn river, while he placed his own men to the north, well hidden behind the bare knolls. He counted on his two rider formations to snare Yellow Hair in a deadly ambush.

The trap was set.

'Move out!' Custer spurred his horse to the head of the column as they moved towards the distant ridge. For some eight miles, Custer and Reno's columns rode in sight of each other, with only the lazy, flowing Sundance Creek between them. It was now 12.15 p.m., and Custer gave Reno a signal with his hat to proceed alongside. The Sundance took them into a stretch of foothills before the creek took a sharp northward turn between two brush-covered hills and a huge cleft in a rock wall, and from there split and passed around a swampy clearing the size of a football field bordered by a heavy growth of trees. Reno led his column across the creek to that island. The air down in the valley was heavy and motionless, and the troop was plagued by a myriad of mosquitoes. All seemed perfectly normal and quiet. On the distant skyline Reno could clearly see Custer's column. They could also see a lone rider dash up to their general. It was the scout Fred Girard, whooping and yelling at the top of his voice: 'There go yer bloody Indians, runnin' like the devils!' What he had actually seen was a group of some forty Indians, whose job it was to keep Custer under close observation. Custer immediately turned to his Crow scouts:

'Go and chase them.' But his ten Crow wouldn't run after a half-hundred Indians, and Custer became red in the face: 'Go and chase them or I will take away your weapons and make women of you!'

The sight of the fleeing Sioux decided Custer – 'there goes my career' may well have been on his mind. He ordered an immediate turn away from the Sundance Creek, and away from Reno's column. Within moments, both columns were out of sight of each other. Custer's sudden move had Reno confused. Then a rider splashed across the creek – Custer's adjutant, Lt Cooke. He carried the commander's final message to Reno: 'PURSUE AND CHARGE THE INDIANS WHERE YOU FIND THEM AND *YOU WILL BE SUPPORTED BY THE WHOLE OUTFIT.*'

This order was entirely misleading, since by now the three individual columns were much too far away from each other to give mutual support. Yet Reno, no doubt competent within limits but utterly unimaginative, interpreted the message to mean that he was to launch a frontal attack on the village – immediately, without waiting for intelligence about the enemy's strength from his own scouts – while Custer's unit would ride around the bare knolls to the north for a simultaneous attack on the tepee town from the rear.

Lt Cooke splashed back across Sundance Creek, where he joined up with Capt. Myles Keogh of 'I' troop, which had fallen slightly back from Custer's column. From their vantage point they could see Reno's column crossing the Little Big Horn and cantering up between the bluffs towards a heavily wooded area. They could also hear gunfire and see Reno's men push a group of Indian sentries from the bluffs. Keogh and Cooke didn't hang around long enough to see what happened next. Instead, they wheeled their horses and rode after Custer, reporting that they 'had seen Reno advancing in face of slight resistance' and that they had spotted a dust cloud beyond the hill, probably from Indians in wild flight. Their report was wrong, a mistake not infrequent in the excitement of a coming battle. They reported what they *had seen* (slight resistance) and *believed* would happen next (Reno advancing), but not what was really to take place, a few minutes thereafter.

Maj. Reno had indeed just engaged a few sentries, who, after letting off a few rounds, disappeared among the bluffs, when a trooper shouted: 'It's the general.' A solitary rider stood on a distant hill and waved what looked like a hat. Because of this, the soldier took him for Custer. However, it is most unlikely that anyone could have made a positive identification of a figure one and a half miles off, distorted by the shimmering heat waves of a midday sun. But, as far as the troopers were concerned, it was their general, and he had given them 'the signal'.[4]

Feeling momentarily heroic and raising himself in the saddle, Maj. Reno gave the order for attack. 'All right, boys, let's go at 'em!' Two troops formed in line, with one slightly behind as reserve. When the first riders reached the top of the embankment, they noticed the same thick cloud of dust as had Capt. Keogh before them. 'Major, they're running!' yelled one of his lieutenants. Reno immediately ordered a fast advance to pursue the cloud – and only then realised his blunder. That cloud was not running away – it was coming straight at him, and from every side! He looked for his native scouts, but they had vanished, leaving his flanks without protection. He still had no idea about the true size of the enemy. Then everything happened at once. A hail of bullets met his lead troop; horses stumbled and riders fell. Sioux riders appeared on the crest line and more on his open left flank and to his rear. The howling Redskins numbered in their thousands! Reno ordered his line to swing right, head for a wooded hill and dismount. The horses were led to safety in a swampy bend of the river and put in the care of horse-holders, while his three companies

[4] The identity of the lone rider remains a mystery. It may well have been Capt. Keogh, since Custer was already too far advanced at this hour.

formed a skirmish line. The Sioux lapped around both Reno's flanks. The trees masked the Sioux' envelopment and Reno did not see it in time. The wildly yelling Indians rode circles around the cavalrymen. A firefight erupted on all sides with the Indians getting the best of it – a case of hide and fire, load and run. Whenever the opportunity presented itself, Indian braves infiltrated the wood to fire off their arrows. Reno's men fought without the 'promised support', and they fought well. Either the Indians were unbelievably bad shots or the cavalrymen extremely lucky, but so far only three soldiers had been killed. Under the incessant rifle fire, Reno's line disintegrated, and the men ran to the swampy river's bend to be near their mounts, a natural reaction for a cavalryman. Had Reno been more decisive and able to organise the defence properly, they could probably have held out for a long time. But the Sioux's surprise attack had taken the initiative from him, plus the uncontrolled expenditure of bullets began to pose a serious threat to his men. Maj. Reno realised that the only salvation lay in retreat. The order for withdrawal and the first touch of panic came at the same moment. He looked for his bugler, but he was nowhere in sight. 'Mount up! Mount up!' Reno screamed. Men scrambled for their horses; others, seeing their buddies on the run, followed them pell-mell. What was intended as an orderly withdrawal turned into what Americans generally refer to as 'getting the hell outta here!'

An Indian brave was taking careful aim with his repeater rifle at the quickly disappearing leader of the white men when Reno's personal Crow scout, Bloody Knife, passed with his horse in front of him. The bullet meant for the major struck Bloody Knife between the eyes, splattering blood and brain over the major's face. He succumbed to a mental paralysis, tore the neckerchief from his neck and wound it around part of his face, in the firm belief that the bullet had pierced him. For minutes Reno was in no condition to issue a coherent order. As a result, he forgot to tell two lieutenants and fifteen men, still holding the flank, to get out.

On the swampy island a company captain formed his men into line-of-four, and they headed for the river ford. This unexpected manoeuvre took the Sioux by such surprise that they momentarily opened a gap in their circle, but then recovered in no time. This forced the cavalrymen 'to run the gauntlet'. Indians, placed up on the bluffs, poured withering fire on to the madly fleeing troopers. Some soldiers tried to reach safety by splitting off from their column; they were immediately chased by dozens of wildly yelling Sioux. The surviving troopers splashed across the ford. That was when the miracle took place. The Sioux stopped, wheeled their ponies and were gone! The troopers couldn't believe their good luck. They didn't realise at the time that the Indians had found themselves a much bigger prey to hunt.

The losses among Reno's column were eighteen killed, forty-six wounded and fifteen missing (those Reno had failed to warn in time). His bleeding, tired troopers drove their exhausted mounts up a hill and collapsed. For the 7th Cavalry the day was far from over; the battle that made history was just about to start.

On that afternoon of 25 June 1876, Custer led five troops of the 7th Cavalry across Medicine Tail Coulee and up a hill, and no white man ever again saw one of them alive. So what *do* we really know? 'What we know for certain is that Custer charged deliberately into a neatly rigged trap.'[5]

With Custer it is near impossible to come to a fair judgment – there are no records to facilitate the historic analysis of what really happened. Most of what we know about the fate of Custer's column came second hand, and often many years after the event, from Indian campfire tales. The most telling story was that of Jack Red Cloud, son of Chief Red Cloud; he gave an account of how he, as a young brave, had spent that

[5] Brig.-Gen. S.L.A. Marshall, *Crimsoned Prairie*, New York 1972. Marshall is an American military historian and Custer battlefield analyst.

day: 'The Sioux kept circling around Custer and as his men came down the ridge we shot them. Then the rest dismounted and gathered in a bunch, kneeling down and shooting from behind their horses.'

As they marched towards the Little Big Horn, Custer and his troops were in good spirits; already it looked as though the usual Indian confusion had begun, for he was receiving reports of small groups running for their lives. A short while before Custer made his final approach, he dispatched his company sergeant, Daniel Kanipe, with a verbal message to Capt. McDougall to hurry up with the pack train. On his way, Kanipe managed to outrace some Indian riders; his first contact was with Benteen's column, moving at a leisurely pace.

'The general, Captain, he wants the pack train to get a move on.'

'What about the Indians, seen any sign of them?'

'Only the half dozen that chased after me, sir.'

Benteen was reassured and sent Kanipe on to McDougall, still trailing miles behind, considering that the general's message didn't really concern him.

Custer's column of hard-muscled regulars continued irresistibly towards their doom. Though some Indian bands tried to hinder their advance, the five companies just shrugged them off without ever deploying. The advance scouts and flankers were enough to drive off these irritants. In fact, it was an easy ride on a lazy afternoon, sweating in the broiling prairie sun. Later on they would water their horses and take a dip in the river, and that was what they really looked forward to. Custer was in the lead next to his regimental standard-bearer.[6] Another ridge was crossed before they made it out to a grassy slope with a tall, bare knoll at the far end. It stuck up like some Indian burial ground, but that was only an impression because

[6] Custer had two flags, that of his regiment and his own as a former major-general.

there was nothing to point to any living thing near by. Just mosquitoes, groundhogs and a few Indians. But it seemed a good place at which to climb and see what lay beyond.

'You wait here,' Custer ordered. He walked his horse across the thick yellow grass to where an opening between rocks led up towards the rise. There was no wind, only silence, and Custer hoped that the next sound he heard wouldn't be a shot from an Indian's rifle. Ten minutes later he got to the top of the hill. At the limit of his vision a dark swath of trees outlined the course of a river. But what was beyond this river held his attention: Scout Bouyer had been right – down in that wide plain were more tepees than he had ever imagined. It must have been at that moment that he finally realised what he was really up against. He dispatched his trumpeter, John Martin, with a message for Capt. Benteen, who by now was trailing behind Reno along Sundance Creek.

BENTEEN.

COME ON. BIG VILLAGE. BE QUICK.

BRING PACKS.

P.S. BRING PACKS.

'Be quick' – this made his urgency clear. Custer was calling for immediate assistance from Benteen's three reserve companies. 'Bring packs' was the obvious call for more ammunition. Did Custer plan to hold his position until resupplied with men and bullets, or did he intend to attack the village in the face of vast numerical superiority and hope for 'Custer's Luck'? We shall never know. When queried by Benteen about the situation up front, Trumpeter Martin stated that he had 'seen some Indians who *skedaddled*'. More errors compounded the situation. Capt. Benteen did not act on the urgent note since to him 'bring packs', repeated, was the keyword of the order, and he had no spare ammunition other than what his men carried, the pack mule train still being well over a mile to his rear.

Custer reached Medicine Tail Coulee through an opening in the bluffs. He crossed the dried-up riverbed about half a mile to the north of the village and thereby failed to spot Chief Gall's massed braves, hidden farther down the same coulee. His column was now in battle formation. 'C' and 'E' troops were in the lead, 'F' with Custer in the centre, 'I' and 'L' as rearguard reserves. The column climbed from Medicine Tail Coulee towards a hill, which was to gain eternal fame. From this hill, a gentle slope led down to the river and the Indian village. It was a stunning sight – hundreds upon hundreds of tepees, smoking campfires and children, staring at the blue formation up on the slope. Squaws raced about, grabbing children and dragging them back into tepees. Women, by the river to fetch water, dropped their gourds and ran. In their eagerness, the troops missed a vital fact: that there were no men about. To the men of the 7th Cavalry, the target of the open tepee town must have looked inviting.

That was when it all went wrong. The attack came suddenly and without warning. One moment it was a lazy Sunday afternoon, and the next a solid line of riders was pouring over the crest of the hill. Custer's troops jumped from their horses, and could feel the hard-packed earth shaking under their feet. To their flanks, from beneath the bluffs and gullies, spilled forth the many thousand braves of Crazy Horse and Gall. They attacked simultaneously, many on foot, in good Indian fashion using every bush, every dip, for cover. From their prone position, the Sioux fired at the dismounted, free-standing soldiers, cutting them down by the dozen. Within minutes all hope of Custer extricating his companies was gone. Thousands against a few hundred on a bare slope without cover – the outcome was a foregone conclusion. The Indians attacked from all sides and the cavalry stood its ground. The Sioux picked off the horse-holders and stampeded the cavalry mounts. With a quickly organised skirmish line, Keogh's 'I' and Calhoun's 'L' troops repulsed a rider attack. That was where the Sioux suffered most of their casualties. They had come whooping down the hill and were met by a solid volley; many were knocked off their ponies, and they were forced to withdraw back up the slope. When there seemed a glimmer of hope for the encircled companies, a new Indian wave stormed up from the river, the victors from the earlier encounter with Maj. Reno's troops. The Sioux set tumbleweed and bushes on fire and under the smokescreen marksmen sneaked up to the company perimeters. A soldier toppled forward. 'Haiii-yi-yi!' sang out a brave in triumph, brandishing his smoking rifle over his head. His war chant was taken up by hundreds of other hidden riflemen, and the volley from their fire struck into the defenders. One by one, they went down in the gale of gunfire. The Indians whittled away at the troops with well-aimed rifle fire and showers of arrows, until they could get in close with battleaxes and knives to finish off the survivors.

It is not clear whether Custer actually ordered the only attack that was attempted on the tepee town; his brother Thomas's 'C' troop and Capt. Smith's 'E' troop tried to get down to the river and use the general confusion to crash out through the unprotected village. This had no chance of success. Before they managed to form up into a coherent attacking unit, the two companies ran into withering fire from hidden sharpshooters placed on the bluffs east of the river. Dozens of troopers died and the rest jumped from their mounts, shooting the horses to use them as a breastwork.

More and more Sioux came on, fast and wild, howling like drunken men and ready to die. They had the courage and they had the numbers. Jack Red Cloud was among the braves coming up on foot from the river bluffs. He was caught up in a sudden move forward as the blue men were falling back. As he leaped from his cover of tumbleweed, a hot slap of air brushed his face. A ball fanned past him and killed the brave behind him. The men in blue were firing madly, but somehow he got through. He raced up to the breastwork and jumped over the dead mounts, while more braves moved with him, hurdling over dead horses and dashing uphill across the backs of fallen soldiers. Some bluecoats had stopped in their mad scramble uphill, kneeling and firing. He saw their guns aimed at him but that didn't stop him. A brave was no more than ten feet from the blue line when he was shot in the chest. All around Jack Red Cloud was noise and a mad rush; hundreds of braves were closing in on the next line, and then the next. A blast from above – earth and stone erupted as more braves crumpled like broken dolls; some rolled down the slope to disappear over the edge into the ravine. Then he was in close. A trooper raised his rifle and Jack just managed to divert the muzzle. There was a blast next to his head and the brave next to him was lifted up and flew through the air. Jack's ears were ringing; he was momentarily stunned by the proximity of the blast. Another brave uttered a savage yell as he smashed in the head of the trooper with his battleaxe. Blood flew across the grass in a savage spray. The blue men were falling all over the slope, for Chief Crazy Horse's braves held a great numerical advantage, and in hand-to-hand fighting they could bring three or four warriors up against any single soldier. In a bloody tangle of sabres, knives and tomahawks, men collapsed in heaps of agonising flesh. Indian lances shredded uniforms, braves staggered under the impact of bullets – the entire slope was a mayhem of yelling, bleeding, twisting and falling. The circle around the US companies grew tighter, the fighting ever more restricted around a ring of dead and dying cavalrymen and Indian braves. Bullets and knives could no longer distinguish between friend and foe. Men in blue and bare-breasted braves clung together in death. Jack Red Cloud felt his scalp; it was matted with blood. He hadn't even noticed when somebody put a hole in his head.

The men of the US Cavalry fought for their lives, battling

with rifle butts, knives and bare fists. They had no illusion about their fate – the Sioux took no prisoners. Their ranks faltered and fell back, a few of them still locked in brutal brawls while more arrows and bullets began to pour into the tight mass. The soldiers fought on bravely until they were overwhelmed by the tidal wave of yelling Indians. Custer's men died where they stood, grouped in their respective companies. The last survivors crawled uphill to join Yates's 'F' troop, positioned on a knoll to be forever known as Last Stand Hill. According to the various Indian versions, these few rallied around the general and every single one performed feats of bravery beyond description.[7] Custer's Last Stand was not the invention of historians; it was a horrifying reality. Crow King said later: 'They kept in order and fought like brave warriors as long as they had a man left.' Then it was over, quick and final.

The entire battle lasted not more than forty minutes.[8] For one more hour, the Sioux roamed the battlefield, killing all those showing signs of life before scalping their victims. 'They made such short work of killing the wounded that no man could give a correct account of it,' was the way that the Sioux Hump put it. They stripped the dead of their uniforms, piled them into a giant heap, set it aflame and celebrated their victory with a war dance around the bonfire.

Two bullets struck Custer, one in the left chest near the heart, the other through his temple. His dust-covered body was caked with blood, his own and that of the men he had probably tried to help. His eyes were aimed rigidly, sightless, up into the topmost depths of a glaring and pitiless prairie sun. He had been stripped but not scalped, though his scalp would

7 In 1983, a forest fire devastated the area. But it helped to expose many spent cartridges which showed the approximate location of the five companies.

8 The fact that around 3.30 p.m. the Indian braves had stopped their pursuit of Reno's routed troops to join Chief Crazy Horse in his main charge established that by around 4.30 p.m. everything was over.

have represented the major trophy of the battle. It is true that he had cut his telltale long blond hair before embarking on this campaign, but he must have been recognised by his buckskin jacket. Therefore, the story that they overlooked him when they scalped and stripped the fallen is highly improbable. Perhaps this honour was reserved for Chief Crazy Horse, and the chief showed a final respect for his enemy because he died a brave man. That would be entirely within Indian custom and is the most likely explanation. It helps strengthen the belief that 'General Yellow Hair' fought to the very end and died a hero.

The rest of the story of that day is muddled. It played out four miles farther south. A shaken Maj. Reno had fled to the top of a hill, which was to carry his name. There he was joined by Capt. Benteen, certainly the more dominant of the two commanders.[9]

'Benteen,' Reno almost cried, 'for God's sake, halt your command and help me. I've lost half of my men.' That wasn't quite true – in fact, Reno's men still numbered 105. He had lost 'only' three officers and forty men, fifteen of whom he had left behind down by the river.

'Where's the general?' Benteen wanted to know, since from where they stood all they could see was a great dust cloud and a few warriors riding around in the far distance.

'He's headed north,' replied the shaken major, 'that's the last I've seen of him.'

'Dammit, Major, we must find out.'

'We cannot, my troop has had it . . .' It wasn't clear who had had it, the soldiers or their thoroughly shaken commander, whose judgment was more than questionable after his own disastrous retreat. Their two units were united at 4 p.m., well in time to head for the sound of gunfire and rush to their commander's assistance. It is certain that

[9] Most of this was revealed during the subsequent official inquiry.

the sudden appearance of several hundred uniformed riders on the slope above Little Big Horn would have altered the outcome and saved a great number of Custer's men. But that was not to be. Instead, vociferous wrangling between the two commanders over who should do what took place, in earshot of their troops. Benteen claimed afterwards that he was not the senior officer on the spot – a lame excuse, since the united seven companies would have had sufficient means to find out at least what was happening to their commander. Such decisive moments show up the quality of individual leadership. That was why the headstrong and arrogant Custer had been handed the command of the regiment, and not Reno. The forceful and decisive Custer would never have sat back as long as he had a platoon and a hundred bullets. But Reno wasn't carved from the same hard wood; he was too shaken to think clearly, his ability to make a decision blocked by his condition of shock. The experienced cavalry officer, veteran of the Civil War slaughter, was suddenly faced by an enemy he couldn't handle – savage Indians.

Added to this critical delay was the normal physiological requirement in terms of the time needed to assess the data, envisage the appropriate action, reach a decision to act on it, then give the order. Inexplicably, the courageous Benteen gave in and put himself under Reno's orders, despite Custer's written 'be quick' directive which he still carried in his pocket. This showed up his own lack of judgment. In these critical minutes, one who couldn't think and one who wouldn't act commanded the regiment. In the end, the two senior officers remained inactive. Only one company commander, Capt. Thomas Weir of 'D' troop, kept on insisting that they rush to the help of their general. Reno refused him permission and even ordered Lt Edgerly to take command of Weir's 'D' troop. Despite the countermanding order, Capt. Weir convinced Lt Edgerly that he had been issued with the order to ride out, and without further ado he headed with his troop to a hill a mile and a half off – Weir Point. And that was where they stopped in shock. Two miles ahead of him, and despite the huge dust cloud, Weir saw thousands of Indian braves riding madly around a hill. He could not make out the precise details, but he could well imagine what was happening to those poor devils in the five troops. He sent a dispatch rider back to Reno to urge immediate action.

In the meantime, Weir's absence had already been discovered, and this finally decided Reno and Benteen to follow 'D' company to Weir Point. When they got there, and Capt. Weir made his report to Reno, the major wouldn't believe him, since by now the distant fight had ended. Instead, the unstable but ranting major tore a strip off his captain for insubordination. Some Indians, having finished with Custer, spotted the presence of a new enemy target, and hundred of riders came galloping towards Weir Point. Weir and Benteen formed a skirmish line. Sgt Callaghan, one of Weir's men, took a bead on a much-feathered brave he took for a leader and shot him out of the saddle. It was the signal for everyone to open fire. Weir knocked five braves out of their saddles. Bullets sang around his head, splintering a dried-up thorntree trunk. He then fired his revolver at a passing rider and blew him from the saddle. Trooper Boone heard the sound of lead hitting solid bone. There was a scream and he turned in time to see Sgt Callaghan falling backward. The whole attack lasted no more than a few minutes. It was nothing but a wild, yelling charge, and ended with a lot of riderless horses.

The pressure proved too much for Maj. Reno's nerves and he called for yet another retreat to Reno's Hill. Yelling and cursing, he waved his Colt, telling his men to fall back. For once he was proved right. Still, his order led to his second disorderly retreat in less than two hours. Once again, the Indians stopped in their pursuit. Out of range, the Sioux wheeled about, most likely to await the arrival of more braves to join in a new attack.

In that moment of the greatest confusion and indecision, waiting for another onslaught by thousands of braves,

Benteen finally took the initiative. This officer, crossing the threshold of mid-life, suddenly awoke to his responsibility. To the troopers, confused by an awareness of imminent danger, Benteen's coolness suggested the first semblance of order since they had been forced to run the gauntlet. The captain stared belligerently at the danger coming at them in the form of a large cloud of dust and shouted an order to dig in. There were no entrenching tools available, so the men used their knives and mess kits to dig and scrape the dry, hard ground in order to put up a breastwork. Experience during the Civil War had taught them that a good, deep hole in the ground always saved lives. Now, with their lives depending on it, every man furiously dug his own foxhole around the crest of the saucer-shaped hilltop. The work proved so exhausting that the only way to keep going was by gulping down great amounts of water, which soon emptied their water bottles. Benteen ordered his sergeant to check the water situation. Within minutes he returned with a worrying report: 'Captain, no water here.'

The men cursed. They could see the life-saving liquid gushing over rocks down in the river, but between the water and them were hundreds of Indians after their scalps. At least with Benteen in charge they were back in command of themselves; they straightened their shoulders in a grim gesture and braced themselves for the ordeal.

'Looks like a stand-off. We've got them outgunned, but they got time on their side.'

A trooper grinned. 'Sir, you think they gonna get tired of waitin', and skedaddle?'

Fortunately, while they had been forward at Weir Point, the pack train had made it to Reno's Hill, and now the ammunition was shared out. They had hardly finished their trenchwork when the Indians struck. They saw them heading towards their hill, their mounts picking up speed. They held their fire until the enemy were a hundred yards from their lined-up rifle barrels. Fire blazed from the hilltop. This time, the shooting from the line of carbines was deadly. But the soldiers also took casualties. A trooper who had not been in his hole walked leaden-footed towards the Indians like a man in a frightening dream before he stumbled and fell. Gun-spooked horses jumped over the cavalrymen's trench line, but without riders. Cursing madly, Benteen stood like a rock behind his men, acting more and more like a real general; he shot as fast as he could work the trigger, and when the hammer clicked on nothing, he threw down his revolver and picked up the gun of a wounded man. The fierce battle cost the Indians hundreds of casualties. For the next three hours, until nightfall, the Indians kept attacking and firing madly at anything that moved. Then they stopped. A trooper called out what none had dared to think a few hours earlier: 'Jeezes, we've got them stopped!'

The water situation was now the worrying problem. The troopers were exhausted; the smoke from their guns had penetrated their lungs, their tongues were dry. They needed water; without it they would surely not survive another attack. During the night, nineteen volunteers braved it down to the river to refill the water bottles. For this feat, every single one was awarded the Congressional Medal of Honor.

The Indians renewed their attack in the early hours of the morning, but the fighting spirit had gone out of them. For eighteen hours, seven beleaguered troops endured, until the Indians became convinced that Reno's Hill could not be taken. They had had their great victory over 'Yellow Hair'; this other general (actually only a captain) was not worth the effort of taking the hill. By noon, the last of the Indians had 'skedaddled'.

Captain of Cavalry Benteen turned away from the picture of horror – the hundreds of dead or dying lying on the slope leading up to their hill – to stare at more blood and wounds among his own troops. Speaking like a man who has fought to hold his breath for a long time, he said: 'Sergeant, get the men some water . . . *please* . . .' Those on top of the hill were mere shadows of the confident regiment of twenty-four hours before. Their final relief came with the arrival of the army of Gen. Terry and Col. Gibbon early on 27 June. Only then did the full dimension of the disaster become known.

The official inquiry into the Little Big Horn disaster turned into a military whitewash. Union generals would never admit that 'savages' had wiped out one of the famous US Cavalry units, one that had been victorious throughout the major battles of the American Civil War. When the verdict was announced, Crow chief Flying Hawk put it plainly: 'All the white men's accounts are guesswork for no white man knows. There was none left.'

While witnesses were called and testimony taken, the court never called upon the only surviving eye-witnesses – the Indians who had taken part in the battle. The court's lame excuse was that Indians were known liars. It was left to some enterprising journalists to come up with the story. When their first account appeared in the *Leavenworth Weekly Times* on 18 August 1881, it created a sensation. It was written after an eye-witness account given by the Hunkpapa Sioux chief Crow King.

> We were in camp and not thinking there was any danger of a battle, though we had heard that the long-haired chief had been sent after us. Some of our runners went back on our trail, for what purpose I do not know. [These were the ones who pilfered the pack mule.] One came rushing back to report that an army of white soldiers was coming, and he had this reported when another runner came with the same story. He told us that the white men's command had divided and that one party was going around to attack us on the opposite side.
>
> The first attack was on the camp of the Hunkpapa tribe [Reno's attack]. The Indians retreated, at first slowly, to give the women and children time to go to

a place of safety. By that time we had warriors enough to turn upon the whites and we drove them to the hill [Reno's Hill] and then started back to camp.

Then the second band of white warriors came. We did not know who was their chief, but we supposed it was Yellow Hair's command. The party commenced firing at long range. We had then all our warriors and all our horses. There were eighty warriors in my band. All the Sioux were there from everywhere. We had warriors plenty as the leaves on the trees. Sitting Bull and Crazy Horse were the great chiefs of the fight. Sitting Bull did not fight himself, *but he gave the orders* [this was afterwards disputed]. We turned against this second party [Custer]. The greater portion of our warriors came together in their front and we rushed our horses at them. At the same time, warriors rode out on each side of them [Gall's hidden riders] and circled around them until they were surrounded. When they saw that they were surrounded, they dismounted. They tried to hold on to their horses, but as we pressed closer they let go their horses [this was the charge by the two companies]. We crowded them toward our main camp and killed them all. They kept in order and fought like brave warriors as long as they had a man left. Our camp was on the Greasy Grass River [Little Big Horn]. When we charged, every chief gave the cry: 'Hi-yi-yi!' When this cry is given, it is a command to all the warriors to watch their chief and follow his actions. Then every chief rushed his horse on the white soldiers, and all our warriors did the same [the final charge]. There was great hurry and confusion in the fight. It was not more than half an hour after the longhaired chief attacked us before he and all his men were dead.

Then we went back for the first party [the attack on Weir's men and Reno's Hill]. We fired at them until the sun went down. We surrounded them and watched

> them all night [this was when water-carriers slipped through their lines] and at first daylight we fought them again. We killed many of them. Then a chief from the Sioux called our men off. He told us those men had been punished enough, that they were fighting under orders, and that we had killed the great leader and his men in the fight the day before, and that we should let the rest go home. Chief Sitting Bull gave this order.
>
> He said: 'This is not my doings, nor these men's. They are fighting because they were commanded to fight. We have killed their leader. Let them go. I call on the Great Manitou to witness what I say. We did not want to fight. Yellow Hair sent us word that he was coming to fight us and we had to defend ourselves and our wives and children.'
>
> If this command had not been given, we would have cut [Reno's] command to pieces, as we did that of the longhaired leader. No warrior knew Yellow Hair in the fight [this is surprising as he was wearing his famous buckskin coat]. We did not know him, dead or alive. When the fight was over, the chiefs gave orders to look for the longhaired chief among the dead but no chief with long hair could be found [because he had cut it off before the campaign].

Another brave, Jack Red Cloud, was found living quietly on a reservation. He substantiated the tale of Crow King: '. . . Then the rest dismounted and gathered in a bunch,' he said, and with that single phrase, 'gathered in a bunch', he started a legend. His story was what led to the version of the final dozen clustered around their general at Custer's Last Stand. How many of the campfire stories were amended by the passage of time remains unknown. The Indian tales differed in many details, yet one thing emerged unchanged: General Custer and his men fought well and died like brave warriors.

Altogether, 261 men died. Custer's five-company unit was

completely wiped out. There were no survivors who could tell the story. Their death toll came to 225 officers and troopers[10] and one civilian, who had been along for the ride, a reporter from the *Bismarck Tribune*, wanting to be the first to cover a great victory. His notebook was never found.

Yet there was one miraculous survivor from the slaughter – Comanche, Captain Keogh's cavalry mount! It was found bleeding from a number of wounds and standing on tired legs next to its master's body. Gently the troops made hoops and then ferried the horse by wagon back to Fort Lincoln, and tenderly nursed it back to health. It was allowed to graze wherever it wanted, was brushed daily, and paraded at ceremonies. It was decorated with the Medal of Honor for its master's heroic stand. But its greatest joy came on pay day. Then the troopers of the reconstituted 7th US Cavalry bought it a bucket of beer.

The facts

Though these events took place in a remote corner of the United States of America, the defeat of the US 7th Cavalry under 'General' Yellow Hair was one of the most glorious moments in the history of the Indians. But Little Big Horn was a Pyrrhic victory. Newspaper headlines stirred up public hatred to a fever pitch. On 6 July 1876, the *Bismarck Tribune* splashed across its front page:

MASSACRED

NO OFFICER OR MAN OF FIVE COMPANIES LEFT TO TELL THE TALE –

SQUAWS MUTILATE AND ROB THE DEAD –

SHALL THIS BE THE BEGINNING OF THE END?

[10] Owing to sloppy army accounting, even this figure has been disputed.

Indeed it was the end – but for the Sioux. On a cold winter's day, 8 January 1877, Col. Nelson A. Miles, with five hundred infantry and two cannon, caught Chief Crazy Horse and his braves on a bluff in the Wolf Mountains. The noise from exploding shells so frightened the braves that they fled and Crazy Horse had to surrender.

And finally, on 29 December 1890 at Wounded Knee, Col. James Forsythe, with the battle-tested 7th US Cavalry, went after Chief Big Foot of the Sioux and massacred an entire tribe. With it, Custer's former regiment gained revenge for its defeat at Little Big Horn. This was to be the last major Indian conflict.

A Court of Inquiry into the Custer tragedy was convened. Its inquest focused on some major points. Why did Custer split his regiment into four columns? Why did he plan to attack without having reconnoitred the enemy's strength? And finally, why did Reno and Benteen not come to Custer's support? It was established that Custer committed his fatal error the moment he ordered Reno to swing away from him to attack on his own, promising him 'support'. By this, he may have meant leading his own charge from the opposite side of the village and thereby relieving the pressure on Reno with a diversionary attack. It is practically certain that Custer did not realise the size of the enemy until the two huge hordes of Crazy Horse and Gall jumped him, although he should have had some indication judging from the size of the tepee town. Still he continued with his attack plans. If he counted on 'Custer's Luck', for once his luck ran out.

Reno was too shaken by his earlier defeat and his effectiveness as a commander was shattered, but why then did not Benteen, always the cooler and more dominant personality, override Reno's earlier decision to hold at Reno's Hill? Benteen carried in his pocket the famous 'Be quick' order from Custer that was still in effect; he had received it before 3 p.m., well in time to speed up and come to Custer's support.

A fighting column of three US Cavalry companies, with freshly watered horses and plenty of ammunition, appearing over the crest of the hill, would have panicked the Indians long enough to enable Custer's encircled troop to break out.

None of these questions was ever fully answered. They became part of the Custer enigma. The Court of Inquiry finally cleared Maj. Reno of the charge of cowardice in face of the enemy; however, it stated: 'While subordinates, in some instances, did more for the safety of the command than did Major Reno, there was nothing in his conduct that requires admonition.' His military career was finished and he took to the bottle. A year later he was court-martialled for drunkenness, slander and trying to seduce the wife of a fellow officer who was at the time absent on patrol. In 1880, he was dismissed from the army. He died a drunkard and was quietly laid to rest at the Little Big Horn military cemetery.

Benteen's career also took a dive, though nothing like as drastic as Reno's, and in the end he was promoted to major. In 1890, the army bestowed on a bitter old man the honorary rank of brigadier-general for his brave action at Reno's Hill.

George Armstrong Custer, 'Brevet Major General United States Army, born December 5, 1839, in Harrison County, Ohio. Killed with his entire command at Little Big Horn, June 25, 1876', was buried in Custer Battlefield National Park, Montana. In 1877, his coffin was removed, and it lies today at the West Point Military Academy, New York.

The virtues for which heroes are celebrated, such commonplaces as courage, generosity, guile, fidelity and faith, hardly ever include aplomb. Custer couldn't tell with any great confidence if he was rising or falling, advancing or retreating, if he was loved or hated, despised or adored. For someone like him, aplomb attained primary importance. Whatever he may have lacked, it certainly was not self-confidence and courage. But he was completely blinded by his drive for personal glory. It is difficult to come up with another case that similarly defies sane military analysis.[11] His example of bad generalship stands as a warning to those in charge of the military selection procedures. Little Big Horn is the chronicle of a 'disaster announced'.

The American Indian Wars produced much bigger battles. Why, then, this irresistible excitement about Custer's Last Stand? It is no doubt the stellar role this modern Siegfried played in his insatiable reach for *la gloire*, which – as in most heroic tragedies – ended in disaster. But it also made him immortal.

Nobody ever found out who shot Custer or how he died. His last-stand spirit lived on and he became a legend, even to his former enemies. It was none other than the spiritual leader of the Sioux nation, Chief Sitting Bull, who paid his nation's flamboyant adversary a final homage: 'He was a great brave who rode foolishly to his death.'

The Hinge of Battle at the Little Big Horn was the boundless ambition of one man who, in his quest for personal glory, sacrificed a regiment.

Little Big Horn, the most famous of Indian victories, also spelled their end.

[11] Perhaps the Chevalier de Ridefort's insane attack at the Springs of Cresson in 1187, as described by this author in his chapter on the Crusades in *The Hinge Factor*.

5

A Washing of the Spears

22 January 1879 – Death in Zululand

'War is the province of danger, and therefore, courage above all things is the first quality of a warrior.'

Karl von Clausewitz, *On War*, 1832

'I do not call animals, which have no fear of danger, because they are ignorant of it, courageous, but only fearless and reckless.'

Plato, 428–347 BC., *Laches*

Lt-Gen. Sir Frederic Augustus Thesiger, Second Baron Chelmsford, sat stiffly in his saddle as befitted a man with the rank of Commander-in-Chief, Her Majesty Queen Victoria's expeditionary forces to Natal Province. He looked ahead and saw no sign of the enemy; even their scouts had melted away. 'They've run . . . nothing else than cowardly,' he said to Col. Richard Glyn, when out of a cloud of dust two riders appeared.

'Milord, they're all dead . . . not one of them left alive . . .' said one of the riders, blood seeping through his dust-covered uniform.

'I . . . I can't understand that,' stuttered a confused Lord Chelmsford. 'I've left over a thousand men there.'

'They're dead, milord, all dead . . .'

* * *

Numerous are the wars that have been started for no apparent reason whatsoever. But there is one that sets a monument to folly, brought about by the whims of a British colonial official and then conducted with such amateurish recklessness that it condemned many of his troops to certain death.

At the end of the nineteenth century, every major power[1] became involved in the active colonial expansion known as imperialism. The imperialist case usually involved several arguments, economic, missionary or strategic, all wrapped in the most powerful motive of all: national prestige and glory. At the height of British colonial expansion, Sir Henry Bartle Frere was appointed the United Kingdom's High Commissioner for South Africa. In 1877, pushed by English business interests and diamond barons, men such as Cecil Rhodes, Sir Henry simply annexed the Transvaal Republic. As a consequence, this brought him into a border dispute with a native warrior tribe, the Zulu. Rather foolishly he appointed a commission, made up entirely of whites, to look into the legal problem, and – to his utter surprise – the judges' verdict was: 'Unquestionably Zulu tribal land.' This so infuriated Frere that he decided to set their verdict aside and create an incident. That wasn't hard to achieve.

A fat and ageing village headman, Sirayo, had dozens of wives and concubines in his kraal looking after his every need. Two of the beauties, hardly past puberty, found themselves younger lovers and together they absconded and took refuge in a far-off village. It is doubtful that they were aware of having crossed into Natal Province as there were neither border stations nor signposts. When Sirayo discovered their absence, he ordered two of his sons to retrieve his 'lost property'; according to Zulu law, adultery was a capital crime. The sons went to this village, killed the two lovers and dragged the women back to Sirayo's kraal.

[1] Except Austria-Hungary.

'Border violation,' raged the High Commissioner. A hopelessly inept Sir Henry demanded reparation from Zulu King Cetewayo in the form of five hundred head of cattle. This the king, who had usurped power in 1872 following the death of his uncle, the great Shaka Zulu, refused, although he sent a bag containing £50 of gold, a hefty sum for the time. The incident didn't end there. Next, two land surveyors crossed into Zululand and were grabbed by the tribesmen. This time the English had violated the border; however, Frere did not see it that way. Once again he demanded reparation for the 'unwarranted arrest' of two of his agents. Cetewayo was understandably insulted and furious; rightly convinced that his position was legally and morally sound, he was as adamant with the British as he had been with the Boers. He began to develop his nation's fighting power. Clouds of war began to gather. Frere panicked; he sent an urgent message to England to ask for reinforcements for his meagre force of a few English units plus his Native Natal Police. His demand was ignored because England was already otherwise engaged in Afghanistan. To gain time, Frere sent his emissaries to Cetewayo's kraal to let the Zulu king know of the commission's verdict about the disputed territory – with one stipulation which was as insane as it was unacceptable: though, indeed, it was Zulu land, the Zulu were not allowed to enter it! Before Cetewayo could catch his breath, Frere's messengers added another clause: the king had to disband his standing army of forty thousand warriors, within twenty days. The English emissaries were fortunate that the king did not have their heads chopped off right there and then.

On 6 January 1879, a British unit crossed the Zululand border and headed for disaster.

Over generations, the Zulu nation had turned into the most fearsome warrior tribe of Africa. When a boy reached the age of about six, he was taken away from his mother and trained in the art of combat. He was forced to walk across thorns to harden his feet and make daily runs of many miles to learn how to keep up with the gruelling pace of the army, which was so fast that they could outrun a horse in broken terrain. Zulu were masters of the stealthy approach, indispensable when stalking wild animals. No European soldier could possibly match the way they used bush or deep gullies for cover or how they defiladed. Their battle units were organised in impis, like Roman legions, every one with its distinctive coloured shield. On the warpath, members of every unit painted their upper bodies and faces with a mixture of chalk and red ochre. Their main armament was the assegai (lance), the knobkerrie (cudgel) for close-in combat, and an oxhide shield. To obtain the shield, the sign of a warrior, the young man had to perform a special feat of heroism; only then was he allowed to take a girl into his hut. Every young man welcomed a raid as the best way to prove himself and overcome his sexual frustration.

King Cetewayo's forty thousand men were an entirely professional army with an integrated command structure; its warriors were fanatically brave, highly disciplined, and incredibly well trained. Reminiscent of the tactics applied by Roman legions, attacks were carried out with the stabbing assegai under a shower of throwing assegais. But the most outstanding feature of Zulu warfare was their highly developed strategy of using the bull's horn. It was said that many years before, Cetewayo had observed thousands of small birds of prey attacking a giant vulture. Their dense cloud spread into something which resembled a bull's horn before its two distinct wings attacked and the little birds brought down the big vulture. The Zulu applied the same tactical manoeuvre: exploiting their incredible speed, their mass would spread rapidly into two wings – the bull's horns – which then drove the enemy against the centre – the bull's chest – to be crushed. This tactic, harking back as far as Hannibal at Cannae, had never failed. Now, owing to the whim of a colonial official pushed by commercial interests, this tough warrior tribe was about to collide with a force of European soldiers who were armed with gunpowder weapons.

Viscount Chelmsford was an arrogant aristocrat whose underestimation of his enemy was truly astounding and who was described by one of his staff officers as 'the general who cannot read a battle beyond the range of his binoculars'. He would have been better suited leading a cricket team in a Test match than a military force of 5,000 British and 8,000 native troops. Having never set foot in the region, and knowing nothing about the terrain or his foe, he prepared a plan that was so full of holes it could never work. Instead of going after the life-blood of the Zulu nation, their cattle herds, and bringing the Zulu impis out into the open to defend what was most precious to them and then using his superior firepower, he chose to march across the scorching veldt in search of flitting shadows. 'They're not fighting fair and standing up' was his initial observation. With his slow-moving oxen train he opted for a three-pronged invasion from Natal and Transvaal to converge on Cetewayo's kraal at Ulundi. His first mistake was that he disregarded the fact that on the veldt there were only stones and cow paths, and no tracks wide enough to accommodate his heavy-wheeled cannon and ammunition wagons, nor bridges with which to cross the mighty rivers.

Lord Chelmsford joined the Central Attack Column, which crossed into Zululand at Rorke's Drift on the Buffalo river, or Upper Tugela. This force was principally HM's 24th Regiment of Col. Richard Glyn; but as Lord Chelmsford was of the party, Col. Glyn was relegated to nominal command, a fact that was only to create confusion. Of his 4,700 men, 1,857 were 'white'. The rest were made up of native battalions, mainly Basuto with a sprinkling of renegade Zulu. The regular troops were boosted by a few companies of NNC (Native Natal Contingent), a non-military outfit which did not fall under military command.

Chelmsford's column dragged itself slowly across the veldt,

a plain covered by yellowed thorns and grey rocks protruding from the ground in needle-sharp points, which had the ugly tendency to shred boots and break wheels. Man-size red termite heaps stood up like sentries. There was no water on the high plateau; everything was dusty and dry. But the gullies, or *dongas*, normally only a trickle of water, had been swelled by seasonal rains into raging rivers. Every *donga* required a separate, delicate operation to cross – sand got into weapons, powder got wet, and uniforms became caked with mud. Then it was up to the plateau again. Soon the column turned into a stretched-out caterpillar that wandered across the plain, then down into the next gully, ferrying the wagons across by pulling on ropes, and on again up the next escarpment. The men slogged through the dust as if it were deep snow. Every now and then their officers wheeled their horses about to glare at the massed array of sweaty faces. For the boys from the outskirts of Glasgow, Manchester or London, life on the African veldt lost its charm, and the spirit of 'adventure in a far-off place' left them. Heat and dust, dust and heat. Day after day, hour after hour, they planted one foot in front of the other, step after dusty step along a track that never seemed to end. And their uniforms, these cursed red woollen coats, acted like a magnet for the African sun! Their comrades in blue, sitting on their horses, had it much easier.

Before sunrise on 20 January 1879, the column had left the last Swedish missionary station at Rorke's Drift before entering the heartland of the Zulu; the missionaries had informed their commander about an increased Zulu presence up on the Nqulu Plateau. Lord Chelmsford left Lt Gonville Bromhead's 'B' Company, 2nd/24th, strengthened by an NNC detachment of Basuto under Capt. George Stephenson, to guard the Swedish mission and its ferry across the Buffalo river and to protect the column's communications. The rest moved on. The track climbed steeply towards the Nqulu Plateau, where it wound through a narrow pass formed by a semicircle of conical-shaped hills, the type the Boers called *kopjes*. One hill was in the shape of a closed fist, or as the natives called it: '*Isandhlwana* – The Hill of the Little Hand'. A rocky spur led from the *kopje* to the high ground on the Nqulu Plateau; crossing the veldt in front of the *kopje* was a deep ravine or *donga*. South of the track lay another hill somewhat similar in shape to the Isandhlwana *kopje*, called Stony Hill. Two thousand yards farther off, and in the direction of the Zulu kraals, was a third outcrop much like a sugar cone – Conical Hill. Isandhlwana, protected by the hill to the rear, the *donga* in front and the escarpment of the plateau to its flank, seemed a perfect position for a camp; furthermore the *kopje* was an ideal observation platform. And yet, not a single man was ordered up for sentry duty. This was not only contrary to the standing Field Rules and Regulations but also ignored the advice from one who knew the country and its natives better than anyone, the famous leader of the Boers. Paul 'Oom' Kruger had warned Chelmsford: 'Place your spies out as far as you can, the Zulu are more dangerous than you think,' and that a Zulu impi, advancing with their ground-devouring trot, could cover fifty miles a day, faster than a cavalry unit riding in the heat of the sun. Chelmsford disregarded the warning; they had seen very few, if any, of these feared warriors. Whenever his troops passed near a kraal of thatched beehive huts, naked-breasted women and barelegged children lined the track to study the Europeans with bold and curious eyes, but in total silence. Chelmsford did not find it strange that there were few or no men around. But those who looked at them from a distance did so the way a lion watches his prey before he begins to stalk it.

After a lengthy discussion with his staff, Chelmsford decided to pitch camp in the shade of Isandhlwana *kopje*, but determined that the Conical Hill was too far off to be of any use. To cover his flank from surprise, a small patrol of local NNC boys was sent to the Nqulu Plateau, but then they were recalled when it was found that they were too far away to be heard.

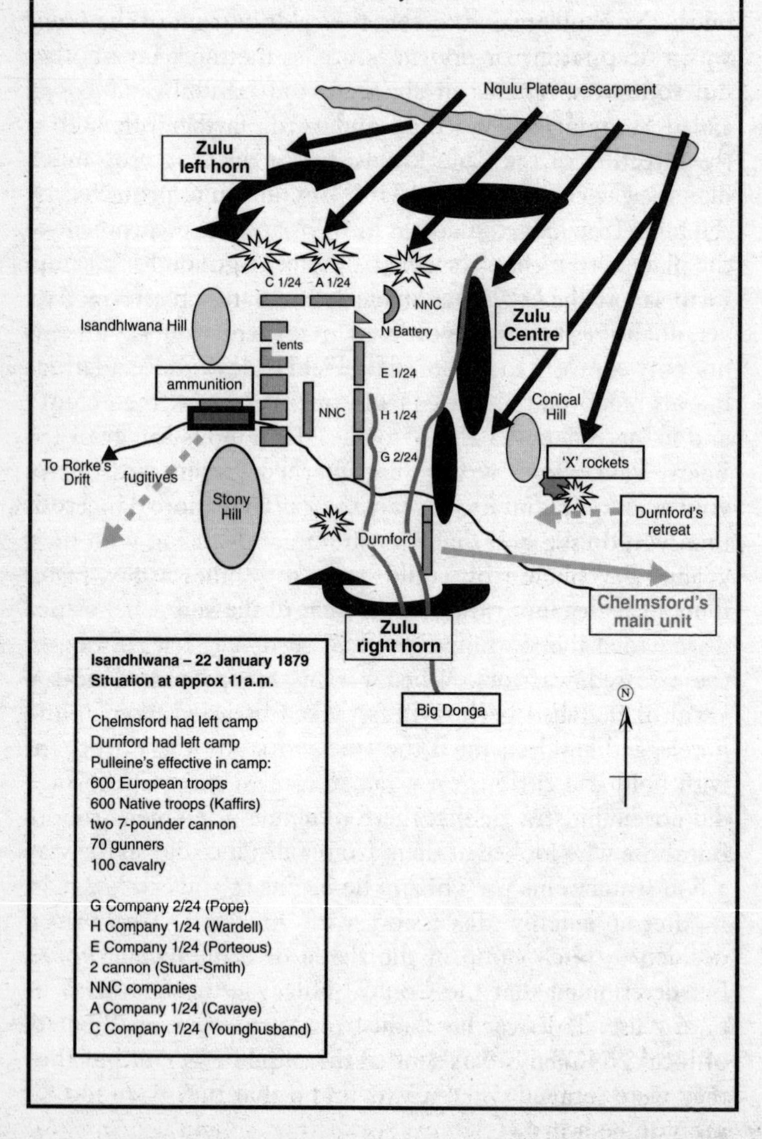
Isandhlwana
22 January 1879
Nqulu Plateau escarpment
Zulu left horn
C 1/24
A 1/24
NNC
N Battery
Zulu Centre
Isandhlwana Hill
tents
ammunition
E 1/24
NNC
H 1/24
Conical Hill
G 2/24
'X' rockets
To Rorke's Drift
fugitives
Stony Hill
Durnford's retreat
Durnford
Chelmsford's main unit
Zulu right horn
Big Donga
N
Isandhlwana – 22 January 1879
Situation at approx 11 a.m.
Chelmsford had left camp
Durnford had left camp
Pulleine's effective in camp:
600 European troops
600 Native troops (Kaffirs)
two 7-pounder cannon
70 gunners
100 cavalry
G Company 2/24 (Pope)
H Company 1/24 (Wardell)
E Company 1/24 (Porteous)
2 cannon (Stuart-Smith)
NNC companies
A Company 1/24 (Cavaye)
C Company 1/24 (Younghusband)

To the dog-tired soldiers, having dragged on wearily in the furnace heat of midday, the *kopjes* seemed like the Promised Land. 'Halt!' yelled the battalion commanders, and 'Halt!' yelled the lieutenants and sergeants. Once again they lined up at the quartermasters' carts to get tenting material and their bed-rolls. After the long hot march, the troops weren't too keen to put up the tents right away. First they wanted a brew-up.

'C'mon, get yer blinkin' bed-rolls, I ain't got all day,' bellowed their quartermaster.

'Silly fucker, 'e's after another stripe,' grinned a soldier. They knew that the quartermaster had never seen action before and his barrack-room harshness cut no ice with them. Regulations worked back in Merry Ol' England, not in the bloody bush. But they knew they had to do it. Soon a row of tents was neatly lined up spaced at a regulation distance measured out by company sergeants. Putting up tents made them work up an enormous lather. They flopped down, sweaty and listless, while someone brewed tea.

The next blunder was the location of the wagon park. When Boers travelled through hostile territory, they put their wagons into a *laager*, or *Wagenburg* circle, around their tents. In case of a surprise attack this could be turned into a formidable fortress. Not so the British. Regulations stipulated they put the wagons *behind* the camp, and at a considerable distance. This looked neat but provided no protection and, furthermore, it separated the companies from their ammunition stores.

After sunrise on 21 January 1879, Lord Chelmsford held another conference. They were now inside enemy territory and only some twelve miles from the kraal of King Cetewayo's military commander, Chief Matayana. It was decided to dispatch Maj. John Dartnell of the Natal Mounted Police with his 150 men on a reconnaissance sortie in the direction of Chief Matayana's kraal, to find out whether there was any Zulu unit in the vicinity. As an afterthought, Chelmsford ordered Maj. Dartnell to return to camp by nightfall. When they hadn't heard from Dartnell by noon, Chelmsford sent two NNC battalions under Commander Rupert Lonsdale after him to find out what was going on. Having done that, Lord Chelmsford climbed on his horse and, accompanied by three of his staff, mounted the Nqulu Plateau, when suddenly a dozen Zulu popped up from the high grass. They seemed quite frightened by the riders, turned and, with their loping stride, made off.

'You see, they're afraid of us,' joked Chelmsford. It was nothing like that; their orders had been to observe the movements of the redcoats, not to engage them in a fight. They were part of a much larger force, hidden away behind the escarpment.

The army of King Cetewayo.

When Chelmsford returned to camp, a messenger from Dartnell had arrived. His reconnaissance patrol had run into 'a strong Zulu detachment of some 2,000', but the Zulu had begun no hostile action and had kept a safe distance. Chelmsford decided to try for an easy victory by crushing the two thousand. He would set out with half of the effective plus four of the six cannon. Col. Glyn was to accompany him, and Lord Chelmsford put the commander of 1st/24th, Lt-Col. Henry Pulleine, in charge of the Isandhlwana camp. To make up for the shortage of men, Chelmsford dispatched a young lieutenant, Horace Smith-Dorrien, to deliver his order to Rorke's Drift for Col. Anthony Durnford: 'YOU ARE TO MARCH TO THE ISANDHLWANA CAMP AT ONCE WITH ALL THE FORCE YOU HAVE WITH YOU OF NO. 2 COLUMN.'

One would have thought that the British might have learned something from their mistake at Balaclava, where a badly worded message had led the Light Brigade to disaster; obviously they had not. Once again a badly worded message was to lead to confusion as to who was to be in command; as Col. Durnford was senior in rank, it should have been him, but since Lt-Col. Pulleine had been put in charge of the camp by the commander-in-chief, he again assumed that he was the Isandhlwana commander. This confusion was to lead to recriminations during the subsequent inquest.

Without sending out *éclaireurs*, Chelmsford set out, stripping the camp of half its men and most of its cannon. It seems from later reports that Chelmsford, a man who saw only as far as his binoculars, had no grasp of the overall situation or the imminent danger. He thought that the Zulu would act by the book and fight him in open battle. But they didn't do him that favour, not on the open veldt where grapeshot from his four cannon in a frontal attack would render them mincemeat. Instead, the Zulu host was hiding to his left flank, only two miles beyond the camp! Once more, Chelmsford rode up to the top of a hillock, and through his spyglass had a look at his camp back at the Isandhlwana *kopje*. All seemed normal, and he thought nothing of the fact that the draw oxen had been herded behind the tents, a procedure normally reserved for an emergency. The viscount turned to Col. Richard Glyn. 'They've run away . . . nothing less than cowardly.' He was sadly mistaken.

The two thousand Zulu that Dartnell discovered had been but a portion of the main force. Should they attack Dartnell's small redcoat troop? 'No,' said the Zulu leader, 'that is not the order of our Great King. He wants every redcoat dead.' The Great King's medicine men had studied the passage of the moon and told him that the constellation was fortuitous for an attack after two more nights (which would have made it 23 January). The two Zulu commanders, Mavumengwana, young, hot-tempered and impatient to dip his spear in the blood of his enemies, and Shingwayo, a veteran of many victorious battles, sent scout parties to keep a permanent tab on the long column of redcoats that had marched from camp early in the morning. While Chelmsford proceeded blind, Shingwayo knew of his every move.

Two events occurred in short order. Chelmsford decided

to move Isandhlwana camp and its supplies closer to his own advancing column. To provide additional manpower for the move, he ordered Commander Hamilton-Browne's NNC battalion to return to Isandhlwana. They were on their way when two NNC riders dashed after a loping Zulu and captured him. While one of Hamilton-Browne's native scouts interrogated the prisoner, another officer from the NNC detachment, Lonsdale, rode back to the British camp to fetch provisions for his native battalion. The interrogation of the Zulu brave proved difficult but eventually successful. He told a puzzled Hamilton-Browne that twelve Zulu impis (regiments of a thousand warriors each) were on the Nqulu Plateau. The NNC commander dashed off a panicky note: 'MILORD, FOR GOD'S SAKE COME BACK WITH ALL YOUR MEN! THE CAMP IS SURROUNDED AND MUST BE TAKEN UNLESS HELPED. (signed) HAMILTON-BROWNE.'

He had ridden to within three miles of the camp when he saw a black wave pour over the edge of the plateau and down the long slope.

Chelmsford, acting on the message, finally reached the NNC battalion. It was 3 p.m. 'What is this excitement all about?' he wanted to know.

'We have a Zulu prisoner who speaks of a Zulu army on the plateau near the camp, milord,' a lieutenant told him. 'Our commander has gone back to take a look.' It was at this moment that two riders appeared out of a cloud of dust. One was Hamilton-Browne, the other was Commander Lonsdale, wounded, bewildered and exhausted. He had come to the edge of the plateau where the Big Donga cut through the veldt and waved to a group of red-coated men on the other slope when bullets began to whistle around his head and he was struck in the shoulder. The redcoats were Zulu! – and beyond them he clearly saw heaps of naked corpses.

'Milord, they're all dead . . . not one of them left alive . . .'

'I . . . I can't understand that,' stuttered a confused Lord Chelmsford. 'I've left over a thousand men there.' These comprised six companies from the 24th Regiment, all regulars who had been trained to kneel and fire volleys, plus six companies from the Natal Mounted Police, well versed in operation on the veldt. Near on 1,300 men – they couldn't be . . .

'They're dead, milord, all dead,' Lonsdale managed to mumble, with red bubbles blistering on his lips and blood seeping through his dust-streaked uniform, before he tumbled from his horse.

Earlier that morning, at 7.30, while an army of Zulu was lying in wait behind the escarpment to the north of Isandhlwana camp, the redcoat soldiers enjoyed their breakfast, glad that they were the ones who had been left behind.

'Another fine day,' joked a man from Lt Pope's 'G' Company.

'Yeah, lots of sun to broil out yer brain,' replied a corporal from Lt Porteous's 'E' Company.

'Poor buggers getting roasted out there,' others pitied their comrades, who had marched from camp at 3.30 a.m.

Lt-Col. Pulleine was having his breakfast served in front of his tent when a dispatch rider from the scout patrol on the plateau brought a message about several small Zulu bands roaming about. The colonel swigged his tea before ordering a 'fall-in' to be sounded. The companies got into formation and marched off to their predesignated location, forming an L-shaped line some six hundred yards ahead of the camp. Since this position had been designed the day before for the entire effective, and they were now down to half, this left a hundred-yard gap between the various companies. Yet nothing happened. The only living things in sight were bugs and vultures, and the soldiers were told to stand down. They put up sentries, stacked their rifles in regulation pyramids and lay down in the grass to snooze.

Lt-Col. Pulleine tore a page from his notebook and was dispatching his first message to Chelmsford, informing him of a scattered Zulu presence near the camp, when another NNC scout dashed into camp. He reported three more Zulu bands, quite substantial, to the north-east and north-west of the spur leading to Isandhlwana Hill. From this report it should have become obvious that something untoward was going on, yet other than to advise his company commanders of the sightings, the colonel did nothing more than to place his two seven-pounders on his line's northern corner – just in case.

At 10 a.m. Colonel Anthony Durnford came up from Rorke's Drift. With his slouch hat, his pistols and his Bowie knife, he cut more of a Davy Crockett figure than that of a stiff-upper-lip British colonel. He brought with him three companies of NNC plus five troops of Natal Mounted Natives and a rocket battery. He also added his own contribution to the half-million rounds of bullets in the quartermaster stores. The ammunition was kept in heavy, metal-lined wooden crates, ringed with metal bands to withstand even the roughest treatment in transport. The crates were divided among the individual company quartermasters. Each box was accounted for and every quartermaster got his share. 'Stack them properly,' ordered Quartermaster Bloomfield of the 2nd/24th, who made sure that not a single ammo box was out of line. Then, like a mother hen, he sat down in front of his neat crate pile to keep a close watch.

Lt-Col Pulleine had asked Colonel Durnford to join him for breakfast in his tent when further reports about Zulu bands came in. Durnford, an old South Africa hand who had helped suppress the 1872 native rebellion, ordered two of his mounted troops to conduct an in-depth reconnaissance of the plateau. One of the groups was under the command of Capt. Barton and Lt Roberts. Within thirty minutes, Barton sent back a message that, yes, they had spotted Zulu bands, but that they were *headed away from the camp* and in the general direction of Chelmsford's flank. Based on this 11 a.m. report, and despite previous rebukes from the commander-in-chief over the many acts taken on his own initiative, Durnford felt he had to protect his general's flank with his unit. When he pulled out, this left Lt-Col. Pulleine once again with only his own companies of the 24th. His effective was now 600 European regular foot troops, 100 cavalry, 600 Native troops (kaffirs), two seven-pounder cannon, plus 70 gunners and a smattering of drummer boys and carriers. His main force of the line, made up of regulars well trained in precision volley fire and steeped in strict British discipline, were: 'G' Company, 2nd/24th (Pope), 'H' Company, 1st/24th (Wardell), 'E' Company, 1st/24th (Porteous), 'A' Company, 1st/24th (Cavaye), and 'C' Company, 1st/24th (Younghusband).

Some commotion broke out near the distant spur north of the camp. Pulleine immediately dispatched a message to Chelmsford, which was so badly worded that it completely misinterpreted the true situation: 'HEAVY FIRING TO LEFT OF CAMP. NNC CAPT SHEPSTONE HAS COME BACK FOR REINFORCEMENTS AND REPORTS *ZULU ARE FALLING BACK*. THE WHOLE FORCE AT CAMP HAS TURNED OUT AND FIGHTING ABOUT ONE MILE TO LEFT FLANK.'

This note certainly gave the impression that Pulleine had everything well under control.

Lt Raw of the NNC, on scout duty along the Nqulu Plateau, was riding along the ridge line when he noticed a dozen Zulu driving their cows across the high ground. Five of Raw's Basuto chased after the Zulu, which brought them to the northern edge of the plateau. They looked over the escarpment – and into the white-and-ochre-painted faces of tens of thousands of Zulu warriors! For a dozen heartbeats they just sat there, mesmerised by the sea of eyes staring up at them, before they wheeled their horses and dashed off, wildly gesticulating with their arms. 'Zulu! Zulu! Zulu!'

Zulu leader Chief Shingwayo realised that their presence had been betrayed, and that the surprise planned for the coming morning was now out of the question. Favourable moon or no favourable moon, he waved his feather-tipped cudgel. 'Kill all redcoats!' he roared, and thousands of half-naked, war-painted warriors rose as one. In a giant black wave, a dozen Zulu impis poured over the lip of the escarpment. The ground trembled under the syncopated impact of many thousands of feet as they came racing down the long slope with their loping stride – a spear-wielding avalanche headed for a red line, facing them perfectly aligned in front of a row of khaki tents.

The redcoats scrambled to their feet as soon as they became conscious of a persistent sound, an indistinct but immense, gurgling rush, resonant and oppressive. The sun was at its zenith when a great black mass appeared over the skyline. The outcry of the Zulu wafted down from the high slope. Their war chant, like the hum of angry bees, was the first sound Lt-Col. Pulleine heard from afar before he noticed a black mass, well over a mile wide, curling over the escarpment on top of the long slope. Dense ranks of shields and war plumes appeared, as if spewed out from an overflowing basin. Pulleine finally realised that he had grossly underestimated the strength of the enemy; he knew that nothing could stop a contest between gunpowder and assegai. Confronted by the Zulu main force, he gave an order which, though tactically sound, overlooked a factor that was to play the decisive role. He moved his line farther away from the camp, towards the edge where the plain sloped down towards the Little Donga. By doing this, he placed the men a thousand yards from the tents; but he also widened the gaps between the individual companies to three hundred yards and gave the enemy the opportunity to enfilade between the companies. Pulleine had no choice; he was strapped for manpower and therefore based his tactics on his well-trained shooters to ensure that nobody got through their curtain of fire.

With his modern Martini-Henry repeater, a British soldier could fire twelve shots per minute and his heavy 480-grain bullet could knock over a target at five hundred yards. On the fields of Europe, this shock of a single volley had never failed to produce an impact. It mattered little that the British were fewer and the Zulu greater in number; this would be offset by repeated salvos. However, rapid fire required a lot of bullets, and Pulleine overlooked the fact that his companies hadn't taken along sufficient ammunition to sustain this rate of fire. Each soldier carried seventy bullets in his individual gun pouch, and, allowing for the occasional break to reload, this meant roughly ten minutes of permanent firing. Even more drastic, the latest forward move of the line had lengthened the distance to 1,500 yards between the fighting men and their ammunition train, parked way behind the tents. At that rate of fire, companies were bound to run out of ammunition, because a round trip for the ammunition carriers, mainly drummer boys and native carriers, would now take a minimum of thirty minutes.

As was predictable, the Zulu host spread into two wings. The right horn came down from the north towards Isandhlwana Hill; the left horn circled around the south of the Conical Hill, where it quickly overran the 'X' rocket battery, then crossed the Big Donga and wheeled around Pulleine's right flank. The first encounter was between the Zulu right horn and a company of NNC with Capt. C.W. Cavaye's 'A' Company as back-up. Suddenly they found themselves confronted by a slope full of dark figures with dancing plumes and brightly coloured shields who divided and swarmed to either side of the company in order to envelop it. The sun sparkled from the spear blades. After firing several volleys, Capt. Cavaye ordered a measured withdrawal. The NNC company pulled back and did precisely what was expected of them – line up in the corner of Pulleine's defensive angle. This put them squarely in front of the two seven-pounders, and this again robbed the gunners of any chance to use their cannon at their most destructive – in face of a massed attack, loaded with canister or grapeshot.[2] It took a lot of screaming to get the NNC to stand aside, by which time the Zulu had advanced to within rifle range.

The red lines held their positions, dropping to their knees to steady their aim. All along the line the same command had been given: 'On my command, volley fire.' The soldiers cocked their rifles, staring at a sea of bobbing black heads adorned with feathers and plumes. The warriors raised their shields high and came racing straight for the red line. 'Fire!' A thousand rifles roared and took a frightful toll. Black bodies went down, tumbling over their shields and burying their lethal assegais in the earth. The Zulu rear ranks jumped over the corpses; their losses didn't seem to dampen their fatal determination. A second volley had a similar effect, and still the Zulu advanced. 'Fire at will!' The British lines increased their rate of fire until they were firing flat out. As on a practice range, the well-trained soldiers pumped out twelve shots a minute, and it was unimaginable that anything living could advance through such a barrage of lead. In fact it didn't; the Zulu attack began to waver. Some foolishly brave warriors kept racing forward, only to die instantly, cut down by dozens of bullets. Then the black tide was no longer advancing and stopped altogether. The Zulu impis dropped to the ground, and lay there, like a black lake topped by a crest of white, bobbing plumes, three hundred yards from the British line.

This moment was greeted with a rousing cheer from the red lines. They had proven their courage. The concentrated gunfire of a few companies had stopped the entire Zulu nation on the warpath. They knew that their heroic stand would never be forgotten.

'The kaffirs 'ave 'ad it now!' shouted one to an ammunition runner.

'Yeah, we's put off the attack till you's arrived.' The

[2] Grapeshot is a metal canister filled with thousands of small steel pellets with an effect similar to a shotgun.

men laughed at the joke, but there was no humour in the laughter.

'They ain't put up much of a fight any more.'

'Those bastards 'ave 'ad it.'

'Don't you worry, they'll be back,' said another, older man who had seen it all before.

Their attention was drawn to a macabre drama that was being played out on the other side of the Big Donga. A corporal from a NNC unit was staggering towards the *donga*. He had been across the gully with a scout party and must have lain wounded in the shrubbery while Zulu surged around him. Now they wanted him alive to make an example and demonstrate to his comrades what would happen to them if caught. He had nearly reached the gully when he stumbled. An instant later the Zulu were all over him and dragging him back uphill. Sgt Jock Sewell of the 1st/24th gave the order to fire on the group. The hail of bullets cut down every single one, including the soldier. For him, it was a mercy killing.

The thudding of scattered rifle fire erupted anew all along the line. The soldiers kept a sharp lookout for heads popping up and picked off individuals as if on a target range. Pumped full of adrenaline and fear, many shot as fast as they could, if only to keep the fearsome warriors at a distance – and in that manner they wasted their ammunition. When the danger of an acute shortage became clear, company commanders dispatched as many as they dared let leave the line to fetch bullets from the quartermaster stores, well over a mile to the rear. Some carriers, mainly drummer boys, managed to make the round trip in the nick of time, but not many.

An outrageous situation, which must go down in the annals of military history as the summit of imbecility, now developed. British Army quartermasters were all trained to keep a precise tally of their stores for Her Majesty's accountants. Everything in its regulated order, and a signed form for everything. They would accept nothing less than an order duly signed by their company commander in exchange for socks, blankets or bullets. In the present emergency, harassed company commanders were understandably too busy to provide their ammo runners with the appropriate requisition form; some of the individual quartermasters simply refused to give out bullets without an officer's signature. Hurrah for military red tape! Worse still, the quartermaster refused to open more than one box at a time, since every bullet had to be accounted for. Instead of handing out boxes, they counted out bullets. The ridiculous became the asinine in the story of drummer boy Billy Cochran, who ran to the nearest supply wagon, which happened to be that of the 2nd/24th, where a red-faced Quartermaster Bloomfield barked at him: 'And what unit may you be from, me laddie?' When it turned out that 'the laddie' was from the 1st/24th and not from the 2nd/24th, Mr Bloomfield sent him on to Quartermaster Pullen – whose wagon happened to be another three hundred yards farther back. By the time young Billy finally covered the added distance, and had stood patiently in line and awaited his turn before heading back into the field, his unit lay dead. Billy did the only smart thing a boy of his age could think of – he turned and ran for his life. He was one of the lucky ones. And finally, there was the problem of the native companies of the NNC – being kaffirs, they didn't belong to anybody, certainly not to a white regiment, so they got no bullets at all.

When Lt Horace Smith-Dorrien heard about the problem of bullet dispatch, he raced on his horse to confront Quartermaster Bloomfield. He ordered him, and the other equally narrow-minded accountant-soldiers, to open all the boxes and allow everyone – 'And I mean everyone!' he yelled – to take as many bullets as they could possibly carry. That was when a new problem cropped up. The boxes were made of solid oak, encased with two solid copper strips, and their lids were tightened down with nine iron screws. These screws had rusted and were impossible to undo. Furthermore, the two quartermasters had been issued with one screwdriver each![3] Soldiers went at the cases with spades, bayonets, rifle butts and rocks. Horace Smith-Dorrien helped out by shovelling bullets by the handful into men's pith helmets.

The red line hadn't moved but the interval between volleys had grown noticeably larger. Those who had bullets continued to take careful aim at painted faces; but the companies could no longer deliver the precision salvos from hundreds of rifles. As the rifle fire slackened, a wave of apprehension passed over the English companies which made itself felt on the opposite side of the battlefield. It didn't take long for the Zulu chieftains to realise that something in the firing was amiss: those devil whites were running out of the devilish lead balls! A black warrior, resplendent in a cloak of feathers and fur and beads, rose in full sight of the red lines. It was Chief Shingwayo. He roared: 'The *Nkosi kakhula* [Great King] has not sent us to the washing of the spears[4] to run away like women.' That insult to a warrior's courage sang in their ears and fizzed in their blood. A deep growl went up from thousands of throats; they had been called women. '*uSuthu! uSuthu! uSuthu!*' they roared – the battle cry of their Great King, the same cry that Cetewayo's followers had used to butcher the enemies of His Greatness and to raise Him to power. Then came that hiss which had terrified so many of their enemies in the past and which always signalled an attack: '*si-gi-di . . . si-gi-di* . . . kill . . . kill!'

'Steady, men, steady!' yelled Lt Melville as the Zulu crept closer, to within a mere fifty yards. Groups of warriors sprang forward to hurl their assegais, which rained upon an English line without protective shields to ward off the missiles. The spears drove into hard earth and soft flesh. A great number of soldiers were struck, which made the parched ground slippery

[3] The only good thing to come out of this battle was that from now on ammunition boxes were sealed with knock-off clamps.

[4] 'Washing of the spears' was the Zulu's way of saying, washing in the enemy's blood.

with the blood of the killed and wounded. '"A" Company,' barked Capt. Cavaye, 'fix bayonets.' The next few minutes would show whether a thin red line of precision-trained modern infantry without bullets could hold off the onslaught of thousands of savages. For this they had only their bayonets, just as their forefathers had at Waterloo. There the *carrés* had stood up to the onslaught of Napoleon's formations. But facing them this time were not European soldiers but savages lusting for blood.

A momentary lull broke over the field as the critical moment approached. Chief Shingwayo growled at some Zulu who hesitated: 'It is time to use your spears for the closing in and tonight we will sing of a glorious victory to our king.' That was when the chief was struck by a bullet, which went in under his shoulder blade and out through his back. It left a big hole and knocked him down. A warrior quickly mixed blood with earth, then scooped up a handful of the red mud and slapped it over his chief's wound to stop the bleeding. It was amazing – the chief got back on his feet and with bloodshot eyes raised his plumed assegai to give the signal for the final rush.

Separated from the Zulu host by less than a hundred yards, soldiers were cursing the kaffirs and the ammunition carriers, the heat, the stench, their thirst and Africa in general, while others prayed in silence. Like the pulsing of the heart, the drumming of assegai on oxhide shields rose to a crescendo. The sound was enough to turn knees to jelly; it sang of death, and drowned out the screams of the dying. The mass of Zulu rose and heaved forward, one shoulder pressed into the hollow of the shield, the other swinging the terrifying knobkerrie. There was a new sound added to the chant, made by the war rattles around their ankles and the pounding of many thousands of bare feet. They lengthened their stride while the English quickly drew up in a tight line, soldier reinforcing soldier, ready to face the impact, their eyes fixed defiantly on the torrent of bodies rushing at them. Only a narrow chasm divided them from the swirls of black heads.

The Zulu came on like a herd of stampeding cattle . . . fifteen yards . . . ten . . . Then, with blundering ferocity, the masses clashed. The black phalanx crashed into a troop of Natal Police; there were so many Zulu that two were able to pin a soldier's arms to his back, while another brought down his hardwood cudgel on the cork helmet. In close, the Zulu lifted their shields high to clear the spear arm for the kill, and then the blade flashed out. More Zulu darted in to stab deep and hard into the mass of red uniforms. Rows of redcoats pitched forward where they stood, to lie still with their faces buried in the bloodstained grass. Others jammed a last cartridge into the breech or swung the rifle as a club. Every one of the dwindling companies was compressed into a killing zone. The sound was no longer one of screams versus gunfire, but the unholy moan of a mill of sheer murder. There was no longer that furious cry which carried before any battle; this was the pumping of breath from heaving chests, a groaning and straining. Many fell down simply from lack of breath. The luckless English companies had nowhere to hide. In the assault by a dozen Zulu impis, they were pushed, shoved and butchered. This was not war, this was not battle – this was raw slaughter on an unimaginable scale. The valour of the English was beyond question, but their bayonets were like harmless toys against the massed savages swirling all over them. Their wall of shields drove into the redcoats, bowling them over in a ram-like assault. Bayonets sliced through oxhide shields and deep into flesh. Soldiers clung to their speared foes, dragging them down in their own death. All around, the trampled ground was littered with corpses, a sea of smashed heads, limbs and torsos, torn apart by gunpowder or slashed off by razor-sharp assegai.

In the end the Zulu came for the cooks, the wounded and the quartermasters. At the wagon park, someone cried out: 'The Zulu are coming!' followed by a booming voice: 'Stand to your guns!' and 'Fire at will!' That was moments before a black tide swept over them. Then the plumed warriors were between the wagons and the slaughter began. The wounded dragged themselves under the wagons, trying to staunch the blood pouring from the awful holes slashed by Zulu blades. Only a few attempted to flee; they were cut off by bands of Zulu, who raced after them like gazelles.

It was 1.30 p.m. The battle had lasted for a little over an hour, when Lt Col. Pulleine called for Lt Teignmouth Melville and Lt Neville Coghill: 'All is lost. Bring the regimental colours to safety.' The two officers galloped off in the direction of the swollen river. They had almost reached the bank when suddenly a fluting sound was in the air. Thrown assegais! One of the weighted heads caught the flag-carrying Melville in his side. His horse reared and whinnied before it plunged into the stream. Melville was so weakened by the spear-thrust that he fell out of the saddle; the flood swept him off and the precious regimental colours slipped from his grip. Lt Coghill, who had already reached the opposite bank, saw his friend's flailing arms above the water and jumped back in to save him. He managed to pull Melville up on the bank, but by this time the riverbank was swarming with Zulu. All became a blur – a milling, shouting confusion. Blood gagged Melville; he was dying, while Coghill fought for their lives with his service revolver until he ran out of bullets. In 1907, both were posthumously awarded the Victoria Cross.

Weeks passed. The waters of the river had subsided when a clean-up party discovered the regimental flag embedded in sand at the bottom of a pool. It was sent to England, where Queen Victoria personally decorated it with a wreath of immortelles to honour the courage of her soldiers. The regimental colours of the ill-fated 24th still hang in the cathedral at Brecon.

Lt Horace Smith-Dorrien, in the forefront of the action, had miraculously come through the battle and sustained no more than superficial slashes and lacerations. This was in part due to a curious coincidence. Just before sending his impis to confront the British forces, King Cetewayo had fired the spirit of his army with a rousing call to 'Kill all redcoats!' The warriors took his words literally – Smith-Dorrien[5] was that day wearing a blue uniform!

> Major Stuart Smith of the artillery came down by me badly wounded, saying: 'For God's sake get on, man, the Zulu are on top of us.' I jumped on my horse and my horse went to the bottom of the precipice, being struck with an assegai. I gave up all hope, as Zulu were all around me, finishing off the wounded, Major Smith among the number. With the strong hope that everybody clings to that some accident would turn up, I rushed off on foot and plunged into the river, which was little better than a roaring torrent. I was being carried downstream at a tremendous pace, when a loose horse came by me and I got hold of its tail and he landed me safely on the other bank. I was too tired to stick to him and get on his back. I got up and rushed on and was several times knocked over by our mounted niggers who would not get out of my way, then up a tremendous hill with my wet clothes and boots full of water. About twenty Zulu got over the water and followed us up the hill, but I am thankful to say they had no firearms. Crossing the river, however, the Zulu on the opposite side kept firing at us as we went up the hill and killed several of the niggers around me. I was the only white man to be seen. A few Zulu followed us for about three miles, but they had no guns and I had a revolver, which I kept letting them know. They finally stopped altogether. I struggled into Helpmakaar, about twenty miles off, at nightfall to find a few men who had escaped.[6]

[5] He was later Corps Commander of the British Expeditionary Force to France in WWI. He recounted his amazing escape in *My Forty-Eight Years in the Service*, published in 1925.
[6] Ibid.

Five officers escaped the massacre, and every single one was dressed in blue.

The last to die was a heroic rifleman whose name will never be known. When the Zulu stormed into the wagon park, he managed his escape up Isandhlwana *kopje*, where he hid out in the crag of a cliff. He had only a dozen bullets. Very carefully he picked his targets among the Zulu leaders with their distinctive signs, lion manes worn on beaded strings over their chests. He eliminated eleven. The last bullet he kept for himself.[7]

Across the rock-strewn plain silence fell. The Zulu army was covered in gore and mud; rivulets of blood ran down their bodies, from their own wounds or those of their slaughtered foes. Before them spread a forest of assegai, planted through flesh into red earth. They gathered their dead warriors, laid them out in the narrow *donga* and covered their bodies with stones to keep away vultures and hyenas. In the midst of the blood-soaked ground stood Chief Shingwayo, staring at the naked bodies of his enemies. His face was impassive, but his eyes were terrible when he issued the order for a final task his brave warriors must perform in order to stop the evil spirit from finding a home: to let their soul fly. Lest their dead ghosts remain on earth and haunt the living. A fatal, ritualistic gesture – the washing of the spears.

Late that night Chelmsford's column halted at the Big Donga, having marched back at double pace. It would have been foolish to cross the river in darkness, and it was only the following morning that an advance party rode up to the camp. The first indication of the disaster was a cloud of carrion birds circling above the plain. The British officers were unprepared for the sight that lay before them – this was no battlefield but a scene of wanton butchery. The fallen had been stripped of

[7] A Zulu told this story many years later; all the accounts from the Zulu side were written down by researchers from tales by old warriors, some as late as the 1930s.

their red coats and were lying face up. In death, they had been disembowelled with the wickedly sharp blades of Zulu assegai, the final act in the Zulu ritual: slitting open the belly of the wounded and dead, they believed, prevented the evil spirit from hiding inside the body.

All the Zulu had left behind was a bloody patch of mud. Chelmsford's horse picked his way slowly between the slain. Her Majesty's 24th Regiment had gone to their deaths where they stood, still in neat lines, company next to company. The camp had been destroyed and the wagons looted. The horses were dead. Corpses lay in a litter of saddlery, smashed equipment, yellow wax paper from ammunition packets and empty brass cartridge cases – but no rifles. Over an ammunition box lay the corpse of Quartermaster Bloomfield of the 2nd/24th. His head and shoulder stuck out from underneath the wagon's axle. A single blow with a battle-mace had crushed his cork helmet and skull. Scattered around his corpse were hundreds of unspent cartridges, glinting evilly in the sun. Over the wagon's wheel hung the body of a young drummer boy with his throat slit, one of the hapless ammunition carriers who had tried in vain to obtain the bullets of the 2nd/24th for another company. A young soldier went behind an overturned wagon to vomit. What a cruel waste this was.

Only six soldiers of the 1st/24th escaped; they were down with fever, had been left out of the company line-up and somehow had been overlooked in a tent. The other survivors, three hundred in all, were native auxiliaries dressed in khaki who had managed to escape. Numbed by the extent of the disaster, Lord Chelmsford climbed from his horse and sat down on a rock. He was to recall with bitterness the promise he had made in a letter to the Duke of Cambridge: 'Your Royal Highness may rest assured that I shall do my best to bring the war in Zululand to a speedy close, so that I may be enabled to send back to England some of the regiments now under my command.'

He had nothing to send back – 1,329 British soldiers with

ripped-open bellies lay on the grassy plain before Isandhlwana Hill. The Zulu had taken no prisoners. The men dug a long trench, a last service for their friends and comrades. It was amazing how hard the earth was, sun-dried and rocky. Afterwards, the soldiers hung around, finding comfort in their common grief. It didn't take much to make them cry like children. They wanted to kill, kill whoever was responsible for the waste of so many lives. Perhaps they realised how absurd war, and especially this stupid, nonsensical campaign against African natives, really was. Many wrote home and told of the horror they had witnessed. The newspapers got hold of some accounts. More than anything, it was the savagery committed in the *washing of the spears* that upset public opinion.

The regimental padre read the burial service. It was a hasty affair. There wasn't much to bury – the hyenas, jackals and vultures had had a feast. When everything was over, what was left of the regiment marched off towards the Swedish mission on the Buffalo river. Chelmsford had no option. The Zulu had not only taken the rifles, but also the reserve ammunition. 'God help our column if the Zulu attack us now,' said Chelmsford to his officers. In fact many Zulu had already dispersed back to their kraals. Many, but not all.

Chelmsford's column headed for Rorke's Drift, where another surprise was in store.

'Thoughtful courage is a quality possessed by very few, but rashness and boldness and fearlessness, which has no forethought, are very common qualities possessed by many men, many animals. Courageous actions are wise actions,' wrote Plato 2,500 years ago. And so it was to be proved at a Swedish missionary station on the Buffalo river, only six miles as the vulture flies from the killing fields of Isandhlwana.

Some years before, when the first white traders came to barter with natives, a certain Jim Rorke had discovered a fordable passage across the yellow-brown waters of the Buffalo river near an easily recognisable landmark, a conical-shaped *kopje* he named the Oscarberg. Eventually, a Swedish missionary station was established near this drift, to look after the spiritual wellbeing of local villagers and slap ointment on snakebites. The compound consisted of several thatched-roof buildings, including a hospital and a general storehouse. The buildings were made of the most readily available material, adobe brick, which, once hardened, was strong and weather resistant.[8] The place was never intended as a stockade and had been left open on all sides. Fronting the main building, and beyond the track that led to the ferry crossing, was a stone wall that had never been finished; beyond this was a vegetable garden studded with fruit trees and surrounded by a simple wooden fence to protect the planted patch from voracious cattle. Behind the station was a cookhouse, and beyond that began a series of terraces leading up to the Oscarberg *kopje*.

At the outset of the Zulu War, the mission was taken over by the British Army as one of its staging-posts for the punitive expedition. The intention was to fortify the buildings, and for this purpose a thirty-two-year-old lieutenant from the Corps of Engineers had recently been dispatched to oversee the construction works.

The acting commander of Rorke's Drift Missionary Station was a moustachioed lieutenant of engineers, John Rouse Merriot Chard, who had arrived at the station in the company of Sgt Milne and a work party of six natives. The fact that he was 'temporarily in command' came about by a series of weird circumstances. Earlier that morning, the commandant, Maj. Spalding, had ridden off to Helpmakaar, ten miles to the south, to drum up some extra bodies in order to bolster the contingent of this small but vital mission on the river crossing. The other officers present, camped with their units next to the vegetable garden, were Lt Gonville Bromhead of 'B' Company, 2nd/24th (older and longer in the service than Chard, but junior in date of commission) and Capt.

8 A mixture of clay and binding straw, left to dry and harden in the sun.

George Stephenson of the NNC native contingent, whose rank did not rate above that of a regular soldier. So it was Lt Chard who automatically became mission commandant in Maj. Spalding's absence. Others at the mission were a doctor, Surgeon-Major James Reynolds, a retired sergeant-major who had been appointed store commissary, Mr James Dalton, the man in charge of the troop's spiritual salvation, the Reverend George Smith, plus a missionary, Mr Otto Witt.

Mid-morning, Lt Chard had taken a leisurely ride up the hill to Isandhlwana camp to have 'a cup of tea' with a fellow officer, but had found that his friend had left earlier that morning with the Chelmsford column. Everything was quiet and normal when Chard left Isandhlwana and rode back to Rorke's Drift. The time was 10 a.m.

It was now 3 p.m. on that fateful day, 22 January 1879. Up on the plateau, everyone was dead, while six miles off, at Rorke's Drift, Lt Chard was sitting down for a quiet meal with the surgeon and the reverend. After lunch, Chard rode to the river crossing, where his work party fixed the guide cables for two shallow-bottomed punts, stretching across the hundred metres of stream. Suddenly he heard a shout from one of his men, who was pointing uphill. Chard didn't know what to make of it as two riders came down the track, pushing their animals as hard as they could, waving their arms like madmen and yelling something that was drowned by the rushing waters. They drove their horses into the Buffalo river. They were Lt Adendorff and Lt Vane of the NNC.

'Hurry back to the mission and warn your men,' they screamed, halfway across the chest-high waters. 'They've butchered our entire camp. Everything's lost!'

'Now hold on a minute, I've just come back from Isandhlwana.'

'What time?'

'Around eleven or thereabouts.'

'That's how you missed it. They came at noon and it took them barely an hour.'

Chard realised that the situation was serious, but he was not prepared for the next shock. Said Adendorff: 'We've managed to outride them, but parallel to us ran several impis – and they are headed straight for you!'

'How many?'

'Four, five thousand I would say.'

'How far away are they?'

'Can't be sure. We lost sight of them. Perhaps only a few minutes.'

Chard shouted orders to his work party to hurry back, then he took off to raise Lt Bromhead. The commander of 'B' Company shook his head at the report; he couldn't believe the story. At that moment, four more riders on sweat-drenched horses and wearing torn, bloodstained uniforms rode up, jumped from their horses and ran up to the two officers. An out-of-breath corporal stuttered: '. . . dead . . . the whole camp . . . every one of them . . .'

'Hold it right there, soldier,' said the colour-sergeant of 'B' Company.

'Here, read for yerself.' The corporal fished a wrinkled piece of paper from his breast pocket.

'CAPT. ESSEX OF 75TH FOOT, TRANSPORT OFFICER AT CENTRE COLUMN . . . GOT AWAY ON HORSE FOUR MILES DOWNSTREAM OF RORKE'S DRIFT . . . HILLSIDE BLACK WITH TROTTING ZULU . . . HEADING NORTH FOLLOWING RIVER . . . AT LEAST ONE IMPI MADE UP OF THOUSANDS . . .'

While he was reading this out aloud, Chard and Bromhead were joined by the surgeon-major, who had ridden up the Oscarberg 'to take a look' and now climbed rather coolly from his horse. 'Rather good visibility towards Isandhlwana Hill. Clouds of natives coming this way. Why d'you look at me this way? I'm only telling you what I saw. Wonder what they're up to.'

'Nothing good, I'm afraid. They're Cetewayo's lot and they're out for blood.'

'Good heavens. You mean rampaging Zulu?'

Bromhead was the first to react. 'Sergeant, get these men out of camp. I don't want our "brave native contingent" to get alarmed, they might just take to the hills. Then get every man of company "B" over here, pronto.'

'Yessir,' the man said without batting an eyelid, before turning to the exhausted riders. 'You men, get on your horses and make for Helpmakaar, tell them what happened. They'll know what to do.' The foursome jumped on their horses and were gone.

Chard made a quick calculation. His effective was made up of a company of Bromhead's regulars, plus Stephenson's company of natives of doubtful value, and two dozen wounded in the hospital ward – 250 men at best. It would have to do.

'I will do my very best to see that all of us survive the next few hours.' He tried to sound positive, but somehow it didn't come out that way.

'You do that, Chard,' replied Bromhead drily, 'but keep an eye on Stephenson's native contingent.'

'With regard to our survival factor?'

'You might call it that.' Bromhead had no time for Stephenson – 'a colonial jock' he called him – just as Bromhead's regulars had no time for Stephenson's scruffy untrained lot, as undisciplined as they were unreliable.

'Let's get the wounded on the wagons and send them off.'

The retired Sgt-Maj. Dalton, who had evidently taken a bath because he was wet and naked save for a pair of drawers, had joined them and intervened. 'With your permission, sir, I disagree. They'd only get waylaid and slaughtered. Keep them here and hand those who can still stand up a rifle and those who cannot, use them to reload.'

Chard had to admit that Dalton had a point and he admired him for his cool head. Thank God for good old British sergeant-majors, even retired ones.

'Right you are,' said Bromhead, 'but we have another asset. Dalton, aren't you qualified to put up field defences?'

'Yessir, I am.'

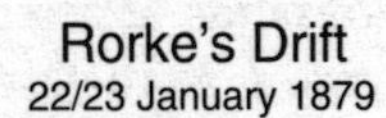
Rorke's Drift
22/23 January 1879

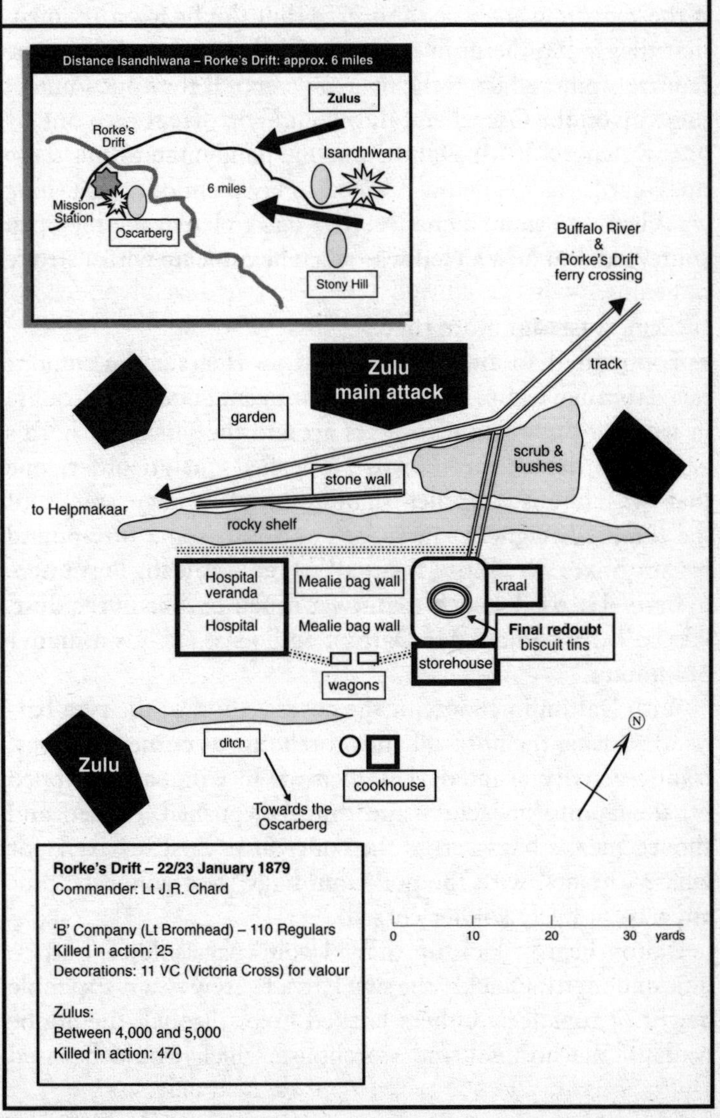
Distance Isandhlwana – Rorke's Drift: approx. 6 miles
Zulus
Rorke's Drift
Isandhlwana
6 miles
Mission Station
Oscarberg
Stony Hill
Buffalo River & Rorke's Drift ferry crossing
track
Zulu main attack
garden
scrub & bushes
stone wall
to Helpmakaar
rocky shelf
Hospital veranda
Hospital
Mealie bag wall
Mealie bag wall
kraal
Final redoubt
biscuit tins
storehouse
wagons
ditch
Zulu
cookhouse
Towards the Oscarberg
N
0
10
20
30
yards
Rorke's Drift – 22/23 January 1879
Commander: Lt J.R. Chard
'B' Company (Lt Bromhead) – 110 Regulars
Killed in action: 25
Decorations: 11 VC (Victoria Cross) for valour
Zulus:
Between 4,000 and 5,000
Killed in action: 470

It would be one hundred Martini-Henry repeater rifles, 1871 model, against thousands of assegai and perhaps a few Snider muskets, as dangerous to the user as to the target. But if the reports were true, and he didn't doubt for a moment that they were, the impi was most likely in possession of the repeaters pilfered from the overrun camp. If they put some of these up on the Oscarberg, they could pop off his men one by one. Defences! If Mr Dalton was the handyman to put them up, Chard was the genius trained to lay them out. One thing was clear – to stand a chance, they had to barricade the open courtyard. But how? That was when he came up with a stroke of genius.

'Let's waste no more time.'

Too many had already seen the four riders and a rumour raced through camp. The whole contingent flooded the square in front of the mission to mass around the officers. Chard's gaze met that of the crowd. He lashed out an order, one that was fatalistic rather than calm. 'We have stacks of the hundredweight mealie[9] bags and also some fifty-pound biscuit boxes. We'll use them all to build a wall. From here to here.' He used a stick to draw a rough outline in the dust. 'You all work under Mr Dalton, and Sergeant, it's a matter of minutes.'

With Dalton in charge of the construction of the two barricades, using the hospital and storehouse as corner bastions, frantic activity erupted. The men of 'B' Company stripped off their uniform jackets and dragged, pushed, carried and shoved mealie bags across the courtyard. 'Bust my back for what? The hell with the goddamn bags! Not gonna help us anyway,' a beefy soldier cursed.

Dalton heard. 'Pick up that bleedin' bag, soldier, and be quick about it!' Quickly the two barriers grew to a respectable height of four feet. Others hacked holes through the adobe walls of the hospital and storehouse which would be used

[9] Mealie is dried corn, a staple food in South Africa.

as rifle pits. In contrast to the final stand by the 24th at Isandhlwana, a specific order was given to break open all the cartridge boxes and pile up a heap of bullets next to every fighting position. Since Rorke's Drift Mission was the supply depot for the entire expeditionary force, at least they wouldn't run short of cartridges. Chard planted himself authoritatively in the centre between the two walls and spaced a man every six yards behind his three hundred yards of mealie bags. A wave of anxiety washed over the engineer. How could one hundred possibly hold out against four thousand? Remember Sparta, King Leonidas and his three hundred? The Spartan had done it with spears, and his men had guns. Outwardly, Lt Chard showed himself a rock in a storm. His voice, irresistible and calm, urged the men to build 'his sandcastle'. When it was finished, Bromhead looked at the fortification. 'This will achieve a decided distinction in the annals of the British Army. It may not be the stoutest fortress, but it certainly is the most edible one.'

'Whatever, it has to do.' Chard had been frustrated by years of impeccable service as an engineer who had never been able to prove his true talent, and finally he was called upon to build his first ever fortifications from flour bags! 'But we're not finished, I'm afraid. I know your men are exhausted, but get me the strongest you can drum up.' He drew another outline on the ground in front of the storehouse veranda. 'Biscuit boxes in a circle. This is where we shall make our final stand.'

A few minutes before 4 p.m. a troop of the NNC Sikali Horse, made up of Basuto natives, with Lt Vause in command, came riding up the road. They seemed in no great hurry. Chard sighed with relief. They would add another hundred rifles to his effective. It brought his defensive strength to 350. Twelve to one was an acceptable ratio. Across the rapidly growing mealie wall, Chard yelled to Lt Vause: 'We've got ourselves a problem. Seems like an impi is on its way. Ride on up ahead and try to delay them as much as you can, then let your horses go and join us inside the wall.' Lt Vause nodded, saluted and then took his riders farther up the track. Suddenly, the native horsemen turned as one and bolted off in wild flight. Lt Vause, chasing after them, reined in his horse and shouted: 'They've disobeyed my order,' before he chased after them. Commotion broke out in the compound, the men of 'B' Company shaking fists and yelling obscenities after the disappearing band of Sikali Horse. Chard and Bromhead stood silently, as if turned into statues of salt. While their attention was diverted, the contingent of Stephenson's native NNC, which had been huddling behind the stone wall of the mission's kraal, slipped away. They were gone before anyone had noticed their flight, shedding their uniforms as they headed through scrub and bush to vanish into the countryside. It was just as well that they ran *before* the fight began; had they done so during the attack the outcome might well have been different. Chard asked a soldier if he had seen Maj. Stephenson. 'When the geezer saw wot 'ad 'appened he near went off his nut. Started blubbin' 'n' then scarpered too. Tryin' to find 'em now, I s'pose.'

'What a show, and that in front of the garrison,' growled Chard. In two minutes, he had lost 60 per cent of his overall effective! From the 350 rifles he had counted on he was now down to 110 actives and 30 cripples from the infirmary. Something like forty to one! For a moment, Chard's mind was drifting on a vast sea of despair. And then he looked at some of the walking wounded who had left their hospital beds; they were leaning on their crutches against the mealie wall. There was even one with bandaged legs who had been carried from his bed on a chair and then had added a few cushions for height to allow him to peer over the bags. Such devotion greatly cheered Chard.

'Fix bayonets!' With a metallic click, one hundred bayonets snapped into sockets. Private Wall, who had been sent to the top of the Oscarberg *kopje* as forward scout, came scampering down the steep slope, stumbling and sliding and waving his arms. 'Here they come,' he screamed, 'black as hell and thick as grass!'

And so it was. Thick as grass, they stepped out from behind the Oscarberg mountain.

Shakala, a chieftain's son, had never expected to take up his father's assegai of impi lordship. He was not the heir apparent; there were older brothers by other wives of higher rank than that of his mother. His body was black steel and muscle, his skin shiny with the grease from the thick rinds of yellow fat applied to protect it from insects. He was a veteran of long marches and bloody battles. Shakala had proven himself as a great brave, with that certain cruelty which any warrior had to make part of his life, and the Great King Cetewayo had bestowed upon him the honour of leading an impi. He had lain before the Great King, face down on the hard clay, and heard Cetawayo's voice ordering him to kill the mamba with its own poison. And he, Shakala, had risen from the ground and had sworn allegiance and loyalty to the death. He had set out with his men to take cattle and women from other tribes. Afterwards he had watched the hyenas wolfing down the flesh of his slain victims and cracking the bones. The seasons passed; dry heat followed the rain. All went well until a group of white men had come along the cattle track on horses, trading beads for yellow metal and those shiny pebbles the boys found in the riverbanks. Shakala had learned the meaning of the popping sound from their guns and the wailing of his mother as she mourned the death of another son. Those men with their wide-brimmed felt hats had brought only misery, and had even taken some Zulu girls with them to serve their pleasure. For this, he hated the white men. He had just proven his value as a leader of valiant warriors, up on the plateau, where they had washed their spears.

Forming distinctive assault groups, Shakala's impi approached the compound. The Zulu army was massive, numbering at least four thousand, if not more. Throwing a choking noose of warriors around their enemy had always been the Zulu's tactic, and the English were aware of it. That was why they had built two walls, one in front and one at the back. Their first objective was to take out some of the Zulu leaders, recognisable by their plumage. Chard's men braced their heavy Martini-Henrys on the mealie bags, then selected the blacks with tall ostrich feathers and began picking them off from a distance. Seeing their chiefs go down so infuriated the Zulu that they ran straight at the barrier.

The first volleys, fired at ten-second intervals, struck home and flung dozens of Zulu bodies to the ground. Not many of the initial wave remained standing. But still the next wave came on; those in front had already covered the better part of the distance between the fruit trees and the mealie bags when a new volley crumpled them. So many Zulu now came across the vegetable garden that their shields seemed to form a continuous mass. But oxhide couldn't stand up to 480-grain slugs. The bullets tore through shield and black skin. Other warriors veered off towards the low stone wall, and stopped just in time to receive the full impact of the next salvo, aimed in anticipation of just such a halt. Scythed by the merciless hail of heavy slugs, the next Zulu wave toppled. The air was acrid with the smell of gunpowder. The shooting had jolted the aggressors, but not all, and hundreds of Zulu managed to break across the track. A full volley hit them, shredding ostrich feathers, oxhide shields and flesh. Still, they kept on coming. Now only the few yards of shallow rock shelf separated the feather-plumed masses from the defenders. Within seconds they had leaped up on to the wall. 'B' Company stood solid, shooting and bayoneting their adversaries as they tried to scramble over the mealie bags.

Assegai wrapped in bundles of burning straw rained down on the hospital's thatched roof, and it caught fire. The flames spread rapidly, and black smoke rose in dense spirals. The fire was to turn into an unexpected bonus. As darkness fell, the flames lit up the enemy for the next few, terrible, hours to come. The immediate emergency switched to the infirmary, where all hell erupted – a fight for possession of the hospital that turned into another epic defence. Dodging bullets and bayonets, Zulu had stormed into the rabbit-warren of rooms. Among the six soldiers defending the hospital there was no shouting, and no orders were given; they reacted as an expert team to evacuate the seriously wounded and kill their enemy. One of them, Joseph Williams, had barricaded himself in the central hallway to face single-handedly a mass of Zulu. He took a few down before they were all over him. His friend, John Williams (no relation), peered through a gun hole in the wall at a scene so horrific it made him vomit. The Zulu stripped Joseph of his uniform jacket and then slit open his belly with an assegai. The example of their comrade in the hands of the savages turned the soldiers into ruthless agents of death. Their faces were grim. They knew they could expect no pity – whatever happened, they were condemned to die, and any condemned man fights harder. They were covered with sweat and blood and pale dust that turned them the colour of the walls. John Williams threw open the last barred window and jumped, his gun roaring even before he hit the ground. An injured man came stumbling after him across the courtyard, took a couple of erratic steps and fell with blood oozing from his chest. A bullet fired by a sniper up on the Oscarberg had hit him.[10] The surgeon-major examined the man briefly and shook his head. 'He's dead,' he said gravely.

The sniping from the Oscarberg increased; Zulu with rifles captured at Isandhlwana, firing down from the heights, became the cause of most of the English casualties. Bromhead chose five of his best shooters and detailed them to pick off the gunmen hunkering on the mountain terraces. They did the job to perfection and the sniping ceased. There wasn't a single

10 Although the Zulu had some guns, notably those captured earlier that day, they never used them with any effect.

soldier whose uniform wasn't stained with dust and blood – his own or that of the many Zulu they had speared with their bayonets. Men fell and others took their place without being told to. A hundred individual acts of heroism took place that night. Everyone did his share. Reverend Smith kept circling the barricades, rushing from man to man and handing out cartridges from his shoulder satchel with a dry 'Bless you, my son.'

And when he wasn't handing out ammunition, he was dragging wounded to the first-aid station, which had had been established on the storehouse veranda. While the attacks carried on unabated, a blood-splattered Surgeon-Major Reynolds cut and patched men up only to send them back to do more fighting. He had to give priority to those who could hold a rifle again; the badly wounded simply had to wait. In his defence it must be stated that he didn't lose a single one of his wounded. Everyone came through.

Byrne, a commissary assistant, was rushing over to Lt Chard, who was clearly visible to all, directing operations and issuing commands from the middle of the compound, when a shot rang out and the young Byrne fell dead. A fraction earlier and the bullet would have struck Chard. Seeing their leader fall could have panicked the defenders, but such is the luck of war.

With the fall of the hospital, the walled-in courtyard had to be abandoned. Lt Chard ordered a withdrawal into the final redoubt, his circular biscuit box barricade, lined with open ammunition crates within easy reach. By the light from the burning hospital, the men continued to pour a withering stream of fire into the Zulu waves that were now beginning to crawl over the mealie bags.

There were still over a thousand Zulu milling around, so thick that they got in each other's way and made for excellent grouped targets. But the spirit that had driven the warriors in the early stage was drying up. No longer did they attack in organised units, but in small groups, a dozen here, then another dozen there; such individual forays were easy to contain with well-aimed rifle fire.

The incessant roar of volleys that had been aimed belly high into the seething masses slackened to intermittent but carefully targeted shots. The rifle barrels were aglow – each soldier had fired for hours without let-up. Thanks to solid English steel and workmanship the rifle tubes held up. From the dark came cries of agony and frustration. Four thousand savages had tried to storm an open missionary building, defended by a mere hundred-odd soldiers, but soldiers armed with modern rifles, and they had taken a terrible toll. The last concerted Zulu attack was launched around 10 p.m. over the stone-walled kraal. Though its defenders finally had to withdraw into the storehouse compound, they left the straw-covered kraal floor littered with Zulu bodies. Chard's men had performed wonders for six hours, but they couldn't endure much longer. They had reached the point of collapse; if the Zulu discovered this, they would come back and overrun them in a final concerted effort.

Then the ululating war cry changed, becoming considerably less insistent. The soldiers stood there with glowing rifles, their chins thrust forward, their eyes peering at the blank wall of darkness. The hospital building, their source of light by which to fight, had finally crumbled to ash. One more attack and they would have to shoot blind . . . but no further attack came. The sound of guns had ceased. In its place was another sound – the rushing waters of the Buffalo river. Chard was tired, deadly tired. All he wanted was to close his eyes and let darkness wash over him.

By 2.30 a.m. it was over. Ten hours of shooting, stabbing, screaming and dying. Ten hours of individual heroism. The mealie-bag brigade had held off an enemy forty times their size, and the world's first edible fortress was still standing. For the survivors, there was no cheering, no joy, only tiredness. Long after the naked hordes had slipped out of sight, the soldiers continued to cower, stunned, behind their biscuit boxes and mealie bags. Many had their faces burrowed into their tightly folded arms, as if there they could find shelter from the storm of blood and violence which they couldn't believe was finally over. And in their midst, stiff as a statue stood a bold medieval knight, wiping his neck and face with a dirty grey handkerchief and letting it flutter as his flag of victory. Time and exhaustion had no relevance in the mind of Lieutenant of Engineers John Rouse Merriot Chard. Everything seemed like a fog-shrouded nightmare. His body moved mechanically, the eyes and muscles taking care of business while his brain numbly tried to accept that many of his men lay dead. It had been a long night and it had aged him. He shook his head to clear it of non-constructive thoughts and attempted to confront the reality of their situation. He knew that his men could repulse no further attack.

Where at first the impi had raced furiously against the low wall, only a few warriors were left for a final charge across the blood-soaked clay. It was a pitifully small band. The rest had turned back and disappeared behind the terraces of the Oscarberg. Shakala, the noble warrior, was sobbing with frustration. He had led his men down to the river, proudly wearing his war plumes, carrying his shield on his shoulder and a bloodied assegai in his fist. Many of his warriors had picked up guns from the dead up on the plateau, and with them they would sting the mamba with its own poison. Until that moment, the only guns they had were a few old muskets that had been manufactured almost a century ago and had been traded for ivory. Their barrels had worn so thin that each shot threatened to tear off the head of the man who used it. But now they were well armed. Shakala had walked with a light spring in his stride as he had surveyed the flat missionary buildings that lay before him. Before he launched his assault, he had sent some men with rifles up the Oscarberg. That had been a few hours ago, and now his impi lay dead around the mission buildings, shot by the white soldiers. He had hardly felt the bayonet that sliced through his side; it was just an irritation that now made him tired. He toppled forward to lie with his face against the ground. When he woke up the sun was coming over the mountain. Leaving a trail of blood, he crawled into the cover of a red-tipped thorn tree and slapped mud over his gaping wound. Many days later he dragged himself into a Zulu kraal. He didn't dare return to the royal kraal and admit defeat, and yet he was one of the few able to tell the tale of his impi's heroic, but futile, charge on the white man's mission.

The night was quiet. Only the whooping cry of a hyena, slinking around in the dark, made the silence that had preceded it even more noticeable. Its cry was answered by a chorus from other beasts that had replaced the Zulu and now surrounded the mission. The whooping and howling, a moan turning to fiendish laughter, sounded like the dead rising. The horrific noise made by animals' carnassial teeth as they sliced through flesh and bone kept the soldiers from their sleep. Chard could see the faces of his men, listening to the hideous laughter and tormented shrieks, their faces frozen with superstitious terror, crouching behind the mealie bags, clutching their rifles. Chard let his thoughts stray to the morrow. What would it bring? More attacks, Lord Chelmsford's column? Dawn came on slowly like the gradual illumination of a stage. To the tired, red-eyed defenders, hanging over their rifles on slashed mealie bags, the morning revealed a corpse-strewn inferno. In front of the makeshift barricade lay a pile of corpses as high as the wall itself. It wasn't a pretty sight. There was no need to search for survivors. Among the slain they found one of the chiefs, but not the leader of the impi. He was identified by his special array of white ostrich-feather plumes, which he wore like a Roman centurion. Save for a loincloth he was naked, and he had a large jagged hole in his breast around which a cluster of flies buzzed.

'Hundreds of them fuckers are dead,' said a bleary-eyed

soldier, 'and ne'er a trace of them left.' There was one final alarm when another impi was sighted, but it soon disappeared behind the Oscarberg. With a deep sigh of relief, Lt Chard turned to no one in particular. 'It's time to brew up some tea, I think. The men have deserved it.'

'Yessir,' answered a strong voice. It was Mr Dalton. 'All right, you've heard the man . . . let's clear out the cookhouse and put some water in the kettle . . .'

Twenty-five soldiers had paid with their lives for the heroic stand. They were buried behind the station houses with full military honours.

'Attention,' Lt Chard shouted. The troop froze where it stood. 'Salute.' The hands went up. 'Fire!' A final volley rang out at Rorke's Drift. It was all they had to offer their fallen heroes.

'We are not heroes, only survival experts,' was the only way Lt Chard could express his deep emotions when he addressed Her Majesty Queen Victoria the day she awarded him, and ten others,[11] the Victoria Cross. With eleven honours for 110 men, Rorke's Drift became the single most decorated action in the history of modern British warfare.

The facts

In a contest between rifles and spears, the gun wins the day. But not always. That was shown on the bloody fields in Zululand. The difference between Isandhlwana and Rorke's Drift is striking. Both battles took place on the same day in the same region and against the same enemy. At one

[11] Lt Chard, Lt Bromhead, Surgeon-Maj. Reynolds, Mr Dalton, Cpl Allen, Cpl Schiess, Pvts Hitch, Hook, Joseph Williams, Jones and John Williams. Some were awarded posthumously.

encounter, a regiment of 1,500 men was overrun and killed in a matter of minutes, while in another a hundred soldiers hung on tenaciously for ten hours. It is not certain that the regiment, caught on the open plain, could have avoided the disaster. Firepower, even with an adequate resupply of bullets is not in itself self-sustaining.

The decisive factor at Rorke's Drift was not only the readily available ammunition but also their fortified position. It took exceptional leadership and quick thinking to make preparations for defence and then to hang on tenaciously until the enemy reached breaking-point. In that, they were lucky to have in Lt Chard an engineer and not a cavalryman in command. With God's assistance and Chard's mealie-bag fortress, they achieved their objective.

The Zulu generals used the classic battle tactic taught in Western military academies: they decoyed Chelmsford's column out of camp while they doubled back and destroyed the depleted regiment at its base. Isandhlwana was a catastrophic reversal of Britain's colonial military might. And yet King Cetewayo's greatest victory also brought about the end of his Zulu empire. Too many of his best warriors had died in the two encounters; there was great sadness in the kraals and the story of the awesome firepower of the British battalions spread across the veldt. Even in defeat at Isandhlwana, the British had achieved much more. Their firepower inflicted enough casualties on the enemy to discourage him from further aggression.

The action at Rorke's Drift will always remain an outstanding feat of arms,[12] although perhaps it would not have become as widely publicised had Isandhlwana gone the British way. The government wanted to hide the major débâcle from its public and found it expedient to stress the heroism of a

[12] The German Kaiser was so impressed that he ordered a lecture on the defence of Rorke's Drift to be given in his officer academies to inspire leadership qualities.

few men in a smaller action. The Victorian press dutifully obliged. For weeks, the British papers published stories of the heroic defence of Rorke's Drift, but also testimony from survivors in letters sent to their families after Isandhlwana which described in great detail the horror of the washing of the spears. What finally focused their full attention on the Zulu was an incident that happened on 1 June 1879. A patrol led by Louis Bonaparte, serving as a volunteer in the British Army, was ambushed and the Prince Imperial was killed and mutilated. Lord Chelmsford set off on one more expedition, and this time he did everything right. On 4 July 1879, within sight of King Cetewayo's royal kraal at Ulundi, he confronted a morally weakened Zulu host and with the musketry of his 4,200 Europeans he blasted the warriors to bits; the British cavalry did the rest. King Cetewayo fled, but was eventually captured.

Only a year later, on 30 December 1880, the Boers proclaimed their independence and England was faced with a much bigger conflict. The war against the Zulu was soon forgotten.

Colonial political ignorance and senile strategy,[13] together with military arrogance, were largely responsible for the outbreak of the Zulu War. For a few months, it had turned the borders of Natal Province into a giant slaughterhouse where the opposing forces did not so much fight as butcher each other, with no mercy given or expected.

And the ammunition boxes . . . the British had clearly not learned the harsh lesson they'd received at the hands of ten thousand Ashanti warriors near Bonsaso in 1824. First, the English general, Sir Charles MacCarthy, tried to halt the tribal onslaught by playing 'God Save the King' to them, and when that had no discernible effect he ordered the reserve

13 Sir Bartle Frere, the colonial official who had provoked this nonsensical war to please some gold and diamond mining interests, was upbraided and relegated to a minor post on the Cape.

ammunition to be distributed. But the men couldn't get the screws out of the boxes, and when they were finally smashed open, instead of bullets they contained biscuits! The redcoats were overrun and their unfortunate general's head impaled on a spear before his skull was converted into a drinking cup for the Ashanti king.

That was not all. In 1885, a British expeditionary force moved against the Mahdi in the Sudan. Near Abu Klea, part of this force fell into an ambush and fought for its life by forming into a square. An ammunition box was opened, and it was discovered that it contained the payroll for the regiment – it was filled to the brim with gold sovereigns. Despite the peril, soldiers abandoned their line to stuff their pockets. The Dervishes quickly slipped through the holes left by the greedy men and killed them all.

The Zulu are not forgotten. Today's sophisticated modern armies run on Zulu time. That, in a way, is a lasting monument to the bravery of a warrior nation.

The Hinge of Battle at Isandhlwana was a rifle regiment caught in the open without an adequate supply of ammunition but with army regulations galore.

At Rorke's Drift it was a rifle company, but one with ammunition, inspired leadership and the tenacity to hold out until their enemy reached breaking-point. And a mealie-bag wall.

The Zulu War revealed British military vulnerability in colonial wars, a factor which encouraged the Boers a few years later.

6

And Raise Your Head with Pride!

24 April 1916 – The Irish Easter Rising

'*. . . so Irishmen remember then, and raise your head with pride,*
for great men and straight men have fought for you and died . . .'
'The Soldier's Song', the Irish national anthem

'*Only in them the first rich vision endures, those over clay.*
Retouch in memory, with sentiment relive, April and May.'
Donagh MacDonagh, Easter 1916

'Billy, me laddie, we're going out to be slaughtered,' proclaimed the stocky man in the emerald-green uniform.

'Is there no hope at all?' asked his lieutenant.

'None whatsoever. *The people aren't with us*,' grimly replied the Commandant-General of the Irish Volunteers and Citizen Army – a forlorn lot, about to march into the history books.

Easter Monday, 24 April 1916. At 11.30 that morning, the Commandant-General ordered his assembled forces: 'Left turn! Quick march!' The Dublin contingent of the outlawed Citizen Army left Liberty Hall, the headquarters of the Irish Transport and General Workers' Union, loaded down with anything from home-made bombs and antiquated Mauser rifles[1] to pickaxes, crowbars and pikes, which lent the column the appearance of a medieval host. Some wore a dark green uniform, sewn lovingly by their wives or sweethearts, or by women dedicated to 'the cause'. Others were dressed in faded blue work trousers and gumboots smudged with grease or splashed with cement. A few women were in the uniform of nurses and wore a Red Cross armband. Many of the men carried wooden ammunition crates; on some could still be seen the faded stencilled inscription 'Hamburg'. The volunteer units were captained by such men as Sean O'Kelly and Michael Collins. In front of the column marched the three commanders: Patrick Henry Pearse, a schoolteacher who would soon proclaim himself president of the Provisional Irish Government, Count Joseph Mary Plunkett, military Chief-of-Staff, and the Commandant-General, James Connolly.

Not all of Connolly's companions shared his impetuosity. They had even tried to dissuade him, pointing out – rightly – that they could not count on popular support. Connolly's disciples accused the doubters of being cowards. That was an insult no good Irishman could accept, and so they marched grimly to their doom.

The entire undertaking had a quixotic quality. It began back at the Plunkett estate, where the Irish Volunteers had assembled their crude arsenal. To face up to the English guns, they needed something heavier than bullets, and somebody came up with the idea of winding copper wire around a cast-iron drainpipe and using it as artillery. During the first test, the pipe blew apart and almost killed Plunkett's daughter. To reach their assembly point at Liberty Hall, Plunkett's fifty-six volunteers commandeered a tram at gunpoint, after which their captain politely asked the conductor for fifty-six tickets. Then he prodded the driver with his bayonet and

[1] Better known as Howth guns after the harbour through which they were smuggled into Ireland. These fired a soft-nose lead bullet which has been frequently, and erroneously, described as the outlawed dum-dum bullet.

asked him to take them 'please, and without further delay', to O'Connell Bridge. The prospect of a non-stop journey greatly upset a lady passenger, who demanded that the driver 'put these men off'.

'Kindly do it yourself, madam. As you can see, I'm quite busy meself,' answered the driver, and proceeded to take Plunkett's company to the bridge.

Dublin was bathed in glorious sunshine that Easter Monday morning. In the music pavilion on St Stephen's Green a military band was playing selections from Gilbert and Sullivan's *Pirates of Penzance*. Most officers and gentlemen had left town for the Fairyhouse racecourse, having beforehand deposited their ladies at the Spring Show of the Royal Dublin Society. That evening Dublin's upper crust would meet for a performance by the D'Oyly Carte Opera Company at the Gaiety Theatre. Yes, it would have been difficult to imagine there was trouble anywhere in the world if hadn't it been for the singing, wafting across town from the miserable slums – the popular tune of Irish soldiers fighting overseas for England:

Full steam ahead John Redmond said
That everything was well, chum
Home Rule will come when we're dead
And buried out in Belgium.[2]

An incongruous column of armed men in funny green slouch hats marched along Abbey Street, before it turned into Sackville Street[3] towards Nelson's Pillar. Dubliners, out for their Easter promenade, stared at them in wonder and puzzlement. A few waved, but most thought of it as just another crazy parade. An officer of the Royal Fusiliers, Lt

2 John Redmond, an Irish politician, had formed an Irish Volunteer Regiment.
3 O'Connell Street today.

Chalmers, was on his way to send a telegram to his wife. He remarked to his colleague: 'Just look at that awful lot.'

At two minutes past noon, the 'awful lot' reached a palatial structure with Ionic columns and (in the prescribed manner of vintage neoclassical Victoriana) adorned by the sculptured figures of Fidelity, Mercury and Hibernia, better known as the Three Apostles of Royal Mail. The building, which had just been renovated, was Dublin's General Post Office (or GPO). James Connolly gave a sharp command: 'Company, halt! Left turn! The Post Office . . .' and after a moment of silence, which seemed to most participants an eternity, shouted: '*Charge!!!*'

Two minutes had passed since the revolutionaries had invaded the Post Office building when a small group of armed men approached the gates of Dublin Castle. From the *Mail & Express* offices across the street, the editor of the paper, H. Doig, watched as Constable James O'Brien tried to prevent them from entering the grounds. A shot rang out and the policeman fell to the ground. The Irish Easter Rising had claimed its first victim. But not its last. Inside the splendid, domed Post Office hall, Connolly yelled: 'Everyone out!' Nobody seemed to take much notice. A postal clerk was eating his sandwich from a lunch box on his knees. He put the last piece of bread into his mouth and talked around it. 'Wot's this?' he said, looking up into a gun barrel. An American tourist, licking a stamp to stick on a postcard, stared amazed at the commotion: 'Hey, this is quite a country you've got.' And the green man, who politely ushered him towards the exit, replied: 'Yes, we're a rather peculiar lot here.' At the telegram counter, Lt Chalmers felt the tip of a bayonet and Volunteer Captain Michael Collins informed him politely that he was now a prisoner of war. 'We don't shoot prisoners,' Collins assured the baffled officer as he had him locked away in an upstairs room. In the confusion, the rebels had forgotten to take over the telegraph machine room, an error that was speedily rectified. Even this created a problem with the Scotsman on duty. 'I'm on guard until six and won't leave my post till I'm relieved.' Since nobody would come this day, or the next, to relieve him, they locked him up.

'Smash the windows and barricade the hall,' ordered Connolly. Anything movable was pushed against doors and windows – tables, benches, file cabinets. As they knocked out the windows, a woman yelled in shock: 'Glory be to God! Will you look at them smashing all the lovely windows!' Connolly waved to Sean O'Kelly, standing idle in the middle of the room. 'Here' – he handed him a flag – 'hoist it on the flagpole.' O'Kelly left while his men continued with their wrecking work. Suddenly all activity stopped. Everyone rushed to the window to watch with great pride a flag unfurl – solid green with a golden harp, and written across it in Gaelic: 'Irish Republic'.

For eight hundred years, ever since Pope Adrian IV, the only English Pope, issued a papal bull that bestowed the country on Henry II Plantagenet, the Irish had been in revolt. When Henry VIII abandoned Catholicism in favour of his own state religion, the Irish clung tenaciously to their faith. The nineteenth century was unparalleled in hardship for the common Irish people. The potato famine, and demands by unscrupulous English landowners, forced thousands of Irish men and women to seek a better existence in America. In 1886, Prime Minister Gladstone launched his Home Rule Bill, which would have granted Ireland some measure of independence. However, the bill was thrown out by the British parliament. Facing the 'Southerners' was Protestant 'King' Carson with his Orange bully-boys and John Redmond with an Irish Regiment in the King's Army, siphoning the best and bravest off the streets of Dublin to take them away from home turf and apply their Irish fighting spirit against Kaiser Willi's Germans on Flanders' bloodied fields. 'Keeps them from mischief, gets them a fancy Australian bush hat, and their families a royal pension, should they not return from the war.'

In 1905, an Irishman, Arthur Griffith, tried to prove to the nation that what Hungarians could do to Austrians, namely quitting the double monarchy, the Irish could do to the British – leave the United Kingdom and form an Irish Republic. Alone! Therefore he called his party Sinn Fein, or 'Ourselves Alone'. Two existing organisations, the Irish Republican Brotherhood (started in 1857 by immigrants in the USA), and the Irish Transport and General Workers' Union, picked up Griffith's idea. There were even more players, such as Eoin MacNeill with his Irish Volunteers and Doug Hyde and his Gaelic League, both mainly parading in native Irish kilts and playing the bagpipes, blathering gibberish and handing out hurley sticks in back yards. There was also the prophetic, unrepentant poet of the Irish Republican Brotherhood, Pádraic Pearse. Not forgetting the Irish National Literary Society, spreading the sacraments of a new religion from its forum at the Abbey Theatre and pretending that Irish freedom was worth fighting for – with words. Such independence play-acting continued until two union leaders founded the Irish Citizen Army.

James Larkin and James Connolly based their movement on a home-grown, honest-to-God class struggle. Towering above all Irish phantom revolutionaries was James Connolly, a forty-six-year-old Ulsterman with a round face, a bushy moustache, narrow, piercing eyes, and a receding hairline. In contrast to Pádraic Pearse, the dreamer (who many thought of as a saint), Connolly was a down-to-earth socialist. In 1910, he wrote his own battle manifesto, *Labour in Irish History*, in which he laid the foundations for future events.

'*The Irish question is a social question*, the whole age-long fight of the Irish people against their oppressors resolves itself in the last analysis into *a fight for the mastery of the means of life, the sources of production, in Ireland.* Who would own and control the land: the people, or the invaders?'

Connolly had learned all about labour unions during his time in the United States, where he had been an active organiser in the rapidly developing labour movement. He decided that the time had come to apply the same revolutionary workers' principles in his native Ireland. He had read Marx, studied the example set by the rioting working classes during the days of the Paris commune in 1871, and, more recently, witnessed the strikes in New York. In contrast to any previous Irish rebellion – the country's century-old struggle for independence from the British crown – Connolly's plan was based on the great class distinction between the haves and have-nots. But he needed popular support and for this he counted on the abject misery in Irish towns. Dublin for the poor was not a nice place to live. Most of it was made up of row upon interminable row of narrow red-brick houses, leaning on each other for reassurance. Over vermin-infested lanes hovered a permanent smell of rotting fish and the yellow smog from peat stoves. The 'Sweet Molly Malones' were in reality women who nagged their husbands and used foul language. Children were grimy and badly dressed, and schooling was something reserved for the rich. As for the men, those who were lucky enough to find employment worked in factories for slave wages. The others sat around, hoping for better times, or went into the nearby pub to fight and get drunk.

The Irish had come to look on suffering and starvation, which they called distress, as part of their social order. 'You starving masses rise from slumber . . .' This was also Connolly's credo, and he was counting on a general uprising from beneath, from the Irish working class. On his return to Ireland he established himself as the leading union organiser, a man possessed by an iron will, capable of incredible feats of audacity. In defiance of police orders he led protest marches through Dublin. In his belief and acts Connolly was deeply Irish. When England tried to recruit Irishmen for their war effort, he showed political astuteness. He hung a huge banner outside Liberty Hall: 'We serve neither King nor Kaiser! Only Ireland!'

The stumbling-block was provided by Connolly himself and his well-known connections with a budding socialism of the working-class left, never on the best of terms with the Irish Catholic clergy. Here he made his major miscalculation, one which was to prove fatal. In the United States industrialisation was quickly replacing a purely agricultural economy, while in Ireland the greater part of the population was still rural, and deeply Catholic. Previous Irish revolutionaries had always been able to count on one rallying point: Catholic identity. The more what the English were doing was seen in religious terms, the worse it became for them; they had to confront religious solidarity. Not so Connolly. He helped mould patriotism to a religion that owed as much to Marx as to traditional Irish values. He saw himself as a defender of true socialism, and equality for all; not only for the Irish, but, as he publicly declared many times, for the working class in general. He spoke of alleviating the poverty and suffering in Ireland, yet his leftist views couldn't count on broad popular support from the rural Catholic majority. Thereby, his messianic mission was doomed from the start. The majority of the Irish did not agree with his violent approach to solving the lingering problem of Irish independence, and declined to lend their support to the rebellion, since they suspected that Connolly's ulterior motive was to put a socialist government into power. How else could he and his working-class rebels act like this in a time of crisis? And was it not downright immoral to attack a country that spoke the same language from the inside while it was engaged in a fight to the death on foreign soil?

Shunning the favourite Irish pastime of telling everyone what was going on, Connolly kept his mouth shut. His reclusiveness masked the temperament of a hot-blooded warrior. How could he get the Irish to rise and fight for their independence? Only an event of a cataclysmic nature could provide the catalyst for the formation of a united front. Therefore, even when his last hope was dashed and he knew they couldn't win, he was still willing to risk all in order to provoke a general Irish rising.

In July 1914, while the Kaiser was getting ready to attack France and England, a ship landed at Howth, carrying 1,500 Mauser rifles of 1870 vintage, plus 49,000 rounds for Connolly's Citizen Army. A month later, on 3 August 1914, Sir Edward Grey, Viscount Fallodon, was to proclaim: 'The lamps are going out all over Europe; we shall not see them lit again in our lifetime,' and then the guns of the First World War rumbled. British regiments were pulled from Ireland to boost the sagging defences in Flanders. An Irish Volunteer Regiment was formed by John Redmond. He plastered the Dublin tram with stirring recruitment posters: 'IRISHMEN ENLIST TODAY!' And: 'FOR THE SMALL NATIONS AND FOR IRELAND, HOW CAN YOU SAY NO?' A number of Dubliners lined up at their local recruitment office, but not everybody. There was other action planned, and it was strictly Irish. The English were well aware of it; they had planted their informers inside McMahon's pub on Sackville Street. There was a lot of subversive talk; everyone had his own opinion and everyone seemed determined to express it at the same time. They thought the British tram recruitment posters an insult. Even if they were all coarse, argumentative and brew-swilling men, there was always the risk that some of them would take advantage of the war conditions, that Connolly's brand of socialist nationalism – not to be confounded with the National Socialism of a later period – would catch on and then spread to other parts of Ireland, even to England itself. The fighting in France was not going well, and now a civil disturbance was creeping towards the borders of the United Kingdom. The English government could hardly be blamed for showing more than a trace of nervousness.

In September 1914, the Irish Republican Brotherhood had

secretly voted for an insurrection and to accept help offered from Germany. The timing for the uprising depended on one of three factors – Germany invading Ireland, the English forcing conscription on Irish citizens, or the war coming to a rapid conclusion. By early 1916, as the war in the French trenches reached a stalemate and the slaughter at Verdun was at its highest, some Irish leaders, with James Connolly in the vanguard, realised that they could no longer restrain their rank and file. Their supporters had had enough of tame parades; they clamoured for action. As England needed more soldiers, Ireland became the logical reservoir of manpower to fill the depleted ranks. Furthermore, the Revolutionary Council had been told to expect an arms shipment from Germany.

'Let's put it to a vote, then,' demanded Connolly. 'We may never have such an opportunity again.' And he added: 'Seize the day, seize the hour.' The Irish Revolutionary Council took a vote, and a date was set for Easter 1916. Connolly's strategy was based on the expectancy that an English capitalist government would never use artillery against civilian targets because of the risk of damage to private property, and secondly on a firm promise by Sir Roger Casement of a shipment of rifles and artillery. Connolly set up plans to assemble his 10,000 men as soon as the arms were available. He counted on the fact that the 100,000 members of John Redmond's Irish Party, who had been admitted as full members to the Irish Volunteers' Council in 1913, would join his meagre forces. In their light green uniforms, they represented a respectable force. Their field commander was Col. Maurice Moore. The authorities saw no reason for anxiety, observing with amusement his well-groomed parades marching through the streets of the capital.

The critical setback to the Irish cause in general, and to Connolly's planning in particular, was the interception by British military intelligence of a coded message: 'Two or three trawlers with 20,000 rifles, ten machineguns and ammunition will land between 20 and 23 April in Tralee Bay. Irish pilot boat to meet them there.' The British reacted and placed their men on the cliffs above Fenit, Spa, Derrymore and Blennerville. Also, patrolling offshore were two Royal Navy auxiliary destroyers, HMS *Zinnia* and HMS *Bluebell*. As advised, on 9 April 1916 a freighter appeared on the horizon, masquerading as the neutral Norwegian vessel *Aud*. It was under the command of German Navy Lt Karl Spindler, and it had sailed from Lübeck with a cargo of rifles and ammunition. Its route had taken it along the coast of Norway, through the Iceland–Faroe Gap and south towards the Irish coast.[4] At the entry into Tralee Bay she was to rendezvous with the *U19*, a German submarine carrying a special passenger. Sir Roger Casement, the intellectual leader of the anti-British movement, was going back to Ireland. The *Aud* and the *U19* never met. Nor did they meet the Irish motor launch *Sea Lark*, which was to pick up the cargo. However, thanks to the cable intercept, the British Navy was lying in wait. For a while, the *Aud* managed to bluff her way out of the trap, but finally her luck ran out, and she was intercepted. When HMS *Bluebell*'s captain ordered Lt Spindler's freighter to follow the British Navy vessel into Queenstown, the German blew up his ship. With it, twenty thousand rifles, ten machineguns and a million bullets went to the bottom. The other disaster was of a political nature, and, in a sense, far more damaging.

Sir Roger Casement was one of the most distinguished Irishmen of his time; a writer, lecturer and former member of the British Consular Service, he was also a founder member of the Irish Volunteers. His name was respected throughout the country, and his voice was heeded in Dublin as well as in the Protestant stronghold of Belfast. This made him the ideal person to become the nominal president of an Irish Free State. He accepted the challenge and went to work.

[4] Captain Spindler's account.

In early 1914, he failed to raise Irish interest on a political level in the United States. Disappointed, he took a ship to Germany, where a spokesman for the German General Staff, Capt. Nadolny, told him that at present Germany had no time for Irish freedom movements. However, they were interested in establishing resupply bases for their submarines in 'Free Irish' ports. Therefore they would agree to give their support to an Irish rebellion, for which they offered the future Irish president rifles[5] but no artillery. The timing was crucial, and called for a precise rendezvous off Tralee Bay. And so it came about that Sir Roger Casement found himself as passenger aboard the German submarine *U19*.

A German naval operator in Bremerhaven had carelessly radioed the instructions for the rendezvous to the *Aud* and given away the plan. The English decided that they would let the landing go ahead in order to score a political point and pull the hesitant Irish Americans into the war by proving that the terrible Hun was about to invade Ireland. Despite their inbred dislike of anything English, the Irish of New York held no great sympathy for a German-sponsored Irish revolution. However, a delay caused by a stormy sea, which made the U-boat late for its rendezvous, and the premature interception of the freighter *Aud*, spoiled the English plan.

On Good Friday, 9 April 1916, a lieutenant of the Royal Irish Constabulary and his constable driver were observing the capture of the *Aud* from Church Hill. The German freighter and its destroyer escort quickly disappeared from view behind Magharee Island. That was when an unbelievable scene played out before the RIC man up on the cliffs. From the dark ocean rose a sleek, black shape. The sight staggered the lieutenant. 'I don't believe it, sir, a bloody submarine,' yelled the driver as water cascaded from the conning tower. But what was a submarine doing on this part of the coast?

[5] The shipment aboard the *Aud* was part of the booty from their victory over the Russians at Tannenberg.

Was it a friendly sub, adrift and about to be smashed up on the rocks of Banna Strand? The ocean currents were strong and the swell rough on this part of the coastline. Through his glasses the lieutenant could make out a number on the conning tower: *U19*. A German U-boat! Then a man stepped out of the hatch, followed by two more. They dumped a small boat overboard. Some German spy was about to land in Ireland! 'Move it,' yelled the lieutenant to his driver, and the car bounced over the dirt track down to where the road snaked from Church Hill towards Banna Strand. They had left the car on the beach and waded into the sea when they noticed a motor launch racing towards them at high speed.

The U-boat captain didn't feel like lingering in hostile waters, and he had set Casement and another man adrift in a collapsible rubber dinghy. They rowed through the strong surf and had almost reached shore when a wave bounced back off a cliff and flipped the light inflatable over. The two men were thrown out. Meanwhile, the fast motor launch had grounded itself onshore and a man waving a pistol came running towards the RIC lieutenant, who pulled out his service revolver and shot him dead. He yelled to his driver, pointing at the heads bobbing on the water: 'Get that one on the left, I'll take this one,' and with that he grabbed the man swimming towards shore by his jacket and hauled him on to the strand. He looked into a haggard, bearded, grease-smeared face, but one familiar to every Irishman.

'Casement!' the lieutenant stuttered in surprise. 'Don't you move, or I'll blow your brains out.'

'Don't, don't. Are you Irish?'

'So what if I'd be?'

'Don't shoot. I've come back only to call it off.'

'Call what off?' asked a somewhat confused RIC Lt Tyrell. His prisoner seemed to be suffering from shock after his narrow escape in the cold water.

'We can't do it,' Casement said. 'We must stop bloodshed

and call off the Rising. The *Aud* was all we had, and now she's gone. Someone's betrayed us.'

'Who?' asked the lieutenant.

'The bloody German Kaiser, that's who. He's called off his U-boat war 'cause he's afraid to bring America into the war.'

'Isn't it because the Irish people will never support your cause?'

'Whatever. I must get through to Connolly and Pearse, tell them it's hopeless, our men will get slaughtered. We cannot expect outside help, and without that our own people will never join us.'

The first man to believe in the Rising was now the first to abandon it. But Casement knew that a deeply Catholic people would never support a hopeless rebellion. They would look upon any killing, undertaken in whatever cause, for whatever religion, as murder.

The young RIC lieutenant didn't know what to do. As an Irishman he wanted to stop bloodshed among his brothers, but as an officer sworn to uphold law and order he couldn't let his prisoner go. Let someone else make this decision. However, being an Irishman, he promised to get Casement's message through to Dublin. He brought his prisoner to Tralee, and from there the unlucky Irish leader went to the gallows in England. With its weapons at the bottom of Tralee Bay and its political head gone, the Rising was now doomed to failure.

Over three centuries of bloodshed, Dublin had mostly remained a quiet haven from the trouble elsewhere in the country. In the spring of 1916, the British government clamped down on growing unrest, banning anti-recruitment rallies and other public demonstrations, and promising to charge protesters with treason. James Connolly did not back down. His Union Headquarters was transformed into a bomb factory, and his speeches left no one in doubt that he was going to use these bombs. As the date set for the Rising approached, his behaviour became more reckless. The Sunday before Easter, he addressed his close supporters: 'The odds against us are a thousand to one. But if we should win, hold on to your rifles because the Volunteers [Pearse's lot] may have a different goal. Remember that *we're out not only for political liberty but for economic liberty* as well. So, hold on to your rifles.' After which stirring speech he had Miss Molly O'Reilly hoist the Irish flag on top of Liberty Hall. Some Dubliners cheered the act of flag bravado, and this had him convinced that he was well on the way to launching an uprising with full popular support. He couldn't have been more wrong.

Looking back, it seems incredible that Pearse, knowing about Connolly's final aims, as well as having been appraised of the full dimensions of the *Aud* disaster, still went ahead with the Rising. But then thirty-six-year-old Patrick Henry Pearse was a dreamer and idealist, never a strong leader. A fight over the date of the Rising had broken out within the Irish Volunteers' camp. Pearse's Chief-of-Staff, Eoin MacNeill, a professor of Gaelic at the University of Ireland, was worried that their plans had been leaked to the British. A confrontation between the two ended in a shouting match, with Pearse yelling: 'Eoin, we don't need you any more,' to which MacNeill threw back: 'I'm still Chief-of-Staff and I'm going to cancel tomorrow's mobilisation.' Pearse didn't take this threat seriously.

On Easter Sunday, the members of the future Provisional Government gathered for a working breakfast at the Connolly house to refine their final plans. While they were having their meal, a Volunteer girl rushed excitedly into the room with the morning's edition of the *Independent*: 'Mr Connolly, it says here "No manoeuvres today."' Connolly went pale. 'What's that?' he shouted. Then he read MacNeill's announcement. 'Owing to the critical position, all orders given to Irish Volunteers for to-morrow, Easter Sunday, are hereby rescinded, and no parades, marches, or other movements of Irish Volunteers will take place. Each individual Volunteer will obey this order strictly in every particular. (signed) Eoin MacNeil. Chief-of-Staff.'

For a moment, everyone sat in frozen silence. Despite the numerous problems, the mere thought of abandoning the Rising had never occurred to them. Tom Clarke said what all thought: 'MacNeill has ruined our plans. I feel like going away to cry.'

MacNeill's proclamation was read across Ireland and the Volunteers stayed at home. Dublin was now on its own. Instead of the tens of thousands it would have taken to make a realistic country-wide stand against the British forces, Connolly was left with two hundred of his hard-core Citizen Army, plus another five or six hundred Dublin Volunteers, those who could still be mobilised by word of mouth.

The Easter Rebellion of 1916 began with a series of confused, individual actions. There was never any co-ordination. When it became clear that not all the men would join in, some commanders waited, others didn't. After the initial assault on the General Post Office, one troop headed for the Magazine Fort to signal the beginning of the Irish rebellion with a big bang. Garry Holohan aimed to set off five bags of gelignite in the fort's powder magazine to achieve his ten minutes of glory. It took planning. To get through the guarded front gate, he and his buddies played around with a football until it rolled to the feet of the sentry. The good-hearted man was about to kick it back when somebody hit him over the head. The rebels then made a dash for the powder room, only to find that the key to the door was missing. The officer who had it had gone off to the races! So, instead of Garry's Big Bang they had to make do with a minor bang, before they left the fort to join up with the rest.

Another troop had taken over Clanwilliam House, which controlled the vital Mount Street Bridge. They were prepared to stage their version of a Spartan Thermopylae against English reinforcements, forced to cross the canal bridge. They were counting on support from a Volunteer battalion under the command of a New York-born mathematics professor, Commandant Eamon de Valera, whose men had barricaded themselves inside Boland's Bakery and a nearby dispensary. (With great gallantry, de Valera informed the wife of the dispensary owner that she had five minutes to pack her valuables and leave the premises.) The men in the bakery didn't take the invaders seriously, not until an English soldier came running up and shouted: 'What the devil are you up to?' to which a rebel answered coolly: 'Shove off!' The soldier committed a fatal error by calling them traitors. That insult was too much for any honourable rebel, so one of them shot the soldier.

The Volunteer Battalion of Lt Thomas Allen had marched past the Bridewell police station under the surprised stares of twenty armed constables before they took Four Courts, the Irish hall of justice, where they barricaded the windows with leather-bound law books. In a poor neighbourhood, the men of Patrick Kelly's 'C' Company were attacked by women, whose furniture they dragged into the street to build a barricade. While this was going on, a troop of English cavalry came blundering through. A ragged volley met them from the barricade; six riders dropped from their horses and the rest fled into side streets, only to run into more barricades. Two cavalrymen galloped madly down North King Street, firing their carbines. Mothers grabbed their screaming children and fled into nearby houses. One little girl was killed. An insurgent planted the lance of a dead trooper between the cobblestones and strung up his Irish flag.

At the Westland Row railway station, some rebels had stopped the 12.15 to Kingstown, which brought out the stationmaster. He was insisting that his train leave on schedule when a party of priests arrived on the scene. 'What are you doing here?' a priest asked the armed men. 'Fighting for Ireland, Father, and ready to die for her. Can you please give us your blessing?' The rebels knelt down, and the priests moved down the row to hear their confessions.

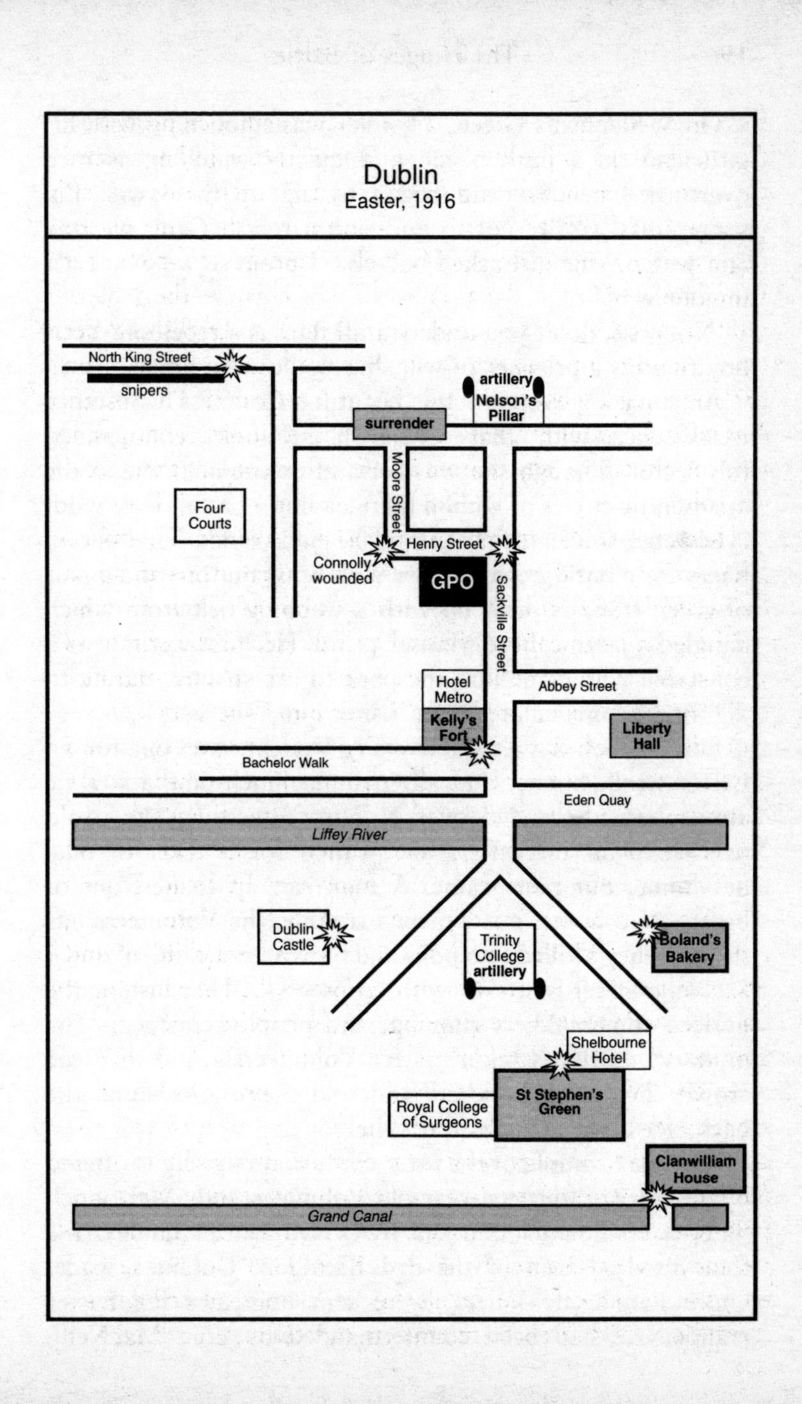
Dublin
Easter, 1916
North King Street
snipers
artillery
Nelson's Pillar
surrender
Moore Street
Four Courts
Henry Street
Connolly wounded
GPO
Sackville Street
Hotel Metro
Abbey Street
Kelly's Fort
Liberty Hall
Bachelor Walk
Eden Quay
Liffey River
Dublin Castle
Trinity College artillery
Boland's Bakery
Shelbourne Hotel
St Stephen's Green
Royal College of Surgeons
Clanwilliam House
Grand Canal

On St Stephen's Green, a soldier was smooching with his girlfriend on a park bench and quietly watching as men overturned benches and began to dig up the lawn. 'I'm sorry, miss, you've got to go,' said a rebel. 'Can't we stay and watch?' the girl asked naïvely. 'I promise we won't get in your way.'

'No, miss, don't you understand? This is a rebellion. Your boyfriend is a prisoner of war, but you can go home.'

An amazing woman, the beautiful Countess Constance Markiewicz, with 'that wild Irish girl look', commanded this sector. Though she was certainly more at home in the aristocratic circles of Dublin than leading a battalion of wild-eyed rebel soldiers, this Easter she had traded her London finery for a dark green sweater with brass buttons and a pair of green trousers, held up with a webbing belt from which dangled a large-calibre Mauser pistol. Her first victim was a constable who came into the park to arrest those daring to dig up the immaculate lawn. 'I shot him,' she said.

Lilly Stokes, a pretty university student, was out for an Easter stroll, bonnet and all. Around lunch-time a strange atmosphere descended over Dublin, something she could never explain thereafter. She waited for a tram to take her home, but none came. A man ran up to her, out of breath. 'Go home, miss, there's trouble, the Volunteers has the city, they's killed two polis and blown up a tram, 'n' down Sackville Street is strewn with corpses . . .' That instant she noticed some soldiers running, and people screamed: 'The military . . . they's takin' us fer Volunteers!' And then the crowd cheered the soldiers and told them: 'Go round the back, yer catch them bastards there.'

A prime example of the utter confusion reigning is offered by the story of fourteen-year-old Volunteer Andy McDonnell (later a commandant in the IRA). On Easter Sunday, the four hundred men of the 3rd Battalion, Dublin Brigade, under Eamon de Valera, were sent home, as the Easter manoeuvres had been countermanded by Eoin MacNeill.

On Easter Monday they were again called up; however, only 120 men joined the battalion. Young Andy was handed a six-foot medieval pike from the city museum and ordered to hold up a tram, which he did – a curious action for a manoeuvre, he said to himself. He still thought they were on a training mission until somebody shot at him. For a week they somehow muddled through, 120 men with little food and even less sleep.

The rebels committed a serious omission when they failed to occupy the telephone exchange that controlled the British Army's entire command structure. Though some cables were cut, the commanding officer, Col. H.W. Cowan, was told of the uprising in a phone call from a police station at 12.10 p.m. Cowan had at his disposal 120 officers and 2,265 well-armed men. It would have been all too easy to put down the thousand rebels with one single blow.[6] A forceful military intervention at this point would have avoided the ensuing drawn-out bloodshed. But Colonel Cowan was not the man of the hour. Instead of ordering his three-to-one superiority into immediate action and putting out the fire, he called for more reinforcements. (Eventually the British were to have a superiority of twenty to one, including heavy artillery and machineguns.)

Another grave mistake committed by the rebels was to overlook the importance of Trinity College, a potentially formidable fortress, located at the vital crossroads that controlled the river crossings as well as Sackville Street, and with it the approach to the Post Office complex. The college sat astride the only possible line of communication between the GPO and the insurgent unit on St Stephen's Green. From a strategic viewpoint, Trinity would have been a better choice than the Post Office. With its tall buildings the college provided excellent gun positions; its spacious campus was

[6] There is no exact account of the number of insurgents involved. Estimates vary from 1,200 to 1,500. The overall army strength is given as 15,000.

ideally suited for the placement of artillery. If only to deny such a choice position to the enemy it should have been regarded as a prime target. It was there for anyone's taking. At the beginning of the Troubles, it was held only by a few Officer Training Corps students. Within an hour, a handful of enterprising Canadians and Anzac soldiers, on furlough from France, moved quickly into the buildings to hold them for the government. Trinity College was the first serious foothold established by regulars within the rebel perimeter. The failure to take this strategic position would prove to be one of Connolly's most costly blunders.[7]

In the meantime, the Post Office had become the hub of insurgent activities. At 1 p.m., its doors opened and out walked Patrick Henry Pearse and James Connolly. Pearse unfolded a paper and began to read out the Proclamation of the Irish Republic:

> . . . we declare the right of the people of Ireland to the ownership of Ireland, and to the unfettered control of Irish destinies, to be sovereign and indefeasible . . . The Irish Republic is entitled to, and hereby claims, the allegiance of every Irishman and Irishwoman . . . In this supreme hour the Irish nation must, by its valour and discipline, and by the readiness of its children to sacrifice themselves for the common good, prove itself worthy of the august destiny to which it is called.

James Connolly took Pearse's hand and shook it. 'Isn't it grand,' he said in a booming voice. But the small crowd that had gathered around the steps of the Post Office did not break out in cheers. There was none of that wild enthusiasm which had greeted the first day of the French Revolution. It was clear that Dublin's General Post Office would never be the Paris Bastille.

[7] *Blackwood's Magazine*, July 1916.

The first serious incident erupted near St Stephen's Green. Facing the two hundred soldiers of Maj. Warmington's and Lt Ramsay's Royal Irish Regiment was young O'Brien and a few fellow rebels. Warmington sent forth a skirmish line. The men advanced according to the military manual, upright in line and with bayonets planted. When they came within fifteen yards of the park wall, the rebels who had been hiding behind it opened up with their heavy Howth Mausers and killed a number of troopers. The surprise was such that a whole company fled into nearby houses, breaking down doors or jumping through panelled windows. A wild exchange took place between the park wall and the adjacent houses in which more soldiers died. Warmington placed a Lewis gun on a nearby high building. Its stream of bullets took the rebels in the flank. 'Get back, boys!' screamed O'Brien. The rebels fled across an open lawn and were mowed down by the machinegun. Seventeen-year-old John Traynor was struck in the chest. 'May Jesus have mercy on my soul,' he whispered, and died. He was lying on his back, his handsome waxen face that of someone who had died too young; a young boy who had sacrificed himself because he had listened too closely to those who were older and should have been wiser. It was the inbred hatred in this teenager which had carried the long crusade against English rule to its logical conclusion; the same hatred which, for countless generations, had kept peace from Irish hearts. When would England appreciate the Irish temperament?

Lilly Stokes, who had witnessed the crowd turning on the rebels, was walking towards St Stephen's Green when a somewhat befuddled policeman stopped her. 'Miss, listen to me, you'd better not go that way, the Germans are having the Green and are after sendin' off a volley.' She turned around but ran into more trouble at a barricade, this one held by four rebels with large guns which they pointed menacingly at the young woman. Two vehicles blocked the street. One was a horse cart, its dead horse near by, the other a laundry van. Baskets of linen and shirts were spread over the street.[8]

As she turned away from St Stephen's Green, more fighting broke out. Lt Ramsay moved in with a frontal attack on the park and broke through a wooden gate. He had hardly taken a step into the park when he was struck down. When Maj. Warmington heard that his lieutenant had been mortally wounded, he took over the attack. Thirty seconds later he too was dead. The soldiers finally managed to get into the park. The situation for the surviving group of rebels became desperate. They barricaded themselves in a wooden shed, and fired through slits in the wall until their rifle barrels were so hot they had to allow them to cool down. The soldiers used a lawnmower as a battering ram to break down the door. As the shack started to disintegrate under a hail of bullets, and soldiers battered their way into it, a voice cried out: 'Don't shoot! We surrender!' Two hundred soldiers had overwhelmed a dozen teenagers!

At the GPO, Connolly was in a pensive mood, sitting on top of the stamp counter. Michael Collins sat down next to him. 'A strange thought occurred to me just now,' said Connolly. 'I was thinking about the future and how everybody seems to think the Germans must invade soon. You know, they won't come. We Irish are on our own, and always will be.' It was something Michael Collins always remembered. Connolly heaved himself off his perch and made a military display of squaring his shoulders and jutting out his chin. A charge by lancers was imminent and he was needed. The riders were lined up near Parnell's obelisk. In the Post Office, every window was manned. 'Hold your fire for my orders!' yelled Connolly. That moment a late-arriving volunteer company from Rathfarnham crossed into Sackville Street. When they spotted the Royal Lancers, one of them yelled: 'Hammer

[8] From there, Miss Stokes went to visit friends to ask what in God's name was going on in Dublin. From her account in *Nonplus*, 1916.

the shit out o' them fuckers!' and the street erupted into wild gunfire. The lancers galloped past Nelson's Pillar and towards the Post Office. Sparks flew off their horses' hoofs, pounding over the cobblestones. The wild rifle fire from the windows and parapets muted the clattering of their cavalry charge. Horses tumbled, lying on the pavement with their legs still kicking. Four riders fell dead from the saddle. Their colonel waved his sabre and yelled: 'Get back!' A young boy weaved his way between fallen horses and dead riders to pick up a carbine. Then he ran up the steps of the Post Office. 'Here yez are!' he yelled, and threw the rifle through a window. Col. Hammond's cavalry had sustained great casualties; many horses had to be destroyed. The colonel rounded up his surviving riders and led them off. No sooner had the firing stopped than a crowd of sightseers came out of hiding.

At the time of the First World War, Dublin had the greatest number of poor per capita in Europe. This slum population surged forth *en masse* – not to fight, but to loot. The women outnumbered the men by four to one. The 'shawlies', named after the black shawls thrown across their shoulders, threw rocks into display windows and helped themselves to undreamed-of luxuries, such as chocolates, smoked salmon or fancy shoes. As most shops displayed only one shoe of a pair, many shawlies found themselves with two left shoes for their thieving effort. A man cursed as he tried to force a pair of fancy tweed trousers over his boots, and then cursed some more when he couldn't get them off. More plate glass burst; more goods were pulled from the shops and scattered all over the street. At some luxury goods stores, people trampled over each other to get inside, or simply lay in wait to rip the stolen goods from the arms of those weaker than themselves. The crowd worked itself into a frenzy. Fights broke out; shawlies tore at each other's hair to get their hands on dresses or pewter tea kettles. Fat women with wispy, greasy hair strutted around in evening dresses that squeezed their voluminous bosoms. One had stripped completely naked and was trying on silk camisoles. Another, attired in Russian red leather boots and a silk nightgown over a grubby dress, wandered around in a drunken stupor, asking any man she came across: 'How do yez like me now?' Men and women sprawled drunk on pavements littered with empty, smashed champagne bottles, coffee beans, sugar and flour. This bawdy lawlessness created a dilemma for James Connolly, a man who had just promised to uphold the protection of the law.

Into this scene of civil disorder walked Dublin's best-known eccentric, a man of great intelligence and integrity – Francis Sheehy-Skeffington. Earlier he had dashed across a bullet-swept street to save the life of a lieutenant of the 8th Hussars, and explained away his heroic action with the comment: 'I couldn't let the man bleed to death.' He confronted Connolly and demanded that the Commandant-General put an end to the looting. Connolly ordered a dozen men to stop the rampaging mob. They fired a volley over their heads. It didn't help. Connolly was upset.

'What did you do?' he asked the men's leader.

'We've shot over their heads,' replied O'Kelly.

'Shooting over their heads is useless,' said Connolly. 'Unless you shoot a few of them, you won't stop them.' And he gave the order to fire into the crowd to protect precisely what he had promised to abolish – the property of the rich. The mere threat of getting shot was enough to calm the rioting in the business district but looting continued in other sectors well into the night. A jeweller's shop was vandalised; youths from the slums paraded in new clothes and fingers were adorned with rings. Little girls hugged teddy bears as if they couldn't believe their good fortune. People were beaten up for a bottle of wine, or a box of chocolates. Private scores were settled. Scenes of raw violence were lit up by fires which had been set deliberately in shops. This provided ideal illumination for the snipers. A man was holding a bottle in his hand from which he was taking the occasional swig when a bullet shattered the glass and the precious golden liquid poured to the cobblestones. 'Jezus,' he said, 'not a drop left. Wasteful bastards!'

After dark, Sean O'Casey was sliding cautiously along the walls of houses towards the bridge across the canal when a tired voice murmured: 'Halt! Who goes?' O'Casey tried to step inside a house but the door was locked. The voice, this time no longer tired, repeated. 'Halt!' and Sean heard the ominous click of a gun bolt. 'F . . . f . . . friend,' he stuttered. A soldier stepped out of the shadows and pointed his rifle straight at his chest. 'Next time, be quicker on the answer. Now, scram!'[9]

The city became a rioting mass. Many young people got caught up in the mêlée without knowing, or caring, why. Many died from stray bullets while waiting in long lines to take home a few loaves of bread.

Under cover of this brouhaha, Capt. Elliotson and a company of 120 troopers quietly moved into the Shelbourne Hotel and set up a number of machineguns with which they could direct concentrated fire at the rebel positions around St Stephen's Green. Elliotson looked down on the Green and remarked drily: 'Well, one thing is certain, no German officer is responsible for the Sinn Feiner strategy. Putting themselves in an enclosure overlooked by tall buildings on all sides . . .'

At 3.45 a.m. Brig.-Gen. Lowe arrived with his 2,000 men of the 25th Irish Reserve Infantry Brigade. He took overall command. He now had 4,650 troops under him, or five heavily armed soldiers for every rebel in Dublin. Two hundred and fifty miles away, in London, Gen. French alerted the entire 59th Division. With maps of Dublin torn from tourist guides, its advance battalions, together with a contingent of artillery, sailed from Liverpool.

'It's a shame to rush youngsters into trouble,' was a widespread opinion. By all accounts, Dubliners, both rich and poor, were much friendlier to the troops than to the Sinn

[9] From Sean O'Casey's *Easter Weekend.*

Feiners. The rich said that the Volunteers all came from the working class and didn't know what they were up to, but were used by some violent socialist types as their tools; and now they found themselves 'in the soup', as it were. And the poor cursed the rebels for everything else, mainly that the Troubles would stop work in the factories and now they wouldn't get their wages. The Dubliners handed out refreshments and cigarettes to the newly arriving troops, who thought that they had landed somewhere in France.

The people were left without news of what was going on in the city. Only one paper was still being printed, the *Irish Times*, which carried no stories whatsoever about the Rising. Only that a toy store 'had caught fire'.[10]

The first streaks of dawn announced the arrival of a new day in a relatively quiet Dublin. The stillness was shattered by machinegun bursts from the windows of the Shelbourne Hotel. The surprise was total, especially to Countess Markiewicz in her command centre in the Royal College of Surgeons, who had forgotten to 'take the high ground' and occupy the high-rise hotel facing her. Bullets caught the men lying exposed on the Green. A young volunteer panicked and scrambled across the lawn. He had almost made it over the fence when the bullets caught him and he flipped on to his back, screaming. A second volley caught him and his screams stopped, although his body kept twitching every time the machineguns swept the lawn and he was struck by more bullets. The rebels were pinned to the ground, or hid behind tall elms. Their leader gave orders to evacuate the Green. They had to leave behind five of their dead and some of their wounded.

Father Aloysius, waving a white apron on a broomstick, tried to reason with a British colonel to let him look after the many wounded and dying. The colonel turned his back on him and left him with the dying and his God.

10 Account by A.J. Cronin in the *Preston Herald* of 6 May 1916.

From the GPO, James Connolly put out a message by Marconi radio: 'An Irish Republic has been proclaimed. Dublin is firmly held and all British attacks have been repulsed.'

Patrick Pearse issued his own newspaper of four pages, the *Irish War News*: '. . . the populace of Dublin are plainly with the Republic . . .' This was a highly optimistic statement. In fact, the good citizens of Dublin were already tired of the street fighting and looting, and were waiting for the military to sort out the insurgents. The rest of the country remained passive, and not a single unit of Irish Volunteers marched to join the Rising.

The *Irish Times*, supportive of the government, finally got involved and wrote: '. . . the authorities have taken active and energetic measures to cope with the situation . . .'

A group of rebels approached Connolly. 'Permission to leave, sir,' they said. 'Where in heaven do you want to go to?' asked a perplexed Commandant-General. 'To go to work, now that the holidays are over.'

An infantry attack was launched from the houses behind the rebel-held *Mail & Express* building. The noise from the machineguns, echoing from the narrow city canyons, was ear shattering. Soldiers with fixed bayonets rushed along the street and were bowled over by the soft-nosed bullets of the terrible Howth Mausers.[11] A second wave reached the *Mail* building and broke through the entrance only to be met by withering fire. Soon the door was jammed with military casualties. Stretcher parties braved the bullet-swept street to evacuate their wounded. The huge powder charges in the Mauser cartridges had a tendency to quickly overheat the Howth barrels, and the insurgents had to use their rifle butts in furious hand-to-hand slaughter. More soldiers poured into

[11] A British officer called them 'an elephant gun'. In fact this type of rifle was used on safari.

the building. The last seven irregulars jumped through a rear window to safety. Twenty-two of their comrades lay dead in the entrance hall and the staircase.

By 3 p.m. rain was beginning to fall. What Connolly had never thought possible now took place. With little regard for 'capitalist property', the heavy English eighteen-pounders opened up. They fired from Trinity College straight down city streets, blowing gaping holes into buildings and barricades. (Connolly finally recognised his blunder in failing to neutralise the Trinity grounds.) The noise, the concussion and the shock were too much for the rebels. They fled. Some joined Connolly at the GPO, but most just went home, realising the extent of the military might that was bearing down on them. Slowly, a noose was beginning to form around the Post Office fortress.

More looting had broken out, and once again the eccentric Mr Sheehy-Skeffington came into the open to stop the rioters. At 5.30 p.m., as he walked towards Portobello Bridge, he was routinely challenged and arrested at a military roadblock. Sheehy-Skeffington may have been an eccentric, but he was no Sinn Feiner. Quite the contrary – he was an anti-militarist and fighting pacifist who abhorred the bloodshed started by those with, so he thought, foolish dreams.

Capt. J. Bowen-Colthurst, a member of a well-known family that owned Blarney Castle, ordered the soldiers at the roadblock to hand over their prisoner. This was to lead to the single most infamous incident of the Rising, and bestowed (unjustly) upon all the British forces a reputation for cruelty and murder. With Sheehy-Skeffington in tow, Capt. Bowen-Colthurst reached Rathmines Church at the same moment as two youngsters stepped out of the door. He yelled at them: 'Don't you know there is martial law?' One of the youths, a boy named Coade, shrugged his shoulders and turned away. Bowen-Colthurst called out to one of his men: 'Bash him.' As the boy fell senseless to the ground, Bowen-Colthurst pulled out his gun and shot him through the head. Francis Sheehy-Skeffington protested at this cold-blooded assassination; the captain screamed at him in a white-hot rage: 'Save your prayers, you'll be the next.'

And so it was to be. On 26 April, Bowen-Colthurst had Sheehy-Skeffington severely beaten to extract a confession. 'He then was taken from his locked cell by Colthurst. As he walked across the yard he was shot in the back, and that without warning by the firing squad of a Lt Toomey and eighteen men. A soldier by the name of Dobbin said to his platoon leader, Sergeant Aldridge: "That man is not dead." Colthurst then ordered them to "finish him off", before he sent in his report.'[12]

A British Army major, Sir Francis Vane, thoroughly horrified by the indifference of the British High Command, attempted to get Capt. Bowen-Colthurst, by now accused of at least five more murders, arrested on a charge of ungentlemanly conduct and wilful murder. Instead, Sir Francis was himself relieved of his command. After a long period in which the army commanders did everything to prevent an inquiry, Mrs Sheehy-Skeffington managed to reach the ear of Prime Minster Asquith, who promised to clear up the accusation. The captain was court-martialled. In a travesty of a trial, where the principal accuser, Maj. Sir Francis Vane, was under the specific order not to testify, Bowen-Colthurst's defence counsel pleaded insanity. Mrs Sheehy-Skeffington would not allow matters to rest. After several newspaper reports had created a public uproar on both sides of the Irish Sea, the case came up before a renewed Commission of Inquiry under Sir John Simon, which cast doubt on Bowen-Colthurst's insanity and censured the conduct of the military authorities involved in the cover-up.[13] 'A martyr fights in death more

[12] Statement made in a letter by Mrs Hannah Sheehy-Skeffington to a Court of Inquiry, 1917.

[13] The account comes from a lecture delivered by Mrs Hannah Sheehy-Skeffington on the murder of her husband, delivered in 1917. Her efforts, and the Simon Inquiry, prompted the eventual removal of Gen. Maxwell.

terribly than many warring saints.' In this way, Francis Sheehy-Skeffington, the troublesome idealist who believed in universal reconciliation through goodwill, did not die in vain. Eva Gore-Booth wrote a famous poem, 'Francis Sheehy-Skeffington'.

> *When driven men, who fight and hate and kill*
> *To order, shall let all their weapons fall,*
> *And know that kindly freedom of the will*
> *That holds no other human will in thrall.*

The Rising was in its third day. On Wednesday morning a loud explosion shook the city. A gunboat anchored in the Liffey, the *Helga*, opened fire on Liberty Hall. Its aim was so bad that instead of hitting a large building on the quayside, the shell struck a railway bridge. A massive, co-ordinated operation, involving *Helga*'s cannon, several machineguns planted on rooftops, and the troops of the Royal Irish Regiment and the Ulster Battalion, was mounted to storm Liberty Hall. For over an hour *Helga*'s cannon fired away while streams of bullets slammed into the red brick. A company advanced cautiously across the open street to storm . . . an empty building![14]

The cross-fire between the rebel position in the Royal College of Surgeons and the Shelbourne Hotel was only halted when – twice each day – Mr Kearney, the park-keeper, went to feed the ducks on St Stephen's Green. However, no ducks swam around the Post Office, and there the chattering of machineguns never stopped. The shooting had abated by noon, and an ominous silence descended.

Clanwilliam House near Mount Street Bridge was held by seventeen young rebels. A woman ran up to the house and

[14] Liberty Hall was emptied when the companies marched out on Easter Monday.

yelled: 'Watch out, the Brits have landed and are marching on Dublin. They now comin' to get ya.' The seventeen had their Mausers, a box of ammunition marked 'Hamburg', and a few assorted revolvers. Against them marched two full battalions. The first volley claimed the lives of ten soldiers.[15] Their captains roared: 'Drop!' and the companies fell flat to the ground. As the seventeen defenders reloaded, Capt. Pragnell jumped up, raised his sword and screamed: 'Charge!' Inside the building the young rebel leader Reynolds yelled: 'Fire!' – and more soldiers fell to the ground. One of the company attempted a flanking movement, but was hit by a stream of well-aimed shots. Col. Fane received a bullet through his arm, but resumed command. A whistle sounded and sixty troopers came storming up Northumberland Road. The men inside fired at the first who came through the door. Reynolds yelled: 'Let them have it with your revolvers.' The troops were knocked down as if in a western movie. The survivors ran for their lives back down the road.

Now that Col. Fane's attack had come to a standstill, the officer signalled Brigade HQ for more bombs and machine-guns. He launched another charge which ended like all the others – nowhere. More lines of soldiers came crawling along the gutters. From their positions in the top windows, the boys in the house fired at the men on the ground. When one trooper died, the next had to crawl over him and became in his turn a prime target. In certain places the bodies piled up. A priest ran across the street to give last rites, and the boys in the house halted the shooting. A big crowd of civilians had gathered on the opposite side of the bridge to watch the amazing stand by a handful of teenagers. Another whistle blew, another attack followed, another slaughter ensued. Capt. Pragnell, who had bravely led most of the attacks, collapsed when his arm was shattered. The rebel leader dispatched a runner to Connolly to ask for relief. The answer came back: 'There

15 Account by Capt. Frank Pragnell of the Sherwood Foresters.

relieve you. Hang on.' And so, as in the tale of Leonidas and his three hundred Spartans, seventeen men held up an entire British battalion for five hours. Gen. Lowe ordered a second battalion into the fray. 'Storm the Mount Street School at all costs. At all costs,' he repeated. Three waves attacked; the third succeeded in reaching the school, but they didn't make it to Clanwilliam House. The two officers who led this attack were killed.

Two battalions were now on the attack. For the heroic defenders of Clanwilliam House time was running out. A machinegun had found the angle necessary to penetrate the living room. The glass chandelier came down in a shower of splintered glass, and the bullets sang in the wires of the living-room piano. The back wall was gone, a water pipe had been punctured and a jet sprayed the room. Patrick Doyle picked up a siphon bottle with which to spray and cool his weapon before he squirted a drink into his mouth. The bottle exploded in his hand and Doyle fell over. While he crawled back, Tom Walsh propped a tailor's dummy against the window. A stream of bullets from a machinegun shredded it. And still the boys behind their windowsills were firing madly at the oncoming waves. Another charge was carried out by Capt. Quibell's men. The carnage on the bridge and the approach to the rebel fortress was terrible. Lt Hewitt's platoon was down to two men. Capt. Cursham had reached the front door and lobbed in a grenade. It bounced back and tore him to pieces.

Shouts of 'Surrender!' came from the outside. Among the insurgents, Dick Murphy was the next to die. Then a bullet split Jimmy Doyle's rifle stock. Reynolds threw him his rifle: 'Here, take mine,' while he stood up and emptied his revolver through the window. He collapsed; a bullet had sliced his femoral artery. He just had time to whisper 'God' before he died. Lt William Foster lobbed more grenades through a hole in the barricade and finally broke through an unguarded window. He shot a man in civilian clothes on the stairs (probably the dead Reynolds) and threw a grenade into the living room. There was an explosion, and afterwards he found only dead defenders sprawled on the floor. The last three survivors, Walsh, Ronan and Jimmy Doyle, clambered through a window into the garden. The sad irony of this heroic stand is that, during their escape, they were set upon by the local population as they tried to reach the GPO.

That day, Miss Stokes had gone to Ranelagh, where she had heard that bread was being sold from baker's carts. For her toil and the danger she braved, Lilly Stokes ended up with only a few dry biscuits and a small bag of pea flour.

At 2 p.m., two cannon began to pound the walls of Kelly's Store across from the rebel headquarters, now proudly flying a tricolour flag and called 'Kelly's Fortress'. Pearse climbed to the GPO roof to encourage the men behind the parapet, trying to silence the cannon and machineguns near Trinity College. A floor down, the prisoner of war Lt Mahony, who happened to be an army surgeon, looked after a roomful of casualties with the primitive means at his disposal. Father John Flanaghan followed Pearse to the roof. And the boys with their powder-smeared faces knelt around the priest and lowered their heads, as streams of bullets from Vickers and Lewis guns flew over them. In its way, this was a true baptism by fire.[16] From then on, the rebels sat, waited, and let the beads of their rosaries slide through their fingers. Suddenly they all stared in puzzlement over their sandbags. Down the road came an iron monster. Months before, the British had tried out their newly invented tanks in France. Now Col. Portal had confiscated two cylindrical iron boilers from the Guinness brewery, drilled shooting slits through the mantle, and had them mounted on to two trucks. Each cylinder held eighteen soldiers. The first Irish tank in history lumbered down Sackville Street. Volunteer Sweeny, a crack shot up

16 As recorded by Father John Flanaghan.

on the GPO roof, aimed for the slit in front of the driver. He fired four rounds before one of his shots hit a bull's-eye. The truck came to a sudden stop and stayed there for the rest of the day, with bullets zinging off its iron mantle and the poor tommies inside boiling in the heat.

The greatest danger during the days of the siege of Dublin, and certainly the one that caused most civilian casualties, came from snipers. Both sides used them to the fullest, shooting at everything moving about in the street. Both sides called it 'potting'. A military sharpshooter in the Bermingham Tower had a score of fifty-three rebels before he was discovered, and killed.

Meanwhile, the infamous Capt. Bowen-Colthurst continued his private extermination rampage. When his men captured a Volunteer, Richard O'Carroll, he had him marched into the back yard, pulled out his gun and shot the prisoner through the lung. The wounded man was found agonising in a gutter. He died ten days later. In defence of the British, Capt. Bowen-Colthurst was the exception.

One of the sections under Commander Daly raided Bridewell police station and captured twenty-four constables. But that was a single action. In general, the odds were now heavily in favour of the army, and Gen. Lowe issued a statement: 'There is now a complete cordon of troops around the centre of town.' From inside the GPO, James Connolly kept directing the battle. He remained cheerful, though he knew only too well the fate that awaited. The ring had closed around them. Brennan Whitmore had an idea: break through the military cordon and start a guerrilla-type action in the countryside. That decision was left for the morning. Another evening of quiet fell over Dublin. Pearse, Connolly and their commanders took turns sleeping on a mattress behind the central counter. While Connolly was soundly asleep, Lord Kitchener put 'the Irish operation' in the hands of a senior commander, Gen. Sir John Grenfell Maxwell. Accompanying him on the troop-ship was a large horde of English and international newspapermen. The Irish Rising was about to become part of history.

Inside the Post Office, most men couldn't remember the day of the week, or even differentiate day from night. Everything seemed to run together. They ate when they found something to eat and they slept when they could. There was a permanent sense of isolation from other parts of the city and other units. Everyone was preoccupied with an overwhelming sense of the need to defend their own sector. Rumour followed upon rumour: the Germans had landed and were marching on Dublin; German U-boats were sailing up the Liffey; the IRA had risen in the countryside. Before sunrise on Thursday, James Connolly tried to raise the men's spirits by making them sing patriotic songs. Michael Collins, trying to sleep, mumbled: 'Put the bloody piano in the other room.'

At 10 a.m. there was the sudden boom of an explosion, followed by a deeper, louder blast. The first artillery shell, fired from Trinity College, smashed into the *Irish Times* building, setting rolls of newsprint on fire. The artillery fire increased in intensity as another gun, this one at Parnell Square, joined in. While Father John Flanaghan said Mass in his church, a woman rushed up to him: 'Father, please come quickly to the Post Office, a Volunteer is dying.' The priest braved sniper bullets and made it into the GPO. Both Pearse and Connolly explained that 'the boys' needed spiritual guidance, and begged the priest to stay on. After only a moment's hesitation he agreed to their request.

The blast came like a sudden hot gale, and when Connolly had regained his feet he had to dodge the lighter bits of debris still tumbling down around him. Near by lay the mutilated body of a fighter. The British artillery had begun to use incendiary shells. Within minutes, most of Lower Abbey Street and Sackville Street were in flames. For the men behind the walls of the Post Office, the heat became unbearable; windows cracked and fabric caught fire. Some shells hit the roof of the building, but the fires were quickly put out.

James Connolly remained calm. He went outside into Henry Street to organise the emplacement of a defensive inner circle in the surrounding buildings. In fact, he was preparing for a last stand on the part of his decimated Army of the Irish Republic. In Princess Street he was hit in the arm by a stray bullet. Without a word, he turned to the prisoner-doctor, Lt Mahony, who bandaged his wound. 'Don't you say a word about this to anyone,' he ordered.

An armoured car lumbered down the street. A young man leaned from a window and dropped a home-made bomb on it. The car stopped. Cannon and machineguns opened up with greater fury than ever before. A solid sheet of lead was sent flying into the sturdy walls of the GPO. In the great hall, a man went off his head. The greatest fear of most was of not dying the glorious death of an Irish freedom fighter but being captured, stood up against a wall and shot as a common criminal. Pearse and Connolly gave a rousing address to reassure their valiant fighters. 'Men, you've held out for three days. By international law, you're now considered belligerents, not rebels.' The men cheered and sang 'The Soldier's Song'.

. . . so Irishmen remember then, and raise your head
with pride,
for great men and straight men have fought for you
and died . . .

The beautiful Countess Markiewicz was lying behind a rampart on the roof of the College of Surgeons from where she looked down on a city on fire. 'It's not Rome, but Dublin's burning,' she mused, 'so where's the fiddler?'

In a basement lock-up lay a military prisoner with a volume of Keats for his headrest. Sean O'Casey. When he heard the artillery, one of his fellow inmates said what they all thought: 'Christ help them now!'[17]

James Connolly realised that the final push would come at any moment now. In the wafer-thin houses turned into sniper positions and strong points, the nerves of the defenders had reached breaking-point. There was one vital position on Moore Street which had to be held at all costs, and Connolly needed to make a final inspection. When he stepped outside the GPO, his visibility restricted by the swirling smoke from the windblown embers of the Metropole Hotel, a gust of wind suddenly cleared the view. Never before had he stood in the centre of such concentrated havoc. The burning houses along Sackville Street flung rippling banners of smoke into the sky; each blaze created its own vicious crackling and growling. Near Nelson's Pillar a tram lay overturned. Shell blasts had blown entire front walls of houses outward, like exploding balloons. They had collapsed into rubble as if a giant fist had shaken them, creating metre-high brick obstacles. Carcasses of horses lay about in untidy heaps, the result of the ill-fated charge by the lancers. In the middle of the road was a crater with the raw earth still gently steaming from the heat of the explosion. The ground shook under his feet from another blast not far away. He moved around the tangle of a splintered barricade, stepped into Middle Abbey Street, and waved to some men to follow him. Disaster struck. One of the many bullets whizzing about like angry bees struck him in the ankle. A hot flame of pain stabbed through his foot, then surged up his whole leg. He went down behind a pile of rubble, where his men couldn't see him. He dug his fingers into the cracks between the cobblestones and dragged himself, inch by inch, a full hundred yards, leaving a trail of blood, before he was pulled inside the Post Office. The POW doctor, Mahony, applied a simple tourniquet to stop the bleeding. Somewhere they found some chloroform, and while Connolly did not go

[17] From Sean O'Casey, *Autobiography*, London 1971–3.

fully under, it was enough to perform the delicate manoeuvre of removing the splintered bone. When Connolly woke up, he looked at Dr Mahony and smiled: 'You're the best thing we've captured this week.'

The men cowering behind the parapet of the GPO could see a gun barrel at Trinity College, big as a factory chimney, belch flame. Instinctively they pulled their heads between their shoulders. Thunder rolled over them and crashed into a house behind their fortress. From the fires, which swept down the row of houses on Sackville Street, tongues of flame roared high into the air; sparks showered the Post Office. The men were ordered to take all grenades and other explosives into the basement. Despite his excruciating pain, Connolly had himself carried into the main hall on a stretcher to be with his men.[18] The pain gushed in waves through his body, and finally he dozed off. When he opened his eyes, he found himself next to a Volunteer soldier who trembled as blood soaked through his bandage and stained his fingers. Why are we fighting? the young man's eyes seemed to ask. He might well ask why, but once a war is declared such a question is redundant.

In a corner, Patrick Pearse sat next to Desmond Ryan. 'It was the right thing to do, wasn't it?' the provisional president asked the young lieutenant.

'Yes,' answered Ryan, 'the right thing.'

'When we're wiped out, the people will blame us for everything, and condemn us. After a few years the same people will see the meaning of what we tried to do.' Pearse may not have possessed the military talents of a Connolly, but he was certainly a prophet.

The focus of fighting shifted to North King Street, where terrible house-to-house combat took place between Irish snipers and men of the South Staffordshire Battalion of Lt-Col. Henry Taylor. It was a night when another British unit would achieve notoriety by going on a killing rampage.

18 A famous painting by W. Paget depicts the scene.

These were the South Staffords, savage men from the worst industrial slums and coal mines. They went into Dublin to 'take care of the Irish buggers'. And they did. In their fashion. The focal point of resistance was a corner pub, 'Reilly's Fort'. The South Staffords suffered heavy casualties from snipers during some of the most vicious and sustained fighting of the entire week. The rebel barricade held and the soldiers got nowhere. The battalion's colonel now ordered his troops to tunnel through a row of houses towards the barricade. While doing so, the men of the South Staffords behaved more like barbaric savages than soldiers. In North King Street and Coleraine Street, people had stayed locked up inside their homes, since these seemed the safest places. These houses were now broken into, and innocent men were ruthlessly bayoneted or shot in front of their horrified families.[19] Most of the army atrocities happened in this sector of the city between 6 p.m. on 28 April and 10 a.m. on the 29th.[20] An old housekeeper in the Hickey residence, Kate Kelly, told the story of an officer and four men who murdered her employer, Thomas Hickey, his son Christopher, and another man, Peter Connolly.

> It was about 6 a.m. on Saturday morning, I heard a noise, and said to Mr Hickey, someone is breaking into the house. The back wall came down and through the hole crawled soldiers with crossbars. They had started four doors down the street, at Mr Hughes' place [172 North King Street]. 'How many prisoners have you

[19] There exist a great number of eye-witness accounts, mostly by widows and relatives of the murdered men, documented by Roger McHugh in *Dublin 1916*.

[20] Positively identified as having been shot were: Michael Noonan, thirty-four, and George Ennis, fifty-one, at 174 North King Street; Thomas Hickey, thirty-eight, Christopher Hickey, sixteen, and Peter Connolly, thirty-nine, at 170 North King Street; Michael Hughes and John Walsh, thirty-six, at 172 North King Street; John Beirnes, fifty, at Coleraine Street (there, a witness heard a soldier cry out: 'Put that fellow out of the way!' before another shot him); Peter Joseph Lawless, twenty-one, James McCartney, thirty-six, James Finnigan, forty, and Patrick Hoey, twenty-five, at 27 North King Street.

> there?' asked the officer. 'Three males and one female,' one of the soldiers said. They pushed us through the hole, which they had broken through the wall of the neighbouring house [170 North King Street]. I stumbled and fell to my knees and Mr Hickey helped me up. I said, 'I hope they're not going to kill us all,' and Mr Hickey, poor soul, he said: 'Very often the innocent suffer for the guilty,' and I heard a soldier laugh. Then I heard Mr Hickey's son, Christopher, a lad of sixteen, say: 'Oh! Don't kill father.' Then they took the two men and the laddie into the next room and I heard the shots, and I cried: 'Oh my God!'

When some of the women who had witnessed the crimes were brought to identify the possible culprits, and the troops were lined up for inspection, the widows couldn't make a single identification. Because by that time the regimental colonel had taken the precaution of shipping anyone suspected of having participated in 'The Massacres of North King Street' back to England. In a letter to Lord Kitchener General Maxwell wrote: 'In one case a sergeant acted like a madman, the redeeming feature being that he reported what he had done.' The man he referred to was a Cpl Bullock.[21]

One thing is certain – atrocities were committed on both sides. If men do not balance feelings and intelligence, they lose command of both. Accounts were settled and blood was spilled. As in every fratricidal conflict since Cain slew Abel, the pent-up hatred of years was vented not only between fighting man and fighting man, but between brother and brother.

Friday, mid-afternoon. The fifth day, and still the remnants of the Army of the Irish Republic held out despite the impossible odds. An entire army division, supported by heavy artillery,

[21] Quoted in Max Caulfield's *The Easter Rebellion*, London 1964.

was combating a few hundred insurgents. More shells poured into the Post Office. 'The flames were soaring higher, till the heavens looked like a great ruby hanging from God's ear,' wrote eye-witness Sean O'Casey. Men were using fire hoses and buckets to douse the flames. It was no use. Incendiary shells were falling on the roof. The artillery was now in plain sight, firing at point-blank range from all sides. By five o'clock parts of the roof had collapsed and the fire was rapidly spreading along staircases and ventilator shafts to the lower floors. Still the men kept up their fire through the slits in the mail-bagged windows. But Connolly realised the building was done for. They had to get out. But how, and where to? Father Flanagan asked about the wounded. Connolly ordered them to be brought to Jervis Street Hospital in the company of his POW doctor, Lt Mahony. 'And what about you?' asked the doctor. 'Your leg must be treated.'

'My place is with my men,' replied Connolly.

Commander The O'Rahilly, one of the commanders, volunteered to lead an assault party to clear the way for an escape. Before he guided his group of men on their sortie, he asked Father Flanaghan to give him absolution. 'I'm afraid, Father, we'll never meet again.' In Moore Street, where the British had manned a barricade, The O'Rahilly divided his unit in half and sent each section along the walls of the houses. When they were spotted and subjected to heavy fire, The O'Rahilly stepped into the middle of the street and stormed towards the barricade, firing from the hip. His bravery spurred the rest of the rebels to follow him. But the British Army was not out of ammunition. Their first burst put five bullets through his chest and killed twenty-one of his men. Nine survived and were taken prisoner.

A street-wise young lad, MacLoughlin, and Michael Collins led another sortie. They stumbled into the same barricade, and their men suffered a similar fate. More died. Lt Chalmers, the prisoner of war, and a few others who had spent their days locked up inside the GPO, were allowed to leave.

Trying to cross the lines, many were shot by their own troops.

Connolly was one of the last to leave the Post Office, on a stretcher. By then, the smoke was so thick his stretcher-bearers couldn't see their hands in front of their faces. Through holes in walls, down into basements and climbing over low roofs, they ended up in a grocery store, which became the final headquarters of the Rising.

Lying on his stretcher, James Connolly concentrated on a spider dangling from the ceiling. A fly had been caught in its web, with no prospect of escape. Then he closed his eyes . . . his patriots had created something new here, he thought, and it would have its effect. He knew his Irish people, he had confidence in them. His endeavour would not be in vain. Obviously there had been excesses – crimes of desperation, brought on by hunger, real, raw hunger. Hell, people had been dying of hunger every day. The Great Famine had emasculated Ireland, and it was said that her people had lost their sense of pride. But that was not so. The Irish had their dreams and they had their poets, great men and famous, a great heritage. No, he was not downhearted; of course, he was sorry about the death and suffering their rebellion had caused. At the same time he was a natural enthusiast and excited by what a few had accomplished in such a brief period. This was his country, his people, and he loved them so much it hurt his heart when things weren't as he would have wished. Soon, his Irish would wake up and find brotherly love and a powerful sense of community in a free Ireland.

Saturday morning – six days since the people of Dublin's world had come apart in a bright flash. Dawn broke over a smouldering city. A man, his wife and daughter fled from their burning home, carrying a white flag. They were shot by trigger-happy soldiers. The Royal Irish Fusiliers of Col. Owen were ordered to storm the Post Office, now an abandoned shell. Thick smoke was still pouring from its windows. At number 16 Moore Street, the last members of the Provisional

Government were standing around Connolly's bed: Patrick Pearse, Tom Clarke, Sean MacDermott, Joseph Plunkett. Volunteer MacLoughlin, back from a scouting trip, announced: 'We've got to get out. They're all around us.'

'We cannot leave, we've got our wounded to think of. Going out there, they'll face almost certain death,' argued one of the men.

'Almost isn't certain . . .' replied Connolly, a sad smile across his tired face. Suddenly, Pearse looked up as if he hadn't heard the argument. 'Can somebody get a white flag?' he asked. Michael O'Reilly, who was shaving in the bathroom, pulled a handkerchief from his pocket. 'Will that do?' The nurse, Miss O'Farrell, offered to take her chances. She made it to the barricade, and was brought before Col. Portal. 'The Commandant of the Irish Republican Army wishes to treat with the Commandant of the British forces in Ireland,' she pronounced. 'The Irish Republican Army? The Sinn Feiners, you mean,' answered the colonel. Nurse O'Farrell refused to be put down: 'No, the Irish Republican Army, and a good name it is, too.'

'Take her over there,' ordered the colonel, 'and search her. She's a spy.' The officer did as ordered and Nurse O'Farrell was marched across the street and searched. They found two pairs of surgical scissors. The colonel phoned Gen. Lowe at his headquarters in Trinity College, who received her in a gentlemanly manner and said to her: 'Tell Pearse, I will not treat at all unless he surrenders unconditionally and that Mr Connolly follows on a stretcher.' He went on to inform Miss O'Farrell that, unless she was to return with Pearse within thirty minutes, the British artillery would shell the city. She left Lowe's HQ to deliver the message. On her way through Moore Street she saw the body of The O'Rahilly, his feet against a doorstep and his head on the kerbstone. Farther down Moore Lane were two shapes covered with a green tablecloth. When she reached Moore Street HQ, she delivered Lowe's message verbally to the men in the room. After some time, Pearse stood up, his face begrimed with soot and dust, his eyes swollen from lack of sleep. He went into the next room to splash water over his tired face, then he took his slouch hat, put it on at a rakish angle, and he and Miss O'Farrell stepped out into the street.

At precisely 2.30 p.m., 29 April 1916,[22] the provisional president of Ireland, Patrick Henry Pearse, met with Brig.-Gen. W.H.M. Lowe behind the barricade at the top of Moore Street. Pearse took off his sword and handed it to the general. He was then brought before Gen. Maxwell. An orderly sat by a typewriter and committed Pearse's words to paper:

> In order to prevent further slaughter of Dublin citizens, and in the hope of saving the lives of our followers now surrounded and hopelessly outnumbered, the members of the Provisional Government present at Headquarters have agreed to an unconditional surrender, and the Commandants of the various districts in the City and Country will order their commands to lay down arms. (signed) P.H. Pearse. 29th April 1916. 3.45 p.m.

Maxwell insisted that Connolly, as military commander, countersign the document. A Capt. Wheeler went to see the wounded Connolly, who scribbled: 'I agree to these conditions for the men under my command. (signed) James Connolly, April 29/16.'

The Irish Rising of 1916 had come to an end. From the top of the Post Office tower dangled the tattered remnants of a green flag with a gold harp.

One thousand three hundred and fifty were killed, or seriously wounded; one hundred thousand people had to be given public relief. Four hundred insurgents, all that was

[22] According to Nurse O'Farrell it was 3.30 p.m. A scratched, badly repaired photograph of the meeting shows Lowe facing Pearse.

left of James Connolly's Irish Republican Army, marched into captivity.[23]

It was a sad sight. The boys who had put up a heroic stand for five whole days were reduced to a thin line of starving warriors in ragged uniforms. Their faces were smeared with soot and powder; there was hardly one without some blood-smeared bandage. They were marched through a cordon of khaki-dressed soldiers with naked bayonets, lining both sides of Sackville Street. The soldiers who led them away didn't know what to make of their unrepentant captives. Rebels against the British Empire? Unheard of!

Pearse's prediction proved prophetic. When the prisoners crossed over the Liffey river, garrulous crowds lining the pavements shouted: 'Shoot the traitors!' and 'Bayonet the bastards!' and 'Down with the Shinners!' The shawlies belted them with rotten vegetables, even poured the contents of chamber pots over their heads. Only Countess Markiewicz kept her head high as she marched in front of her men into captivity.[24]

Connolly was carried on his stretcher to confront the English commander-in-chief. Gen. Maxwell, straight as a ramrod, stared down at his beaten foe. 'Why?' the general barked at him.

'I did what I thought was my duty.'

[23] For the authorities in the middle of a devastating world war, it was in the interests of public morale to minimise the real dimensions of the Rising. The official count was 52 rebels, 129 army troops and nearly one thousand civilians. There are discrepancies in the statistics. Let us take a closer look. Perhaps as many as 1,500 rebels took part, but only 400 marched into captivity. The army used heavy artillery and machineguns, which suggests a high attrition rate. This is substantiated by personal accounts from specific encounters: Clanwilliam House (14 IRA killed), *Mail* building (22), Moore Street (21), etc. The high rate of civilian casualties suggests that some IRA members in civilian clothes were counted as non-combatants. Also, a number of IRA members were quietly buried by families or friends for fear of future reprisals.

[24] There was also a scene of compassion. One hefty woman, noticing young Andy McDonnell march past, yelled: 'Lord, look at the child going to be shot!' She pushed through the armed cordon and hugged McDonnell. Eventually, McDonnell was sent home to his parents.

There was a thin smile on the general's aristocratic face. 'Hm, but now it's all over and done with.'

'Not to me,' replied the defiant Connolly, who saw that the despotism of the English upper class was out of touch with modern ideas. 'The Irish are not beaten. Our uprising marks only the beginning of the fall of the British Empire.' He was to be proven right.

It took a great Irish writer, George Bernard Shaw, to express it appropriately.

> *At Easter 1916 a handful of Irishmen seized the Dublin Post Office and proclaimed an Irish Republic. If all of Ireland had risen at this gesture it would have been a serious matter for England, then up to her neck in the war against the Central Empires. But there was no response; the gesture was a complete failure.*
>
> *Having worked up a harebrained romantic adventure into a heroic episode, the victorious [English] artillerists proceeded to kill their prisoners of war in a drawn-out string of executions. Those who were executed accordingly became not only national heroes, but the martyrs whose blood was the seed of the present Irish Free State. Nothing more blindly savage, stupid, and terror-mad could have been devised by England's worst enemies . . .*

Certainly, for the military authorities, a cautious reaction, not a strong line, was called for. Given Gen. Maxwell's stubborn paternalism and punctiliousness, it was hard to envisage any peaceful outcome. The Irish people's expectation, that English judiciary would uphold the rule of law, was sadly unfulfilled.

On 3 May, Patrick Henry Pearse, Thomas MacDonagh and Thomas Clarke were executed.

On 4 May, at 1.30 a.m., Grace Gifford married Joseph Plunkett. At four o'clock he was shot, as were the brother of the provisional president, Willi Pearse, Edward Daly and Michael O'Hanrahan.

On 5 May John MacBride died. The same day, a death sentence for Countess Markiewicz was commuted to life in prison.

On 8 May, Edmund Kent, Michael Mallin, J.J. Heuston and Cornelius Colbert went to the wall.

On 9 May, Eamon de Valera, because he was technically an American citizen, was sentenced to life imprisonment. (A footnote to history: his life spared, Eamon de Valera eventually became the nation's President and kept the Irish Republic out of the Second World War.)

On 12 May, John MacDermott was shot.

Until that moment, the people of Ireland had been in a state of shock and quietly endured the harsh punishment meted out by Gen. Maxwell. Perhaps he was misled by a famous editorial in the *Irish Times*, traditionally a Unionist paper, and took it as the average popular Irish opinion: 'In the verdict of history, weakness today would be more criminal than the indifference of the past few months. Sedition must be rooted out of Ireland, once and for all. The rapine and bloodshed of the past week must be finished with a severity which will make any repetition of them impossible for many generations to come.'

The paper and the general couldn't have been more wrong. What finally woke the Irish from their lethargy was the fate of their national hero, James Connolly. The US Senate demanded that their President send a note to London, asking for clemency. Even Connolly's mortal enemies, among them the Protestant leader of Northern Ireland, 'King' Carson, appealed in the House of Commons. But Gen. Maxwell, the undisputed overlord of Ireland, remained unforgiving.

James Connolly's wife and daughter were allowed to see the wounded man on 9 May. The wound had become infected and his strength was rapidly fading, yet he seemed in good spirits and tried to cheer his family up with the story about the man who had come into the Post Office to buy a stamp. 'What has Dublin come to,' the man complained, 'if one cannot buy a stamp in a post office.'[25] The last to see him was Father Aloysius, his confessor. 'I was sure there would be no more executions,' the priest said afterwards. 'Then came the night of 12 May. An ambulance picked me up in the middle of the night and brought me to Connolly's bedside. It was a terrible shock to me, but I will always thank the Lord that he permitted me to remain by his side until the very end.'

The guards put Connolly on a stretcher and loaded him into the waiting ambulance. He was driven to Kilmainham Jail and carried on the stretcher into the prison courtyard. Near the wall stood a wooden chair with lanyards around the uprights. The soldiers lifted Connolly from his stretcher and propped him up on the chair. He was so weak one soldier had to hold him while they pulled a strap around his chest and tied him so that he wouldn't fall forward. With a final effort, he lifted his head and raised his eyes to heaven. 'Father, say good-bye to me.' He tried to raise himself upright. 'God save Ireland.'

Then they shot him.

The facts

James Connolly was the last of the fifteen leaders of the Easter Rising to be executed. His death caused a wave of uproar, and from that moment on Gen. Maxwell became known as 'Bloody' Maxwell.[26] He may well have changed his mind had he only known that, by shooting James Connolly, he had turned him into the very symbol of Irish martyrdom. 'Life springs from death; and from the graves of patriot men and women spring living nations . . . the fools, the fools, the fools! They have left us our Fenian dead, and while Ireland holds

25 Account by his daughter Nora.
26 Maxwell was quietly moved to a posting in northern England.

these graves, Ireland unfree shall never be in peace.'

Words written years before by Patrick Henry Pearse. How well he knew his Irish. Soon unrest broke out throughout Ireland. London renewed its suppression, but this time it didn't quite turn out the way they had planned it, and the world learned that No. 10 Downing Street was out of touch with the Irish problem and political reality. In a major blunder, police began to round up Irishmen in cities and villages, their constabulary began to tear up the countryside, and Ireland slipped hard and fast into anarchy. While Connolly's following had been, at best, sparse, following the arrests[27] and summary executions, opposition to British rule began to unite. It took the deaths of many more patriots for Connolly's call to find fertile soil, sowing a seed of Irish patriotism so powerful that no number of guns would ever be able to silence it.

Of heroic deeds we speak and great heroes we sing . . . but some were sadly overlooked, because they didn't carry guns. At the height of the battle, while mayhem and terror befell a city, while relatives searched the rubble for the bodies of their beloved, some of the same women went knocking from door to door, trying desperately to raise popular support for their fighting men. No pleading, no reasoning would make the mainstream come out in support of the 'Irish cause'. Day after day the women tried and day after day the Dubliners shouted abuse at them and slammed doors in their faces. Ireland simply wasn't ready to achieve its freedom by violent means – and without popular support the Rising never stood a chance.

In this moment of great sadness, one voice could be heard, ringing out like a bell all across Ireland. Cathleen ni Houlihan, Daughter of Houlihan, in her tattered gown and with ashes in her hair, walked firmly in her bare feet across the land, singing:

27 In the days following the Rising, over 2,000 were arbitrarily arrested and put into camps.

Ready in heart and ready in hand,
march with banner and bugle and fife,
to the death for their native land.

For things were changing now. Younger men, such as the ferocious and unforgiving military mastermind of the IRA, Michael Collins, emerged. It wasn't revenge he was after, it was reckoning. Soon every cottage became a hideout and every hamlet a hotbed of unrest. A bloody free-for-all engulfed village and town, English and Irish. Gunfire rattled throughout the countryside, creating confusion and chaos. English soldiers pointed their weapons at any crowd larger than three. They didn't take any chances and arrested them all. An appeal by the English authorities for people to turn in their weapons went largely unheeded. A few rifles were handed over, but with thousands still out there, the British had a long way to go.

Then the British tried police terror. To stop the IRA they set loose the equally ruthless Black and Tan.[28] Michael Collins answered with an eye for an eye. He promised for every Catholic tuppenny milk store burned to the ground the destruction of two Protestant residences; for every Irish patriot killed the hooded execution of two members of the Protestant gentry; and he carried out his threat.[29] The British government stood by helplessly while a reign of terror and torture, murder and devastation swept the Irish countryside. The Black and Tan arrested and killed in the name of authority, and the IRA treated the Black and Tan as common killers and slaughtered them in country lanes and city streets. Police informers were eliminated, politicians assassinated. Collins' men burned and fought and killed, until the champions of Ulster separatism couldn't stomach any more, and the Irish

[28] Black and Tan owing to the colour of their uniform and belts.
[29] He ordered the execution of Capt. Lea Wilson, himself an Irishman, who had maltreated all his Irish prisoners after their surrender in 1916.

problem was resolved, to quote G.B. Shaw, 'not as civilised and reasonable men should have settled it, but as dogs settle a dispute over a bone'. The English had come to the same grief in Ireland at the beginning of the twentieth century as their predecessors had in the United States at the end of the eighteenth.

In 1921, Britain having failed to crush the Irish independence movement, and after four months of haggling, Michael Collins[30] made the government concede the creation of an Irish Free State, based on the constitution of Canada. But the British government would not grant the creation of an Irish Republic. Also, a specific clause allowed the six Ulster provinces to opt out and remain loyal to the United Kingdom and the English crown. The bloodshed hasn't stopped since. *Sunday, bloody Sunday* . . .[31] There is one more reason why the Rising won't go away. And it has little to do with the Rising itself. For the Irish, it has turned into a symbol with which to express frustration and discontent with government leaders regarded as not being patriotic enough.[32]

Of all the Irishmen who participated in the Easter Rising, James Connolly is the most enigmatic and the most fascinating. Here was a leader inbued with the impetuous Celtic temperament. His virtues were richly Irish virtues, his flaws deeply Irish flaws. That is why history can never let him rest. He is both vilified and canonised. His thinking was beguilingly innocent, his creed to make Ireland an independent paradise of free people. Few leaders have failed as dismally as did Connolly, yet soon after his death his dream came true. After his execution, all of Ireland finally believed that

[30] Michael Collins was killed in an ambush – probably accidentally – during combat between two IRA factions a few years later.

[31] Refers to a notorious incident between British troops and Catholics in Londonderry in 1972.

[32] Today, any Irish government has to be fiercely patriotic on one hand, while it looks to Great Britain for finance and technology on the other.

violence was inevitable, that their problem could no longer be solved by peaceful means.

Thus, the Easter Rising became the defining moment in Ireland's political showdown. Some patriots stood up and died. And, unless London was prepared to offer alternatives, other Irish patriots would surely follow.

Foreigners had come to Ireland, an endless procession of the same nationality on the same quest. To conquer and rule. From the gay-coloured Elizabethans with pikes and bows, Cromwell's men in their drab leather jerkins with spears and swords, and King William's red-coated men with their muskets, to the khaki-clad soldiers with their machineguns and big cannon.[33] Ireland had suffered them all, helpless, passionate and contemptuous. Then, for one glorious week, Ireland had been free. In a sunburst of freedom, some had dared to throw off the ancient symbols of miseries, the Silenced Harp and the tears of Dark Rosaleen. Future generations were to recall their great heroes in tales and songs.[34] The dreamer Pearse, the visionary de Valera, the poet MacDonagh, the pacifist Sheehy-Skeffington and the firebrand Countess Markiewicz.

But most of all they would remember that troublesome idealist, James Connolly.

Theirs was a story of achievement, triumph and ruin, of vain hopes torn apart by the tides of history, both master and slave of their destiny. There are lessons in their lives far greater than their influence ever was. They are their lasting monument.

The Hinge of Battle of the Irish Easter Rising lay in its failure to raise popular support. It was a glorious if futile gesture where patriots went knowingly to their death.

The Dublin Easter Rising moved the people of Ireland into

[33] These days it is special forces, in camouflage, with night-vision goggles and sniper scopes.

[34] Sean O'Casey, James Joyce, George Bernard Shaw, James Stephens, George William Russell, Roy McFadden.

action. Following civil war, conducted by both sides with utter brutality, it led to the creation of the Irish Free State in 1921.

7

'Since This Morning We Are Shooting Back!'

31 August 1939 – The Gleiwitz Caper

'The importance of this special mission exceeds anything our department has been asked to undertake to this day.'
Reinhardt Heydrich, Chief of the *Reichssicherheitshauptamt*, 24 August 1939

'Seit heute früh wird zurückgeschossen!'
('Since this morning we are shooting back!')
Radio broadcast by Adolf Hitler, 1 September 1939

It was a damp, humid summer evening in Silesia that 31 August 1939. Heinz Klausen, a locomotive engineer, was sitting near at his kitchen table, spooning soup from a bowl, when he heard the shot. It came from somewhere near by. But where? Across the small green was only the local radio station, and, at this hour of the night, only the cleaning people were in there. There was nothing worth stealing. Then he heard yelling and engines springing to life. He dropped his spoon, rushed to the window and saw shadows dashing from the entrance of the Radiohaus. Two black cars spun off with screeching tyres. Klausen rushed downstairs and across the green; that was when he saw the crumpled figure lying just inside the entrance to the building. A soldier in a foreign uniform with blood seeping from a wound in his neck. Klausen looked down on the corpse, unable to take in what he had just witnessed. More people crowded around, villagers who had been out for a late stroll. 'What happened?' they asked, moving closer to the broken body, while others kept well away, averting their eyes. A strange sensation overcame him, a foreboding that this was not at all what it appeared. There was more behind it, much more. *The unknown is always more fearful than the reality*. Klausen sprang to his feet and pushed past the startled onlookers. He had to get to the police, warn the people . . . tell them that the Polish Army had attacked the German Reich!

The drama on the road leading to the Second World War was played out by many. There were the mega-stars, Hitler, Chamberlain, Stalin and Daladier, and their assistants, Ribbentrop, Halifax, Henderson, Molotov, Coulondre. Many were overlooked. SS officer Alfred Naujocks was one such.

The stone of contention was created by the Allies on 28 June 1919, at Versailles. A real granite border stone was planted as the 'Three-Country-Mark' at Weissenberg an der Weichsel, granting Poland access to the Baltic through a wide strip of land. This Polish Corridor cut through predominantly German-settled territory and separated the bulk of Germany from East Prussia. The German port of Danzig was declared an international free zone. This political blindness on the part of the victors after World War I provided extremists like Hitler with a valid reason for plunging the world into a monstrous holocaust.

Already in 1922, German Gen. von Seeckt, chief of a truncated Home Army, had declared before an assembly of World War I officers: 'The very existence of Poland is unbearable and incompatible with the living conditions of Germany. It has to disappear and that with our help. It would be most beneficial for us if Poland had Russia in its neck.' With these words he laid the foundation for Hitler's strategy. A pact with the Devil himself – Stalin. If he could achieve that goal, nothing and nobody could stop him from eliminating the corridor and annexing large swaths of eastern *Lebensraum*.

On 23 March 1939 Prime Minister Neville Chamberlain addressed the British Parliament: '. . . should Germany, in a series of successive measures, try to rule Europe so would this call for the successful resistance of England and other nations that value their liberty . . .' This was followed by British Foreign Secretary Lord Halifax's speech before the members of the Royal Institute of International Affairs: '. . . in case of further aggression must we be prepared to use all our forces to fulfil our obligation and to resist the aggressor . . . we're standing accused of isolating Germany, fact is that Germany has isolated itself . . . under the threat of military adventurism they're holding the world to ransom. Our duty is, and will be, to resist.'

Encouraged by this bellicose warning, on 25 March Poland ordered a general mobilisation of its armed forces. The Poles were a proud nation. Some even believed in a Polish victory; after all, they had shown what they were capable of when they beat the Russians in 1920. If Hitler must bear responsibility for his devious juggling, it should not be overlooked that the Polish were playing into his hands. With their mobilisation, the German dictator could pretend that Poland had taken a definite stand. Especially after the Polish Army chief, Marshal Rydz-Smigly, declared: 'For centuries, Danzig has been united with Poland . . .', despite the fact that the League of Nations had voted overwhelmingly in 1933 and again in 1935 to 'return Danzig to Germany'. Hitler was ambitious; he had the machinery for war, Poland had not. Following his invasion and annexation of the Sudetenland (1 October 1938), he instructed the Polish ambassador to Berlin, Lipski, to inform his foreign minister, Colonel Beck, of the German claim for the '*Korridor*' (24 October 1938). In exchange, he offered Poland a twenty-five-year non-aggression pact which he never intended to keep, since his goal was always to extend Germany's *Lebensraum im Osten*.

1 April. The 'Polish crisis', started by Hitler on a date of his choice, would, so he thought, be contained and offer little threat to international security. In any case, he had assured the Allied protagonists that they would never have to confront German forces in France. His ambitions were focused on the east, not the west. Thus he thought and thus he acted.

The word 'crisis' had been so much overused and so badly defined that it had become a cliché, almost an abuse of the language. For Hitler, the 'Polish crisis' was no different. Certainly, he listened to the Allied threats. But had they also not threatened before he marched into Czechoslovakia? They had made a lot of noise – and then did nothing! At Munich, Chamberlain had even signed on the dotted line, 'Peace in our time!', and then he had waved a worthless piece of paper to appease his own people. Why would they act differently now? Their nations were faced by depression, strikes and economic hardship; why would they worry about the affairs of a country with which they had almost zero trade? 'England will never go to war. At best, it will threaten us with an economic war,' he stated. Thus he went ahead with his invasion plans. He made matters clear during the launching ceremony for Germany's fourth battleship with his chestnuts-from-the-fire speech: 'Those declaring themselves willing to pull the chestnuts from the fire must also be willing to get their fingers burned.'

6 April. England replied to this open threat with a declaration of possible mutual assistance between Great Britain and Poland.

11 April. Hitler raised the stakes with a secret address to his chiefs of staff: 'The task of our Wehrmacht is to annihilate the Polish forces. For this it will be necessary to prepare a surprise attack . . .'

28 April. Hitler rescinded the Polish–German non-aggression treaty he himself had signed in 1934. It stunned the world

and brought about a complex round of negotiations in which the major powers scrambled to align themselves. England and France's aim was to head off war by forming strong alliances and agreeing to act, if necessary, against Germany. Hitler's only aim was to open the way for an invasion of Poland. And Russia needed to buy time to rearm, following its devastating purge of its officer corps; Stalin promised to use 'his influence' over the parts of eastern Europe which he was out to incorporate into his own empire. In this chess game among nations, where diplomats bluffed, bargained, threatened and prayed, nobody remained neutral and Poland became the centre square on the board.

3 May. Poland felt so strengthened that it broke off further talks with Germany. During a troop parade in Warsaw, the masses howled: 'March on to Danzig! On to Berlin!' Anti-German incidents multiplied, especially under the leadership of the nobleman, Voyvod Graczinski: 'We shall burn the Germans' eyes before we chase them across the border.'

17 June. Propagandaminister Joseph Goebbels flew to Danzig. Addressing a delirious crowd, he exhorted them to resist: '. . . you are all of the same race and want to return home into the Reich . . . I've come to tell you that the full might of the Reich is behind you . . .'

27 June. Premier Daladier spoke before the French Senate: '. . . it is our duty to combine, to arm ourselves and to remain vigilant . . .'

4 August. The Poles foolishly played into Hitler's hands when they issued an ultimatum requiring the Senate of Danzig to permit Polish customs officials access to the free port. Danzig said no and Poland closed the harbour facilities for all German shipping at Gdingen. Danzig replied by calling up its men to form the 'Self-defence Unit Eberhardt'. The *Völkische Beobachter*, the Nazi paper, splashed the headline: 'DANZIG IN GEFAHR . . . Danzig in danger'.

18 August. Hitler ordered his military strategists to his private residence in Berchtesgaden: 'We have nothing to

lose and everything to gain . . . prepare for an attack on 26 August . . . *der Stärkere hat das Recht* . . . the powerful rules the law!' Generaloberst von Brauchitsch tried to change Hitler's mind by telling him that the army was far from ready. But Hitler would listen to reason no more. The politician had taken over from the strategist. He simply refused to believe that England and France would enter the conflict.

Superpower diplomacy cranked up but its engine was running in neutral. A series of charges and counter-charges were levelled between London–Paris–Warsaw and Berlin. While the haggling went on, Hitler exploded a bomb: on 21 August 1939, Germany and the Soviet Union signed a friendship pact and parcelled out Poland. This momentous agreement was set up during a meeting between Stalin and Joachim von Ribbentrop.

Ribbentrop: England has always attempted to interfere in the internal matters of our two countries and thereby hinder any friendly approach.

Stalin: That is so. The English Army is weak, the English Fleet can no longer fulfil its ambitions. Their air arm is under reconstruction but it suffers from an acute shortage of seasoned pilots. If England still controls the world this is due to the stupidity of countries that let themselves be bluffed. It's absurd that a few hundred Englishmen should rule a country the size of India.

Ribbentrop: I may tell you in confidence that England has once again put out feelers, insinuating a repeat of its alliances of 1914. I have suggested to the Führer to let the English know that any interference into our affairs will be answered with the bombing of London. [Stalin seemed highly satisfied with the development of the situation.]

Ribbentrop: Our people know of no points of contention between Germany and the Soviet Union, and that only the interference of England has put a stress on our past relationship.

Stalin: Yes, I believe you are right. The Germans wish for peace and therefore call for a friendly relationship between the Reich and the Soviet Union. The Soviet government takes its engagements seriously and I can give you my word, the Soviet Union will never betray its partner.

Stalin's sentence was hardly out of his month before Ribbentrop was on the telephone to Berlin.[1]

The English–French military commission, in the Russian capital since 11 August to negotiate a non-aggression agreement, was expelled from Moscow. Comrade Voroshilov gave a declaration to that effect: 'The talks have ended without an agreement. The military mission of the Soviet Union is of the opinion, as we do not have a common border with the (by the Allies so named) aggressor, it can only come to the military assistance of England, France and Poland by allowing Soviet troops to march across Polish territory. This was denied. All further discussions seem futile and the Allied military commission has left Moscow.'[2]

Hitler knew that with his new partner, albeit up to that moment the arch-enemy of fascism, Poland had to cave in. The German press were jubilant. But Hitler and his advisers had it all wrong – the real triumph was Stalin's. With sheer cunning the Red Tsar helped to strengthen Hitler's position before the world, allowed him his '15 minutes of glory', and encouraged him to adopt a forceful solution to the Polish issue which could only benefit Russia. Also, Stalin realised that England and France had to honour their defence promise to Poland, or lose all credibility for ever.

25 August 1939. A day of decision, a hot summer's day. In Berlin girls wore gaily flowered dresses and businessmen took off their ties. The beaches along the Spree were jammed with bathers and the cafés on the Kurfürstendamm were crowded.

1 *Akten zur Deutschen Auswärtigen Politik*, Serie D.
2 *Izvestia*, 27 August 1939.

Berlin was at the peak of its glory, proudly showing off its wealth. But it was also living on the edge of a volcano and didn't know it – or chose to ignore it. In the vastness of the Reichschancellery, Hitler issued his final instructions to attack across the Polish border. *Y-Tag* (D-day) was to be 26 August, at 4.30 a.m. He felt certain that he could hold off the West with more proposals and promises. With this uppermost in his mind, he offered his Polish options to the British ambassador, Sir Neville Henderson. '*Diesmal wird Deutschland nicht an zwei Fronten kämpfen* . . . This time, Germany will not fight on two fronts. This is because our agreement with the Soviet Union is binding and has changed German foreign policy for a long time to come. Russia and Germany will never again raise their weapons against each other. The German–Polish problem must, and will be solved. Should England attack, then it will find a resolute Germany.'

Hitler then provided Henderson with a German plane to carry his proposition to London.

That same afternoon, a meeting was held in London between Lord Halifax, First Secretary of State for Foreign Affairs in HM Government, and Count Edvard Raczynski, representing Poland. There and then they signed a pact for military assistance, and England guaranteed in Article 1 'the existence of Poland in its present form and a mutual assistance in case of an aggression of one of the partners of this agreement by a foreign power . . .'. 'Mutual assistance' was to become the key phrase in the coming drama. Added to the pact was a secret addendum: 'under "foreign power" is understood Germany'.

Shortly after the departure of Ambassador Henderson, and shortly before the French plenipotentiary was due to present himself for a similar discussion, Hitler suffered two serious setbacks. At 5 p.m. he was informed via his London embassy of the mutual assistance agreement between Great Britain and Poland. And he received the special envoy of Italy's Duce,

Bernardo Attolico, bearer of a personal letter from Mussolini: '. . . it is one of the more painful moments of my life to let you know that Italy is not ready for war . . .' Hitler was furious and broke out in a fit of temper, pacing the marble floor and screaming at those around him. It was perhaps the refusal by his 'faithful and trusted Italian ally' which led to his fateful decision: he would show the world – Germany would go it alone![3]

6.30 p.m. Hitler next talked to France's plenipotentiary, Robert Coulondre.

Hitler: I have no hostile intention towards the French Republic. I have shown my goodwill when I personally renounced all claims to Alsace-Lorraine and recognised the existing borderline. I will not attack France, but should it interfere I will march all the way to Paris . . . please tell this to your Premier Daladier.

Coulondre: To leave you not with the slightest doubt, Reichschancellor, I give you my word of honour as a soldier, should Germany attack across the Polish border, France will stand on the side of Poland. But I can also assure you that our Republic will do all it can to avoid a conflict.

Hitler: Why do you allow Poland a blank cheque?

Coulondre: The events of last March [Czechoslovakia] have left a deep impression on France and awoken a feeling of insecurity which forced us to forge new coalitions.

Hitler: Concerning the events of last March, it was a matter of honour for the German Reich. As I said, it would sadden me to have to fight your country. But the choice is not mine, please convey this message to your Premier.[4]

Daladier's threat altered only one thing. Hitler had planned

[3] There is an anecdote to the effect that Ribbentrop said one day to Churchill: 'Beware, the Italians are our allies.' 'Good for you,' replied Churchill. 'We had them last time.'

[4] *Livre Jaune Français*, Paris 1939.

to open hostilities against Poland on 26 August, but now he tried to postpone matters.

25 August, 7 p.m. Zossen, forward headquarters of the German forces (OKW). The phone rang. Berlin was on the line.

General Heusinger at OKW: What is the matter?
General Jodl with the Führer: The Führer wishes to know if the movement can be stopped and the troops brought back into their original positions.
Heusinger: Why, what gives?
Jodl: The English once more got involved.
Heusinger: I have to check with General Fellgiebel . . . I'll call back.
Fellgiebel: Have they gone completely mad up there? I cannot command such a large front line like a battalion. Tell those idiots, I will guarantee nothing, especially not along the army wings in Slovakia and East Prussia.
Heusinger to *Jodl*: Perhaps we can hold the centre, but not the army wings.
Jodl: Tell Fellgiebel to try his utmost.

That the troops were called back in time was due to a well-organised, perfectly functioning network of field communications which was to make all the difference at the beginning of the war. It was at this point that many of Hitler's officers got the impression that once more their Führer had bluffed. He had not! In fact, even at this late stage, Hitler still hoped for a way to make England come to an agreement. At a heated meeting, where Hitler threw a tantrum at the mere suggestion that England really wanted peace, he yelled at Göring and Birger Dahlerus, who had offered to leave for London on a final peace mission: '*Ich bin fest entschlossen* . . . I am unconditionally decided to break Polish resistance and to annihilate the Polish nation.

If the English want to negotiate, I'm prepared to listen. But they don't seem to understand that it is in their own interest not to pick a fight with me . . . I'm prepared to do battle with them, even if it takes us ten years.'

There can be no doubt that Hitler took the decision to invade Poland on his own, without consulting his advisers, his government or the German nation. The oft-repeated *Ich* (I) in all his speeches points to his egocentric character: '*Ich habe beschlossen* . . . *I* have decided . . . *I* will conduct this fight . . .' It would be unwise to confound the *Führergewalt* (Hitler's power) with *Staatsgewalt* (state power). It was Hitler, and Hitler alone, who issued the fateful '*Fall Weiss*' (Operation White) order:[5]

> OKW/WFA Nr. 170/39 – *Geheime Kommandosache*
> Para 1: '*Nachdem all politischen Möglichkeiten erschöpft sind, um auf friedlichem Wege eine für Deutschland unerträgliche Lage an seiner Ostgrenze zu beseitigen, habe ich mich zur gewaltsamen Lösung entschlossen* . . . Having failed to achieve a peaceful solution of this unbearable situation on Germany's Eastern border, *I have decided on a forcible action* . . .'
> *Angriffstag* (day of attack): 1 September 1939
> *Angriffszeit* (time of attack): 4.45 *Uhr*
> *(gez)* Adolf Hitler

The die was cast, and Germany cranked up its mighty war machine. Once again, from its headquarters at Zossen, every unit of the Wehrmacht received the order to open hostilities with a mighty bang on 1 September 1939.

26 August. In a final attempt to resolve the crisis with the Western powers, Herman Göring became involved, and with him a new man entered the scene: the Swede Birger

[5] He reconfirmed it on 31 August at 12.40 p.m.

Dahlerus, a friend and close adviser of the Reichsmarschall. Göring collected his friend at his residence and drove to the Reichschancellery just after midnight. Hitler was asleep, but they got him out of bed and held a brief conference. Hitler outlined to Dahlerus six points to be taken to London and the Swede scribbled these on the back of an envelope. In it, the Führer offered England a quick treaty in exchange for Danzig. 'Tell them, a war does not frighten me, they cannot encircle me, I will build U-boats and more U-boats, tell them that my nation adores me and my people will follow me. With your intricate knowledge of England, what is it that bothers the English?'

Hitler's ignorance about Great Britain in general was baffling to the Swedish diplomat, who found that, more than anything else, it was Hitler's inability to understand the English character which led to catastrophe. 'Excellency, their position is founded in the lack of trust in you and your government's statements.'

'Those idiots. Have I ever pronounced a lie?'

Dahlerus left by special plane for London and was almost immediately ushered into 10 Downing Street to meet with Chamberlain and to read him the points on his envelope. While this discussion took place, and Dahlerus was on the phone to Berlin for instructions, the British parliament was in heated discussion over the possibility of an appeasement. Finally, Dahlerus was given an encouraging reply by Lord Halifax. He was back in Berlin by 11 a.m. on 28 August. He carried two important messages: '*Yes*, England is ready to discuss a treaty with Germany. *But* whatever the outcome of these talks, England will stand by the Poles.'

Later that same afternoon, Hitler received Sir Neville Henderson, who had also returned from London on the last English plane to land in the German capital for a long time. He carried a similar reply from Prime Minister Chamberlain. He was received with great pomp by an honour guard with fife and drums on the monumental steps leading to the Reichschancellery, and ushered into the huge marble reception room of Germany's strongman.

Henderson: I wish to state from the outset: Berlin's position that England wishes nothing but the annihilation of Germany is based on completely absurd presumptions. At the same time, London finds it difficult to understand that the German government doubts England's determination to stand by its allies and fight on the side of Poland. Our word has always been our word . . . we offer friendship, but on the basis of a peaceful solution of the Polish question.

Hitler: I'd be willing to deal with a Polish government if there was such a thing. I will be satisfied with nothing less than to settle the Danzig problem.

Henderson: Then you will have to choose between England and Poland . . . you have been offered a corridor, everything else is not for discussion. I beg you to reconsider before you raise the price.

Hitler: I have already made an offer and it was rejected. I will not repeat it.

Henderson: You've put it in the form of an ultimatum. That makes all the difference . . . if you are not willing to make a sacrifice, there is nothing more to discuss.

Hitler, quite angry: I have to follow the will of my people. My army is ready and thirsts for battle. My people are solidly behind me and *I will tolerate no more Polish incidents* . . .

With this phrase one man set the stage. Now it only required 'the incident'.

31 August, 6.30 p.m. The Polish ambassador to Berlin, Josef Lipski, delivered a message to Ribbentrop to the effect that his government was carefully studying the latest German proposal.

Ribbentrop: Do you know that the German government,

upon request by London, has given its understanding to discuss this matter with a Polish plenipotentiary and that we've waited since yesterday noon for his visit?

Lipski: I have not had any instruction to that.

Ribbentrop: Then there is nothing else to discuss between us.[6]

31 August, 9.15 p.m. Ambassador Henderson and the French plenipotentiary, Coulondre, were called to meet with Germany's foreign minister, Joachim von Ribbentrop, at the Foreign Office. Hitler had added ten more points to the original six points presented by Dahlerus in London. He was fully aware that neither the Poles nor their allies would ever be prepared to accept this extension. Ribbentrop read 'Hitler's 16-point suggestion' aloud to both ambassadors: 'Article 1 – Without further delay, Danzig returns into the fold of the German Reich . . .'[7] If the ambassadors still believed in a last-minute miracle, their hopes were now sadly dashed. Hitler wanted war and Hitler always got what he wanted. The German chief interpreter, Dr Paul Schmidt, suddenly realised the full dimensions of the game being played by Hitler and Ribbentrop. Before the ambassadors had a chance to ask further questions, Ribbentrop turned and walked away from them, saying: 'In any case, *this suggestion has already been overtaken by recent events*!'[8]

What was he talking about, and what were these events?

Hitler had made no bones about his *acte provocateur*. During a meeting with Molotov, the German leader made his plans clear: 'Demonstrations can always be produced – and afterwards nobody is any wiser who the real instigator was . . .'[9]

* * *

6 *White Book of Polish Government*, Basel 1940.
7 All other points were a direct follow-up to this demand.
8 P. Schmidt, *Statist auf der diplomatischen Bühne*, Bonn 1949.
9 Ibid.

Midsummer, 1938. SS guest-house Wannsee, near Berlin. The dinner had been delicious, the ladies had withdrawn, and the men had retired to the smoking lounge where cognac was served. The chief of the Reichssicherheitshauptamt (RSHA), Reinhardt Heydrich, better known as the 'Nazi party's evil young god of death', lit a cigarette and blew smoke rings into the air. With the firelight from the chimney carving clefts of shadow on his ascetic face, he said: 'We live in unconventional times, and must adapt ourselves . . .' His voice drifted off and he stared after his smoke rings. 'What kind of an operation do you have in mind?'

'Something spectacular and significant.' Reichsführer SS Heinrich Himmler spoke in a low, schoolmasterly voice. 'You make any arrangements you deem necessary. I take full responsibility before God and the Führer.' How generous of him, Heydrich probably thought – he takes the responsibility, but for what? Success, or failure? Heydrich, who many called the 'half-Jew', despised his superior for his prissiness. Himmler's eyes were glazed behind his pince-nez. With his pinched face, sparse hair and paunch he hardly matched the Führer's ideal of a Germanic hero figure. Himmler rattled on: 'You will have every opportunity to familiarise yourself with the problem, but the general outline is, it has to look highly provocative. It is essential that proof be ruthlessly established. Once the German population is more frightened of the enemy than of going to war, our Führer will have achieved his objective.'

Hitler was beset by a profound hatred for anything Slavic.[10] That he had expanded his plan into the arena of political action had not really surprised Heydrich. This was necessary. Heydrich didn't express his feelings; he never did. He just looked at his boss and nodded.

'I was sure you'd see it my way,' said Himmler. 'We've

[10] J. W. Borejsza, *Antyslawizm Adolfa Hitlera* (Adolf Hitler's Antislavism), Warsaw 1988.

had the benefit of good advice from some highly experienced people. Of course, you will need someone you can trust.'

Heydrich had got to know his chief's way of thinking only too well. 'Of course – and he will be expendable,' he replied. They hadn't needed to apply this stratagem during the invasion of Czechoslovakia; there they had just walked across the border. But Poland was a different problem. Bigger and more complex. Heydrich recalled last summer's conversation. Stir up anti-Slav feelings, give the German nation something that bound them together, then serve it up as the cement to hold all of western Europe under Germany's rule. 'The world will swarm with pro-German sentiments and follow us blindly,' Goebbels had said. Most countries abounded with anti-Slav, pro-Nazi movements; they considered anyone east of the Oder as nothing but the miserable leftovers of the Huns.

No, it wasn't difficult to produce a reason for an invasion. The Nazis were well versed in that sort of operation – after all, they had set fire to the German Reichstag building to serve their specific needs. For months, provocative acts by members of the SD had been committed at the German customs posts of Hohenlinde, Pfalzdorf and Geyersdorf. The Amt VI in the SS Reichssicherheitshauptamt (Heydrich) under Brigadeführer Heinz Jost planned and executed over two hundred such minor provocations. But this next one was to be big enough to unite public opinion in support of the Führer's directives 'to shoot back'. Speed was essential – the RSHA didn't even bother to plan an operation that would stand up to international scrutiny. In any case, that wasn't needed. The Nazis didn't care about the world's reaction; what counted was for Hitler to justify himself before his German nation.

The overall command of the operation was handed to Heydrich, a paragon of intrigue. In the next few days he drew up a plan and picked its executioner. The scheme was simple: fake an attack by regular Polish troops across the upper Silesian border. The Abwehr (the counter-espionage department under Admiral Canaris) was ordered to provide 150 Polish Army uniforms. Lt-Col. Helmut Groscurth, in charge of Abwehr procurement, wrote: 'The provocation for war will be supplied by 150 inmates from the Konzentrationslager (KZ); they will be dressed up in Polish uniforms and sacrificed. That is the job of Heydrich.'[11]

For what was to become the overture to the big drama, Heydrich selected two main players, Heinrich Müller, his chief of the Gestapo (secret police), and Alfred Naujocks of his SD (Sicherheitsdienst). Plus a dozen bit players to be wasted – specially selected KZ inmates in Polish Army garb. They would be 'shot while illegally crossing the border into Germany'. These bodies, supplied by Müller to the SD Sonderkommando, were given the cynical codename of '*Konserve*' (tinned meat).

'Alfred Helmut Naujocks, born in Kiel, son of a grocer, joined the SS in 1931 and was seconded to Sicherheitsdienst since its creation,' read SD general Reinhardt Heydrich, sitting in an enormous Berlin office hung with red, white and black banners and a giant portrait of the Führer. He looked up at the man standing to attention before him. Naujocks had already proven his immense value when he mounted 'Operation Tukhachevski', which drowned the entire Soviet military high command under its leader, Marshal Tukhachevski, in a Stalinist orgy of blood. Now the same Naujocks, who knew how to temper his fanatical belief in Nazism with great lucidity, had been picked for an even more difficult task: to start a war! Although he didn't like him at all, Heydrich knew that Naujocks was the indispensable man for the job.

Heydrich allowed himself almost a smile, albeit a grim one. 'Alfred,' he said, addressing him on a first-name basis to get the man's full attention, 'Alfred, I've got something for you, which is in your line, almost as if it was designed for you.'

[11] H. Groscurth, *Tagebuch eines Abwehroffiziers*, Stuttgart 1970.

He opened a folder: '*Geheime Staatssache*'. 'The importance of the mission pales beside anything you may have ever done, or even heard of. It is a commando raid – and the Führer's political and military decisions depend entirely on its positive outcome. Have I made myself clear?'[12]

'*Jawohl.*' Naujocks was trying to digest what he had just been told.

'You understand that failure cannot be tolerated.'

'*Verstanden!* I understand.'

'Good.' A slight pause. 'It is Poland. The war starts next week. We need an incident.'

Naujocks just nodded; he had understood. It was his role to provide the motive.

'There have been a number of incidents along the German–Polish border. All minor. This has to change. You are going to light the fuse.' With this, Heydrich got up from his desk, picked up a red pencil, walked to the wall map and circled a place name: Gleiwitz.

'Gleiwitz is in Germany, just across the border. The place is of no importance other than it has a radio transmitter linked to the Deutschlandfunk. Now, let us assume that Polish troops were to attack this radio station and then transmit a message, insulting our Führer and promising an attack on everything that is German in Danzig, that would be a serious provocation.'

Naujocks stared into the sharp, dark features and ice-blue eyes of a man he would never be allowed to forget – a face he saw often in the bad dreams that filled tormented nights. He knew well enough where Heydrich was leading. 'Especially if the Deutschlandfunk were to pick up the transmission and dispatch it over its network across Germany.' He paused for a moment. 'It will add impact if a few bodies were to be found . . .'

Naujocks was petrified. The realisation that he had become

12 From transcripts of Naujocks' Nuremberg trial on 20 November 1945.

involved in something of such incredible magnitude struck like a bolt of lightning. The significance of the task – to provoke a war! He hardly heard Heydrich's final phrase: 'You are not given a choice, of course. The decision is not yours to make. You are ordered to do it! And you will not fail.'

'I will try.'

'Oh no, you will do better than that.'

Both men were feeling the strain. They had been told to solve a problem and theirs was now an alliance that would become vitally important for *Führer und Vaterland*. After swearing to keep the plan secret, Naujocks gave a Nazi salute and marched from the office to put the scheme into action.[13]

Naujocks assembled his crew. Four of them he chose himself; Heydrich sent two: Karl, a radio technician, to facilitate the radio broadcast, and Heinrich, who spoke Polish, to read it. Six men, plus sundry corpses . . . Sonderkommando Naujocks.

Six men checked into the Hotel Oberschlesischer Hof in Gleiwitz. It wasn't much of a hotel, but then Gleiwitz wasn't much of a town. They signed the hotel register under the aegis of a geological research team. Naujocks took pains to check the guest list and found it to contain mostly workers in essential services and minor Nazi politicians. Although the place was close to the border, there was a conspicuous absence of foreigners. For the next days the team scouted the town and 'collected earth samples'. Most of their digging was done around the tall, soot-smudged building of the local radio station. Naujocks left only once to meet Müller in nearby Oppeln to arrange for delivery of the '*Konserve*'. He was assured by Müller that a selection of suitable victims had already been lined up.

'How many?' asked Naujocks.

[13] G. Peis, *The Man Who Started the War*, London 1960.

'One is plenty, and you'll have the *Konserve* at the time you need him,' replied Müller, a Gestapo brute who assisted frequently in the medieval torture of prisoners by his henchmen, and who copied Heydrich's dry, nasal voice. It made him feel important. 'This is what I shall do for you. Two minutes after the start of your operation, a black Opel will pass before the entrance of the radio station. I will be in it and will personally deposit a body. He'll be dressed up as a Polish soldier. By the way, you have never seen me.' This sinister killer neither looked nor acted like a madman. He was quite rational about killing.

'And who will that body be?'

'Don't worry about that, the *Konserve* has already been picked,' replied Müller, ever the efficient provider.

31 August, 4 p.m. Room seven in the Oberschlesischer Hof. The room was crowded and the air stale with cigarette smoke. They could feel the excitement; a heightening of perception that led to fear, to apprehension. They all felt a sudden chill and tried to envisage how the day would end. If they failed . . . they didn't even want to consider that. Despite the heat, the windows were tightly shut. They were six – three sitting on the bed, two on chairs, plus Naujocks, with his back to the window. This ordinarily steely-eyed man wore the same expression of suppressed anxiety on his face as all the rest. The electricity of the moment passed from him into the others. 'I've just received the go signal. Tonight at nineteen-thirty precisely.' The loudness of his own voice surprised him. 'We move into the station, neutralise the staff, and remember, you shoot anyone who puts himself in your way. No questions asked, just shoot. We are Polish terrorists and are expected to act as such. Karl and Heinrich will stick with me. Heinrich, here's your text.' He handed a few stapled sheets of paper to the newsreader. 'Make sure you know it, there will be no mistakes on the air.' He thought back to when he was still in training. *Well planned is well executed*, the instructors in boot

camp had pumped into him. But nothing ever goes according to plan. '*Verstanden?*' he asked. Everyone nodded. 'Oh, and one final thing: don't get caught, shoot your way out – or shoot yourself!' He didn't need to outline the consequences for anyone caught; Müller's Gestapo clean-up squad would eliminate the unfortunate man. Naujocks was nervous; sweat was running down inside his shirt. He had always told his crew that their chances of success were excellent. He only wished he believed it himself. There were bigger minds at work, all the way up to Hitler, and he was only a small cog in the whole – but the explosive cog! This late in the game it would take an earthquake to stop them.

The 'geological survey vehicles', two black Fords, left the hotel at 6.30 p.m. They drove out of town and into the nearby forest, where they pulled up in a clearing. The wood surrounding them was dark and forbidding, without a sound; even the animals seemed to be asleep. There was another hour before the action was to begin. Naujocks got out of the car and paced nervously on the soft, leaf-covered ground. He was deep in thought, adrenaline pumping through his veins. He had registered what he had been told . . . that he must perform exceptional feats. He was overjoyed. In Heydrich he had found a commander who obviously appreciated his special qualities. Yes, he would do his duty and this would lead to promotion – perhaps he would become a SS colonel. No, he wouldn't allow anyone to stand in his way . . .

They changed into Polish Army uniforms and armed themselves with guns. The uniforms didn't fit, but that was of no importance. One of the suitcases contained a radio. Karl, the radio specialist, clamped on the earphones to listen to Müller's countdown: 19.25, 19.26, 19.27. 'Go!' he yelled, and the cars raced from the woods. Three minutes – they had timed it precisely. Three minutes and the dark building loomed before them. The cars skidded to a stop. Six steps led up to a glass door. Naujocks was running ahead; right behind him were Karl and Heinrich. From the end of the hallway appeared a guard in blue uniform. Heinrich jumped him and bashed his head against the wall. The man slid to the ground without giving a sound. Karl stood around, motionless, the pistol shaking in his hand. His eyes were darting from side to side and his body was trembling. Panic had seized him. It was a critical moment. 'Move, you stupid bastard! Move!' The moment of indecision was gone and Karl barrelled up the main staircase. The surprise was total. Naujocks burst through a door and found a man sitting behind a desk. Naujocks' pistol whipped him over the back of his head and the man pitched forward, splattering blood on the notes for next morning's local newscast. Naujocks pivoted around with the pistol levelled in front of him. While the rest of the group raced off to neutralise the remaining staff, Heinrich and Naujocks sprinted towards the radio studio to join up with Karl, who was already behind the thick glass panel of the transmitting room. A bout of frustration awaited him in the dimly lit space, where Karl was studying the control panel. Confusion showed on his face as he stared at a row of switches. Which was the one that plugged into the wavelength of the Deutschlandfunk transmitter of Radio Breslau? '*Scheisse* . . .' Karl fumbled with relays. A high, piercing sound filled his earphones. All he was getting was static over the entire spectrum of the radio band! He grabbed, almost blindly, for buttons and switched to alternative channels, but they were filled only with more static.

'What's the matter?' fumed Naujocks, looking out of the window for activity outside the building. He saw none. The town was quiet, but wouldn't be for much longer.

A curse came from the man at the switching panel. '*Die Verbindung* . . . the connection, I cannot locate the switch . . .'

'What switch?'

'The one that opens the main channel to Breslau . . .'

'Find it . . . you must find it! I thought you knew your job . . .' yelled a riled Naujocks. An image of total disaster filled his brain and nearly numbed him. Everything depended on that broadcast – his future, his career, even his life.

'I know my job, but I must find the switch . . .' Panic was building. No broadcast was equal to total failure.

Heinrich waved the pages of his text frantically. 'When do I start?'

'Wait, we've got a problem . . .'

'Cannot find it . . .' fumed Karl.

'Can you go out on a local channel?'

'Yes. But it's strictly local, it won't be captured beyond this town . . .'

'Do it!' Naujocks tried to sound calm. His heart pounded in his chest from excitement. He looked past Karl and out into the open hallway. He hadn't counted on a stupid technical problem caused by a stupid radio technician who didn't know his bloody job! Nobody had. If they couldn't get the message on the air, and soon, the local police might come and there would be some real shooting. Something had to be saved from the disaster. That's when Karl yelled: 'The line to Breslau is open . . .' Naujocks signalled frantically through the partition glass to Heinrich: 'Ready? Scream, make it sound like total panic, I'll fire off a few shots . . .' before he raced into the newscaster's room. Heinrich, white as a sheet and under great stress, didn't have to be told to behave in a panicky fashion. He screamed into the microphone at the top of his voice . . . '*Danzig ist für immer polnisch* . . . Danzig is Polish for ever . . . Wrozlav [Breslau] is Polish . . .' A deafening burst flamed from the muzzle of Naujocks' automatic and slammed into the ceiling, dusting both with plaster. Heinrich broke off as Naujocks fired the shots before again finding his voice. '. . . *Hitler ist ein schäbiger Verbrecher* . . . Hitler is an evil gangster . . .' He kept reading his text while his eyes smarted from the powder fumes in the confined room. Certainly somebody must've heard the shots and was on their way to notify the police. 'Everybody out of here . . .' Naujocks yelled. They raced downstairs and nearly stumbled over a body that lay crumpled up just inside the door. Müller had delivered his '*Konserve*', blood-smeared and dying. He was Sonderkommando Naujocks' 'seventh man'.[14]

For a moment, Alfred Naujocks found himself staring down at the corpse before he and his gang sped out into the night. In front of them was the square, stretching out into darkness . . .

On this night, people across Germany made love or got drunk or did whatever they did any other night, before they stumbled into their beds. Only a few sat in front of their *Volksempfänger*, a radio that was designed specially to bring every good German citizen close to his Führer's voice. Those who did were privileged to listen to a broadcast of a highly inflammatory nature about their sacred Führer being a gangster, a killer, and the fact that Poles were about to cross the border in order to help their nationals held prisoner in Danzig, before a shocked technician in Breslau threw the switch: '*Wir unterbrechen dieses Programm* . . . we interrupt this programme . . .', the usual announcement to prepare the population for the worst. Minutes later, this was followed by a German newscast about the barbaric treatment of ethnic Germans, describing in great detail the rape of Aryan maidens by Poles and Jews in the German Corridor (it wasn't yet German!).

Within the hour, the Führer was advised of 'the murder of innocent Germans in a raid by Polish terrorists on a German radio station'. This was his 'first good news of the day'. The door was now open for his plans. He knew Russia would not oppose him since Stalin was happy with the concession he had made. He went to bed. When he woke up, Germany was at war.

* * *

14 Statement given by Naujocks before the Allied Commission on War Crimes, 20 November 1945.

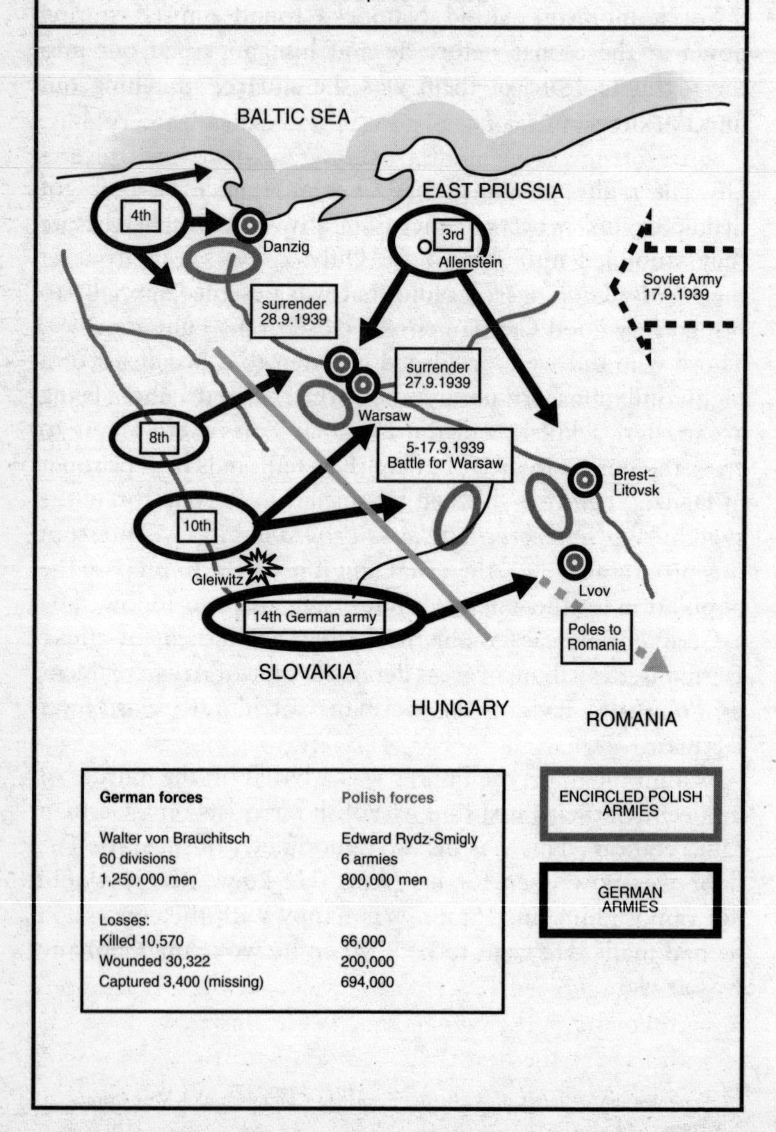
Battle of Poland
1–28 September 1939
BALTIC SEA
EAST PRUSSIA
4th
Danzig
3rd
Allenstein
Soviet Army
17.9.1939
surrender
28.9.1939
surrender
27.9.1939
Warsaw
8th
5-17.9.1939
Battle for Warsaw
Brest-
Litovsk
10th
Gleiwitz
Lvov
14th German army
Poles to
Romania
SLOVAKIA
HUNGARY
ROMANIA
German forces
Polish forces
Walter von Brauchitsch
Edward Rydz-Smigly
60 divisions
6 armies
1,250,000 men
800,000 men
Losses:
Killed 10,570
66,000
Wounded 30,322
200,000
Captured 3,400 (missing)
694,000
ENCIRCLED POLISH
ARMIES
GERMAN
ARMIES

1 September 1939. At 4.45 a.m. German forces crossed the border into Poland without a declaration of war. The German battle-cruiser *Schleswig Holstein* opened the hostilities by firing at point-blank range with its mighty twin-turret cannon at the Polish defences of the Westerplatte, straddling the approaches to Danzig. The earthen bulwarks crumpled and hundreds of Polish soldiers were buried beneath the rubble.

A terrorising level of destruction rained down from the air. The streets of Polish cities were turned into scenes of hell, people screaming and running in all directions while Stukas made strafing runs over people fleeing before the advancing German columns. The Luftwaffe inflicted heavy civilian casualties. A mother sat in the rubble, amidst the lifeless torn bodies of her entire family, cradling a child and rocking it back and forth until all signs of life had left it. She kissed its bloody head, then lay down and waited for the end. The horror of it all was shattering, a sickening vision of what modern weapons could – and would – do to human bodies.

In Berlin, 1 September dawned with a fine drizzle. The German nation woke up to its first day of a war that was to last five years and end in a sea of blood. At 10 a.m., speaking from Berlin's Kroll Opera House, his voice relayed around the globe by Germany's overseas transmitters, Hitler addressed his nation:

> *Ich habe mich nun entschlossen, mit Polen in der gleichen Sprache zu reden, die Polen gegenüber uns anwendet! Polen hat nun heute nacht zum ersten Mal auf unserem eigenen Territorium auch durch regelrechte Soldaten geschossen. Seit heute früh 5.45 wird jetzt zurückgeschossen!* . . . I have now decided to speak with Poland in the same language they have been using with us. For the first time, *Poland has used its regular soldiers to shoot on our own territory. Since 5.45 this morning, we are shooting back!*

And his fanatical followers broke out in patriotic cheers and roared in thunderous unison: '*Sieg Heil! Sieg Heil! Sieg Heil!*' That day, 1 September 1939, Germany turned into a mad carnival procession willing to follow a despot on the road to a holocaust.

Ein Volk – Ein Reich – Ein Führer! And the lamps went out all over Europe.[15]

'Ghengis Khan with a panzer' was on the move . . .

The facts

'A war, waged in defiance of every ethical consideration, can never be won. There is still a divine justice made manifest on this Earth.'

The man who wrote these lines was none other than Hitler's chief of espionage, Admiral Wilhelm Canaris, shot on Hitler's orders one month before the end of the war.[16]

The 'Polish Blitzkrieg' was an unprecedented success in modern warfare. Hitler's generals called it the 'War of 18 Days'. The key to the tragedy lay in the lightning penetration by German panzer forces into Poland. They progressed like a knife through butter. The Germans cut up the Polish Army in ten days with tank–plane teams operating under ideal conditions of weather and terrain.[17] There was little in the way of natural barriers to stop the German push, and the Poles were never given the time to recover. A Soviet invasion on 17 September, in conformity with the Nazi–Soviet agreement, dashed the Poles' final hopes. (The Russians' poor showing in the early stages was due to political miscalculation, but left Hitler with a false impression of the Red Army's capabilities.)

[15] A phrase used by Foreign Secretary Viscount Grey in 1914.
[16] Canaris was executed on 9 April 1945.
[17] The losses: Germans 10,000, Poles 66,000.

Russia went on to occupy her share of Poland.

For the first time, Hitler, and his propaganda minister, Josef Goebbels, employed a psychological weapon – filmed propaganda. Hundreds of cameramen documented scores of victories to convince the world of Hitler's military genius and the invincibility of German armies.

Seven hundred thousand Polish POWs started on their long march into German camps. SS gangs began a systematic recruitment of forced labour for Germany's war industry and the ruthless execution of hostages, political enemies and Jews.[18]

Despite his overwhelming military triumph, Hitler didn't achieve what he wanted most: a political victory with peace forced on the Allies.[19] This time, the English–French alliance didn't flinch; they took the menace quite seriously. They were left with a painful decision. But Churchill remained adamant. England simply wrote off Poland and refused to come to the negotiating table, demanding Hitler's abdication: 'There can be no peace as long as the Hitler regime is not eliminated.' What made London and Paris think that the much-heralded victor of a blitzkrieg would step down from his pedestal? By issuing this demand, the Allies practically forced Hitler into an attack against the West and France, and with it both sides were well launched on the path towards all-out global conflict.

The Western Allies saw little hope for Poland, but hoped that her resistance might give them up to six months to prepare, and perhaps even blunt Germany's striking power. Poland's fate, they concluded, would depend on the ultimate outcome of the war. They were wrong in both respects –

[18] In 1939, the Jewish population of Poland was 3.74 million, or 10 per cent of the total population. Compared to this figure, the Jews of Germany made up only 0.7 per cent.

[19] Not all Germans supported Hitler's radical views. One, Count Fritz-Dietlof von der Schulenburg, the first President of the new Silesia, was soon so upset by the brutality of SS and Gestapo squads that he became a ferocious anti-Nazi.

the Polish campaign lasted three weeks and Russia had the final say.

In the East, Russia's foreign minister, Molotov, announced in a speech before the Supreme Soviet that the real instigators of the Polish drama were the imperialists of England and France. Russia speedily annexed 196,000 square kilometres with their 13,000,000 Poles. Neither England nor France protested. The League of Nations kept its usual silence. That encouraged Russia to incorporate another 165,000 square kilometres of Latvia, Estonia and Lithuania, with 5.5 million inhabitants. Stalin's NKVD killer squads, who shot 14,000 Polish officers in cold blood in the forests of Katyn, accomplished the final destruction of the Polish Army.

Poland disappeared from the map – *Finis Poloniae!* In this, Poland's allies played a shabby role. While German strategy was based on the blitzkrieg, England and France practised a 'Sitzkrieg' (sitting down and doing nothing). Germany's defences on the Rhine were stripped bare; had the Allies struck there and then, and the Wehrmacht suffered an initial setback, Hitler might have changed his mind. But they didn't. From Poland, Hitler marched with flying colours to another world war. The world woke up to the sobering realisation that it was once again in the midst of a madness from which it had escaped only twenty years before . . .

In a sense, the Gleiwitz Caper was a failure, since the transmission never did go out the way it had been intended by Hitler and planned by Heydrich. The provocative address failed to make the national radio network; it never reached the international short waves. Only some confused sentences were broadcast on a local radio waveband that couldn't be picked up far beyond Gleiwitz. But for Hitler that was sufficient. Naujocks' *acte provocateur* provided Germany's dictator with the moral justification to announce to the world his invasion of Poland, and in that sense the act of terrorism fully achieved its intended purpose.

'*Das Einzige, was man aus der Geschichte lernen kann, ist, dass die Menschen aus ihr niemals etwas gelernt haben* . . . The only thing which history teaches us is that humanity never learns from history,' wrote the philosopher Heinrich von Sybel.

Gleiwitz proved that if a dictator needs a pretext, a dictator always gets what he wants.

The Hinge factor at Gleiwitz wasn't a monumental battle, but more of a bank hold-up – six gangsters and one corpse.

But it was important to history, as it supplied a dictator with his fig leaf before world opinion, the 'moral grounds' on which to tell his people: 'Since this morning we are shooting back!' From that moment on, nothing – but nothing – could halt the frenzy with which the nations of the world marched to the cataclysmic funeral pyre they had built with their own hands.

Gleiwitz brought about a monstrous holocaust and the end of Poland.

8

All Warfare Is Based on Deception

19 November 1942 –
Stalin's Secret Army at Stalingrad

> 'All warfare is based on deception.
> Hence when we are able to attack, we must seem unable.'
> Sun Tsu, *Military Writings*, 500 BC

> '*Gehorsam ist ein Prinzip, aber über dem Prinzip steht der Mann.*
> Obedience is a principle, but above the principle stands the man.'
> General von Moltke, 1871

'*Shto novovo?* What's new?' asked the man in the plain ochre uniform, bereft of any sign of rank, as he stuffed a wad of Golden Fleece tobacco into his curved pipe and lit it. He walked to a huge wall map covered with small flags which showed the present front line and stabbed the pipe at a precise point where the Volga turned sharply from a southerly to an easterly direction. 'What's new – here?' The stem of the pipe pointed at a town that had been named after him: Stalingrad.

Thousands of miles away, a man in a pin-stripe suit, inhaling smoke through a cigarette holder, posed a similar question to his adviser, Harry Hopkins. Then, in the unique manner of personal relationships between world leaders, President Franklin D. Roosevelt scribbled a message to Josef Stalin: 'I HAVE IN MIND A SIGNIFICANT MILITARY PROPOSAL INVOLVING OUR ARMED FORCES. PLEASE SEND MR MOLOTOV TO LONDON. WE SHALL SEND YOU A SAFE PLANE. TIME IS OF IMPORTANCE IF WE ARE TO HELP IN AN IMPORTANT WAY.'

Stalin, his usual suspicious self, wondered: What was the American up to? Was he proposing opening a Second Front or was he once again trying to draw his attention away from it? And why offer to fly Molotov out on an American plane? Stalin had an inborn mistrust of the good intentions of his allies and refused to respond immediately. He went into a lengthy discussion with his number-one adviser, a grey man in a grey suit with a grey moustache who blended perfectly into the wallpaper. But appearances can be deceptive. Mr *Nyet*, Vyacheslav Molotov, was anything but grey and naïve. In 1939 he had aptly persuaded Hitler to sign the German–Russian non-aggression pact; at the time, Russia wasn't ready to confront Germany's war machine. And now once again, Molotov was to play his dubious role. When Stalin finally did reply to Roosevelt's offer, it was only to announce that: 'UNCERTAIN WEATHER CONDITIONS ARE POSTPONING MR MOLOTOV'S PROPOSED LONDON TRIP.'

Stalin continued to deceive his allies. It began when Marshal Timoshenko's army became encircled near Kharkov and cried for help. Nikita Krushchev, the political commissar on Timoshenko's military staff, wrote an urgent appeal for assistance. Stalin's reply sounded desperate – and then he made quite certain that a copy of his reply was leaked to his Western allies: '*WE HAVE NO RESERVE DIVISION READY FOR COMBAT.* THERE ARE OTHER FRONTS TO THINK OF BESIDE YOURS. OUR RESOURCES IN MEN AND EQUIPMENT ARE LIMITED . . .'[1] It was a blatant lie. Stalin could call up strategic reserves, and quite

[1] S. Shtemenko, *General Shtemenko Notes from Stavka*, Ministry of Defence Papers, Moscow 1968.

a few, but he didn't want anyone to find out, and certainly not his allies Churchill and Roosevelt. It was Stalin's master plan for a deception on a gigantic scale.

It seemed that the flying weather had finally improved when, on 20 May 1942, thirty-eight days after having received Roosevelt's invitation, Stalin dispatched Molotov to London, but on a Russian plane. He had waited impatiently for the final piece of his master plan to fall into place, and now that it had Molotov could meet with Churchill and complete the deception.

At the Oberkommando der Wehrmacht (OKW), Hitler's Supreme HQ, the *Wolfschanze* (wolf's lair) hidden in the dense forest near Rastenburg in East Prussia, the Chief-of-Staff of OKH (Oberkommando Heer), Generaloberst Halder, was preparing notes for the *Führer Lagebesprechung* (Hitler's daily situation briefing). To obtain the latest estimates of enemy movements, Halder was in conference with Oberstleutnant Reinhard Gehlen, the newly appointed Head of Army Intelligence for the Eastern Front. Halder checked his intelligence officer's briefing notes. 'What is your reading, Gehlen? Is Stalin finished?'

'Far from it, General. He has hidden reserves.'

'Confirmed?'

'Not confirmed – but on paper we're missing nearly two million men from the enemy line-up. They must be somewhere.'

'Explain, please.'

'Well, it's all a simple matter of numbers. We know of an initial Russian call-up of seventeen million men. Up to this point, the enemy has lost seven and a half million in dead, wounded or POWs, and another 450,000 in the winter war against Finland [1939–40]. He's got as of this moment six million deployed in the army, one and a half million in the air force and about 300,000 in his navy. That leaves 1.7 million to be accounted for. Where are they?'

Generaloberst Halder frowned. 'If that is true, then ...

what is Foreign Army East's[2] estimate of Soviet reserve strength?'

'We cannot come up with an exact number for Stalin's reserve divisions, we can only surmise that they are massive.'

'What do you call massive? Be more specific.'

'At least forty – possibly as many as sixty divisions.'

'Sixty divisions! We'd better inform Hitler.'[3]

'I wouldn't do that, Herr Generaloberst.' Halder was well aware of the danger of mentioning anything of that sort to Hitler. Oberstleutnant Gehlen's predecessor, Oberst Eberhard Kinzel of Foreign Army East, had dared to disagree only once with Germany's self-proclaimed military genius, and for such an offence he was sacked and put into an active unit in General von Paulus's 6th Army.[4] When Hitler insisted that Stalin was finished, Kinzel had tried to point out to him that Stalin was forming a new army east of the Volga. He had called for caution, but Hitler was allergic to those who dissented from his divine inspirations.

'The Führer won't believe you,' Gehlen warned Halder. 'Things are going too well for him right now.' Indeed they were. The German panzer spearhead was pushing irresistibly towards the Don. From there it would speed across the narrow land bridge to the Volga, cross that last water barrier and fan out into Russia's vulnerable hinterlands, catching Stalin from the rear. Nothing could stop the German Army now. The final barricade where the Russians could make a stand was an industrial town on the Volga named Stalingrad. But towns had never presented much of an obstacle; the Wehrmacht had overrun much bigger cities, like Kiev.

'*Herrgott*, don't you see? If your estimates are anywhere

[2] German army intelligence, Eastern Front.

[3] A. Hillgruber, *Kriegstagebuch des OKW 1940–1945*, quotes Gehlen on 28 June 1942: '*die vermutliche Stärke* . . . the estimated strength of the Soviet Russian Army at the beginning of winter 1942 is forty reserve divisions . . .'

[4] 29th Army Corps, 6th Army.

near correct . . . our genius is sending our men straight into disaster.'[5]

Halder tried to give his leader a hint, but Hitler wouldn't listen. He never did. Yet confirmation of the Russian build-up was readily available from an independent informant. A 'deep Swedish source' had told Col. Kinzel that Stalin held at least thirty-nine divisions in readiness east of the Volga, poised to bounce on Hitler's Don advance. This relevant secret message was handed to the OKW as early as 1 May 1942.

At the same time, Propagandaminister Joseph Goebbels arranged a leak. A trusted journalist, Dr Otto Kriegk, was dispatched to ostensibly report on the progress of German troops on the Eastern Front, after which he was sent to Lisbon for 'general reporting'. There he got drunk in a bar and in his (pretended) alcoholic stupor disclosed that the German High Command was planning its major '42 offensive in Russia's central sector, aimed at Moscow,[6] an option not even discussed by Hitler's generals. The main objective was the Caucasus and its vast oil reserves, vital to keep Germany's war machine running. On 5 April 1942, Hitler issued General Order 41: '. . . THE VITAL OPERATION FOR THE YEAR WILL BE THE ATTACK INTO THE SOUTHERN SECTOR TO REACH THE OIL WELLS [Baku], AND SMASH THE REMAINING SOVIET FORCES.'

Generaloberst Friedrich von Paulus of the 6th Army sat stiffly in the back seat of his open car. To appear normal cost him dearly. He mustn't allow his worries to show and thereby infect his staff. His assigned duty was to be their general and a leader of nearly half a million men. Whether or not he liked the present situation was irrelevant. The wellbeing of his army and its fighting spirit were the responsibility of a general. If an army failed, for whatever the reason, be it

[5] R. Gehlen, *The Service. The Memoirs of General Reinhard Gehlen* (transl. D. Irving), NY 1972; F. Halder, *Generaloberst Halder, Kriegstagebuch*, Stuttgart 1964.
[6] J. Goebbels, *The Goebbels Diaries* (trans. L. Lochner), NY 1948.

by *force majeure*, human error or an encounter with an overpowering enemy, all responsibility rested on a general's shoulders. Paulus's situation was complicated by the fact that he was an experienced military man who had to obey the orders of a megalomaniac politician, and unquestionably so. Sometimes it was difficult for a German aristocrat and professional officer to obey the orders of a former corporal. But von Paulus was a man steeped in the age-old Prussian military tradition of blind obedience, laid down by his oath to the Nazi Party leader as head of Germany's armed forces. Paulus knew that his new command of the 6th German Army was a no-win situation. Should the outcome of the battle prove positive, Hitler would achieve fame; but he would bear all the blame should things go wrong.

Seventy-four of Germany's 217 divisions operating along the German–Soviet front were ordered to prepare a spring offensive against Stalin's southern front and push across the Don and Volga rivers. One million men, thousands of panzers and 1,600 aircraft were all headed for a rendezvous with history at a town called Stalingrad. Stalin was informed of Hitler's plan thanks to a ferociously anti-Nazi major on the German general staff. This forced Stalin into a panic option; he ordered his South-west Front into an immediate counterstrike (12 May 1942). The South-western Group of Soviet Armies under Marshal Simeon Timoshenko was responsible for the defence of the entire front line from Kursk to the Black Sea. With three armies, Timoshenko launched an offensive near Kharkov, badly planned and even more badly executed. The Russians attacked without flank protection and without reserves. The Germans struck back (17 May) and within a week Timoshenko's Russians had been smashed and three armies annihilated. The remainders of the Soviets' 6th Army under Gen. Lt Gorodnjanskij, the 57th of Gen. Lt Podlas and the 9th of Gen. Maj. Charitonov, altogether 240,000 officers and men, marched into German captivity; 1,249 tanks and 2,026 guns were captured or destroyed. This débâcle stripped Stalin's south-western sector of any viable defence and proved the decisive factor in the forthcoming German push over the Don and towards the Volga. Despite continuous reverses, the Red Army was not smashed. In a series of cleverly executed manoeuvres, the remnants of many divisions withdrew, as had their forebears 150 years ago before the might of Napoleon's *Grande Armée*. The result was that the enemy was sucked ever deeper into the immensity of Russia. Encouraged by its victory, Generaloberst von Kleist's Army Group A launched an attack towards the Caucasus. They were helped by a mutiny that broke out in General Lvov's Kuban Cossack division, assigned to block a vital road bottleneck. Once another Russian force had managed to stabilise the front, the 15,000 officers and men of the mutinous Cossack division were lined up and every third one was shot.

On 23 July, Hitler once more changed his mind. In the firm belief that the Russians were finished, his new General Order 45 called for the main strike to be delivered against Stalingrad. Generaloberst von Paulus's 6th Army and General Hoth's 4th Panzer Army were ordered to swing towards the industrial centre on the Volga. Within days, a copy of this order was relayed to Stalin via his Soviet spy inside the German OKW. On 28 July, the Soviet supremo issued the order: 'STALINGRAD MUST BE HELD. NOT A SINGLE STEP BACK.'

On 31 July the German panzers attacked on the Don river.

Inside the peasant hut, the general and his staff officers pored over maps. A Fieseler Storch scout plane circled the hamlet and settled on a dirt road. It had holes in its wings and was leaking petrol like a sieve. As the propeller stopped, the aerial observer jumped from the cockpit and came on the double towards the group of men who had gathered outside the makeshift HQ of Germany's 6th Army.

'What is it?' asked the officer standing next to the one with the red stripes running down his trousers.

'Scattered artillery fire and farther to the east some motorised columns moving about, but nothing heading in this direction. Along the riverbank only holding companies.'

'Is that where you got shot up?' asked the colonel.

'*Jawohl,* Herr Oberst, we came down to have a closer look and that's where they almost got us.'

'And you are quite certain nothing headed our way?'

'*Ohne Zweifel* . . . without doubt, nothing in this direction.'

The Oberst turned to the Generaloberst to make his report, before turning back to the aerial observer. 'That is not possible.'

The airman stuck to his guns. 'Well, Herr Oberst, then please tell the Herr Generaloberst, I shall be pleased to take him up so he can have a look for himself.'

'That will not be necessary. You'd better get your machine patched up, we shall need you up again within the hour.'

The 6th Army's leader was worried. He had counted on heavy resistance, and now he was being told there was no enemy ahead of his army. Something was wrong. Either previous reports of enemy concentrations were exaggerated, or they were where he least expected them, ready to pounce on his stretched-out units. He wanted the enemy quickly brought to battle and utterly defeated in order to have an open road into the city that lay within his grasp.

'Get General Hoth at 4th Panzers on the line,' ordered the army general. 'Hoth . . . Paulus here . . . yes . . . yes . . . we're moving out.'

He turned to his ADC, Oberst Schmidt: 'How far are they with the bridging operation? Make sure the Pioneers get the pontoon bridges across as soon as the infantry secures a bridgehead. We need the armour to give full support to our advancing infantry. We must break out from the bridgehead and move fast in an easterly direction. That is our present objective.' With that, General von Paulus, head of Germany's 6th Army, stabbed at a point on the map. Stalingrad.

Dust-covered figures rose all along the front line. From a distance came the thunder of heavy howitzers. A Russian observer plane was chased by a brace of Messerschmidts before it curved down in flames. Its pilot tried to eject, but the cords of his parachute got caught in the plane's tail fin. Hauptmann Hubschmidt's 3rd Company of Pioneers were the first to push their boats into the water. Their battalion's order was to establish a bridgehead and allow the Pioneers to throw a bridge across the wide river. They crossed the majestic Don without further ado. On the opposite shore they jumped into the waist-deep water and scrambled up the riverbank, then combed the bushes and the fields for hidden enemy. In the hot sun of the Russian steppe their clothes soon dried on their bodies, and now they were wet again from their sweat. Somewhere on their flank a machinegun rattled and bullets whipped up the surface of the river. They dived for cover; after all, they were not bulletproof. They discovered a few stragglers running back along a path that wound along by the river, the way cows had trod it out. From out of a cloud of dust came a camouflaged car. A heavy machinegun spurted flame and the vehicle cartwheeled into a field. Next to the dead driver was another body with a gold-embroidered star on his sleeve. '*Gucke mal*, hey, look.' The voice was heavy with a strong Berlin accent, 'Karl just bagged himself a commissar.' From farther south they could distinctly hear a rumbling noise. The tanks were across. That was indeed good news. They came to the first village; the straw roofs of its log cabins were on fire and a few dead horses lay sprawled about. Womenfolk with their typical headscarves cowered against walls and stared at them with fright. Next to a dead Russian soldier was the body of a woman; the smouldering remains of a truck with its dead driver hanging out were in front of a brick structure adorned with sickle and hammer. A motorcycle dispatch rider raced past, disappearing into a cloud of dust. Suddenly heavy firing erupted on their flank. '*Deckung!* Take cover!' yelled the company commander. Two medium-sized enemy tanks had infiltrated their advance platoon and the battalion had taken casualties before anti-tank guns blasted the Russian tanks at point-blank range; they blew apart in a shower of sparks. When everything was again quiet the company commander ordered a brief halt. They had played their part; they had opened the way across the river.

The Germans crossed the Don. The flat terrain between the two main Russian rivers, the Don and the Volga, was perfectly suited to motorised advance; there were no natural barriers to stop Germany's panzers from storming across the hard surface. Rain could have helped the Russians, for most access routes were dirt roads and mud would have slowed up the enemy's armoured columns, but it hadn't rained for months and there was no mud. While Generaloberst von Paulus's foot-soldiery marched across the flat, dusty steppe between the great rivers, Hoth's panzers raced on to clear the way. A steady stream of messages came into 6th Army HQ from its motorised units reporting on their rapid advance. 'There is hardly any resistance. *Unglaublich,* it's truly uncanny . . . where is the enemy?' asked the Generaloberst. Nobody had the answer.

So complete was the Russian collapse in the corridor leading to Stalingrad that control of the city could have been secured with great ease in mid-July. But Hitler's fantastic changes of objectives, and his insistence on an overextended offensive, led to a strategic blunder. He ordered Hoth's 4th Panzer Army away from the Stalingrad front to lend its support to the 1st Panzer Army, which was headed for the Caucasian oilfields; thereby he slowed up Paulus's progress. Then Hitler had another change of mind, brought about by a conversation with his propaganda chief, Goebbels, who pointed out the city's moral importance; its propaganda value the city of that ogre Stalin greatly outweighed its strategic value. For Goebbels, and through him, Hitler, bringing about the fall of Stalin's city would be equivalent to defeating Stalin himself. Hoth's 4th Panzers were once more ordered north to lend their support to the 6th Army in the Stalingrad sector. This shuttling back and forth cost huge amounts of fuel and time, and this was not something the Germans could afford.

While Hitler shuttled his armies back and forth, and some moved irresistibly towards the Volga, he counted on the fact that his penetration deep into the heartland of his enemy would bring about a moral crack in the Soviet High Command. The opposite happened; it pushed Stalin into a reorganisation of the Red Army, perhaps the turning point in the German–Russian war. He finally got rid of 'Uncle Joe's ageing civil war buddies', and in their stead put young, dynamic generals such as Zhukov, Vasilievski, Golikov, Voronov, Vatutin, Eremenko and Rokossovsky. He decided that Stalingrad would be the new Verdun, unyielding, a fight to the last man and the last bullet – not only because of its strategic importance, but also because of its moral significance for the Russian people.

Stalingrad, an industrial centre of half a million, snaked eighteen miles along the western bank of the Volga; it was (and still is today) a city of tall smokestacks and square workers' flats. Its main importance lay in the three groups of factories located in its northern suburb, which produced a quarter of all tractors and tanks in the Soviet arsenal. The strategic key to the town was a rolling hill, the Mamayev Kurgan, which overlooked the factory complex and the ferry crossings. Whoever held it controlled the city. Now the city was to get a new commander. In a brief meeting with Lt-Gen. Vasili Chuikov, Stalin was brief and to the point. 'You will take up the position of commander of Stalingrad and you will make certain that the enemy does not gain possession of the town.'

Vasili Chuikov, one of the most capable young Russian commanders, was selected because he had led the toughest division in his corps. Where others retreated, he had stood and fought. Chuikov was described as an exemplary Soviet patriot. From that point of view much could be overlooked in him. His outstanding value lay in his inner strength; he followed his own rules for survival: don't make your inferior officers your friends, never get involved with other generals' problems, and flatten those who try to intimidate you. It turned out to be a successful formula. Chuikov quickly realised that he had two main problems to contend with: stopping the Germans crossing the river to the north and thereby cutting his communications with the rest of Russia and then starving the city into submission by closing the river to his vital supply traffic; and holding the Kurgan hill. He converted workers' flats into bunkers, dynamited entire districts to gain an open field of fire, and used bricks and rails to construct anti-tank barricades across major highways. He ordered the steep west bank of the Volga tunnelled to create a command complex with secure communication facilities, a field hospital and bunkers for ammunition storage. It was to prove a decisive move.

The German steamroller approached the city. Dust, petrol stench and heat; gleaming tank tracks, oil fumes and more red dust. It got into the men's hair and eyes, into oiled gun barrels and engine crankcases. They sped along dirt tracks and across trampled fields of rye and oats. Nothing could slow them; broken-down vehicles were simply shoved aside by the next tank. A never-ending stream of panzers thundered past infantry lying at rest at the side of the tracks and covered them with a thick layer of dust. Only the drivers remained inside their tanks; the rest of the crew hung out of the turret, their faces caked with sweat and dust. Only their teeth were white, but they tried not to open their mouths since then dust ground between their teeth. '*Denn heute gehört uns Deutschland – und morgen die ganze Welt* . . . Because today we are masters of Germany – and tomorrow the entire world,' they hummed.

All were part of the great German war machine. On it droned, a confusing din rolling eastward, objective Stalingrad. The first two days after crossing the Don, the Germans covered thirty kilometres. Then they ran out of petrol and water. The next fifty kilometres took them a month, while Stalin used the precious delay to reorganise his armies and Chuikov blasted, tunnelled and recruited.

The survivors of the 2nd Guard Rifle Company were spread out on the ground in a country lane. Altogether they were a sorry sight – their uniforms hung loose on their skinny frames, their trousers were soiled and ripped. They had been lying in wait for forty-eight hours – waiting for the first Germans to appear over the rise. During daytime they could see the heavy dust clouds, they could hear the rumble of tanks, but nothing so far had come in their direction. A quarter-mile in front was the crater of a giant bomb. When the Stuka had come down in a dive, they thought it was all over, but the bomb had missed them and instead killed a farmer and four oxen. During the night they had ventured out for the meat of the dead animals. Since they couldn't make a fire, they had to chew it raw; it tasted delicious, their first meal in days. They had eaten so much and so greedily that quite a few suffered. They moved away from the others to let down their trousers. The unit was out of contact with the battalion. Lt-Capt. Vassarov had been killed and Sgt Rybatov was in command. Vassarov was not the only casualty; so many had been killed that every man now had his own rifle. Rybatov was only a poor peasant's son, but he had been to school and told the others that the Motherland was in grave danger and that they had to make a stand, 'or the Fritzes would go swimming in the Volga'. The Volga, holy mother of Russian streams, was only ten kilometres behind them.

An unreal stillness lay over the land, almost as if the place were uninhabited. The six tanks of Lt Klinghofer, followed by mounted infantry on trucks, moved over ground that had been flattened by retreating Russian units. Farther up the track the crater of a giant bomb barred the way to transport vehicles. The column stopped and Pioneers with shovels had gone ahead to fill in the hole when a burst of rifle fire cut them down. The main guns from two Mark IVs opened up and silenced the small holding unit of Sgt Rybatov. A rumbling that shook the ground crept along the road – a Soviet battery firing. The German soldiers leaped from their trucks and took cover away from the track; the explosions stopped before they reached the Germans. The single Russian gun between them and the river had run out of shells. Finally, on 19 August, near Rynok north of Stalingrad, the driver of Lt Klinghofer's panzer stared through the driving slits at water ahead. 'The Volga!' he yelled.

In military river crossings, the determining factor is almost never the width of a river. Fast boats and highly specialised attack formations can overcome that. It is the length of river frontage held by the one who attempts to cross the water. He can feint points of attack, draw the enemy to these and then cross at others. This is something that the Germans failed to exploit on the Volga. Instead of spreading out, they jammed their forces into a narrow strip of riverbank and exposed themselves to the concentrated hail of explosives from Soviet guns, hidden along the opposite shore.

Anna Blumenthal was born in Vienna at the turn of the century.[7] During a Congress of Young Socialists she had met her future husband, Mendel. When Hitler marched into Austria, they took their baby son and fled across the Czech border; in a roundabout way they ended up in Stalingrad, certainly far enough away that the long arm of the Nazis would never reach them. It was not to be. Mendel was called

[7] The author met her in Volgograd and recorded her story.

up and mortally wounded during the battle for the Ukraine in 1941. Anna went to work on the assembly line in the tank factory, one of many women who took up a man's job while their men were fighting the invader.

> The days of early summer '42 were particularly hot. In some ways it seemed that life continued as usual, the kind of routine we were used to, but in truth, life wasn't normal. I stocked up on whatever items became available, some red beets and cabbages, in case we had to go down into a shelter; everyone was grabbed by the same fear. On my day off from the factory I walked with my little Avi up the Mamayev Kurgan from where we could have a splendid view over our city and on the Volga, shimmering in the sun like a huge silver snake. At the beginning of the war, we were the lucky ones, so far from the actual fighting not many worried about their future. Suddenly, we were in the front line. In mid-July German bombs tore our neighbourhood to pieces. By a miracle, our building was left standing. More than bombs, it was the sound of screaming German Stukas that had a psychological impact on the civilian population. The streets were a scene of madness, people were screaming, crying and running in all directions. I am not someone who panics easily, maybe it's denial. But somehow, this was different. Those terrifying planes made low strafing runs right into the tangled mass of people; piles of corpses were lying everywhere. I was sickened by the sight of what a weapon could do to a human body. Streams of refugees poured from the city, trying to get on some embarkation to flee across the river towards the east. Many were drowned on makeshift floats, others were dive-bombed or strafed. Fleeing men were rounded up by GPU squads and put into punishment battalions or shot as deserters. But nothing seemed to stop the flow of refugees; any

> personal danger was acceptable if only to get away from the advancing Germans.

Anna's mind struggled with the sobering realisation that she was again in the midst of the madness that she had already escaped once before. She eventually managed to take her son across on an old fisherman's rowing boat. The fisherman's wife agreed to take good care of little Avi, because by now Anna Blumenthal had come to a decision. She, like so many other women, went back across the river, back into beleaguered Stalingrad. 'Hitler had chased me from my native Vienna, now he was once again trying to chase me from another home. This time, I wouldn't run; I was adamant that I would help stop Hitler and his German hordes. I did it for my son's future.'

Today, the first thing a visitor sees from fifty miles off is the statue of 'Mother Russia'. It crowns the top of Mamayev Kurgan, the sacred Hill of Heroes. It is without doubt the biggest single monument ever built by man. In sheer height it compares favourably with the Eiffel Tower. Stalingrad, until 1925 called Tsaritsyn, is today Volgograd, a town that has risen from the ashes in the style of a people's commune, with its grey socialist-style apartment blocks, bereft of shops, with wide avenues and plazas boasting statues of its heroic past, surrounded by endless suburbs of wooden houses, all served by a ramshackle tramway. Tall factory smokestacks belch toxic fumes, and its citizens still form long queues for bread, sausages, cabbage and other vital necessities.

But it was in the autumn and winter of 1942/3 that the city made world history. The Russian historian Victor Nekrassov remembered it like this:

> As a direct participant of the historic Battle of Stalingrad, there can be no doubt that it was in fact the decisive turn of the Great Patriotic War. Until then, our army was driven helplessly before the might of the German war machine. When all seemed lost and we were called

> to make a stand, perhaps to many of us this seemed a heroic if utterly futile gesture. We didn't know that our sacrifice was intended to gain time, a month, a week, even a few precious hours. It wasn't an hour or a week, we held out for five and a half months. *And then all of a sudden, as if by miracle, appeared from Siberia fresh Red Army reserves, and all without the Germans noticing. I must admit, we didn't know about these reserves – I don't think anybody knew.* The sheer size and amount of material with which Stalin and his marshals launched the great counter-offensive was as much a surprise to us as it was to the Germans.

Nobody knew! And that included Stalin's wartime allies. The only one who had predicted the coming storm rightly was a German Oberstleutnant, Reinhard Gehlen. But his people considered him a doomsayer, and nobody has ever listened to the wisdom of a prophet. The Trojans failed to heed the warning of Cassandra and Hitler didn't listen to Gehlen. 'You don't have to have the gift of a prophet to foresee what will happen when Stalin unleashes a million and a half men against Stalingrad and our Don flank.' When Halder dared to point this out to Hitler, the German leader flew at him with clenched fists and foaming mouth. He threw a tantrum. Halder was bitter: '23 July. The situation is getting increasingly intolerable. There is no room for serious work. This "leadership" is characterised by a pathological reacting to the impressions of the moment and the complete lack of any understanding of a command machinery and its possibilities.'

A week later, Hitler again changed his mind when he grandly announced that the battle of the Caucasus would be decided at Stalingrad. 'This is rankest nonsense. The enemy is running for dear life and will be in the foothills of the Caucasus . . . and then we are going to have another unhealthy congestion of forces before the enemy front.'[8]

[8] Both quotes from F. Halder, *Kriegstagebücher*, Stuttgart 1964.

Gen. Halder dispatched one of his own men, Maj. Count von Kielmannsegg, to take a personal look. What he saw didn't worry him. But he missed the vital factor. On the eastern bank of the Volga, ever more Soviet divisions were being put into place – all part of Stalin's 'non-existing manpower reserves'. By mid-July, ten divisions had already been placed to the north of Stalingrad; by mid-August there were sixty Soviet divisions concentrated on the Volga's east bank with another thirteen on their way. In fact, the Germans rushed unaware into a disaster. Not even Stalin's allies knew – there is nothing written about the Soviet build-up in English or US war diaries, official or secret reports. By withholding the information about his real strength, Stalin could now induce an Allied concession to open a second front in order 'to relieve pressure'. In other words, the British and Americans simply didn't know that Stalin had already put six full and fresh armies into position and was about to add three more.[9]

At the beginning of the war, when the Russians allied themselves with the Germans against Britain and France, any pretension of friendship between the West and the East was abandoned. Stalin was vilified, and perhaps rightly so. He outsmarted all the politicians of the time and everyone had him wrong. And when, at the end of the Polish campaign, Poland was parcelled out among the victors, they got it wrong again. Unlike the Western Allies, Stalin never had qualms about the collusive aspect of his non-aggression treaty with Germany. Behind all his pretensions was a hard determination to gain time. Nothing showed this more clearly than the alacrity with which he sucked the German Army deep into Russia. And the claim that he was powerless to stop the invaders – certainly true in the opening stages of the war – was but a clever mantle for his ultimate design. As Germany was to discover to its cost, the acquisition of vast spaces of Russia was more of a liability than an asset. Because as important as

[9] 60th, 62nd, 63rd, 64th, 6th, 5th Tank.

a lightning advance by its tank forces was the security of its lines of communications. This demanded the maintenance of military bases throughout the wide spaces and the deployment of vitally needed forces to guard the extended supply lines, which drew manpower from its fighting machine. While the supply line in the French campaign had been a manageable two hundred miles, in Russia this was stretched out over two thousand miles. As Hitler's forces were thinning out, Stalin had an ace up his sleeve. For this he would make his stand on Russia's Mother of Streams, the Volga.

Meanwhile, as Germany's generals continued to fight Hitler, and Stalin's men were retreating, the Western leaders decided that the situation for their Russian ally was serious enough to warrant a desperate measure. They agreed that a personal talk with Stalin in Moscow was called for. If Stalin's army collapsed, vast German forces would be freed for other theatres of war. And that was why Prime Minister Churchill insisted on a head-to-head meeting with Uncle Joe. The whole world was witness to the fact that the Russians had taken over the backbreaking task of confronting Hitler's mighty spearhead, and Stalin wanted to know when his Allies would open a Second Front in Europe. To sell a delay wouldn't be an easy task, certainly not to the leader of a country fighting for its life. Fortunately, Hitler had committed a dumb and unprovoked act the moment he declared war on the United States. That brought America and its industrial might in on England's side, and meant it could send Stalin tanks and planes. When Churchill met Stalin, arguing about the price of such military aid was not on – the communist would always accept the price, however high it was, but he would also remember. And such remembrance would carry into the after-war days. But what if the conservative, red-threat-conscious US Congress balked at the Lend-Lease Act? Roosevelt had warned Churchill that this could happen. What if Stalin, with his manpower resources pushed to the very limit and beyond, was to turn around and sign a separate peace with the Germans? Hitler would turn his entire might against England! Such an explosive situation had to be diffused, and for this to happen required the right man to keep matters on an even keel. There was but one man he could fully trust – himself. Churchill was willing to undertake the task and 'visit the sullen, sinister Bolshevik state I had once tried so hard to strangle at birth'.[10] He cabled to Stalin: 'I AM WILLING, SHOULD YOU INVITE ME, TO COME MYSELF TO MEET YOU IN ASTRAKHAN, THE CAUCASUS, OR SIMILAR CONVENIENT MEETING PLACE. WE COULD THEN SURVEY THE WAR TOGETHER AND TAKE DECISIONS HAND-IN-HAND. I COULD THEN TELL YOU OF PLANS WE HAVE MADE WITH PRESIDENT ROOSEVELT FOR OFFENSIVE ACTION IN 1942. I WOULD BRING THE CHIEF OF THE IMPERIAL GENERAL STAFF WITH ME. CHURCHILL.'

For once Stalin seemed quite eager for a top-level meeting and asked Churchill to meet him in Moscow, 'pressing matters preventing me from leaving my capital as the war has reached a special degree of intensity'. Churchill took this to be Stalin's desperate situation along his south-western front. In fact, Stalin's pressing business was that of creating shock armies from his secret strategic reserves. He appointed an overall commander for the Stalingrad front, Andrei Eremenko, for a change not one of his cronies. Eremenko was informed of his new assignment while recovering from a serious wound in a Moscow hospital. He was collected from his bed and driven to the Kremlin to meet Stalin, who just looked at him and said: 'Stop them and don't spare the men.' Eremenko was then put on a plane and flown straight into the battle zone.

The summit meeting was set. On 9 August, Churchill left London for Cairo, whence he continued on to Tehran to have 'lunch with the Shah'. Just before leaving Egypt, he sent

[10] W. Churchill, *The Second World War*, vol. IV: *The Hinge of Fate*, London 1951.

a message to President Roosevelt: 'I WOULD GREATLY LIKE TO HAVE YOUR AID AND COUNTENANCE IN MY TALKS WITH JOE. WOULD YOU BE ABLE TO LET AVERELL [Harriman] COME WITH ME? I HAVE A SOMEWHAT RAW JOB . . . AM KEEPING MY IMMEDIATE MOVEMENTS VAGUE. CHURCHILL.'[11]

After lunch, the Shah accompanied his famous guest to the airport. Churchill's aircraft rose into the air, then it simply vanished.[12] Nobody knew where Churchill was, or whether his plane had been shot down. At 1647 hours on 12 August, Muscovites ran in panic for the nearest air-raid shelter as three heavy bombers roared at a mere 250 metres over the towers of the Kremlin; until someone recognised their white-star markings and yelled: '*Amerikanski!*' Indeed, these were American-made B-24s, yet no one but Stalin knew what this flight was all about. There was no forewarning, except that Moscow traffic controllers had chased cars off the road; but that was nothing unusual whenever a government cortège was on its way. An hour later a line of black limousines drove along Gorki Prospect. In the first car sat Russia's foreign minister, Vyacheslav Molotov, and next to him Winston Churchill, smoking a cigar! In the second car was Roosevelt's special envoy, Averell Harriman, whose greatest worry was that Stalin wouldn't believe a word of what Churchill told him about a Second Front. He was quite right. Churchill's mind was also beset by other worries – how to keep another secret so deep that he couldn't possibly share it with Stalin. It might set off a violent reaction. Churchill was well aware of the advances made by Americans with their Manhattan Project;[13] but even more worrisome was a recent British intelligence report about a similar nuclear crash programme under way in Germany, in addition to their programme, now

[11] Loewenheim *et al*, *Roosevelt and Churchill*, New York 1975.

[12] The first word about Churchill's Moscow visit came long after he had left, from Russian newsreels.

[13] It was on Churchill's personal order that secret research documents were shipped to the US to be included in the atomic weapons programme.

in an advanced stage, for a rocket delivery system.[14]

In 1938, the German physicist Otto Hahn found that uranium atoms bombarded with neutrons would give off an enormous amount of atomic energy. In the Reichspost Laboratory, Professor von Ardenne envisioned the possibility of a superweapon, and proposed it to the military. He was discouraged from building such a bomb. But one man at the top of the Nazi pyramid recognised the potential. What eternal glory would be his if his Luftwaffe planes could wipe London from the map! Hermann Göring was prepared to take a bold risk and affront Hitler by pursuing strictly 'non-Aryan' theories. But by this time, the men who were to build the bomb, German Jewish scientists, had escaped via France or Sweden to England, and from there emigrated to the United States. Germany still had a number of brilliant physicists, and an émigré Nazi scientist, Leo Szilard, had warned Churchill that the Germans *could* build a bomb. What if the Allies failed to stop Hitler before he had the means to deliver the ultimate deterrent? How would the West reply to sudden death from the sky, and what would be left afterwards? There would be such massive political disorder that there would be no losers or winners, only one survivor: Stalin and worldwide communism. The spectre was real.

Stalin also had a deep secret, and it was for imminent use. He needed trucks and guns and ammunition and plane parts and all the many accoutrements necessary to continue a war – but he didn't need men. He had more than he could use on any single front line, only nobody knew about them. Certainly not Roosevelt or Churchill. And Old Joe wasn't about to tell them either. If he was to throw them into the fray, the Americans would have to pay for it.

The cars pulled up outside the Kremlin. The entrance hall was shrouded in that kind of semi-darkness and living silence that comes seconds before the theatre curtain rises. Stalin, Molotov and Marshal Voroshilov, three dyed-in-the-blood

[14] Churchill was right about the rockets but not about Germany's nuclear capability.

Bolsheviks from the days of Red October, met Churchill and his delegation; beside Averell Harriman as the special envoy of President Roosevelt was the British ambassador to Moscow, Clark Kerr. Stalin, in a plain uniform, greeted them warmly and shook everyone's hand, then motioned them to the opposite side of a long baize-covered table complete with notepads and bottled water. Churchill sat down; Stalin bowed to them with a slight nod of the head, then lowered himself into his chair, slowly at first, as if bending his knees with difficulty to give the impression of a man worn down by stress. Molotov and Voroshilov took their places beside him. After the usual 'we're grateful that you could come and visit us . . .', Stalin's marshal gave a briefing on the military situation. The picture that emerged was shattering. Churchill had not expected much else, but it still left him speechless. The Red Army had been crumpled in a series of badly planned battles. Following the setback at Kharkov, the south-west sector was stripped bare of troops and material. The Volga crossings were in acute danger, and with them the Russian hinterland.

A military aide walked into the room, bent over and whispered into Stalin's ear; the dictator shook his head petulantly as if annoyed at the interruption. Molotov observed his rival Harriman closely, blinking his eyes behind his glasses. In contrast to Harriman, whose close friendship with President Roosevelt was widely known, Molotov never boasted of his personal contacts with Stalin; he just acted like an obedient schoolboy and faded into the background, all the while planning the strategy that would force the West to rush to Russia's support and offer serious financial and material concessions. He had advised Stalin that they could negotiate for as long as they had something to negotiate about. 'Whatever, don't tell them about the reserves.' Stalin had seen his chief of diplomacy's point and nodded. 'If they arrive too late to save Stalingrad, they will still be in plenty of time to help us drive them out of the ruins.' He remembered this when he said to Churchill: '. . . to the last man and the last woman and the last drop of blood in our sacred cause . . .' – his emotional finale to show his savage determination to hold the city.

Stalin was smart. He didn't want to open the proceedings by having to give answers. He offered the floor to Churchill, who knew that this was likely to happen and had come fully prepared. He began with the bad news and then came to the good news, news that would greatly cheer up his host. The Americans pledged to ship tanks, trucks and fighter aircraft, mostly by naval convoys on the dangerous 'Murmansk run', but also on the safer route through Iran. Stalin smiled. For his secret stratagem the availability of US-made weapons and equipment was essential. Despite the great industrial effort Russia was making, she could not possibly have provided the material needed for successful defence followed by successful offence without the great quantities of equipment supplied by her Anglo-Saxon allies.

Having noticed Stalin's positive reaction to the pledge of arms, Churchill launched into the difficult part, the vague promise of a 'Second Front' with a possible invasion of France. He knew this to be false promise since the planned Anglo-American invasion of North Africa would preclude any full-scale invasion of France, even in the coming year, 1943. But he didn't say so, and this proved to be a grave error, since it established the mistrust between East and West that was to last fifty years. Instead he said it would be militarily unwise to move in 1942 as it would endanger the 'bigger undertaking we're planning for 1943'. He certainly implied that by early 1943 a million Americans would have been stationed on UK soil – twenty-seven American divisions, half of them motorised units. But if Churchill had thought this would appease Stalin, he was sadly mistaken.

'Why are the Americans and British so afraid of the Germans?' Stalin asked through his interpreter. This left Churchill with no choice but to outline 'Operation Torch', the invasion of North Africa by a combined British–American force.

'When?' snapped Stalin.

'Not later than 30 October, and perhaps as early as 7 October. If we can score a decisive victory in North Africa, we *could* make a deadly attack upon Hitler next year.' In this duel of two foxes, Churchill was most careful to weigh every word. *Could*, he said, not *would*. Stalin certainly caught the nuance but wouldn't comment on it. Now that he had a date, he knew that it was vital to precede this with a move designed to score a psychological victory over his allies. Compared to burying the German might at Stalingrad, his allies' North African campaign was, militarily speaking, peanuts.

Two days passed before the group met again. This time a touch of chill had entered the conference room. The ashtrays had been emptied but the rancid odour of stale tobacco remained. There were large circles of moisture where glasses had rested.

Stalin said, 'Mr Prime Minister, we are most interested to hear of your plans to open a Second Front.'

'We have decided . . . I mean, it is not easy for me to talk about it, but . . .'

Stalin interrupted: 'We have strong nerves, Mr Prime Minister.'

'Well, the invasion in this year is virtually impossible . . .'

From across the baize table his announcement was met by cold stares. With a deep drag on his pipe, Stalin rasped: 'You mean to tell us that the sacred promise given to us by the British and American statesmen last spring will not be honoured?'

Churchill was taken aback by Stalin's harsh manner. 'We are thinking of a landing in Sicily.'

Stalin frowned. 'This is certainly more of a political than a military option.'

Churchill knew that it was time to offer something. 'Plans are well advanced for an invasion of western Europe by the spring of 1943.'

'Are you giving us an assurance that this time your sacred

promise will not be broken as have been all the others before?'

To which the silent grey man Molotov added: 'The British Prime Minister will prove once again to us that his country is not willing to sacrifice its soldiers.'

That phrase did it! It riled Churchill, and he knew that nothing further would come from his trip to Moscow.[15] Stalin handed Churchill a sheet of paper. The memorandum was blunt and to the point: 'It will be easily understood that the Soviet Command *built their plan of summer and autumn operations* calculating on the creation of a Second Front in Europe in 1942.' This wasn't a memorandum, it was an ultimatum. Stalin couldn't put it more clearly, and Churchill and Harriman were taken unawares. The Prime Minister recovered, but felt that it was time to go beyond his usual diplomatic firmness. Harshness might be required. 'What plan of operation are you speaking of?' he snapped, in a tone perceptibly less cordial. 'We know of none.' His response was understandable, given the fact that Churchill still believed in the inherent weakness of the Red Army based on battle results and recent British intelligence estimates.[16] Both Churchill and Harriman overlooked the obvious question: 'How many divisions do you really have?', to be immediately followed by: 'On the front *and in reserve*?'

The conference in the Kremlin had reached its dramatic climax. It had produced too many divergent views, conflicting ambitions and grey ambiguities. It was now that the meeting nearly collapsed. Stalin couldn't allow that; he still needed Allied material to equip his strategic reserves. In a last-minute effort, he changed tactics and offered to show Churchill and his party some of the new Soviet arsenal. The Prime Minister was not interested in inspecting 'military apparatus and such',

[15] *Deutsche Aussenpolitik,* vol. 10, Berlin 1961.

[16] The Germans knew that Stalin was lying; the British, allies of the Russians, did not!

but in returning to London with a clear picture and a firm promise.

'Will you defend the Caucasus?'

'Of course.'

'With what?'

'Twenty-five divisions.' Churchill's Chief-of-Staff, Sir Alan Brooke, shook his head; he didn't believe that Stalin could muster another twenty-five divisions from his inventory. But Stalin had more, much more. In the defence of the Caucasian oilfields, he had aligned twenty-nine rifle divisions, eight cavalry divisions, fifteen rifle and eight tank brigades, with another thirteen brigades on the way. And yet that was only a minute portion of his true reserves. At the beginning of 1942 Stalin's reserves were *three times larger than the entire US Army at the start of the war*! Nobody, of course, was aware of this! Not Hitler – and certainly not Stalin's allies.

The conference broke up. It had not been a good meeting. Visible proof was a pencil that had been broken in two in a fit of surprise or anger. Stalin didn't trust his ally; this showed in the tightening of his mouth. Only one man in that room seemed totally unmoved by what was going on – Molotov. Silent, motionless, his eyes hidden behind glasses and gazing beyond the table into a space that was inaccessible to others, he sat in his chair as though he were fulfilling an unnecessary and tedious duty. On the opposite side of the table, Churchill was left with a strange sense of suspicion. He was studying Stalin carefully and thinking of the abyss into which the logic of autocratic power led a country. They would sign a communiqué, but history tended to laugh at these scraps of paper. There had been an almost too-obvious effort by the Russian to pass over some critical information. He had come to get the facts; he had got the facts, but not all of them, of that he was certain. In the final analysis, he came away believing that the major burden of the war would have to be carried by the Western powers. At the time he was right in his assessment, since at just about the time that the farewell dinner began in the Kremlin, Stalin's 4th Tank Army holding the Don front was overrun near Rodinov.

The final banquet was a disaster. Special care had been taken to invite diplomats and highly decorated generals, assembled beneath the magnificent crystal chandeliers in the Tsars' grand banquet hall, to give proof of the eternal friendship between East and West. Stalin, wearing the grey uniform of a marshal of the Soviet Union, arrived shortly before his guest of honour. The assembled guests gasped when Churchill made his entry. In complete defiance of protocol, the British Prime Minister, angry about the negative results of the talks, showed up in a blue boiler suit, and then added insult to injury by refusing to stand up while his ambassador proposed a toast to the Red dictator. By 1.30 a.m., after meaningless speeches and vodka toasts to enduring brotherhood, Churchill had had enough. He took a deep pull on his cigar, blew out the smoke and bent to Harriman, saying almost indifferently: 'Well, I've had it.' He got up and simply walked away from the banquet table. This time Stalin was the one with an open mouth; it left him with no option but to chase after Churchill along the long corridors of the Kremlin to shake hands with the British Prime Minister. He reached Churchill as he was about to climb into his limousine. The lit-up gilded cupolas of the Church of Ivan the Terrible, that white-stone fairytale of Russian architecture, rose up before Churchill as from the depths of Russian history. From Ivan to Stalin, cruelty and deceit had ruled Russia. The next day, while Churchill was still in the air, Stalin forwarded a memorandum via the Soviet ambassador to London: 'Following our debate I have come to the firm conclusion that the British Prime Minister excludes the establishment of a Second Front in Europe for 1942. This is a severe shock not only to me, but to the fighting spirit of the entire Russian nation.'

Churchill replied: 'It would serve no purpose and certainly would not help the Russian people, if we were to sacrifice 100,000 men in a hasty and misplanned Channel crossing.'

To which Stalin answered: 'It needs no words to state that the government of the Soviet Union cannot accept such disregard of its interest vital to its country's survival, in the fight against our common enemy.'

Stalin was possessed with a notion based on a secret report from his intelligence apparatus, which had either read it wrong or had slovenly pursued the line taken by their dictator, that the initiative for an invasion of western Europe lay with the Allies, but the true intention behind such an invasion was not strategic but entirely political. Their aim was not to draw the strength of the German panzers from the Russian front and relieve some of the pressure on Stalin's sorely tried troops, though this could be a consequence; the aim was to stall as long as they could and then conquer Europe, while Russia bled so that it would never become a postwar power. That, and only that, was the key. Russia had to go it alone!

A meeting between wartime allies, based on mistrust, cannot succeed. And so it was in Moscow in the summer of '42; all their meeting produced was a conversation between two plug-eared men who didn't even try lip-reading. Only one piece of information emerged from the encounter – Stalin was planning something big, and this thought had Churchill worried. At one point in the discussion he had put a specific question to Stalin: 'I wish to discuss the Polish question.' All he had received was a vague reply from Molotov: 'We are looking into it.' A few days after his return home, Churchill had his answer. Stalin broke off diplomatic relations with the London-exiled Polish government and formed his own Polish government-in-exile, consisting of communist hardliners friendly to the Soviet Union. Stalin's plan couldn't be clearer – he was out to set up a satellite state. But what made him so sure he could turn the war around and then head straight for Warsaw to install his puppet regime?[17]

[17] *Deutsche Aussenpolitik*, vol. 10, Berlin 1961.

* * *

For one last time the outcome was in the hands of the German panzers. On 29 August Hoth's 4th Panzer Army managed to penetrate the flank of Eremenko's Stalingrad defences – and then the German advance stalled. Their panzers ran dry! Hitler's indecisive shuttling about of Hoth's mechanised units had wasted their fuel supply. The 16th Panzer Division, the armoured spearhead of Paulus's 6th Army, suddenly found itself surrounded by several Russian divisions, thrown into the fray by Eremenko in a desperate countermove. Now something took place which was quite unique in the annals of the German Wehrmacht. In a moment of extreme confusion bordering on mutiny, General Hans Hube of the 16th Panzer Division called his officers to a staff meeting: 'The shortage of ammunition and fuel is critical. I absolutely refuse to fight a pointless battle that must end in the annihilation of my troops. I therefore shall order a breakout to the west. *I absolve you, gentlemen, of your oath of loyalty* . . . I am acting contrary to the Führer's orders.'[18]

Stalin's order to Marshal Georgi Zhukov and his chief-of-staff, Gen. Aleksandr Vasilievski, was open to no misinterpretation: 'ENEMY TROOPS TO BE SURROUNDED AT STALINGRAD. MUST BE LIQUIDATED IN ORDER TO FREE THREE ARMIES FOR OUR OBJECTIVE.'

The overall plan, to use Stalin's huge strategic manpower reserve and turn a defensive action into a carefully executed Red Army offensive, was taking shape. While Stalin was still in conference with Churchill, confirming his lack of effectives, hundreds of thousands of Soviet reserves moved into the salient north of the Don and into the flank of the thinly protected German spearhead. This massive reinforcement was dictated by a large-scale offensive aimed at the annihilation of

18 Heinz Schröter, *Stalingrad – bis zur letzten Patrone*, Klagenfurt 1955. This mutiny was averted with the arrival of 250 fuel trucks – too late to be of much use. The push had stalled.

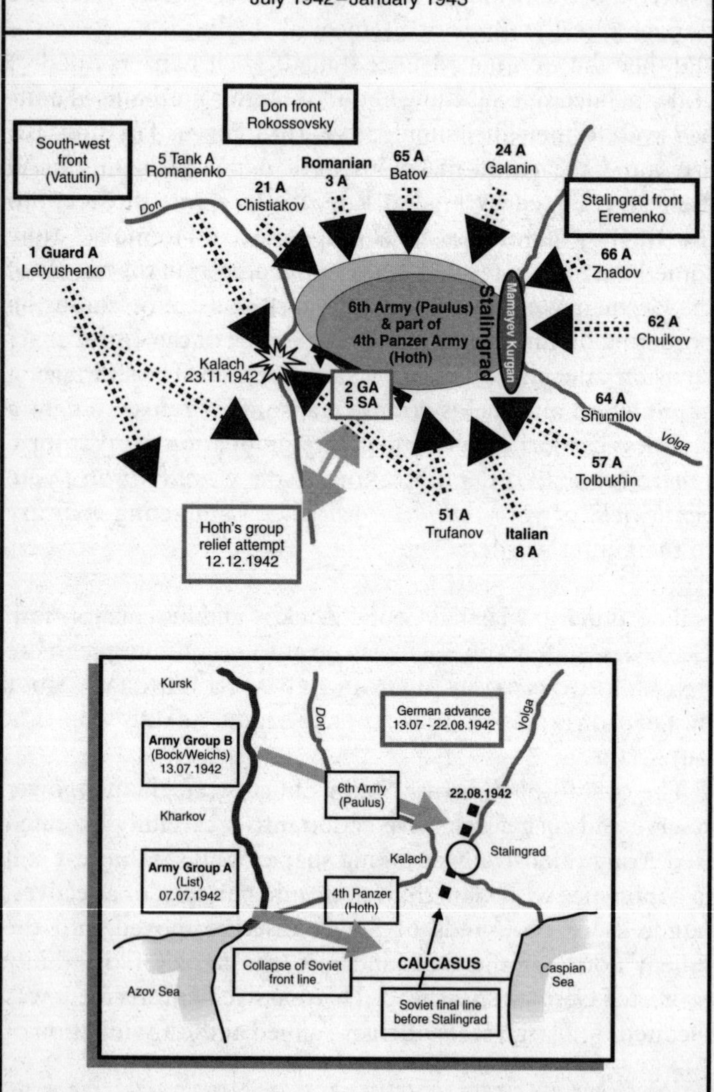

Stalingrad
July 1942–January 1943
Don front
Rokossovsky
South-west
front
(Vatutin)
5 Tank A
Romanenko
Romanian
3 A
65 A
Batov
24 A
Galanin
21 A
Chistiakov
Stalingrad front
Eremenko
Don
1 Guard A
Letyushenko
66 A
Zhadov
6th Army (Paulus)
& part of
4th Panzer Army
(Hoth)
Stalingrad
Mamayev Kurgan
62 A
Chuikov
Kalach
23.11.1942
2 GA
5 SA
64 A
Shumilov
Volga
57 A
Tolbukhin
51 A
Trufanov
Italian
8 A
Hoth's group
relief attempt
12.12.1942
Kursk
Don
German advance
13.07 - 22.08.1942
Volga
Army Group B
(Bock/Weichs)
13.07.1942
6th Army
(Paulus)
22.08.1942
Kharkov
Stalingrad
Kalach
Army Group A
(List)
07.07.1942
4th Panzer
(Hoth)
Collapse of Soviet
front line
CAUCASUS
Caspian
Sea
Azov Sea
Soviet final line
before Stalingrad

Hoth's 4th Panzer Army and Paulus's 6th Army. As autumn drew to a close, Stavka (Russian Army HQ) completed the deployment. The initial assault was to be undertaken by massed Soviet artillery, thousands of guns and hundreds of batteries of Katyusha rocket-launchers.

On the ground an ominous lull continued, though the air war rapidly intensified. But a serious problem had to be solved first, one of a political order which concerned Stalin's personal contacts with Churchill and Roosevelt. There had been one final attempt to establish courteous relations between Churchill–Roosevelt and Stalin. On 3 October Stalin received a coded message from Churchill and Roosevelt querying the situation. While plans were being finalised to throw his vast reserve forces into a gigantic counteroffensive Stalin wired back: 'I MUST INFORM YOU THAT OUR POSITION IN THE STALINGRAD AREA HAS CHANGED FOR THE WORSE . . . DUE TO THE FACT THAT WE ARE SHORT OF PLANES, ESPECIALLY PURSUIT PLANES.'

Roosevelt wired to Churchill: 'I FEEL STRONGLY THAT WE SHOULD MAKE A FIRM COMMITMENT TO PUT AN AIRFORCE INTO THE CAUCASUS . . .'

Their proposal was met with utter silence. It was clear that Stalin didn't want anyone, especially not his 'dear allies', to have their air force tramping around in his vegetable patch. But the time had come to reveal his real strength. His 'last twenty-five divisions in the Caucasus' suddenly became almost as many shock armies, with thousands of tanks and over a million men. The Allies suddenly realised that they had been led around by the nose. Churchill suggested to Roosevelt a conference of the three leaders around 15 January 1943, but Stalin would have none of that. Given that the Allies had become aware that he could most likely repel the Germans on his own, he didn't want to become embroiled in arguments and allow his allies to back out of the promised invasion of France. Therefore, he replied: 'I AM AWAITING YOUR REPLY TO MY PRECEDING LETTER DEALING WITH THE ESTABLISHMENT

OF A SECOND FRONT IN WESTERN EUROPE BY THE SPRING OF 1943. STALIN.'

Stalingrad was holy, and Stalingrad had turned into a battle of prestige. If Stalin insisted on holding the town carrying his name, Hitler wanted it destroyed for the same reason. But his offensive had stalled, not due to a lack of panzers and men but to a lack of petrol brought about by his amateurish interference. The Führer was furious; he blamed everything on the incompetence of his generals. To revive the momentum, he ordered that troops be pulled from the 6th Army's flank protection and be pushed into the spearhead. It was the blueprint for disaster. A bragging Reichsmarschall Hermann Göring assured Hitler: 'The Luftwaffe has had difficulties in finding enemy forces at all, just as if the country was entirely without cover.' Generaloberst Halder claimed that he didn't believe a word of the pilots' report; Hitler did because he wanted to. He was suffering increasingly from nervous exhaustion. 'Today once again, the *Führer Lagebesprechung* was the occasion for abusive reproaches against the military leadership abilities of the highest commands.'[19] On 20 September, Halder wrote: 'We are beginning to feel the approaching exhaustion of our assault troops,' and he added two days later: 'He and I must part. Hitler feels a necessity to educate the General Staff in a fanatical faith in the Nazi Idea. He is determined to enforce his will on the Army.' One more Hitler tantrum was followed by a shake-up in the OKW. It happened like this.

Spymaster Reinhard Gehlen had received a worrying message from his undercover source, which confirmed without doubt his suspicion: masses of Russian reserves were gathering to the north of the extended German flank. He informed his direct superior, Generaloberst Franz Halder, at OKH, and Halder went to see Hitler at OKW. It resulted in a face-to-face

[19] 30 August 1942, reported by Gen. Greiner (OKW) quoting Field Marshal Keitel.

confrontation which, in OKW chief Keitel's words, was the worst bust-up he had ever witnessed. When Halder insisted on halting the 6th Army's advance and protecting its vulnerable flank, Hitler banged the table and became red in the face to the point of choking. The discussion ended when the 'greatest military genius since Napoleon' ranted: '*Hier bestimme ich und Sie können gehen* . . . I decide here and you can go. *The little affair of operational command is something that anybody can do.*' The best strategic planner of the Wehrmacht, the one who could have avoided the looming disaster, was thus kicked out in the shabbiest manner.[20] Gen. Kurt Zeitzler replaced Franz Halder as head of Oberkommando Heer (OKH).

Halder was removed because he dared to point out to Hitler that he worried – worried about the men inside Stalingrad, worried about supplies not reaching them, worried about the long northern flank of the Stalingrad salient, where Germany's satellite armies had failed to liquidate a number of Russian bridgeheads over the Don and one just south of Stalingrad across the Volga. Hitler interpreted Russian activity along the salient's flank as strictly diversionary – because he couldn't admit that he had committed a strategic blunder. The shake-up at OKH did nothing to solve the real cause of the problem. Without giving the slightest thought to the survival chances of his men, forced to attack under the most unfavourable conditions, along a narrow front through a field of rubble, Hitler ordered a general offensive for 4 October. It produced minimal results and resulted in massive losses. In a single afternoon, Mamayev Kurgan, that controlling height, changed hands six times! Hitler's insistence on bombing and shelling every building, every inch of ground, helped only to erect an impassable barricade of smashed concrete and broken rubble. The fighting was

[20] Halder retired to Bavaria where he was arrested on 21 July 1944, the day after the attempt on Hitler's life. However, he never faced trial for complicity in the plot and survived the war.

carried from street to street, house to house, room to room, hand to hand. In that notorious 'Bloodmill of Stalingrad', no pity was offered and none expected. The losses on both sides were staggering. While the Germans were winning some meaningless yards of rubbled streets, the Russians were bringing up ever more fresh reinforcements – more men, more guns, more tanks. Only nobody knew about them since Stalin and his generals held them back on the other side of the Volga, patiently awaiting the appropriate moment.

Hauptmann Karl Kretschmer had just taken his Ju-88 into a sharp dive and released his bombs when he discovered two Russian fighter planes on his tail. He pulled back on the stick and managed to climb into a cloud bank. His navigational instruments hadn't worked for days and his mechanics weren't given time for repairs. Always out on missions, day after bloody day. He was flying blind, what pilots called 'by the seat of your pants'. When he exited the white cotton fog, he found that he was some thirty miles east of the Volga, deep inside enemy territory. As he banked back to the west, he saw a great cloud of dust. It was a huge column of vehicles, stretching way into the distance. He brought his plane down for a closer look and then skimmed above the ground next to a country road. All he saw were tanks and guns, and then more tanks, great columns of them. He began to draw scattered fire, reversed his direction and made it safely back to his base at Gumrak. He reported his sighting. Within an hour he was ordered to report to Corps HQ.

'What is this report?' an intelligence officer asked him.

'Tanks, and more tanks, I'm telling you.'

'What he's seen were probably columns of refugees fleeing from the city,' said a harassed general over his shoulder. 'The Russians are finished! They have no more tanks.' In his recent speech, their Führer had declared that the Soviets were smashed 'and never again would be able to recover their strength'. Why go against the words of the Führer? A military genius had spoken and he must know.

Hauptmann Kretschmer's sighting was never passed on.

'Here the sky burns over your head and the ground shakes under your feet,' wrote a Soviet reporter from inside the city. Gen. Chuikov led a heroic defence, his immediate worry being to stop the Germans from crossing the Volga. His perimeter shrank, then shrank again. His units were split up, encircled, fought their way out only to become once more cut off from the rest. Chuikov hoped for reinforcement from the 193rd Division. It never came. He called for ammunition and got none. Then the unimaginable happened. Col. Tarasov's 92nd Brigade had to pull out and the Germans immediately filled the gap. With it, they held the Volga embankment from the Tsaritsa river all the way to the central landing stage. The same afternoon, Col. Gorishny's 95th Division attacked twice and then twice lost the summit of Mamayev Kurgan. In a final attempt to secure the controlling heights, Col. Batiuk's 284th Division was used up on the same blood-drenched slopes.

In a final, heroic charge, the remnants of a division under the inspired command of thirty-eight-year-old Col. Nikolai Batiuk stumbled up the hill and managed to throw the last Germans from their trenches near the top. A horde of screaming wild men pounced on the Germans – rifle butts cracked skulls, bayonets ripped tunics and flesh, and corpses piled high. Dirty and ragged, the survivors crouched down behind earthen walls and then waited for the counter-attack, which they knew had to come. The colonel sent a runner to Chuikov's HQ to ask for reserves and ammunition. Within the hour, the messenger was back. 'Colonel, we're ordered to hold.'

'And where is our support?'

'We're to hold with what we've got.'

The colonel put his dead-tired survivors to work and set up a defensive position. One half of the unit was used to clear the trenches of dead Germans; they threw the corpses over the parapets and into bomb craters, while the others went down the slopes to recover grenades, guns and bullets from the dead, Russians and Germans. Especially useful was a German MG-42 machinegun with some five hundred rounds; its crew had been blown apart by a grenade after firing only fifty shots. They were fairly safe from the German artillery, because guns firing in a straight line, even if they were aimed at their trenches, could not have closed the angle of the hill. It was only mortars they had to worry about; those came straight down from above. A lieutenant came in and saluted. 'Comrade Colonel, I have inspected the troops and found them fit and eager for battle.' The colonel waved a tired hand. 'Have you now?' The young man didn't seem even vaguely aware that out there the worst kind of a bloody disaster awaited them, and that there was no way he could avert it. An elderly sergeant showed up and from under his uniform jacket pulled out a bottle. He poured the crystal-clear liquid into a water glass, up to the rim. The colonel nodded appreciatively, picked up the glass and downed the vodka in one go. At least he wouldn't be going down sober. Apart from a faraway rumble of artillery there was not a sound near by; all was quiet, uncannily so, before an explosion shattered the silence like a bolt out of the clear sky. More mortar bombs zeroed in on the Russian line. A mass of German infantry, several battalions, appeared down the slope; with their helmets they looked more barbaric and invincible than ever. An opening salvo of gunfire broke across the hill; the first wave of Germans was met by the sharp staccato rattle from the captured MG-42 machinegun and soldiers were bowled over like ninepins. The rifles barked. The first gun became two, then six, until there were so many they could not be counted. But Batiuk's men also suffered greatly, the gunners and the belt-tenders. Others rushed up to take their places. A German officer rose, waving his pistol, and was running up the hill when a well-aimed shot knocked him down. The whole crest of Mamayev Kurgan erupted in a line of flashes. The Germans went spinning and tumbling down the slope.

Worn out as the 284th Division was, following thirty minutes of unbroken effort they still managed to ward off the German attack. But then the Germans brought up armoured vehicles and heavy artillery. A flight of Stukas appeared and hurled its bombs into Batiuk's trenches. The rest of his men were either torn to pieces by aerial bombs or pinned down by artillery; under cover of a murderous bombardment, more waves of German infantry advanced until the last defenders were hit by small-arms fire from a few yards away. Under the assault of German Schmeisser submachine-guns, Batiuk's line dissolved. The Russian survivors tried to fight their way through to their own troops. They had only their bayonets to do it with. What took place in the next ten minutes is near indescribable. The assault and defence were undertaken with clubs and knives and boots. Hand grenades exploded.[21] The last dozen were compressed into a dugout near the summit around Col. Batiuk. His only choice was to surrender. They all knew what happened to political commissars, but there were also stories that the Germans hanged regular army officers. So when the first German appeared near his dugout, Col. Batiuk, this heroic divisional commander, raised the Nagan pistol to his temple, pulled the trigger and collapsed.

Down from the Kurgan, along the riverbank, the Red Army's 13th and 34th Regiments were cut off. The remnants realised that their position was hopeless and that no relief would come. Yet they kept on fighting to the last man and the last bullet. The final message from their last surviving regimental officer, Maj. Dimitri Panikhin, was left unfinished in an ancient Underwood typewriter: 'ENEMY AT COMMAND POST. THEY ARE THROWING GRENADES . . .'

A historic tank duel took place inside the giant assembly

21 In the war museum at Stalingrad is a wall panorama of the heroic last stand on top of Mamayev Kurgan.

halls of the Red October tractor plant. German panzers were shooting down the line at Russian tanks. Each lathe, each steel press was defended to the last. The battle ended in a stand-off. Like gasping mastodons, each side was too exhausted to advance another metre, unable to take the plant or evict the aggressor. While the Germans held the northern end of the assembly line, the Russians barricaded themselves down the opposite end behind smouldering tank carcasses, fallen roof beams and dead bodies piled up like sandbags.

Along the steep embankment of the Volga were the remains of a red-brick house that had suffered a series of direct hits.[22] It served a regiment from the 62nd Soviet Army as their forward observation post. Their perimeter had shrunk to a thin slice of land, a final redoubt with its outer edge not farther than two hundred yards from the riverbank. Since dawn they had been under steady attack by a battalion of Sturmgrenadiere. From the command centre on the first floor of that red-brick house, Capt. Rastanko could see German troops advancing towards both his flanks. He gave orders to hold the line to the last bullet and then use bayonets. The Germans mustn't get hold of the central sector of the Volga embankment, the thinnest of lifelines for the beleaguered garrison. Rastanko heard rapid shots from downstairs. Lt Vassilev ran to the staircase in time to see a German steel helmet racing up towards him. He fired and a body was blown back down the stairs to end up next to the Soviet guards that had been killed by the Germans. 'Grenade!' someone yelled, and then there was an awful explosion behind him. He turned to see his commander being knocked into the wall before he flopped to the ground. Lt Vassilev dropped his gun and knelt down beside his captain, whose eyes were fixed and dilated. The lieutenant touched a finger to the open eye. There was no reflex response. Rastanko was dead. Vassilev ran back to the telephone to take control of the situation, but the

[22] It is still there and is now part of a museum.

explosion had cut the line. He had moved to the hole that served as their lookout point to give a hand signal when a burst hit him squarely in the chest, splattering his blood on the wall. Moments later more steel-helmeted Germans climbed up the stairs. They dumped the bodies through a hole in the floorboards and took possession of this strategic position. From here they could guide their artillery fire – high on the embankment they had a perfect view of the riverbank and, with it, the last three ferry crossings. The Germans were now in the city centre and a mere two hundred metres from the Volga! And that was as far they got . . . because they too were so exhausted that they could advance no more. In a desperate counter-attack by a group made up of tankers without tanks, factory workers and students with guns they had collected from the dead, the Germans were thrown out and the red ruin was once again in Russian hands – and all for the loss of some three hundred lives.

This was 10 November. From now on, both sides fought the type of battle imposed on them by exhaustion, conducted with utter brutality. The wounded were left to die and many prisoners were shot. Companies and battalions were wasted in a final head-on charge. They came on in a frenzy, men bunched together, crouched low to avoid the bullets or to pick up guns. The first line were prone to getting snagged on the barbed wire they tried to crawl over, or pushed into it by the men behind them. There they hung, writhing, with bloody hands and faces, tearing at the needle-sharp strands lodged in their bodies. Both sides fired into the mangled bodies from behind walls or sandbags. A lot of the fighting was done from basement windows and sewers, and that was why the Germans called it the '*Rattenkrieg*', the war of rats.

No place was safe from bombs and shells. Women and children who had failed to flee in time and who hid out in basements had to dig themselves from beneath buildings that had collapsed on top of them. They tried to reach the shoreline, piled high with twisted corpses from artillery bombardment and burned ferry boats. In the rubble of the city, the situation worsened by the minute. Behind every window lay the enemy, from every doorway came a stream of deadly bullets. Every house became a bunker, a fortress, a cemetery. Germans stormed a building's first floor, Russians retreated to the second floor; Germans took the kitchen and Russians took the living room. Then the Russians stormed into the kitchen and the Germans fired through the adjoining wall. Buildings, shattered by shells, buried friend and foe alike. At night-time the city was brightly lit by the fires in buildings and factories.

Anna Blumenthal was terrified of the screaming dive-bombers. Death fell from the sky; bombs hurtled on to the tiny perimeter still held by the groups of defenders. Hour after hour she could hear the drone of engines, the noise of heavily laden machines. And she found herself right in the midst of the howling aircraft, in a basement taking care of some wounded, not able to see what was going on up top and wondering when the next bomb would crush her. When she emerged from her hole, she was blinded by the white incandescence of a burning city. The heat was tremendous, and wherever she went the smell of burning corpses wafted around her. She was asked to collect bullets from the dead, Soviet and German alike. 'Sometimes I found a few dozen, sometimes only two or three, but it kept our valiant defenders in ammunition.' She walked until her feet were blistered. Around her were broken cement and shattered dreams. She kept thinking of her little son. Would she ever see him again?

At the beginning of November she had just taken a submachine-gun with half a magazine from a body when she saw three shadows rushing at her from a ruin. She didn't know if they were Germans or Russians; she just fired. No one knew friend from foe any longer. And then she ran as one who is marked for death.

He looked like a singed ghost rising from the grave, this

young Soviet lieutenant, his uniform blood-splattered and in shreds and with a deep cut on his forehead, who erred across the rubble. His eyes stared listlessly at the three men who confronted him.

'Where is your unit?'

'Dead . . . all dead.'

'So you abandoned them?'

'But comrade, what is there to abandon, they're all dead.' The lieutenant began to sob.

'I'm not your comrade and you are a deserter,' the man barked. '*Rastelryat!* – Guilty!' They shot the young lieutenant on the spot.

On the slopes of Mamayev Kurgan, a young German soldier put down his weapon, sat and wept. Three times they had stormed up those cursed 'Iron Heights' until not a single man was left of his company. 'I knock your teeth in if you don't move, *du Feigling* – you coward,' said a voice, kicking him in the shin. The young soldier looked up at a bully of an SS Scharführer. To him this SS thug represented the sum of all this confusion, of mad orders and personal frustrations. Slowly he picked up his rifle and then shot the SS man. With this gesture he hoped to expiate his suffering and that of his comrades. Then he walked slowly up the fire-spitting hill, alone.

When Stalingrad seemed lost, an Allied-induced miracle happened. On 5 November 1942, Gen. Montgomery attacked at El Alamein and on 8 November Gen. Eisenhower invaded Algeria; Hitler's attention was suddenly diverted from the Stalingrad front to North Africa. For forty-eight hours he forgot all about his major theatre of war, and these hours were to prove decisive. Halder's greatest fear, an attack against the exposed flank of the Stalingrad salient, was about to become reality. Despite his horrendous losses in the city, Hitler prevailed: 'Not a square metre of ground will be given up.' That choice was no longer his. Stalin was about to unleash his secret weapon: a million men, ten thousand guns and thousands of modern T-34 tanks. That this was also to come as a total surprise to Stalin's allies was confirmed by a cable, sent by Churchill only twenty-four hours before the start of the Soviet offensive: '. . . WE HAVE GIVEN STALIN TO UNDERSTAND THAT THE GREAT ATTACK ON THE CONTINENT WILL COME IN 1943 . . . I NEVER MEANT THE ANGLO-AMERICAN ARMY TO BE STUCK IN NORTH AFRICA. IT IS A SPRINGBOARD, NOT A SOFA . . .'[23] Nothing in Churchill's resolute invasion message, intended to relieve pressure on the badly mauled Russians, shows that the Allies knew or even thought that the Russians were able to go it alone. *They were unaware of Stalin's reserves.*

The forces at Stalin's disposal were huge. These comprised north to south:

Vatutin's south-west front: 1st Guards Army, 5th Tank Army and 21st Army
Rokossovsky's Don front: 65th Army (partly 4th Tank Army), 24th and 66th Armies
Eremenko's Stalingrad front: 62nd and 64th Armies in Stalingrad and 57th and 51st Armies
In reserve: Malinovski's 1st Reserve Army plus 8 Tank Corps with another 1,600 tanks

Their main objective: 5th Tank Army and 21st Army to attack from the north and 57th Army and 51st Army from the south to join up near the town of Kalach on the Don.

Marshal Zhukov and his chief-of-staff Vasilievski were hard at work, planning the massive counterstroke. On 18 November a message went out from Stavka HQ to Gen. Rokossovsky (Don front), Gen. Vatutin (south-west front) and Gen. Eremenko (Stalingrad front). Vatutin then instructed

23 W. Churchill, *The Hinge of Fate*, op. cit.

the generals Batov (65th Army), Romanenko (5th Tank Army) and Chistiakov (21st Army): 'SEND THE PERSON WHO IS TO RECEIVE THEM FOR THE FUR GLOVES.' Decoded, this read: 'START INFANTRY ATTACK 19 NOVEMBER '42 – 0805 HOURS.'

'*Nachalos* . . . it has started, Vasili Vasilievich! Can you hear?' These were the first words in months to cause a thin smile to flicker on the face of the defender of Stalingrad, Gen. Vasili Chuikov. He stepped outside his command tunnel. The sound of distant gunfire and the thunder of many explosions could clearly be heard. The deafening chorus was once more increased by the release of thousands of Katyusha rockets. Their high and increasing rate of fire set up a continuous roar. '*Nachalos!*' he said in a quiet voice, almost as if in prayer. The time was 0732 hours on a bitterly cold morning, 19 November 1942. Chuikov, in a highly relieved state, watched formations of silver planes flying over the ruins of his city. These were not German attack aircraft but Russian fighter-bombers. The men gathered around their general; they were grey faced, hardly able to keep their red-rimmed eyes open; their cheeks were hollow and unshaven, but still they managed a rousing cheer.

At 8.05 a.m. the Soviet Army struck the flank of Paulus's 6th Army near Serafimovich on the Don. Units from the 5th Romanian Army Corps of the 3rd Romanian Army, a country allied to the Germans, had been allotted the defence of this sector on the northern flank of the Stalingrad salient. These troops were poorly armed, but then no great danger was expected to come in their direction, and for many weeks all had been quiet on that sector of the front line. That morning was to be full of surprises. The first came with warm food from a field kitchen, their first warm meal in weeks. The second surprise was less pleasant. Most of the Romanian troops were sitting down to a leisurely breakfast, when from the swirling fog appeared white-clad Russian fighters.

The mass of soldiers began to flow forward. Suddenly there were Russians everywhere; a whole front poured over the Romanian trenches, into their dugouts. The Romanians struggled and fell. There were acts of heroism and others of treachery, yet no one beyond the chaos would ever know about them – not that anyone cared much about the fate of the valiant but inadequately equipped Romanians. Following brief hand-to-hand combat, conducted without mercy, the Soviet infantry pierced the Romanian position in three different places. Through these holes poured the tanks of Gens Romanenko and Chistiakov. A wave of T-34s swept the Romanian 5th Army Corps from its defensive positions. With the Romanians' rout, Paulus's northern flank suddenly developed a gaping hole. Encountering no further resistance, the Russian tanks raced for Kalach and the Don. More units struck the 3rd Romanian Army of Generaloberst Dumitrescu at Kletskaja and the 4th Romanians of Gen. Konstantinescu at Beketovka. The Russian tanks rolled over the helpless Romanians and crushed them into the ground.

So far no German unit had been in contact with the advancing Russian juggernaut. In the Corps HQ of Gen. von Seydlitz-Kursbach, opinions were voiced, but the overall situation was still unclear. Earlier that day, a snowstorm had prevented the Luftwaffe from launching reconnaissance flights. According to initial ground reports, some Red Army units had struck at the German flank. But nothing was said about their size or strength. Seydlitz thought his tank forces strong enough to carry out a manoeuvre against the enemy, as they had done time and again in the past. The Germans held only a small reserve to back up their Romanian allies, the panzers of Generalleutnant Heim, mainly captured, thin-skinned Czech Skodas, no match for the heavy T-34. The general didn't realise that he was actually ordering parts of two divisions to go up against a full tank army and a rifle army – his hundred panzers against thousands of the enemy. The Germans were getting ready when they heard the drone of aircraft engines and looked up. 'Hermann and his Luftwaffe will soon put order into this,' said a staff officer, before the first explosions shook the ground. 'Russian planes! *Deckung!*' Petrol dumps, ammunition dumps – the world exploded around them. Hundreds of Russian planes dumped a shower of explosives and everywhere chains of destruction were set off. Seydlitz's mobile units were obliterated, his infantry buried under fountains of earth. A car pulled up with a divisional general who looked as if he had emerged from hell.

Seydlitz pointed to the devastation around him. 'General, it's an entire army that comes down on us. We need ammo and fuel.'

'And where do you expect me to get it? Go back to your division and hold. That's an order.' As the size and scope of the Russian attack became known, they left no doubt about its final aim and outcome.

There was the continuous roar of a thousand motors as more Soviet tanks and self-propelled weapons lumbered in waves across the frozen steppe. They came out of the early mist, quickly extending the forward edge of the battle area, and blasted everything in their way. For the first time since the beginning of the war, Soviet planning was solid. The army commanders recognised that changes would be forced upon them as the action developed and they had planned flexibly. The operational plan of attack could be radically altered in a matter of hours, as a new, younger generation of commanders responded to the developing situation. Even logistical support – a huge tonnage of material, from fuel and ammunition to food and medical supplies – followed in good time the flow of the battle. The fresh Soviet divisions pushed on fast and every hour deeper into the back of the German 6th Army. Paulus was still in the dark, but not for long. The picture soon became clear – two Russian tank armies had struck a decisive blow and routed his flank protection.

The chief-of-staff at Army Group B (Weichs) suggested an immediate withdrawal of the German spearhead from the

Stalingrad salient. But this required specific permission from Hitler. Until such could be obtained, Generalfeldmarschall von Weichs issued an order: 'THE SITUATION DEVELOPING ON THE FRONT OF THE 3RD ROMANIAN ARMY DICTATES RADICAL MEASURES . . . ALL OFFENSIVE OPERATIONS IN STALINGRAD TO BE STOPPED . . . CONCENTRATE ON ATTACKS TOWARD NORTHWEST AND WEST.'

That was the moment when a secondary Soviet attack smashed into the Italian 8th Army protecting the Germans' flank on the Volga, south of Stalingrad. Paulus's 22 divisions were up against 114 divisions of 'non-existing reserves'. It is an ancient truism that in war nothing goes according to plan; Hitler was left with a disaster based entirely on the 'peculiarity of false positions'. With no other option, his only hope was that the enemy might commit a blunder.

While the attack built up momentum, Stalin paced up and down in the situation room of the Kremlin, waiting for more reports. He looked at the map and then again at the telephone. Why didn't it ring, and what would be the message when it did? Gen. Eremenko had assured him of success, but until he received confirmation there was always the possibility of yet another disaster. With all the promises and failures of the past, Stalin had learned to trust nobody but himself. There was another worry that preoccupied him, and it was of a political nature. How would he explain to his allies the sudden appearance of a million men on the battlefield? Roosevelt and Churchill had shown a certain amount of confidence, and he hadn't been quite open during his recent meeting with Churchill. This the Englishman had detected, and that was why he had behaved so angrily before his departure. What must have irritated Stalin most was the thought that the Western leaders always debated among themselves before letting him in on their next move. Surely (such was the working of a paranoid's mind) they considered him as nothing more than some oriental potentate, and not their equal as leader of a European power. Why did he have to justify his every move to them? His 'dear allies' knew, as did he, that war was a temporary condition, but politics were not. He had proven his political prowess to the likes of Bukharin and Kamenev, Trotsky and Tuchachevski. Since the beginning of this war he had had to act like a fox with his allies. But now a change in the fortunes of war was within his grasp. Once victory over the fascist wolf was his, it didn't matter by what means he achieved it; he'd be above worrying how to explain his deception to his Western allies. At the dawn of his greatest military triumph, a paranoid Russian dictator locked himself in a dungeon of his own mental creation, and would remain its prisoner for the rest of his life. What played out in the next few hours inside the walls of the Kremlin can hardly be imagined. Tension, stress, nervous electricity were everywhere – in the courtyards, in the hallways, in the strategy rooms. The entire fate of the state created by Lenin hinged on one phone call. Stalin was plagued by terrible stomach cramps. Why hadn't Eremenko called? What was wrong? When the phone jingled, its shrill sound was heard throughout the Kremlin . . .

Winter held sway. The temperature dropped to –15°, –20°, then –35°C. As always in times of greatest peril, as when the country reeled under the attacks of Carl XII of Sweden and, after him, Napoleon, General Frost and General Winter had come to the assistance of Mother Russia. The icy storm blew snow clouds across the battlefield. The great Nazi plan of world hegemony ground to a halt in the frozen plain between the Don and the Volga. For Gen. von Paulus, the surprise was sprung at the most inopportune moment; in Stalingrad a heroic stand by a makeshift army of soldiers and factory workers had broken his troops' offensive spirit. A lot had to do with the sub-zero temperatures. Anna Blumenthal had been put in charge of the wounded, and she was finally evacuated by ferry when the defensive perimeter had shrunk to within two hundred yards of the river.[24] 'It was the coldest winter in memory. Anyone left in the open for more than thirty minutes was certain to perish. Many of our wounded boys froze to death before they could be got at, but then the Germans suffered even greater losses from the cold. They couldn't evacuate their wounded and their front-line units were ill equipped to deal with the Russian winter. They were dependent on their machines,[25] we were not.'

On 21 November, Generaloberst von Paulus dispatched an urgent request to Hitler's OKW to pull his army back and punch a hole through the ever tightening ring with his remaining panzers. As fate had it, that day the military brains of the Wehrmacht were spread all over the map. Gen. Zeitzler held the fort at OKW in East Prussia but did not have the necessary authority. His operational staff was in Salzburg, while Hitler, the only one who could take such a decision, was in his eagle's nest at Berchtesgaden. Isolated from his military strategists, and without further counselling, Hitler denied the request for a withdrawal and issued his infamous *Igelbefehl* (porcupine order): 'THE COMMANDER IN CHIEF [PAULUS] WILL PROCEED WITH HIS STAFF TO STALINGRAD. THE 6TH ARMY WILL FORM AN *IGEL* (porcupine).'

A second cable followed this initial order almost immediately: 'THOSE UNITS OF THE 6TH ARMY THAT REMAIN BETWEEN DON AND VOLGA WILL HENCEFORTH BE DESIGNATED *FESTUNG STALINGRAD* (Fortress Stalingrad).'

Paulus replied instantaneously:

GEHEIME KOMMANDOSACHE, 6. ARMEE AN OKH . . .

24 She took the author on a tour of the many plaques on house fronts which show the real extent of German penetration.

25 While the engines of German armoured vehicles were machined to perfection, pistons in Russian petrol engines were notoriously loose and thereby didn't seize up in the cold.

> *DIE ARMEE GEHT IN KÜRZESTER ZEIT DER VERNICHTUNG ENTGEGEN, WENN NICHT UNTER ZUSAMMENFASSUNG ALLER KRÄFTE DER VON SÜDEN UND WESTEN ANGREIFENDE FEIND GESCHLAGEN WIRD. BITTE AUFGRUND DER LAGE NOCHMALS UM HANDLUNGSFREIHEIT.* (signed) PAULUS 23.11.42 23.45 *UHR* . . . The army is condemned to annihilation in short time, should it fail to assemble all its forces and defeat the enemy attacking from south and west. Based on situation request once again freedom of decision. Paulus.

Hitler was now irretrievably engaged at Stalingrad. His reply came as no surprise:

> *DIE ARMEE DARF ÜBERZEUGT SEIN DASS ICH ALLES TUN WERDE UM SIE ENTSPRECHEND ZU VERSORGEN UND RECHTZEITIG ZU ENTSETZEN. ICH KENNE DIE TAPFERE 6. ARMEE UND IHREN OBERBEFEHLSHABER UND WEISS, DASS SIE IHRE PFLICHT TUN WIRD.* (signed) ADOLF HITLER 24.11.42 . . . The army may be reassured that I will do everything to supply it and deliver it in due course. I know the brave 6th Army and its courageous commander and also know that it will stand up to its duty. Adolf Hitler.

With this, Hitler sealed the fate of an army and pronounced a death sentence on 250,000 brave men. And Paulus, steeped in Prussian military discipline and blind obeisance, did nothing to act contrary to the specific order by a superior commander, suicidal and foolish though this directive may have been.

One person did act. Field Marshal von Manstein, the newly appointed commander-in-chief of Germany's Don front, crossed to a large wall map. Pins of various colours represented divisions dotted across the stretches of white, with a heavy concentration of red pins coming down from the north into the back of the 6th Army. Stony faced, Manstein studied the map. He knew what he had to do. He defied Hitler's order and radioed Paulus to take what was left of his army and break out. But Generaloberst von Paulus's brain was no longer working along rational lines; the stress had become too much. Arguing over the simplest issue with the bosses at OKW, and trying to keep his army from annihilation, was more than any man could bear. He felt abandoned at this most climactic moment of his life when all his energy should have been directed to reaching a decision. A sense of the visitation of doom was upon him. What was he to do? Disobey an order? He recalled the pertinent words of Count von Moltke, the military genius of Bismarck: 'Obedience is the principle, but above the principle stands the man.' When the only way to save his men was to turn will into action, he became despondent over this question of 'obedience' versus 'above the principle'. He was caught in a mental prison that others had built around him years ago during his strict upbringing; he was a general steeped in the Prussian tradition of giving orders to those below and obeying orders from those above. Such was not the reasoning of his number two, Artillery General von Seydlitz-Kursbach. In earshot of the staff at 6th Army HQ he had a heated confrontation with his superior. 'For God's sake, Paulus, let us take our men out of here. We still have time and the means to do it.'

'I have the Führer's orders. I will not go against them.'

Every one of his divisional commanders urged Paulus to listen to Manstein and Seydlitz, and not to that political madman Hitler. Paulus answered them with the lame excuse that his tanks had fuel for only twenty miles. 'So we dump them and walk out on foot. We can always replace a tank but not an army of brave German soldiers.' Paulus remained adamant. What was the value of principle if it was not directly connected to obedience? It was dishonour! He simply wouldn't consider leading a breakout from the pocket without the specific order from his supreme commander,

Adolf Hitler! Thus he missed the last chance to deliver his 6th Army from certain destruction.

Hitler's refusal and Paulus's blind obeisance created the worst possible scenario and played into the hands of the Red Army. On 23 November the trap snapped shut. Shortly after midday, the Soviet 36th Brigade of Gen. Volski's 4th Mechanised Corps reached the southern bank of the River Karpovka, and at 4 p.m. that same afternoon they saw white-clad men running towards them from the opposite shore, waving wildly. They were from the 45th Brigade of Gen. Kravchenko's 4th Tank Corps. It was an historic encounter, immortalised by Soviet newsreel cameras. Caught on the inside of the ring of steel were parts of Hoth's 4th Panzer Army and von Paulus's entire 6th Army, twenty-two German divisions, an anti-aircraft corps, two mortar regiments, two Romanian divisions and a Croat regiment.

Hitler's decisions were always based on his political thoughts, but now these decisions lost their last shred of coherence. Everything he ordered was on the spur of the moment or in a panic. Rather than withdraw Army Group A from the Caucasus and head for Paulus with everything they'd got, Hitler went for the worst possible option. He ordered a makeshift panzer force under Gen. Hoth to break through the iron ring around von Paulus's 6th Army. Operation Wintersturm began on 12 December. For this task, Hoth's force was frightfully weak; lacking transport, petrol and ammunition, his men made a superhuman effort and fought themselves to within twenty-two miles of Paulus's position. While this relief operation was going on, the nervous tension in OKW was tremendous; with the noted exception of Hitler, who showed little concern about the fate of Paulus and his men, his generals knew what was at stake. A major defeat of the invincible Wehrmacht! They willed Hoth on, another mile and then another. Only ten more miles and Paulus could break out with a concerted attack from inside the ring. This still seemed a distinct possibility when Hoth received a report about a new Guard Army forming up to his north-east. The information about this threat to his flank was correct, but its reported location was not. The 2nd Guard Army had indeed moved into position, but they were to Hoth's south-east. On Christmas Day 1942, just as he thought his panzers had finally broken through the blockade, his spearhead ran into the combined forces of three Soviet armies: the 2nd Guard, the 5th Shock and the 51st Rifle Army. It resulted in a massacre. The turning point in the battle for Stalingrad had come. By executing a brilliant tactical manoeuvre, Hoth managed to extract his depleted force, thereby abandoning the trapped men inside the *Festung Stalingrad* to their fate. Nothing could now save Paulus's 6th Army from annihilation.

The German forces inside the *Festung* were exhausted from lack of sleep and nights of bitter cold. They suffered severe and irreplaceable casualties. Corps Commander von Seydlitz-Kursbach dispatched a message to Generaloberst von Paulus:

> *. . . DIE ARMEE STEHT VOR DEM EINDEUTIGEN ENTWEDER-ODER. DURCHBRUCH NACH SÜDWESTEN, ODER UNTERGANG IN WENIGEN TAGEN . . . DIE VÖLLIGE VERNICHTUNG VON 200.000 KÄMPFERN UND IHRER GESAMMTEN MATERIALAUSTATTUNG STEHT AM SPIEL. ES GIBT KEINE ANDERE WAHL.* (signed) SEYDLITZ . . . The army is at the point of either-or. We have to break out towards the south-west or face total annihilation of 200,000 fighting men plus all their matériel. We have no choice. (signed) Seydlitz

Generaloberst von Paulus tried to put on a brave face despite his dejection at the size of the calamity. Now his self-control was all that he had left, and it had to last until the final blow of destiny would shatter it.

* * *

Two dozen T-34 battle tanks thundered, creaking and clanking, through the smoke from burning buildings and the dust from explosions. Multi-barrelled rockets brought down an enormous concentration of fire to cover the advance of Guard infantry. The smoke of exploding shells and impacting rockets obscured the position of the German enemy. Waves of foot-soldiers followed closely behind the tanks and rushed from ruin to ruin. The Germans were firing from well-chosen positions behind makeshift barricades. Men were bowled over; flames and black smoke poured from a T-34 tank. All over town, what was left of it, the terrifying whiplash of automatic rifle fire and the clash of iron filled the air.

A hundred Soviet divisions from Stalin's strategic reserve compressed the Germans inside a constantly shrinking perimeter. Soon they were holding only a few city blocks. On 10 January, the Russians cut Paulus's army into two separate pockets. Hauptmann Kerner, the senior officer of a Sturmtruppe battalion, could hear the approaching rumble of truck engines, carrying more troops to deliver death and destruction. And always more of the same rumbling. Was it a dream, was it reality? For days they had been on the run, bone tired, scared and too exhausted to care, leaving behind them piles of grotesquely frozen bodies. They had found shelter in a factory ruin. There they fell asleep. Kerner emerged from his nightmare still more asleep than awake. But the sound remained . . . rumbling. His eyes opened and he stared out of the hole in the wall. The dawn was beginning to break. He was out of the dream now and still he heard the sound of engines. The sound was real. Russian tanks! – this dreadful clanging noise spreading terror and confusion. 'Tanks,' he yelled, and again: 'Tanks!' His men jumped up, sleep drunk, staring in confusion at their leader. 'Tanks!' He pointed to the back of their ruin. Carrying his Schmeisser submachine-gun levelled, he raced towards the big hole which served as the entrance to the factory building. Several men were outlined against the opening. Kerner fired a burst and the men were blown back through the hole. Around him were his own men, crouched down, ready to fire. A soldier moved with a Panzerfaust to a hole, took aim, and fired his rocket. It was followed by a blast as a Russian T-34 tank burst into flames. '*Hinter uns*, behind us,' yelled a soldier. Half a dozen Russians sprinted across the empty factory halls. The Germans fired. 'Decker, Baumann, follow me,' yelled Kerner, and tore after the Russians. The two men sprinted behind their captain across the shattered bricks littered with the frozen corpses from an earlier battle; Corporal Decker pulled the fuse of a grenade and tossed it over a heap of rubble. As it exploded Baumann raked the hall with automatic fire. His clip empty, he was about to exchange it when he threw up his arms and fell over. He lay rock still on the factory floor, his eyes open. Hauptmann Kerner signalled to his corporal to move around the wall before he pulled a grenade from his satchel; he was priming the fuse when a burst struck him in the shoulder. He fell on his own grenade and thereby saved the lives of his men at the cost of his own. An Unteroffizier (corporal) was now the new battalion commander. Corporal Wilhelm Decker survived Stalingrad only to starve on the road into Siberian captivity.

The day was grey and cold. The thermometer showed minus 30°C. The storm broke over the city, and a martyred town was for the last time buried under a deluge of fire. It announced the final act of the drama. On 10 January 1943, seven thousand Russian guns lobbed shell after shell into the Germans' last stand. Within five days, their outer perimeter had crumpled, and in another week the Soviet 21st Army met the heroic defenders of Stalingrad, Chuikov's 62nd Army, in the centre of the city. Paulus hung on with 'a herd of stumbling, frost-bitten men'. Hour after hour, his perimeter shrank.

Yuri Skropatkin was a machinegunner, one of the few survivors from a company of riflemen. Throughout the fight he had carried a Russian pennant wrapped around his body under the uniform. Their order was to clear Mamayev Kurgan of the remnants of the enemy; today he would plant the flag on top of the hill. Like some fire-spitting dragon, he and his comrades progressed in line up the hill. They were met by rifle fire from higher up the ridge. Bullets whistled overhead; some fell and others stormed forward to fill the gaps. But no bullet could reach him, of that Yuri was convinced. The enemy's fire became thinner before it stopped altogether. Ghosts rose from trenches with hands raised high above heads, the limping remnants of a German battalion. The summit was tantalisingly near. Yuri Skropatkin pulled out his red flag and rushed ahead. Then he stepped on a mine.

For four days the small group of Panzergrenadiere had fought valiantly – four days in hell. They hadn't eaten and were down to five bullets a man. Their acting commander was Klaus Kunze, a twenty-two-year-old corporal from Nürnberg. He was so tired all he could think of was sleep. One of his group had taken slivers from smashed timbers to light a fire, and then he had spread the hot ashes on the stone floor and lain down on their warmth. The others had followed his example. Klaus closed his eyes and recalled the day seven years before when, as representative of his *Hitlerjugend Fähnleins*, he had been honoured to participate in the grandiose 1935 *Reichsparteitag* on the Luitpoldhain in Nürnberg.[26] The Führer had walked down the centre aisle, between thousands of party standards and the hundred thousand men of the SA and SS lining his route. How they had cheered the saviour of the nation and prophet of a New Germany. Now the same prophet had abandoned them to their abject fate – an army of the forgotten. The tip of a boot kicked Klaus. He opened his eyes and saw a gun

[26] As portrayed in the famous documentary film *Macht des Willens* by Leni Riefenstahl.

pointed at him. Klaus no longer had the strength to put a bullet into his brain as he had intended to do. He just raised his arms. His Russian captors locked him and his group into a cold basement. There they left them to go on fighting. They forgot all about their prisoners, or were probably themselves killed in some street battle. Some days later a Soviet clean-up squad came to check the cellar; they found a group of frozen Germans.

For the remnants of the 6th Army, used to marching to a seemingly never-ending string of victories in three hard years of war, their world was dying before their eyes. The wounded starved first since they were the weakest. It almost didn't matter when or how they died – their situation was hopeless. If they fought on they were going to die by the bullet, and if they surrendered they would perish on the road to the camps. Many of them chose the hero's alternative and fought on. They kept the last bullet for themselves. There are no pictures of their suffering. No wonder the Nazi leaders prohibited photography – the effect on national morale would have been devastating. The picture would have been one of sheer horror. The dead were stacked outside their foxholes like firewood; the biting cold did the rest. It was a vision from hell, this 'fight to the last bullet'. The final messages from General von Paulus to OKW portrayed the hopelessness of the situation:

> 20 JANUARY: . . . I REQUEST FREEDOM OF ACTION IN ORDER TO RESIST AS LONG AS POSSIBLE OR CEASE MILITARY ACTIVITY IF CANNOT BE CONTINUED, WOUNDED CANNOT BE CARED FOR AND TOTAL DEMORALIZATION AVOIDED. PAULUS.
>
> 22 JANUARY: NO MORE FOODSTUFF. 12,000 WOUNDED INSIDE PERIMETER. WHAT ORDERS AM I TO GIVE THE TROOPS WHO HAVE RUN OUT OF AMMUNITION AND SUFFER FROM CONTINUED ATTACKS BY TANK FORMATIONS, HEAVY ARTILLERY

> BOMBARDMENT AND MASSES OF SOVIET INFANTRY. RAPID DECISION REQUESTED. DISSOLUTION HAS ALREADY BEGUN IN MANY SECTORS.

There was one commander who took it upon himself to go against Hitler's orders. General der Artillerie von Seydlitz-Kursbach, second in rank to Paulus, issued a directive that left it up to individual commanders to take responsible action to protect the lives of their men:

> STALINGRAD 25.1.43 21.00 *UHR – KORPSBEFEHL* (corps order) *DIE REGIMENTSKOMMANDÖRE ERHALTEN HIERMIT DAS RECHT, JE NACH ÖRTLICHER LAGE, DEN REST DER MUNITION ZU VERSCHIESSEN UND DAMIT DEN KAMPF EINZUSTELLEN.* (*gez*) von Seydlitz, General der Artillerie . . . Regimental commanders are herewith authorised, depending on the situation, to fire off the rest of munitions and then stop the fight. Seydlitz

That night, elements of the 64th and 57th Soviet armies cut through the city centre. The decisive day was the 26th, when the 22nd Army met up with the 62nd Army of Chuikov on Mamayev Kurgan. (A photograph, much like the famous photograph of the flag-raising on Iwo Shima, shows a single Soviet soldier waving his submachine-gun next to a red flag tied to a fence post on top of the blood-drenched hill.[27]) With this, the 6th Army was cleanly cut into two pockets. Whatever was left of Germany's pride was falling apart. Hitler's 'undefeatables' surrendered. First to put down his arms was Gen. Drebber of the 287th Infantry Division, followed by Gen. Dimitriu of the 20th Romanian Infantry. The commander of the 113th Infantry, Gen. Stempel, went into his dugout, pulled out his gun and, in front of his

27 APN photo.

shocked staff, blew out his brains. Gen. von Hartmann of the 71st Infantry chose a hero's death; he grabbed a submachine-gun, jumped on top of his trench and kept firing at the advancing Russians until he himself was struck in the forehead. The picture inside the circle of fire was one of total collapse; officers and soldiers put an end to their suffering by turning their arms on themselves. Many surrendered, only to be instantly executed by the Russians.[28] Others were shot by their own execution squads. Such was the case of an infantry captain. His unit had been overrun, his men lay dead in the trenches, and his nerves had finally given out. He was ordered to report to battalion command, where he tried to explain his predicament and that of his men – fifty against a regiment of many thousands. '*Halt die Schnauze, du feiger Hund!* Shut your mouth, you cowardly dog!' growled an SS lieutenant, seconded to battalion to keep up morale. The captain babbled on about his loyalty to the Führer, his proven obedience and the many battles he had fought for his *Vaterland*. Nobody cared. In his final desperation, he turned to his commanding colonel: 'What . . . what is going to happen to me . . . *Bitte, Herr Oberst* . . .' he pleaded with tears running down his cheeks. The colonel shook his head; confronted by Himmler's SS executioners, he was powerless to intervene. He turned away and the SS man answered instead. 'Whatever happens to cowards and deserters.' He gave an order to his sergeant: '*Knall den Hund ab* – shoot the dog.' A shot rang out. The former captain of infantry, Herbert Blank, stood for another moment with an unbelieving expression on his face before his knees buckled. The SS lieutenant kicked the inert corpse. 'I've seen men die with more dignity.'

Goebbels' propaganda machine was grinding out daily ideological hogwash. It was of no use – the German nation no longer believed in the invincibility of its army.

[28] N. Khrushchev, *Krushchev remembers: the last testiment*, Boston 1974.

On 25 January von Manstein called Hitler: '*Mein Führer*, willpower alone cannot overcome military logic. Your soldiers have reached their end.' Hitler rejected the logic. If a prime example of the mind of a maniac needs to be provided, it came in the single phrase the infuriated Hitler screamed down the wire: '*Die Pflicht meiner Soldaten in Stalingrad ist zu sterben* . . . The duty of my soldiers in Stalingrad is to die!' He ordered one last overflight of the pocket. It didn't bring bullets, it didn't bring food or medicines; it dropped a box of Iron Crosses intended to keep up the troops' morale!

The Deutschlandfunk (All-German radio) announced: '*Die noch kampffähigen Teile der 6. Armee verkrallen sich in den Trümmern von Stalingrad* . . . Those units of the 6th Army, still able to put up a struggle, hang on in the rubble of Stalingrad . . .'

Paulus sent a pleading message to Hitler: '26 JANUARY: DEFENCE IN NARROW CITY PERIMETER WITH 40,000 WOUNDED NEAR IMPOSSIBLE.'

When he received no reply, he followed it up with another message, one clear and to the point. '28 JANUARY. *WEITERE VERTEIDIGUNG SINNLOS. ZUSAMMENBRUCH UNVERMEIDBAR . . . ARMEE ERBITTET, UM NOCH VORHANDENE MENSCHENLEBEN ZU RETTEN, UM SOFORTIGE KAPITULATIONSGENEHMIGUNG . . .* All further defence senseless. Disintegration unstoppable. To save further lives army asks for immediate permission to surrender. Have stopped feeding wounded to keep fighters alive. Paulus.'

In OKW, the entire planning staff was assembled around the Eastern Front map table. Hitler's face was frozen; his staring eyes held everyone present transfixed. His voice was cold and impassionate as he turned to an assistant by his side, notebook in hand. 'To Generaloberst von Paulus,' he dictated. This time he left Paulus in no doubt of his role. '*KAPITULATION AUSGESCHLOSSEN. DIE 6. ARMEE ERFÜLLT DAMIT IHRE HISTORISCHE AUFGABE, DEN AUFBAU EINER*

NEUEN FRONT ZU ERMÖGLICHEN. KAMPF BIS ZUR LETZTEN PATRONE! . . . Surrender is out of the question. The 6th Army is to fulfil its historic mission that will allow us to regain our strength in the east. *You are to fight on to the last bullet!* Adolf Hitler.'

'How are we to handle the Paulus situation?' asked Hitler, showing his frustration over this officer's obstinacy and refusal to die as a hero. He didn't consider the fate of three hundred thousand of Germany's best. Chief of General Staff Zeitzler suggested: 'Make Paulus a field marshal. Never in Germany's glorious history has a Feldmarschall surrendered his baton.'

That same morning, Goebbels' propaganda machine issued an announcement designed to prepare the nation for the worst: '*In Stalingrad die Lage ist unverändert. Der Mut der Verteidiger ist ungebrochen* . . . Inside Stalingrad the situation is unchanged and the heroism of its defenders intact. The Führer has appointed the heroic defender of Stalingrad, Friedrich von Paulus, to the rank of a Generalfeldmarschall. Meanwhile in Stalingrad our troops are heroically defending their position to the last. They present a shining example to all soldiers of Germany.'

Friedrich von Paulus stepped outside the Univermag department store, his final redoubt. When his ADC, Oberst Schmidt, had informed him that OKW was on the line, he had just waved his hand. He no longer wished to speak to them. What could he tell them? That what he had been ordered to do was a crime? It was as if Hitler had taken a knife and cut the throat of his valiant men. Two-thirds of his proud army lay dead, unburied and frozen under the open sky. For the rest, there was no turning back. Why hadn't he disobeyed the mad dictator's orders and led his army as they fought their way out? It was too late for such thoughts. His first act as Generalfeldmarschall would also be his last. He gazed up at the frost-chilled night sky. Dawn crept up over the frozen

Volga. How beautiful the earth is under the sky of a newborn day, especially when that day is to be your last.

On 31 January 1943, a twenty-one-year-old Ukrainian sub-lieutenant, Fedor Ilchenko, leading a detachment of fifteen men armed with submachine-guns, was dashing under the protection of a low wall towards a flat building, the Univermag department store, when a side door was pushed open. What Fedor saw took his breath away. 'Hold your fire,' yelled the young sub-lieutenant. His men kept their guns trained on the three Germans emerging from the door. One waved a white napkin tied to a stick. The one in the middle with a fur cap pulled down over his ears was obviously a high-ranking officer. The third was the interpreter. '*Mein Chef will mit Ihrem Chef sprechen* . . . My chief wants to talk to your chief.' Young Fedor didn't know what to say. Had they stumbled perchance on the elusive German HQ? The chief – was that Paulus? The Soviet sub-lieutenant caught his breath. 'I'm the chief here. Take me to your man!' The officer with the fur cap shrugged his shoulders and signalled Fedor to follow. 'With that we headed for the door but some Germans yelled to stop as the entrance was mined,' Fedor related soon afterwards to the American war correspondent Walter Kerr. 'I had fifteen men with me, but the Germans would only allow one man inside. I wasn't happy about that, but I went anyway. Inside I met General Roske and Colonel Schmidt. "Where is Paulus?" I asked and they replied: "We're negotiating in his name." So we did.'[29]

A Soviet photographer snapped the picture that made headlines around the world. It showed Generalfeldmarschall von Paulus in a long winter coat with the epaulettes of a Generaloberst, a white scarf tightly wound around his throat, hands buried in his pockets, in the company of his ADC, Oberst Adam, and his Chief-of-Staff, Oberst Schmidt,

[29] W. Kerr, *The Secret of Stalingrad*, London 1979.

approaching Gen. Chumilov's 64th Army headquarters at Beketovka. He replied only to two questions:

'What is your first name?'

'Friedrich.'

'What is your age?'

'Fifty-two.' That was all he would say.

Hitler, who had so disastrously interfered in command decisions in order to ensure that military operations coincided with his political aims, had the final word:[30] 'I don't understand his [Paulus's] act of cowardice. To have surrendered! I have no respect for such a man. If the nerves fail, then there is nothing left but to kill oneself just as the leaders of the past fell upon their swords. Even Varus ordered his slave: Kill me! In an extreme situation, one uses the last bullet to kill oneself . . . you will see, he will now make proclamations of how he has been betrayed and we will see his lack of character down to the last degradation. I can only say, a bad deed can only bring on more evil. No, there was only one way out for him, he should have shot himself.'[31] Hitler's smear on the honour of an extremely brave man was made while a heroic field marshal, who had stood up to the enemy when all hope was gone, was leading thousands of his starving, bleeding men into captivity over the ice of the Volga.

A German army was finally crossing the 'Mother of Rivers'.

The facts

For Germany, destiny lay in the hands of two men – one who ordered and one who obeyed. The brutality and inhumanity of Hitler's behaviour transcends historical explanations

30 In OKH to Gen. Zeitzler, 1 February 1943.

31 From documents found after the war, partly burned, in the Berlin Reichschancellery.

and is only comprehensible in the context of strategic and political choices made by an élite group of power-mad Nazis. Germany, they argued, could only survive if it controlled its own destiny. 'Today Germany belongs to us, and tomorrow the whole world,' their children sang, marching through the streets of Berlin, Hamburg and Vienna. Germany never possessed enough military power to control its own destiny, which was shaped by global economic processes. Once it engaged in a fight with both the East (the manpower resources of the Soviet Union) and the West (the industrial productivity of the United States) it must have become obvious to even the most narrow-minded of Nazis that Germany would perish as a nation. And Hitler was quite willing to take his valiant soldiers down with him.

In Hitler's world there was no room for redemption, and he never showed respect for human lives. '*Die Pflicht meiner Soldaten in Stalingrad ist zu sterben* . . . The duty of my soldiers in Stalingrad is to die!' had screamed a megalomaniac despot. With one phrase, Germany's dictator sacrificed a nation's best fighting men. The tragedy was compounded when his commander in the field obeyed this insane, suicidal command. Had Generaloberst von Paulus disobeyed and succeeded in effecting a breakout, he might have been court-martialled and executed, but he would have saved the lives of hundreds of thousands.

The disaster was total, and the only one to blame was Hitler himself. His constant changes of objective, his insistence on an overextended offensive culminating in the senseless order to hold Stalingrad at all costs, wrecked his best troops. Had Hitler's army been victorious at Stalingrad, Germany's forces would have become sucked farther into the immensity of the Russian continent and, just as a river dries up in sand, they would have been swallowed up and eventually gone down to defeat.

For seventy-two days the world held its breath. Of the

330,000 Germans who set out to conquer the city of Stalin, 90,000 went into captivity between 31 January and 2 February 1943. The rest succumbed to the wounds of war, hunger or bitter cold.[32] Some preferred to die standing up in their trenches rather than face the horrors of Russian captivity. The rest set off, marching in ankle-deep snow across the windswept steppes of Russia to reach their destination, an endless column of tired, starving, defeated men who had been the cream of the German war machine. Along the way 25,000 stragglers fell over dead from cold, exhaustion or summary executions; 60,000 arrived in the Siberian camps, of which 20,000 were placed in isolation wards. Most of them died from malnutrition and lack of hygiene; others suffered mental breakdown and catatonic withdrawal. Those who did survive the years of forced labour that were to follow, on rations close to starvation level, spent their days living out their tragedies, and their nights with dreams of indescribable horror. For years the shadow of death hung over their lives. To their tormented minds and their pain-racked bodies, death seemed almost a mercy. A mere 2,500 were to return to Germany.

For the German people, Stalingrad was a foretaste of hell, and the will to fight went out of its people. The fact that Hitler had knowingly abandoned 300,000 Germans could not remain a secret. Before the final surrender, 35,000 wounded had been evacuated to Germany by air – and they talked. For the first time, the fascist leaders experienced a noticeable weakening of their elaborate communication control. It didn't help that Goebbels tried to raise morale with a fiery speech: '*Wollt ihr den totalen Krieg?* Do you want total war? Do you want it, more radical, more total than we can even imagine today?' Two years earlier he had been answered

[32] Nobody will ever know how many really died; the figures given by German and Russian sources vary greatly. Completely destroyed was the XIV Panzer Corps, the Armee Corps IV, VIII, XI and LI, the Panzer Divisions 44, 71, 76, 79, 94, 100, 113, 295, 305, 371, 376, 384, 389, the Romanian 1st Cavalry and 20th Infantry Division. The German Luftwaffe lost 488 transport planes.

by a nationwide cheer; this time he was greeted with silence. A lapse in Goebbels' tight mind control was illustrated by an uncensored broadcast by General Dietmar put out over Radio-Berlin: 'The tragedy of Stalingrad lies heavy on our souls. For the first time, we have experienced defeat. For the first time, a German army has been annihilated. This is a fate we normally reserve for our enemy, and he made us suffer this terrible fate.' Yes, the 'invincible German Army' had suffered a crushing defeat and nothing, not even the stream of lies pumped out by the Nazi propaganda machine, could change that fact. Germans knew that they had entered a dark tunnel.

Hitler declared four days of national mourning (3–6 February 1943). As a direct consequence of the débâcle, his alliances fell apart. Hungary was stalling on its pro-German commitments. Romania was attempting to shed German influence and Bulgaria, until Stalingrad tempted to join Hitler, now declared war on him. But his troubles weren't over. The climate for a rebellion was in place, and the senseless sacrifice of an army at Stalingrad, ordained by Hitler, set off a wave of anti-Nazi sentiment within the army hierarchy. On 22 January 1943, a group of dissident German general officers gathered in the Berlin residence of Count von Wartenburg to plot the elimination of Hitler. 'Our conspiracy was a great tragedy,' stated one of the conspiring officers who survived the war. 'The world might have ended the war a year and a half earlier – if only the Anglo-American government would have given us some encouragement.' A secret memorandum was passed (via Sweden) to Anthony Eden, asking for acceptable conditions. The dissident officers were out to convince the Western Allies that Hitler had been wrong in the way he ran the war but not in his identification of the true enemy of all humanity: the brutal Bolshevik regime. Some hardliners among German plotters were even discussing the possibility of continuing to fight the Russians with Anglo-American help. The Western leaders did what was expected of them – they did not reply, at least not to the German conspirators. Instead, the day the message reached London Churchill and Roosevelt announced that the Allies would accept nothing short of 'an unconditional surrender of Germany'. That was something no proud Prussian officer could accept, and it robbed the conspiracy of all chances of support from the officer corps. This Western political ineptness buried any hope of settling the conflict by 'a rising from the inside'.

In Russia, the victory of Stalingrad brought on a mood of euphoria. 'Stalin! Stalin!' they shouted, and bore his picture aloft in triumph. But one man did not save Stalingrad. It was the Russian people, resolute and stubborn, who saved it. Few had not responded to the emergency in some positive way. Bravest and most determined were the defenders of Stalingrad. They had become accustomed to death and knew how easy it was to die. Their courage in the face of peril, and their willingness to expose themselves for the sake of others, were what truly saved Russia.

Several elements in this war of movement stand out: the methodical progression of the Russian masses in a war of attrition closely directed by the Soviet High Command. The amazing tenacity and ability of the German commanders, fighting a campaign they all knew was lost through their Führer's madness. And the simple devotion by soldiers on both sides.[33] Hitler had sown the wind of bitterness; now he was to reap the whirlwind of revenge. Stalingrad was less of a defeat for the Wehrmacht and its obedient commanders than for Hitler himself. Not since Napoleon had the outcome of a battle been so much the product of a single man. He had rejected the advice of the best brains in the German Army and swept away their plans. By turning Stalin first into a

[33] E. Dupuy and T. N. Dupuy, *Military History*, New York 1986.

martyr, then into a hero, Hitler had raised the Red Tsar to the pinnacle of power and prestige. Both men knew that there was no room for two systems as alike as fascism and communism to exist side by side. With Hitler going down to defeat, the Soviet dictator was now free to plan his own grand design: the Global Communist Empire. This implied that the day would come when he had to take on his own allies.

The blindness of Western statesmen was staggering. They misjudged the true importance of Stalingrad, the turning point of the war. From the shores of the Volga, a Russian juggernaut now raced towards Prague, Vienna and Berlin. Once the politicians realised that the onrushing Red Army constituted just as dangerous a threat to the West's ultimate aims, they still left it up to generals in the field to take strategic decisions. As a consequence, large sections of central Europe and Germany were left for the Russians to conquer, with far-reaching political consequences.

Stalingrad had proved a pivotal point in an already uneasy relationship between the Allied powers. While Stalin believed that the West was holding off on its 'promise' of a Second Front in order to bleed Russia white, the West felt duped by Stalin's secrecy about his available reserves. The hidden secrets between 'trusted allies' cut both ways. The Western powers were just as secretive about their ultimate weapon – the atomic bomb. In July 1945, while the victors, Russia, the USA, Great Britain and France, haggled in Potsdam over the partition of Europe, the United States entered the nuclear age. Stalin had to be told. This signalled the end of any pretence of friendly co-existence between the victorious nations. But it was at Stalingrad that the foundation for the mistrust between East and West had been laid.

'Is there anybody in the centre of Europe, in that mosaic of countries without consistency or unity, who could contain the ambitions of Stalin?' dared to ask Count Jordana, General Franco's Spanish foreign minister. He was quickly reassured by the British ambassador to Spain, Sir Samuel Hoare: 'The victory at the end of this war will be Allied, not Russian, a victory in which the British Empire and the United States of America will exercise the greatest possible influence. Moreover, Mr Stalin declared on 6 November 1942 that it was not the future policy of Russia to interfere in the international affairs of other countries . . . I make the confident prophecy that Great Britain will remain the strongest European military power . . .'

Four days after a war that he had greatly helped bring to a victorious conclusion, Winston Spencer Churchill, a man who had tried so hard in the crucial days of 1942 to achieve a status quo with Stalin, sent a secret message to President Truman: '*An iron curtain is drawn down upon their front* and we do not know what is going on behind . . .'[34]

Only one man had read up on history. Stalin took a lesson from Ivan the Terrible and Marshall Kutusov:[35] 'Suck your enemy into the immensity of Russia and then destroy him.' Stalin's strategic masterpiece, the sudden appearance of huge reserve armies, which nobody – except a German intelligence officer – even suspected existed, changed the course of the war. Once unleashed, they destroyed what may well have been the best army the Germans ever put into the field.

As already in 1918, the Germans had been only a few kilometres short of destroying socialism in Russia. The German leadership underestimated the Soviet war potential and thus engaged in a campaign that was poorly planned from the start and doomed to failure. German forces found their limits not only in the industrial capacity of the Soviet Union and its allies but also in its ability to send wave after wave of recruits into battle. Stalin's victory was the concept of a whole country mobilised for war. Effective resistance by the entire

[34] W. Churchill, *The Hinge of Fate*, op. cit.

[35] In 1709 at Poltava against Charles XII of Sweden, and again, in 1812, in Napoleon's great retreat from Moscow.

population, fully aware of the behaviour of the Nazis towards the Slavs, buttressed the efforts of the Soviet Union's forces at the front. In seeking support from the population, Stalin dropped the distinction between proletarian and peasant, communist and nationalist.

Hitler's strategy of racist war permeated every aspect of the struggle in the East, strengthening the resolve of the Soviet people, making it possible to unite them under an all-Russian banner in one gigantic struggle for holy Mother Russia, a struggle that had been waged many times in Russian history. However ambivalent the military might be about ideological terrorism, dictated by unscrupulous party hacks, its course led inexorably from war as a means of attaining a rational end to its use as a means of extermination. The unpremeditated outcome of the German practice of war was to escalate force and terror to the point where they stiffened the resistance of old enemies and created new ones.

In retrospect, the fact that the German advance fell short is in itself a remarkable occurrence, the result of Russian tenacity and of German strategic, operational and political errors. The battle for Stalingrad was simply too big and took too long; it was where two giants bumped into each other in a mechanical remake of the Charge of the Light Brigade. But more than anything, the battle was conducted for a symbol, a name: the City of Stalin. Hitler needed it and Stalin didn't want to give it up. For both, failure meant admitting defeat.

As to inter-Allied relations, the war ended as it had started, in political controversy and mistrust. While Russia did most of the fighting, lost twenty million in war dead, and waited for its allies to open a Second Front in Europe, the West's bungling policies made the Russians believe that the promised invasion had been stalled on purpose to eliminate Russia as a postwar power by letting it waste the country's manpower potential. Some historians have placed this turn for the worse in Allied relations at Yalta, others at Potsdam. But, in reality, the pivotal point was Stalingrad. On the banks of the Volga, Stalin produced the decisive change that was to shape not only the outcome of an armed conflict of monumental proportions, but also alter the course of the postwar world.

If Stalin had thought he *could* win a battle, he now knew he *would* win the war.

The Hinge of Battle at Stalingrad was the blind Teutonic obedience on the part of a Prussian Junker to the insane order from a maniacal dictator, who was quite willing to sacrifice an entire army to his brand of '*Götterdämmerung*'.

But the real key to the battle was contained in a single comment by Germany's spymaster: 'We are missing 1.6 million men from our enemy line-up. Where are they?'

Victory at Stalingrad was due to a deceptive Red Tsar's stratagem of hidden reserve armies.

Stalingrad sounded the death knell of Hitler's Nazi Germany and fanned a mistrust in East–West relations that was to last for fifty years.

Epilogue: What happened to the main players?

German

Friedrich Wilhelm Ernst von Paulus (1890–1957) took command of the 6th Army in January 1942. In a Soviet POW camp he joined the group of dissident officers *Freies Deutschland*, calling for Germany's surrender. After the war, many of his staff officers were instrumental in guiding the German Democratic Republic from Nazism to communism. Paulus was considered an outcast. He died in East Germany, abandoned by all.

Erich von Manstein (1887–1973), one of Hitler's most brilliant strategists and the principal planner of the Blitzkrieg of 1940 in France, was unceremoniously sacked by Hitler in 1944, arrested by the Allies after the war and sentenced at the Nuremberg War Crimes Trial to eighteen years in prison. He was released early owing to bad health.

Hermann von Hoth (1885–1971), the brilliant panzer commander who commanded the 4th Panzer Army in January 1942, was sacked by Hitler in November 1943. He played no further role in the war.

Adolf Hitler shot himself in his bunker in Berlin on 30 April 1945.

Russians

Georgi Konstantinovich Chukov (1896–1974), without doubt the most brilliant of all Soviet strategists, supervised the attack on Stalingrad, and then received Germany's capitulation in 1945. Because of his immense popularity he was dumped by a jealous Stalin, but brought back after Stalin's death as Minister of Defence.

Vasili Chuikov (1900–82), head of the heroic 62nd Army defending Stalingrad, stormed into Berlin at the head of the 8th Army in 1945. He served as Soviet Commandant of Occupied East Germany from 1948 to 1953.

Andrei Ivanovich Eremenko (1892–1970) commanded the Stalingrad front and eventually liberated Prague.

Konstantin Rokossovsky (1896–1968) commanded the Don front, and afterwards took Warsaw. After the war he adopted Polish citizenship and became Poland's Defence Minister.

Nikolai Fedor Vatutin (1901–44), an outstanding strategist, reconquered Kiev in 1943. He was killed in an ambush by Ukrainian nationalists.

And finally, Iosif Vissarionovich Dzhugashvili, aka Josef Stalin (1879–1953). His most fervent supporter, Enver Hoxha, the Albanian communist, wrote his eulogy:[36]

> Khrushchev was so shameless as to accuse Stalin of being a person 'shut away' from the reality, who allegedly did not know the situation in the Soviet Union and who did not know where the forces of the Red Army were deployed . . .

[36] E. Hoxha, *With Stalin*, Tirana 1984.

> What slander did the external enemies not invent against the great Stalin, the continuer of the work of Marx and Lenin, the talented leader of the Soviet Union, whom they accused of being a 'bloody tyrant' and 'murderer'. All these slanders were remarkable for their cynicism. No, Stalin was no tyrant, he was a man of principle, he was just, modest and very kindly and considerate towards his people . . .

During the 'Great Patriotic War' (World War II), twenty million Russians died. Another twenty-five million were killed by Stalin's henchmen during the 'Great Terror'.

Stalin died in 1953. He was put on exhibition in a glass coffin in the Kremlin mausoleum next to Lenin. In 1961, upon order of Khrushchev, his body was removed from Lenin's side and buried in a small cemetery outside the Kremlin walls.

A black marble slab with a small bust bears his name.

Appendix: Stalin's strategic reserve armies

It is amazing to note that German Army intelligence had pinpointed all Soviet Front units, yet Stalin's allies were kept in total ignorance of his front troop line-up. Neither Germans nor Anglo-Americans were aware of his strategic reserve power of twelve reserve armies.

Unit	Locations (N-S)	Activated as	Commander
2nd Reserve	Vologda	1st Guard Army	Kiril Moskalenko
4th Reserve	Kalinin	38th Army	Nikandr Chibisov
10th Reserve	Ivanovo	5th Shock Army	Markian Popov
9th Reserve	Gorki	24th Army	Dimitri Kozlov
1st Reserve	Tula	64th Army	Vasili Chuikov
3rd Tank Reserve	West of Tula	3rd Tank Army	Prokofi Romanenko
5th Tank Reserve	East of Orel	5th Tank Army	Aleksandr Lizukov
3rd Reserve	Tambov	60th Army	Maxim Antonyuk
8th Reserve	Saratov	66th Army	Rodion Malinovsky
6th Reserve	Don river	6th Army	Fedor Kharitonov
5th Reserve	Don river	63rd Army	Vasili Kuznetsov
7th Reserve	Stalingrad	62nd Army	Vladimir Kolpakchi

(A number of these army commanders were changed or demoted during the battle.)

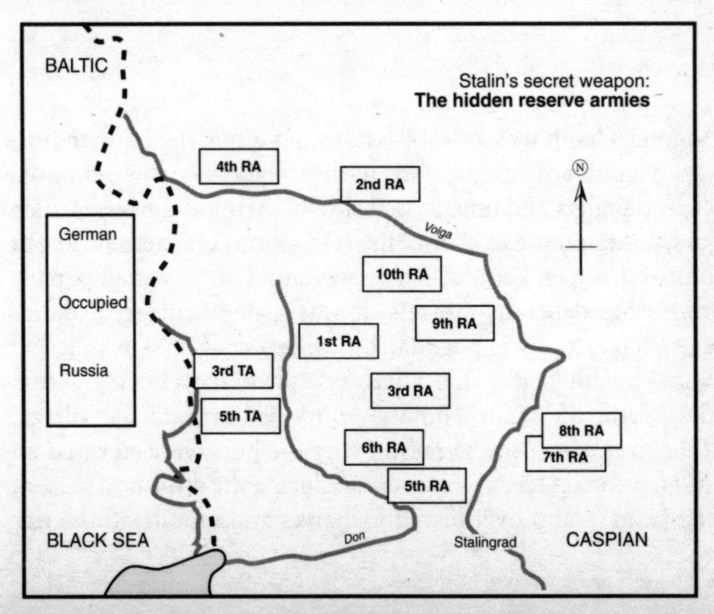

9

A Mousetrap That Caught the Cat

13 March 1954 – The Last Day of Diên Biên Phu

'Je me suis fabriqué une plaine, maintenant je vais casser les Viet.'
('I've built myself a battlefield, now I'm going to bust a few Viet.')
Colonel de Castries to his minister, René Pleven, at Diên Biên Phu, February 1954

'Strike to win, strike only when success is certain, or do not strike at all.'
Viet General Vo Nguyen Giap, Diên Biên Phu, February 1954

Muong Thanh was a sleepy backwater along the Laotian border, a hamlet of *paillotes* (straw-thatched huts) where children chased piglets and time passed slowly. Around the big earthen jars, containing a year's rice harvest, skinny chickens picked at bits of dropped kernels. Black pigs snouted for rotten papaya and other delicious morsels. It was a poor village; it didn't even have its own pagoda, only the occasional wandering *bonze* to look after the villagers' spiritual wellbeing. From the north, the Nam Youm river looped around the village. This river was also the reason why the huts were elevated on stilts, some six feet above ground; during the monsoon season, the Nam Youm overflowed its banks and inundated the rice paddies along its banks, depositing the fertile soil washed down from the highlands. The river's waters supplemented the simple diet of rice with their bounty of fish. From both sides of the shallow valley, hills covered with dense jungle pressed down on to the village. The jungle was no enemy to the locals; for ages the villagers of Muong Thanh had ventured into its denseness in search of food and wood for their stoves. But the jungle was also a source of death – snakes and scorpions, armies of white and red ants, collapsing trees or the occasional voracious tiger. The indigenous population had learned to survive in this jungle and at times considered it even as its friend. It provided them with a place of refuge whenever a village was exposed to raids by Laotian bandits. They had cut narrow trails through its interwoven foliage which could be used as escape routes. Only those familiar with the jungle could cross it. It was full of evil spirits, coming forth from the earth and down from the trees, whispering, howling and devouring. They knew that the spirits were there because their dank odour drifted into the village, foul and rotten. That was why, at night-time, the locals fled back into their stilted huts and pulled up their ladders.

The French colonial authorities had first heard about the hidden valley from Catholic missionaries, travelling upriver with their cross and their bag of miracle medicines to convert the locals to the true faith and save them from cholera, *tajh* fever and the most terrible of all killers, malaria.[1] For the villagers of the Nam Youm valley, everything was peaceful. Their lives were regulated by the seasons – when it rained they got stuck in the mud and when it didn't rain, the sun fried their brains. Then things began to change the day a stranger walked into their village. His hands were not scarred like those of a peasant and he didn't talk about Jesus Christ the Saviour, but about 'throwing off the domination of the white man's exploitation' and other strange things they didn't really

1 Worldwide, more people die annually of malaria than from any other cause.

understand. Then he left, but a few moons later he returned in the company of men carrying guns. They came armed with Chinese-made rifles and mortars, English Brownings and French MATS. The newcomers were followed by more and then some more, until well over two thousand of them were camped around their hamlet. The stillness of the sleepy Nam Youm valley was shattered. Little did the locals realise, this autumn of 1953, that their hamlet would go down in history as a milestone in the defeat of colonialism, but under a different name – Diên Biên Phu.

On 20 November 1953, a Dakota of Task Group 2/64 was flying through fog as thick as pea soup. Its propellers cut a swath through the clouds. Sitting in the plane was Gen. Jean Gilles, better known as 'the man with the glass eye', head of the French Airborne Troops and in charge of Operation Castor. Next to him sat Gens Decheaux and Bodet, special envoys of the *commandant en chef*, General Navarre. The three men stared at the map spread across their knees; from time to time they threw a glance out of the porthole. They saw only fog, and it gave them no indication as to where they were or what they could expect to find on the ground.

'Has anybody done ground reconnaissance?' asked Decheaux.

'Negative,' replied Bodet, the headquarters man. 'For that we were too pressed for time.'

'So they're going in blind . . .' Gilles cursed under his breath. It was a hazardous gamble, and Gen. Gilles knew it. If present weather conditions prevailed, it would be too dangerous for a parachute drop. The targeted drop zone was circled in red on their plastic-covered map; along the banks of the Nam Youm river, two parachute battalions were to take possession of a series of hamlets and set up a base perimeter. The observer plane broke through the clouds, but everything below them was impenetrably white. Only the summits, marking the high border region between

Tonkinchina and Laos, stuck up through this opaque milky ocean like islets of green in a white sea.

Gilles looked at his chronometer. '0540 hours. Another hour before we have to come to a decision. If it stays like this we must abandon the operation.'

The order had come through from Gen. Navarre personally last night: 'Castor is a go,' he had told Gilles by phone. The two battalions of paras, the 6th BPC (*Bataillon Parachutistes Coloniales*) of Col. Bigeard and the 2/1 RCP (*Régiment Coloniale Parachutistes*) of Col. Bréchignac, were kept on stand-by on an airstrip along Indochina's coast, ready to board the planes and pounce on a zone that was marked on the French map as 'departmental centre of the regional border administration', or under its Vietnamese name: Diên Biên Phu.

In the valley of the Nam Youm, visibility was close to zero. Not a good day on which to hold the manoeuvre planned by Viet Minh Gen. Giap for his 148th Regiment. Several thousand heavily armed *bo-dois* (Viet Minh soldiers) were spread out in the rice paddies, boiling their breakfast rice, when they heard the drone of aeroplane engines above the clouds. It sounded like a single reconnaissance aircraft. Their company captains ordered the men to go under cover, something at which the Viet Minh excelled.

0637 hours. For the first time their view down to the valley was clear. The French generals could see the square shapes of paddies along the banks of a looping river. Rows of black-dressed figures with wide conical hats, typical of Vietnamese rice farmers, were working in the paddies. In the deep grass other farmers grazed their buffalo. As military men, Gilles and his generals didn't appreciate that it hardly took a dozen conical hats to guard a single buffalo. To them up there in the plane, all was serene, a piece of cake for the paratroopers.

Down on the ground, eyes stared at a plane flying straight

down the valley before it banked in a shallow turn and came back, straight over the position of a regiment of *bo-dois* hidden in bamboo shrubs, in high elephant grass or crouching under conical hats in the paddies.

In the reconnaissance aircraft, Gen. Bodet took up the microphone to relay an order: 'Operation Castor – it's a go!' Destiny was on its way, only nobody knew it yet.

'Battalion load up!' Col. Bigeard gave the order and his 651 paratroopers climbed aboard a fleet of C-47 transport planes. The armada lifted off and headed for the big loop in the Nam Youm river and Diên Biên Phu.

'What's our dropping speed?' Col. Bréchignac asked the pilot.

'170 kph at altitude 750 metres.'

Bréchignac made a quick calculation. It took twenty-four men just under two minutes to drop from a Dakota. That would spread his contingent over almost six kilometres of paddy. Pretty thin on the ground. Not to worry – according to Gen. Gilles's report, the worst they could expect to meet on the ground was a small band of guerrillas.

It wasn't a small contingent that was down below them, this 20 November 1953, but two thousand well-trained *bo-dois* with twelve heavy 120mm mortars and four 75mm recoil rifles. They possessed one further advantage – they were tightly grouped in coherent units, while the paratroopers would be spaced out and would have to act individually without support.

Six hundred kilometres to the north-east, in a tunnel cut into an ancient quarry, Gen. Giap was in a meeting with the *Tong Bô*, the Superior Committee of the Revolution, when a message was passed to him. 'Diên Biên Phu.' He cursed and slammed his fist on the table. 'Not where I had expected them.' His information was derived from many sources. Almost his best spies were kids playing football near a military installation who, instead of kicking leather, counted tanks and planes. They had duly advised him of the packet of transport planes that had been assembled at a coastal airstrip, but he had counted on a strike farther south. He had enough men in the Nam Youm valley for a medium-size action. The entire 148th VM Regiment was his mainstay in controlling the vital border region and keeping open his lifeline, but they were held in reserve and, like every reserve unit, they lacked the ammunition for a bigger action. Now it was too late to do anything about it; they would have to fight it out as best they could. If things turned out badly, and the French decided to remain, then he would have to do something about it, since a French base there would threaten his vital supply lines. Just in case this was what Navarre had in mind, Giap ordered the 316th VM Division, still some eighty miles from the Nam Youm, to march on the battle zone in support of the 148th VM Regiment.

'Are we to attack as soon as we get there?' came the query from his divisional commander. Giap was only too aware of the awesome firepower a '*hérisson*' (fortified defensive position) could bring down on his men and that it would annihilate any attacking force. 'Under no circumstances are you to attack without my express order. The fundamental principle of a revolutionary war is to attack and win, and then only when the certitude that this can be achieved is given. Otherwise, wait for the propitious moment.' This was his philosophy, and it was to prove the correct one.

For Bigeard and Bréchignac's men, the projected landing zone, 'Natacha', was an expanse of paddies and deep elephant grass. The Dakotas levelled at an altitude of 750 metres, their ideal dropping height; the doors opened and the first wave jumped. If they considered this another routine operation that would end in a cheap victory, they quickly learned differently. While dangling on their silk parachutes, a number were killed by rifle fire from the conical-hatted 'farmers' who suddenly turned out to be heavily armed guerrillas.

The first paratroopers to make it safely to the ground ran into a platoon of *bo-dois* led by a Viet Minh officer who moved his hand forward in the order for an attack – his last conscious act, because a moment later he doubled up and fell, hit by a salvo from a MAT submachine-gun. A short burst of withering fire from other Paras shredded belts, conical hats and flesh, and the Viet Minh platoon went down, the first victims of a battle that was to cost thousands of lives in the months to come. Other groups of Paras, formed by chance rather than by unit, stormed into the hamlet of Bach Mai, where they were met by a murderous mortar barrage, owing to curious circumstances. Three days earlier, the hamlet's headman had died and was buried in the local tradition with a flag stuck into the top of his tomb. Wind agitated this flag and the Viet gunners took this as a signal to rally the French units.

The mortar barrage stopped as suddenly as it had begun. The Viet had run out of ammunition, and the Paras encountered no more organised resistance. They charged into the village and sprayed its huts with machinegun fire, changing magazines as they ran. No orders, no shouting, no confusion – these were professionals demonstrating expert teamwork. Though the defending Viet had a variety of weapons, they were never given a chance to use them with effect. A similar situation prevailed in the paddies. A human avalanche of screaming *bo-dois* splashed through ankle-deep water and was cut down by a deluge of bullets from French submachine-guns. But the French also took casualties. Near the village of Ban Khéo, the fire of a heavy machinegun located on top of a hill, code-named 'Alpha', pinned down the platoon of Lt Trapp. Before the lieutenant could call up reinforcements, a heavy slug tore through the chest of his radioman, Cpl Peressin. Col. Bigeard was caught in crossfire from the first row of huts in Diên Biên Phu, which the Viet had converted into earthen bunkers. For a moment his situation was critical, since all his heavy weapon support had been dropped six kilometres farther to the south. He ordered rapid fire to divert the attention of the defenders from a platoon of Paras moving into the flank of the Viets. In the village all hell broke loose. Grenades were flung into huts and set them on fire; hens, dogs and pigs panicked and raced through a mêlée of fleeing *bo-dois*. Several dozen Viets managed to break out, running across the open paddies towards the riverbank. Bracing their hand-carried light machineguns against trees, the Paras raked the fleeing Viet Minh mass. Most went down.

'Friendly casualties?' snapped Colonel Bigeard.

'*Oui, mon colonel*. Our casualties are fifteen killed and forty-six wounded.'

'And the enemy?'

'We haven't been able to count them as yet, but they are in the hundreds.'

The French did not realise how close they had come to ending the war right there. The headquarters of the 148th VM Regiment contained the battle order for the planned Viet Minh campaign, and this would have given the French high command an unsurpassable advantage. Unfortunately, the unit designated to capture the headquarters was dropped too far off to get into the action, and the Viet Minh regimental commanders managed to effect their getaway. For the time being, euphoria reigned in the French camp. A relatively minor French force had annihilated a Viet Minh regiment. That afternoon and the next day more paratroopers arrived,[2] bringing the total French strength to 4,560. The initial battle in Navarre's overall design, to force the Viet Minh out into the open to face destruction by superior French firepower, had proven a success. Sappers began to erect fortified emplacements of some permanence. Friendly casualties were given a military funeral; the smouldering fires in the village were extinguished; bunkers went up and trenches were dug. The

[2] 6 BPC (Bigeard), 2/1 RCP (Bréchignac), 1 BPC (Souquet), 1 BEP (Guiraud), 8 BPC (Tourret), 1 CEPML (Molinier), 5 BPVN (Leclerc). 1 BPC, 6 BPC and 2/1 RCP were evacuated to Hanoi in early December.

village took on the air of an anthill in a kind of victory jamboree. Groups of Paras, stripped down to their T-shirts, were busy at work opening lines of fire and supplying logs for sandbag-covered bunkers; others were digging ditches in which to lay communication wires. Some groups went outside the perimeter to collect parachutes; others did their laundry and then hung it on telephone wires strung between bamboo poles. Soon it looked as if nothing could disturb the future tranquillity of the Nam Youm valley.

As an operation, Castor was a great tactical success, but one that was to cost the French dearly, because the victory over 'a bunch of *autochtones* [natives]' engendered in them the arrogance of over-confidence and a white-man superiority complex. They did not reckon with a brace of old foxes who knew just how to play this game and bide their time: Gen. Giap and his boss, Ho Chi Minh.

Nguyen That Than's amazing career began with him working as kitchen help in the fashionable Carlton Hotel in London. From there he went to Paris, Moscow and China, before he founded, together with a professor of French, Pham Van Dong, the Vietnam Doc Lap Dong Minh, the League for the Independence of Vietnam, or, abbreviated, the Viet Minh (19 May 1941). Nguyen That Than, Mr C.P. Hoo as the Chinese called him, became a household name under the sobriquet the Americans bestowed on him: Ho Chi Minh. His military deputy, Vo Nguyen Giap, practised history long before he taught it. Jailed at eighteen for having organised a student strike, Giap became a history professor at the lycée in Hanoi and offered his knowledge of military history to Ho's new party. In the climate of a looming Cold War, the Americans had sent a plenipotentiary to Hanoi to make a deal with Ho Chi Minh. He readily agreed to a proposal that called for the 200,000 Chinese, on occupation duty in Vietnam, to be exchanged for 15,000 French. When some of his party members challenged his decision, he exploded: 'You imbeciles! Don't you realise what it means to us if the Chinese stay? Remember your history! The last time the Chinese came they stayed a thousand years. The French are foreigners, they are weak. Colonialism is dying out. Nothing will be able to withstand world pressure for *doc lap*, independence.'

The Vietnamese loathing for everything remotely Chinese was amply demonstrated during the Chinese troop withdrawal from Vietnam. Angry mobs confronted the units filing out of Hanoi. They had looted Vietnamese homes of everything, from furniture to plumbing fixtures, even ripping the tiles from the roofs. At that moment in time, the United States would have been in a good position to rush to the aid of Ho's Vietnamese, but Washington's attention was focused on another part of the globe, and it thereby missed its unique political opportunity. France jumped into the vacuum, but instead of food it brought troops. Ho Chi Minh made one final attempt to reach a mutual understanding with France when he sailed for Paris in July 1946. While these talks were going on, a phrase uttered by General de Gaulle set the stage for the coming drama. 'United with its overseas territories which she opened to civilisation, France is a great power. Without these territories she would be in grave danger of no longer being one.' With this he eliminated any remaining chance for a political settlement and a disheartened Ho returned to Hanoi. Fighting between the Viet Minh and the French expeditionary corps broke out on 20 November 1946 over control of the customs house in Haiphong harbour.

The Battle of Diên Biên Phu had its roots in France's monumental political misunderstanding of its strategic situation in the Far East in 1953. French Indochina, made up of Annam and Tonkinchina, had been annexed by French gunboat diplomacy in 1880 to open a permanent trade route to China. Ever since the 1942 invasion by the armies of Japan, the country had been in permanent armed conflict. World War II had spelled *finis* to the era of colonial rubber barons, and the nations of South-East Asia were striving for independence. The end of the war had brought no peace to the region; British and Dutch troops were fighting groups of guerrillas in the jungles of Malaya and Indonesia. For the revolutionary forces of Ho Chi Minh, the dense border jungles provided safe bases for their Viet Minh guerrillas.

The bells of independence tolled loud and clear across all of Asia at 0830 hours on the morning of 15 August 1947. The Viceroy of India, Lord Mountbatten, entered the great hall of his magnificent palace in New Delhi and ordered the lowering of the union flag as the colours of a New India went up. From his headquarters in the *maquis*, Ho Chi Minh addressed a message to Pandit Nehru: 'The independence of India fortifies the people of Viet Nam in its struggle for independence.' The ceremony was not repeated in Hanoi. France missed its opportunity to arrive at an acceptable deal with the independence movement. Instead it opted for all-out war.

During World War II the Americans had lavishly provided the Vietnamese with weapons to help in the struggle against Japan. Once the war was finished and French administrators returned to Hanoi, the guerrilla hid his gun. Raids on police outposts supplied the revolutionary with his ammunition. For food he had to rely on voluntary contributions from the local peasantry. When these were not forthcoming he used the strong-arm method to get his quota of rice. Villagers were beaten up and the village chiefs executed, their sons abducted and forced to join the guerrilla bands, operating as small units. Though this precluded major encounters, such bands were sufficiently strong to carry out sporadic ambushes and wear down their enemy. French rubber plantation managers were terrorised and frequently murdered. Despite their highly mechanised army, well supplied with aircraft and helicopters, the French were unable to put enough troops into the jungle to deal with the many tiny bands. The French tried to riposte by attacking known guerrilla bases, but such raids proved futile as there were too many camps and they contained nothing of value; under attack, a guerrilla slung his bag of rice over his shoulder and vanished. Next, the French colonial authorities tried to pursue a policy of tolerance, a kind of Hearts and Minds campaign.[3] They offered social reforms, to a point where they even recognised local trade unions even though these were under communist control. A further attempt to persuade the local population that it would be considerably more profitable to support the colonial officials than some barefoot bandits ended in failure, because the only French officials the Vietnamese had ever met were tax collectors and policemen. The local population remained loyal to their brothers in the jungle, and the military attempted to enforce a rigid curfew. This only helped to upset the locals, who began to supply the Viet Minh with another vital commodity: information.

In contrast to the conventional war the French had fought during World War II, this unconventional war was largely dependent on the direction of operations in the field. The choice between civic action and military attack, reprisal versus persuasion, reform or coercion, what town to defend and which village to abandon, the use of napalm or pamphlets – such political decisions should have been left up to a commander on the spot and not directives from Paris. Yet recommendations from subofficers patrolling the rice paddies were ignored; statements to the effect that guerrilla groups were capable of great military feats were rejected as being incompatible with the idea that only a mechanical force could sustain and win a modern war. That, more than anything else, stifled the French effort to hold on to Indochina, where a professional soldier receiving his instructions from Paris, General Henri-Eugene Navarre, faced a history teacher and committed

[3] This was not an American innovation, but proved just as futile as the French attempt – another example of the Americans not learning their lesson.

revolutionary, Vo Nguyen Giap. The French marshals, Salan, de Lattre and Navarre, who had recently emerged from a monumental victory over Hitler's Germany, regarded the 'Communist peasant rabble' at best as a distasteful nuisance. But their disdain and arrogance helped them little, as a history teacher's rabble was about to sweep them to an ignominious defeat.

The message that awaited the first commander-in-chief of French forces, Marshal de Lattre de Tassigny, upon his arrival in Indochina, came from the district capital Vinh-Yen. A guerrilla band under the leadership of an as yet unknown quantity, a Viet Minh leader called Giap, had overrun a French army outpost at Bao-Chuc, held by a garrison of Senegalese colonial troops and some loyal Vietnamese scouts. The Viet Minh general had planned the move well; by taking out one French force he had lured another into a deadly ambush. When a Foreign Legion battalion rushed to the relief of Bao-Chuc it was wiped out. This was the first time the world was to hear about this insignificant-looking man, Vo Nguyen Giap.

It has been frequently stated that Giap was Asia's Napoleon. That is not so. His good fortune was that he faced up to generals who assumed a prominent place in the hierarchy of military incompetence. Giap carefully planned every one of his operations; he never ventured into a battle where he risked a major defeat, and he gradually forced the French on to the defensive while he consolidated his forces and steadily increased the size of his units, transforming them from guerrilla bands into regular battalions capable of attacking larger enemy units. His political boss, Ho Chi Minh, was able to acquire the necessary arms for Giap by skilfully playing one side of world communism off against the other, Russia versus China, both of which had an openly expressed interest in the region. Each successful strike raised the Viet Minh's morale, restored the confidence of the civilian population and reduced the French forces to a state of desperation. Each side was fully aware that the outcome would depend on its military ability, but even more so on the will to win. The Viet Minh was possessed of such will. Also, timing was crucial. Ho and Giap depended on the political and strategic shortsightedness of the French. Of this the French were true masters.

By the spring of 1953 Josef Stalin had died and the new masters in the Kremlin were becoming worried about China, a country that had emerged from the Korean War stronger than ever, flexing its muscles. Communist China was now in a position to supply its Red comrades in Indochina with arms to help them achieve a decisive victory. Their goal was to bring Chinese-style socialism to power, leading to Chinese hegemony over South-East Asia, as had been the case for thousands of years. For this, Beijing supplied Ho with vast quantities of weapons, together with military advisers to keep a close tab on Ho's ambitions. Chairman Ho used the supplies to expel the French from the border regions, while Giap took no notice of his Chinese advisers. When things began to go well for Indochina's communists, Russian leaders, having become acutely aware of Beijing's attempts to dominate Asia's communist empire, were willing to offer the West their help in working towards a negotiated settlement in Indochina.[4]

History was not decided, as one might assume, in Indochina but over a working lunch in Paris. In a floundering *Quatrième République* beset by internal political pressures and a failure to come to grips with the strikes by the Viet Minh, the discussions focused on a *sortie honorable* – an honourable way out of the mess with no loss of face. This had to be accomplished before the major powers, the USSR and the USA, participated at a forthcoming Geneva Conference to dictate a solution that would 'assure lasting peace in Indochina', but on their terms. The French Council of Ministers had demanded an overall

[4] Those who eventually benefited from France's defeat in Indochina were the Austrians. The Russians, still looking for a way to appease the West, agreed to Austria's peace treaty in 1955.

military strategy to combat the communist Viet Minh. Such a plan had been developed by Gen. Léchères, and it called for the concentration of a powerful French effective along the littoral of Annam, where the population density was greatest and resupply of military bases by sea presented no problem. From Vinh in the north to Cap St Jacques in the south, French units would establish a series of coastal strongpoints (*hérissons*) to control traffic along the only highway between the north (Tonkin) and the south (Annam). They would stay for three or four years, then declare victory and pull out. In this manner, France would save honour and face. The ministers agreed on the plan in principle and the meeting broke up. The president of the state council, René Mayer, shook hands with his military advisers. As Gen. Léchères and his ADC, Col. Gallois, were about to close the door, René Mayer called after them: 'Of course, *mon cher* Léchères, you will keep us Laos!'

The general was stunned. Laos – how could he possibly keep Laos, hundreds of miles from the nearest supply base, without viable access along one narrow road that was impassable during the rainy season? '*Mais, Monsieur le Président*, the coastal zones of the Gulf of Tonkin, from Annam to Cochinchina, constitute the only essential of Viet Nam . . . only their possession will dictate the outcome of the war . . .'

Mayer would not even listen. He continued: '*Mon cher général*, you certainly recall our school atlas, those *pink places indicating the French colonial empire* . . . it would be most difficult, even impossible, to present myself before a French electorate, certainly that in Algeria, if only a fraction of these pink areas were to be found missing.'

Once more, Léchères tried to defend his strategy of littoral defence: '. . . the only way to defend Laos would be with *camps retranchés* [entrenched camps] which again would become entirely dependent on supplies flown in by air, and for that we simply do not have the means.'

'No, believe me, General, you must keep me Laos.'

Gen. Léchères left the meeting aghast. In the car back to the Ministry of Defence, he confided his worries to his air strategist, Col. Gallois: 'We act in complete incoherence, but we must accommodate,' he sighed, before he pronounced the fateful phrase: 'I fear for the worst.'

At about the same time, a meeting was held between Ho Chi Minh and his military commander, Gen. Vo Nguyen Giap. Ho asked the general: 'Our forces grow stronger day by day, but we mustn't let the enemy destroy our strength – can you do it?'

Giap replied instantly: 'The enemy won't be able to destroy our strength. The difficult thing will be to take the initiative.'[5]

What neither knew was that France had already taken it and was playing into their hands.

The fateful decision to establish a *camp retranché* at Diên Biên Phu, along the Laotian border, was taken on 12 November 1953; Defence Minister René Pleven left the execution of the operation to Gen. Navarre, who had taken over when Gen. Léchères resigned over the 'Laos demand'. Unfortunately, Gen. Henri Navarre painted for himself a picture of a situation that suited him but was nowhere near reality. He never even considered that a guerrilla force would be capable of gathering enough men and matériel at a given point to engage in a 'stand-up' battle, and on this false assumption he based his entire strategy. He would force Giap into the open and destroy him with superior firepower. He disregarded the fact that the Viet general was no longer leading a guerrilla band but a fully integrated army with sophisticated logistics, artillery and divisional units. And that Giap had one decisive advantage: his army could move on foot; the French could

[5] Interview with Gen. Giap.

not. Thereby, in a country without roads, only jungle paths, transportation was the key to victory, or disaster. The French had to depend entirely on their air force to supply outlying bases. During a council of war, Col. Pierre Gallois was asked to give his assessment of aircraft availability. 'We have ten air transport squadrons, altogether sixty-five C-47 transport planes, which could possibly be used to supply one garrison.[6] They are stationed at our bases at Bac Mai, Goialam, Dojon and Cat Bi. That is hundreds of miles from the Laotian border. Haiphong, our major supply port, is four hundred kilometres from Diên Biên Phu. We must also take into consideration that our planes do not possess an all-weather capability and that we use metal-strip runways. During the monsoon season, soft ground makes landing on our forward airstrips impracticable if not outright impossible.' Nobody would listen to him.

Diên Biên Phu base, only thirty kilometres from the Laotian border, was located in a shallow pan, about a mile wide and surrounded by hills covered by dense jungle vegetation; the region collected more rain during the monsoon season than almost anywhere else in South-East Asia. On 3 December 1953, Gen. Navarre issued the order to establish a defensive position and to hold it at all costs. It was intended as the army's stepping-off point for launching incursions into the flank of Gen. Giap's Viet Minh forces and to prevent supplies from reaching Giap's units. As his base commander, Navarre appointed a cavalryman who had proven his valour on many occasions. Col. Christian Marie Ferdinand de Castries was a highly decorated scion of French nobility who considered everyone *autochtone* (native) below his class and not worthy

[6] The total number of aircraft available to the French military command in Indochina was less than what a US battalion could deploy fifteen years later. Furthermore, these aircraft were relatively unsophisticated and could not detect enemy supply depots or troop concentrations, and they were not all-weather planes.

of being addressed. If such was possible, his deputy was even more arrogant. Col. Charles Piroth was an artilleryman who bragged that no gun manned by little yellow men would be able to fire three rounds before his French batteries would blast it to hell. Alas, matters were to turn out quite differently.

Final plans were being discussed between Gens Navarre, Cogny and Gilles. 'We must wiggle them out of their jungle redoubt and make them fight us in the open.'

'Beware of Giap,' warned Gilles, 'he has developed a new type of guerrilla warfare that just could defeat a modern European army. I'm not so sure about this wiggling him out.'

'Then we go after him into the jungle. We must screw up his operation,' said Navarre.

'The notion of imitating the Viet Minh guerrilla in the jungle is playing into their hands. We cannot reply with a half-baked idea someone else has cooked up.' Gen. Cogny was referring to the instructions from Paris. 'The Viets gave the Japanese a bloody hard time.'

'Because the Japs could never deploy their full strength. They were embroiled in war with a much bigger enemy. We are not. The Viet Minh is our foe, and the only one France has. Suppose we had started using carpet bombing on their known training bases from the first day on – the whole thing would have ended right there. But Paris subverted the programme.'

Gen. Navarre's strategy of a Diên Biên Phu *hérisson* was based on two vital contingencies: that such a base could be supplied with all its needs by *terrestrial* means, and that the surrounding jungle was indeed *impenetrable* and would thereby provide a protective wall around the base. In both his assessments he was sadly mistaken, with a disastrous result for France. On the question of supplies it soon became apparent that the only way to get anything through to the base was by air, and for that the French Air Force was not equipped – anyway, for many months monsoon rains made flying impossible. And in his concept of what a guerrilla army could transport on its back through hilly jungle terrain he proved to be completely wide of the mark.

The Viet Minh military chiefs mobilised a force of People's Carriers. Duong Quynh Hoa, a medical student who had joined Ho's army on strictly nationalistic grounds, was put in charge of forming a 'brigade of iron horses', bicycles that were converted into *xe tho* (pack bicycles) by adding a contraption of bamboo sticks, and capable of taking a load of two hundred kilograms. 'The first night out our tyres burst. I pondered the matter, then tore the legs of my khaki trousers into long strips which I wound around the inner tubes before pumping them up. It worked, and none of our tyres ever burst again, though from now on all of us walked in shorts.' They found a way to move through the jungle to avoid strafing runs by French planes on the main roads. For secrecy they moved only by night. To bring one kilo of rice to the men at the front called for an additional four kilos to feed the transporters. Giap was a careful planner; his motto was: 'Strike to win, strike only when success is certain, or do not strike at all.' He did achieve 'the impossible'. In the months of November and December 1953, he moved thirty-three battalions of infantry and six artillery regiments across a terrain that outdated French maps indicated in white and marked 'unknown – insurmountable jungle region'.

Navarre overlooked the lesson the Germans had taught his predecessors during the 1940 Battle of France – those French generals who had considered the Ardennes an equally 'insurmountable obstacle'. The jungle was certainly impassable to modern mechanised transportation – but not to human muscle pushing sturdy pre-war Peugeot bicycles that could carry big loads. Thousands of human ants carried, tugged, dragged and pushed, on their backs and on their bicycles, 150 pieces of dismantled artillery, as well as their shells, bags of rice and machinegun bullets, across the insurmountable obstacle. Giap himself stated that 'I won because the French were always badly informed, they were forever one army behind in their evaluation of our true means.' The French Deuxième Bureau (Military Intelligence) estimated that, given the narrow jungle paths, at the very best a maximum of 5,000 coolies could overcome the difficult terrain. It wasn't 5,000 or 10,000 but 75,000 men who built tracks and then, by bicycle, ox cart, truck or on foot, pushed and pulled prodigious loads across the wilderness. They cut a negotiable road through the vines which they named in honour of their leader the Ho Chi Minh Trail. When the brand-new Molotova trucks, courtesy of their brotherly comrades of the Soviet Union, got stuck in the wet or on steep hills, 150 men threw ropes around them and pulled them from the mud or up the incline. As for the heavy guns, these were moved an inch at a time, a kilometre a day. But they did reach the pre-positioned firing pads, secreted in caves and behind earthen walls, on the hillsides facing the French. The French never knew they were there; they never saw them coming. French intelligence offered an estimate that the Viet Minh couldn't fire more than 20,000 rounds of medium calibre from guns such as the 75mm US mountain howitzer; they fired ten times more – 200,000 shells, and from the heavy 105mm artillery tubes. While the Viet were using the foliage to hide, the French had flattened all vegetation in front of their position to create fire lanes. This revealed their every move to Giap, looking down on them from his balcony. The French sent up reconnaissance aircraft. All they ever filmed was the dense canopy of leaves; they never got a glimpse of the uninterrupted line of porters carrying shells and bags of rice through the entanglement of vines and bamboo. Some French patrols did get in fairly close and reported some movement. Their reports were filed away as sheer fantasies.

In mid-December, a mobile unit, the GM 9 of Col. Gaucher, replaced some of the parachute units. Two-thirds were from the shock 1st and 3rd Battalion of the 13th Brigade which had received its baptism of fire against the Germans at Narvik and then had fought the Battle of Bir-Hakeim against Rommel's Africa Korps. After the end of World War II, seasoned veterans from the defunct German Wehrmacht had joined these Foreign Legion units. Because of their experience, many were promoted to *sergent-chefs* (master sergeants) and put in charge of platoons. Their arrival was greeted with a cheer. Three of these veterans, Sgts Schweiger, Soos and Osterlich, formerly subalterns in a German panzer division, weren't overly impressed by what they saw, which was mainly engineers strengthening the base perimeter.

Schweiger had returned from a sortie into the jungle. He hadn't talked much about it. Now he took a look at the newly built defences. '*Grossartige Scheisse* . . . great shit,' he said to his buddy, Sgt Soos. 'The French are truly the biggest builders of useless fortresses. They must've learned that from their medieval knights and haven't discovered that since then things have changed. With all their pillboxes and minefields, it'll take them about ten years before they kill just about as many Viets as we do on a single patrol in a week . . .'

Soos, Schweiger and Osterlich had been on an interdiction mission[7] with thirty of their '*Alten Kameraden*', all German legionnaires. This bunch of headhunters, armed only with three light machineguns, went after bands of Viet Minh and eliminated them without asking questions. In the denseness of the jungle they preferred to operate independently and silently, with knives and clubs. This time their patrol had been keeping to the Nam Youm river, but well inside jungle cover, when they stumbled on a large enemy detachment camped on the opposite shore. From the way the Viets crowded the riverbank it was obvious that these were either green recruits or thought themselves invulnerable by virtue of their sheer number. To Schweiger it became clear that the planners back at HQ had vastly underestimated the real strength of

[7] The Americans were later to call them search-and-destroy missions.

the 'commies'. What was camped there, some five hundred yards off and ready to cross the river to threaten the rear of the Diên Biên Phu defences, was at least a brigade-size force. For the ex-Panzer sergeant and his men, this was too big a horde to tackle in their usual way, yet it was also too good an opportunity to miss. The sun was low behind them and the bulk of the enemy was still on the opposite shore, therefore in no position to interfere; and Schweiger's men were under cover with a clear field of fire across open water. Schweiger and Soos discussed the situation and decided on brief bursts in a traversing arc from their three machineguns placed on tripods. It had to be done with precision and quickly, but the veterans from Russia were masters of the art. They designated one shooter and one feeder for each gun; the rest of their group was told to safeguard their getaway. They set up their three guns behind bushes on a ridge from where they could slide back into the dense forest and make good their escape. On Schweiger's hand signal, their machineguns opened up simultaneously and fired two five-second bursts. Their chatter was dull, but not their effect. During these ten seconds, five hundred bullets slammed into the massed enemy ready to cross the river. The Viets never knew what hit them, but they received a grim lesson in a cruel war.

The monsoon arrived with a vengeance. It stopped all movement, and the war ground to a halt. The French supply planes could no longer take off or land; even Giap's bicycle caravans got stuck in knee-deep mud. The rain came down so hard that it penetrated the overhead foliage like bullets, and everyone had to seek shelter under groundsheets or hastily thrown-up huts made from big leaves. The rain hammered so hard on the leaves that they had to shout to make themselves heard. Wild torrents rushed down and emptied into the Nam Young, which turned into a raging torrent, while the long metal ribbons of the runways disappeared under two feet of water. The soldiers in the trenches swallowed sulfathiazole pills by the handful to head off diseases, while their enemies in the jungle chewed on quinine bark to keep away the killer malaria. Whenever the downpour stopped, the sun turned jungle and plain into a steam bath and an ideal breeding ground for the leech. Then the soldiers stripped and used glowing cigarettes to burn off the purple bloodsuckers and hung up shirts and socks to dry on the telephone wires strung between bamboo poles.

On 19 February 1954, a last-minute effort was undertaken to abort the disaster. French Minister of Defence René Pleven had himself flown into Diên Biên Phu to inspect the base. On the airstrip he was greeted by Col. de Castries with a cheerful announcement: '*Je me suis fabriqué une plaine, maintenant je vais casser les Viets* . . . I've built for myself a battlefield, now I'm going to bust a few Viet.' Pleven took one look at the surrounding hills. 'What if Giap gets up there?'

'He never will. My artillery would blast him from the top.' Pleven was not convinced. As a non-military observer, he alone saw the fatal trap. He returned to Paris, where he confided his fears to Col. Gallois. 'At Angkor Vat they once showed me a granite statue that had been cut from a single block of twenty tons and then carried on the backs of a thousand coolies from the quarry, some hundred kilometres distant. Why couldn't Giap perform the same miracle with a cannon?' Pleven demanded that his staff immediately devise a plan to save the base. For that it was already too late.

A telling story comes from Australian journalist Wilfred Burchett, the only Westerner to meet with Ho Chi Minh at the time. The chairman took off his sun helmet and turned it upside down on the table: 'This is Diên Biên Phu, a valley, surrounded by hills. The cream of the French military are in it, and we' – he felt around the brim of the helmet – 'we sit around them.'

At the beginning of March 1954 the rains abated and Giap

was ready to make his move. His ground superiority was three to one. Three infantry divisions, or 60,000 men, facing 11,000 defenders, of which only 8,500 could be counted on as reliable. Giap's superiority in artillery was even more pronounced – eighty 105mm howitzers, forty 75mm howitzers and twenty 120mm mortars. To their arsenal the Viet Minh had added thirty-six anti-aircraft guns that could effectively prevent any aircraft from even trying a landing. The French had four 155mm howitzers, twenty 105mm and twenty-four 120mm mortars. They had added ten heavy tanks, which proved quite useless; already on their first outing they had sunk axle deep in mud. Most important of all was the question of morale. While the French had in their units a considerable number of auxiliary Thais, Senegalese and Algerians, Giap's forces were made up entirely of Vietnamese, pumped up in their belief (after a solid dose of indoctrination) that 'heroism was the best answer to superior firepower'. Still, the Vietnamese supremo knew only too well that open assault against well-defended, fortified positions was suicidal, and he opted for the slower method of a formal siege by first weakening the defences with artillery (as the Turks had done at Constantinople, five centuries before). His batteries would remorselessly pound the enemy and herd them into the hollow of their fortresses, where the morale of the French and their auxiliaries was sure to collapse. Only then would he allow frontal assaults. That, at least, was his plan.

In the base PC (HQ) of Diên Biên Phu, Col. de Castries, in shirtsleeves and open collar which showed off his famous red silk scarf, was surrounded by his closest advisers – his Chief-of-Staff Guth, his artillery commander Piroth, and the battalion chiefs Allioux, Noël, Trancart and the newly arrived Gaucher, who voiced his doubts. 'Uncle Ho has a million ants moving his equipment around. Why should they not be able to move a dismantled 105mm cannon? Those ants crawl, sometimes a metre, sometimes a mile, but they do get there.'

'Don't be silly, nobody gets through that jungle, or up and down the hills.'

'How do we find out?'

'Do you have anything that will push aside the leafy cover and tell us if a line of communists are moving down a jungle trail carrying a disassembled 105mm howitzer? No, somebody has to go in to find out, and I can only hope they'll come back out.'

Three reconnaissance parties went out and did come back; they had discovered three camps under the roof of the jungle foliage, each with about five hundred heavily armed Viet, *only five miles to the north-east and east near the top of some of the hills surrounding the French base*. The patrols marked the enemy emplacements on a map. But they had also brought news of something else: the Viet were there with batteries of 105mm howitzers!

If final proof were needed, de Castries now had it: the enemy held the high ground. At least three hills around Diên Biên Phu were crawling with Giap's men. De Castries called for an air-strike. Napalm rained down on the first hill marked for destruction by the reconnaissance patrol. For the Viet Minh, this was a unique, if horrifying, experience. Shortly thereafter more planes struck the second hill. A French sortie that went in the following day found among the hundreds of charred bodies the diary of Van Vinh, a Viet Minh political commissar. 'Hell opens up in front of my eyes, fire falls from the sky in the form of cigar-shaped containers, sheets of flames extending throughout the forest, burning my soldiers and panicking the rest. My men are fleeing in all directions, they know the jungle but are afraid of planes. I try to regroup them, in vain, they run. Those of us that have escaped the inferno have found refuge with our comrades.' And that was where he died. The *bo-dois* knew about snakes and scorpions, barbed wire and bullets, but fire from the sky they could not take. It demonstrated what carefully planned and executed carpet bombing by several hundred planes could have achieved. But the French never had a hundred planes.

A new element entered the political scene. Ho Chi Minh was suddenly faced with a deadline. The 'Big Four', the USA, the Soviet Union, Great Britain and France, agreed to meet in Geneva in late April to discuss Cold War issues, including Indochina. If the French could be seriously defeated at Diên Biên Phu, and Ho presented this *fait accompli* at the table in Geneva, this would win him the war. Ho knew that it would mean accepting much bigger losses in men and more immediate assistance from both Russia and China. Giap's clock began to tick.

The initial phase of the siege began with a mighty bang at 1745 hours on 13 March 1954. One hundred pieces of medium and heavy artillery opened up and poured a withering hail of shells on to Strongpoint Béatrice. Some pieces were firing in a straight line and hit blockhouses, bunkers and machinegun emplacements. They struck the battalion command centre, easily identifiable by its aerials. The men of 11th Company, crouching down in the trenches, could do little more than pray. The younger, less experienced legionnaires began to curse God and Giap.

'Don't bitch, keep your strength for later, you'll be needing it,' scolded the *sergent-chef* of 1 Section,[8] Sgt Schweiger. He had already survived an onslaught by tall Russians and he was sure that he could overcome some little yellow bastards. His radio came on. Capt. Pardi was trying to arrive at an assessment of the situation: 'Schweiger, how goes it over at 1 Section?'

'Funny sort of picnic, the cabin has fallen on the dog. Guess it wasn't meant to stand up to 105s.' In the jargon of the legion, this meant we're under fire and in a mess.

[8] The 11th Company of 3/13 Battalion, holding Béatrice, was commanded by Lt Turpin, with two *sergent-chefs*, the master sergeant of 1st Platoon, Schweiger, and the 2nd Platoon of Keil, nine sergeants, eleven corporals and eighty-five legionnaires.

'Need artillery sup . . .' Pardi was trying to pass on the message to battalion when an 120mm mortar bomb struck his command post. It came through the roof and exploded inside the command bunker. There were no survivors. A runner came up to Schweiger, his old comrade Keil of 2 Section. '*Wir sitzen in der Scheisse* . . . we're deep in shit.'

'You're telling me.' The radio crackled.

'*Béatrice, Béatrice, répondre Béatrice* . . . what's going on?'

'*Ici Béatrice 3* . . . or what's left of it,' answered Schweiger, who suddenly found himself in charge, '*alles tot* . . . they're all dead.'

Two men came stumbling out of the dust cloud – a young soldier supporting Lt Turpin, who had suffered a concussion and was bleeding from a gash in his head. He grabbed the microphone. '*Ici Béatrice*, Turpin speaking. Lt Carrière on Béatrice 1 is dead, Sgt Kubiak is in command. Sgt Bartoli is manning the heavy machineguns. On Béatrice 3 are Schweiger and Keil. I'll try to organise defences.'

'Why no news from the PC?'

'*Ils ont pris l'obus plein dans le buffet* . . . They had a shell served on their dining table. They're all gone.'

At 1915 hours, just as the sun was setting, an outpost on Béatrice 3 reported that hordes of Viet Minh were pouring down from the mountains to the north-east in the direction of their position. With this began the 'Night of Béatrice'. The voice of Col. Gaucher came on the line. 'We need an estimate of enemy numbers.'

'Two regiments.'

'Calm yourself,' came the cool voice over the radio, 'they haven't got that many in this sector.'

'Then bloody well come up here and count them yourself!'

A quick calculation came up with six thousand *bo-dois*. The attackers were quickly identified as the 141st and 209th

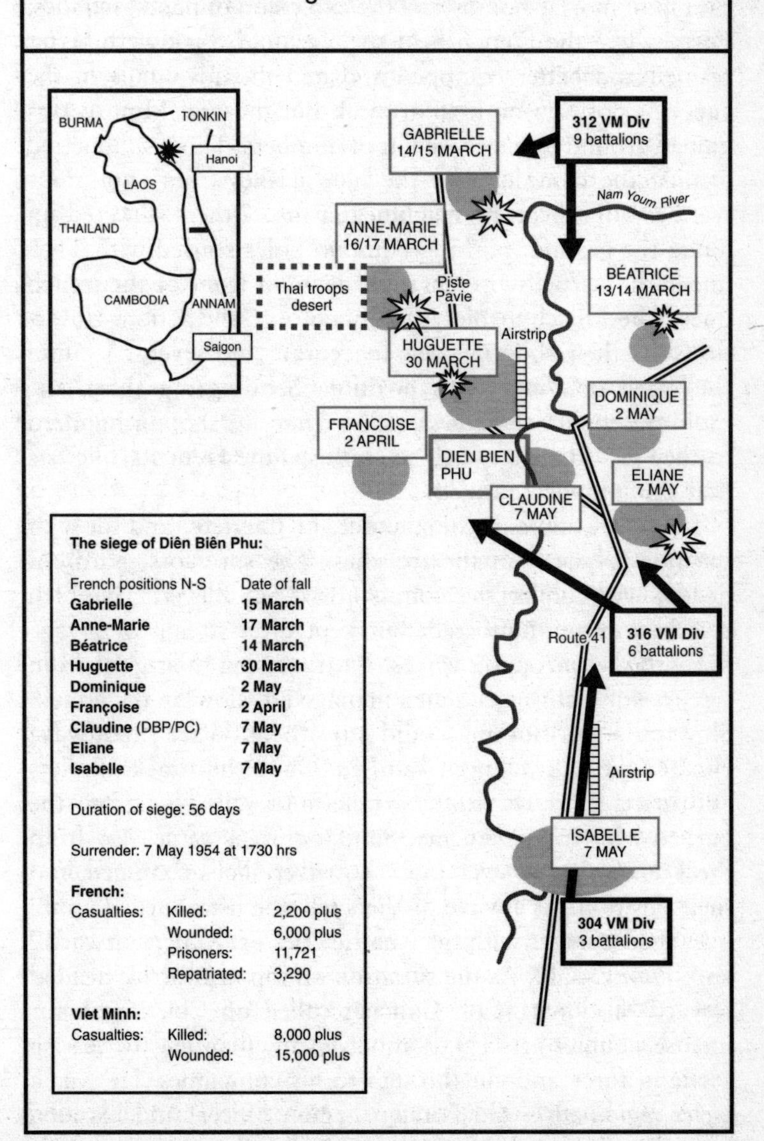
The Siege of Diên Biên Phu
BURMA
TONKIN
Hanoi
LAOS
THAILAND
CAMBODIA
ANNAM
Saigon
GABRIELLE
14/15 MARCH
312 VM Div
9 battalions
Nam Youm River
ANNE-MARIE
16/17 MARCH
BÉATRICE
13/14 MARCH
Thai troops
desert
Piste
Pavie
Airstrip
HUGUETTE
30 MARCH
DOMINIQUE
2 MAY
FRANCOISE
2 APRIL
DIEN BIEN
PHU
ELIANE
7 MAY
CLAUDINE
7 MAY
The siege of Diên Biên Phu:
French positions N-S
Date of fall
Gabrielle 15 March
Anne-Marie 17 March
Béatrice 14 March
Huguette 30 March
Dominique 2 May
Françoise 2 April
Claudine (DBP/PC) 7 May
Eliane 7 May
Isabelle 7 May
Duration of siege: 56 days
Surrender: 7 May 1954 at 1730 hrs
French:
Casualties: Killed: 2,200 plus
Wounded: 6,000 plus
Prisoners: 11,721
Repatriated: 3,290
Viet Minh:
Casualties: Killed: 8,000 plus
Wounded: 15,000 plus
Route 41
316 VM Div
6 battalions
Airstrip
ISABELLE
7 MAY
304 VM Div
3 battalions

VM Regiments of Gen. Lê Trong Tan's 312th VM Division. The darkness roared with the clatter of machineguns, the thump of mortar bombs and the explosion of hand grenades. For a while the French held their ground; they were better trained and better equipped and had the advantage of the superior position on high ground. But the Viet Minh waves gained ground by sheer weight of numbers. Those silhouetted against the moonlight or the blue flashes from explosions were rapidly felled by machinegun fire. Others slithered up along the ground, pushing bamboo poles stuffed with TNT under the barbed-wire entanglements in front of the trench lines. The French artillery finally got into the action. Unfortunately, their shooting was inaccurate and several 105mm shells fell on the French position. Schweiger grabbed the radio microphone: '*Schiesst 100 weiter* . . . shoot a hundred further . . .' His angry call so confused the French artillerists that they stopped altogether.

The 9th Company commander, Lt Carrière, and most of the rest lay dead in the trenches. The survivors, hardly a dozen, were under the command of Sgt Bleyer. The 11th was heavily outnumbered, but kept up a stream of savage fire into the oncoming waves. By traversing their guns from side to side, Schweiger's men managed to slow up the attack. Slow up – but nothing could stop them. Wave after wave climbed the hill, yelling: '*Tien Lên!* On to the attack!' Bullets and grenades dealt death; shrieks and yells rose from the barbed-wire entanglements. Similar shrieks came also from the French side as ever more howitzer shells slammed into their position. As a wave of Viets fell, the next hurtled uphill over their corpses with their battle cries of '*Xung!* Forward!' and '*Phong!* Kill!' As the situation on top of Béatrice headed towards a climax, Col. Gaucher called up Col. Piroth for intense counter-artillery bombardment, planning to lead a sortie in force and cut through to his companies. He was a *vieux légionnaire* (old Foreign Legion officer) and his men knew that he would never abandon them to their fate. 'We cannot leave Béatrice without . . .' Nobody will ever know what *le vieux* wanted to say, since a shell slammed through the roof and killed most of the battalion command, including Col. Gaucher, Lt Bailly and Lt Bretteville.

De Castries ordered up a communication link with Hanoi.

'Who do you wish to speak to, *mon colonel*?'

'Just get me through and don't worry about the rest.'

'You mean you're going to talk to *le commandant-en-chef* at four in the morning?'

'A Corsican never sleeps when the enemy kills his soldiers. Remember that.'

'*Oui, mon colonel.*'

On Béatrice 3, the last of the defenders were being compressed into a tiny area, providing an easy target for Giap's massed artillery, while more Viet Minh charged into their belching machineguns. They fell and slithered down the hill, but others came on. Soon they were only a dozen yards from the final trench. The French had no more time to change magazines. The moment for rifle butts and knives had come. '*A la baionette!*'

'Legionnaires, *haut les mains! Rendez-vous* . . . hands up! Surrender . . .' came a shrill, heavily accented voice. Any further defence was useless, and the very few still alive put up their hands. Lt Turpin was found next to a destroyed blockhouse; he was bleeding from many wounds. Two *bodois* lifted him under his arms and dragged him before a high-ranking Viet officer. 'Rank, name, unit?' the Viet Minh barked.

'Turpin, Lieutenant, 11th Company.'

'French?'

'Yes.'

'You didn't think we had artillery . . .' He spoke with a grim smile. 'President Ho Chi Minh has ordered us to treat wounded with leniency. You were quite brave.' The Viet Minh officer took a folded paper from his shirt pocket.

'A message for your Colonel de Castries. I want you to deliver it.'

It contained a hastily scribbled request for a *trêve* (ceasefire).[9]

From nearby hills, other French companies looked in horror on the carnage, clearly visible in the ghastly white-blue light of magnesium flares. They watched as up on Béatrice the defence faltered and the struggle came to a dramatic halt. Viet Minh and French dead littered the hill; shells and bullets had made no distinction between friend and foe. A few survivors of the hand-to-hand carnage came bouncing down the steep slope, only to be caught in the crossfire from the new occupants of the bloodied copse. By 3 a.m. it was over. The flares went out and darkness blanketed the horror, a horror fully revealed in the light of a new dawn. Along a front line of only three hundred metres, partly hanging from the barbed wire, lay the mutilated, bleeding corpses of 1,800 Viet Minh next to two companies of legionnaires. By noon the tropical sun had turned them into black and bloated cadavers. One of the *miraculeux* who had managed to slip away was Legionnaire Osterlich. He tore a page from a notebook and wrote on it:

> *Heldentaten, Heldengräber reihen neu sich an die alten*
> *Künden wie Legenden erstanden, künden wie Legenden erhalten . . .*
> Heroes' deeds and heroes' graves align along the old
> Announce how the legend came to be and how the legend will continue . . .

This he nailed to a pole which he stuck in the ground. It was his way of paying final homage to his *Alten Kameraden* Schweiger, Soos and all others who had survived Stalingrad and Kursk but not the hell at Diên Biên Phu.

[9] The question of this ceasefire has never been settled. It was denied by Gen. Giap during an interview. 'Why should we have asked for a *trêve*, we had won and were on top of the hill.'

* * *

Now that Giap had Béatrice, the key to the Diên Biên Phu supply line, he could practically spit down on to the airstrip, and his 37mm anti-aircraft guns could blast any aircraft from the sky or on the ground. With the fall of Béatrice the fate of the defenders was sealed.

The attack on Gabrielle in the early hours of 15 March was a repeat of the action on Béatrice. Following a furious artillery bombardment, Viet Minh battalions swept up the hill. Hundreds were cut down and hundreds entangled on the razor-sharp wire and left there to die as the fight moved up the hill. Nothing could stop the suicidal masses of two VM divisions, the 308th and 312th. The commander of Gabrielle, Commandant Kha, who had been wounded by a bazooka shell fired from fifty yards at his HQ bunker, was found still alive among the many dead. A Viet Minh officer ordered him moved down the hill. While they put him on a stretcher, Kha mumbled: '*Mon pauvre bataillon* . . . my poor battalion . . .'

The Viet Minh officer answered in impeccable French: 'Your hill has cost us dearly.'

Indeed it had. The Viet Minh lost 9,000. But Giap had 25,000 more to replace them. For the French it was a different story. Of Gabrielle's 877 defenders, 501 were killed, and the rest were wounded and taken prisoner. Commandant Kha died of his injuries. Only sixty-five POWs from Strongpoint Gabrielle were ever to see France again.

Down in the valley, one-armed artillery colonel Piroth stumbled around his shattered gun emplacements. Everything had gone so badly wrong. Piroth stared in disbelief at his batteries, which had been blown apart by precision fire from the surrounding heights. He told anyone willing to listen how sorry he was about his flawed counter-fire plan. Nobody cared to listen; everybody was too busy trying to stay alive. In the end the colonel staggered into his bunker, pulled a pin on a hand grenade and held it against his chest.[10] The news spread quickly throughout the camp. Two men were sitting in a trench on Strongpoint Eliane. 'Hear about Piroth?'

'*Oui.* Curious manner *de filer à l'anglaise* [to take French leave],' said Sub-Lt Canton, swigging a mouthful of coffee.

'I guess he felt responsible for a plan that never worked,' replied Lt Bergot, who was in charge of a company of 120mm mortars.

Canton just shrugged his shoulders: 'If all those idiots who feel responsible for their blunders kill themselves, that's gonna blow a helluva hole between here and Paris.'

Both sides were too exhausted to continue at this furious pace. The captured hills seemed more lifeless than the paralysed French base lying below them. The airstrip, with its peppered runway, resembled a picture of the craters on the moon. A smashed plane had been flipped on its back and opened up like a neatly split lobster shell – a bull's-eye hit from an 120mm mortar. From 23 March onwards both airstrips were out of action. This also eliminated sizeable *médévacs* and supply planes. Only smaller aircraft made occasional overflights to drop ammunition and medicines. These were dangerous missions, since every attempt to supply the base by air-drops was met by a curtain of anti-aircraft fire. Nothing moved on the roads. The valley floor was empty – no buffaloes grazing, for they had been slaughtered, no palms blowing in the wind, because these had been cut to built redoubts, and no people dashing across the paddies, for this would have spelled their certain death. Giap's cannon commanded the valley and everything that moved in it.

Out of the cover of a monsoon cloud came the sharp droning of a plane, its engine revving into the high pitch of a dive. The cloud parted with a flash of wings and the chatter

10 Gen. Navarre cabled Paris: 'Colonel Piroth fell on the Field of Honour.' When Paris enquired about the true circumstances, Navarre replied curtly: 'I reconfirm, Colonel Piroth fell on the Field of Honour!'

of her guns. A Hellcat was back, her 50mms spitting death from her wings. She was raking one of the lost strongpoints. The Viet had spotted the danger. Their 37mm Peking Piano anti-aircraft guns spat eight hundred rounds a minute. The noise was tremendous – the clatter of the breeching and the creak as gun carriages swivelled. The heat was permeated by the smell of cordite and hot grease. The guns were well hidden, but from the sound they were on or near Béatrice. Having made her run, the aircraft banked and in no time was back out of sight in the clouds. The plane's attack had been noisy but without visible effect. She had waved the flag and given the beleaguered French something to cheer.

On 16 March, Col. Bigeard's six Bataillon Parachutistes Coloniale jumped on to a thinly protected drop zone from high-flying transport planes. Bigeard, still suffering from a leg wound, hobbled around the field, encouraging his men. But what was to have been the relief of the beleaguered base led only to more wounded and additional mouths to feed.

More horror awaited the defenders. Another invasion, something even more appalling than the spectre of Viet Minh battalions: maggots issuing from hundreds of unburied corpses. The slimy white worms crept into uniforms, under bandages and into plaster casts. At night they crept across hands and faces and into ears. The invasion drove some soldiers mad. The scene in the field hospital was one from Dante's *Inferno*.[11] The infected limbs that had to be cut from living bodies in the operating theatre were dumped into a hole, six feet square. It was called *le trou des amputés*. During these days of extreme hardship, acts of incredible heroism were common; one of the few women still present, Geneviève de Galard, was honoured as 'heroine of DBP', after a seriously wounded lieutenant bestowed on her his own Croix de la Légion d'Honneur (Medal of Honour). Some night sorties were undertaken by the Paras of Cols Bigeard and Langlais

[11] Cdt Grauwin, *J'étais médecin à Diên Biên Phu*, London 1955.

– small groups of legionnaires armed only with knives who slipped into Viet Minh trenches to slit throats.

The focal point of battle shifted from Indochina to discussions held in Paris and Washington. From a series of secret meetings in the Pentagon came a personal encounter between the American Secretary of State, John Foster Dulles, and his French counterpart, Georges Bidault. During this meeting Dulles, a man who loved French culture and had studied at the Sorbonne, threw out a sentence which took Bidault by such surprise that he didn't know what to answer. 'And if we gave you two atomic bombs to save Diên Biên Phu?'

'Atomic bombs? But we would also destroy our own people,' Bidault stuttered, not quite certain whether the American had made a sick joke, or was serious.

The tall American in his grey suit, with a face as cold as granite, snapped: 'We shall no longer tolerate a progression of communism in Asia. That is finished, finished for ever. If we don't stand up to them, right away and by all our means, we shall be swept away.'[12] John Foster Dulles, a minister of the Presbyterian Church, had seen red. His was a holy mission to save the West – and how many statesmen have ever believed in their mission on earth? 'He loved France in his way,' Georges Bidault was to state years later of his friend Dulles. Bidault, a disciple of Richelieu and steeped in his Carthesian upbringing, held to seeking a solution by diplomatic efforts. Yet it was one of his own, Voltaire, who had penned some words of good advice to France's Maréchal de Turenne (1770): 'It is said that God is always on the side of the big battalions.'

In Washington, the anti-Chinese lobby was hot on the down-with-the-Red-threat idea: 'We've got to finish with Mao sooner or later.' US Vice-President Richard Nixon joined forces with Dulles: 'We've got to step up to the threshold

[12] The text of this conversation comes from French archives and also from a private talk with Gen. Pierre Gallois. It has also been quoted in J.R. Tournoux, *Secrets d'Etat*, Paris 1960.

in order to safeguard the peace.' He formulated his policy around four critical points:

1. China has no bomb.[13]
2. If they want to use one they have to go to Moscow, which they will not.
3. Russia is way behind the US in atomic weapons [America had the H-bomb].
4. The communist camp will consider it out of proportion to go to war over Indochina; thereby they will accept the diplomatic option of talks in Geneva.

At the height of the Cold War, and in the midst of the anti-Red hysteria raised by Senator McCarthy's Committee on Un-American Activities, the Indochina Affair quickly reached a point of extreme crisis. Admiral Radford, as acting Chief-of-Staff, presiding over a military conference at SHAPE HQ in Rocquencourt near Paris, was a fervent advocate of a permanent bridgehead in Asia. French Gen. Ely, just back from Washington, where he had been in discussion with the chiefs-of-staff at the Pentagon on behalf of his Minister of Defence, René Pleven, hastened to the Hotel Matignon, where he met with French Premier Laniel. 'The Pentagon is ready to launch an immediate intervention with its heavy bombers. All that's left for us to do is push the button.'

In fact, President Eisenhower, who had taken office in January 1953, was initially in favour of adopting a hard line to communism. In a memo to Prime Minister Winston Churchill he wrote: 'If I may refer again to history, we failed to halt Hirohito, Mussolini and Hitler by not acting in unity and in time. That marked the beginning of many years of stark tragedy and desperate peril.'

Col. Pierre Gallois was called in for consultations. He suggested a plan that had possibilities: drop a 'big one' on the

13 China got the bomb in 1964.

uninhabited jungle, avoiding causing any casualties. It would show the Chinese and the Viet that the West meant business. It was a strategic alternative, but politically unacceptable. The French were only too aware that the Americans hadn't used the ultimate deterrent in Korea in order to save their own divisions from annihilation when the Chinese swept across the Yalu river. They would hardly sanction its use to save a few battalions of French foreign legionnaires in a region where the USA had no strategic interest. Vice-President Richard Nixon confirmed this in his memoirs: 'In Washington, the Joint Chiefs of Staff devised a plan known only as *Operation Vulture*, for using three small tactical atomic bombs to destroy Viet Minh positions and relieve the French garrison . . . [I told] the President that he should not underestimate his ability to get the Congress and the country to follow his leadership.'

So it was back to conventional bombing. In effect, the Pentagon had readied for this operation a veritable air armada: three hundred fighter-bombers and sixty heavy bombers, capable of spreading a carpet of 2,000kg bombs (compared with the maximum 500kg capability of the French Air Force).

'Will these planes carry French identification?' Paris wished to know, and Gallois gave them a reply they didn't like: 'Negative, our pilots aren't trained for this kind of operation.' More transatlantic calls reached a compromise: French colours, American crews. Operation Vulture was ready to go. Bombers of the US Air Force flying from Manila would 'zap the Viets' with conventional explosives. But unfortunately, alongside the secret negotiations another, ultra-secret negotiation was taking place: any intervention by conventional arms was to be linked to an intervention by nuclear means, or, as the French called it, '*le sous-entendu atomique*' (the hidden atomic understanding). For the chiefs-of-staff, to combine nuclear with conventional deterrent was a fatal error, since it robbed the politicians of any chance of falling back on the 'classical option'.

The chiefs-of-staff argued the options: Radford (Navy) and Twining (Air Force) were for the attack, Ridgway (Army) was against it. 'Never get involved in a land war in Asia,' he counselled. Another negative voice was that of Prime Minister Winston Churchill, who called Ike personally by phone: 'You've got to stop that nonsense.'

Now it was up to the men of the US Congress. And there the military ran into a solid wall. 'The bombing scheme was stopped by leaders of the Congress, above all by House Leader Lyndon Johnson.'[14] But the one who tilted the balance was a young senator from Massachusetts: 'No amount of American military assistance in Indo-China can conquer an enemy which is everywhere and at the same time nowhere, an "enemy of the people" which has the sympathy and covert support of the people.' A few years later, it was left up to this same man, John F. Kennedy, to make a decision about this situation; by then he had forgotten his own prophetic lines.

The decision was up to US President Dwight Eisenhower, who thereby became the first American President to make a decision on Vietnam. French ambassador Henri Bonnet went to see Eisenhower, who was vacationing in Kentucky. After the meeting, he cabled Paris: 'The US President feels that an intervention at this time would make the Americans look like raving imperialists. He cannot see an American intervention in our conflict in the Far East.'

In a cable dated 24 April 1954, John Foster Dulles dotted the 'i':

> . . . any war action can only be effected with the full consent of Congress . . . such a consent cannot be obtained in the hours to come, and in my opinion, cannot be obtained at all if we cannot establish an organisation for the defence of South-East Asia, which must include all the nations concerned . . . already, the valiant defenders

14 Jean Lacouture.

> of Diên Biên Phu have inflicted such heavy casualties on the aggressors in human lives and equipment, that the balance from a strictly military point remains favourable to France . . . I'm persuaded that France will overcome this temporary setback . . . John Foster Dulles.

French Foreign Minister Bidault replied immediately the same day:

> The advice by our military experts, one of whom has just returned from Diên Biên Phu, has it that the US Airforce could still save the garrison . . . for the first time, the Viet Minh has massed all its effective to attack. A concerted effort by the airforce could destroy a great part of the enemy's effective, *an occasion which most likely will never again present itself* . . . it is not to be excluded that such action would carry a decisive and fatal strike against the Viet Minh . . . Georges Bidault.

With Eisenhower's *nyet* died the last chance of settling the issue in a war that was to continue for another twenty years and cost the lives of millions. The Americans were to recall their 'non-intervention' in the years to come. Fifteen years passed before the United States had to pay for it with 55,000 of their own dead in the jungles of Vietnam. It led to America's greatest trauma and caused one President (Lyndon Johnson) to fall and another (Richard Nixon) to admit to America's first-ever military defeat. It finally shaped a country's conscience.

A new crisis had developed in the besieged garrison with a sharp decline in the loyalty of North African units. Using loudspeakers, the Viet broadcast across the lines in Arabic and German (for the benefit of the legionnaires): 'Brothers, your days are numbered. Do you really want to die for the

French colonialists?' Many Algerians discovered for the first time that non-whites, in this case *les jaunes* (yellows), could beat *les blancs*. On 30 March, the Algerian battalion simply disbanded. It was as a result of Indochina that Algerians developed ideas which were to lead directly to Algeria's struggle for independence from France.

The final phase began with the longest and bloodiest combat, the struggle for Strongpoint Huguette, held by the battalion under Col. Bizard. On 30 March an entire VM division, the 308th, began their attack on the fortified hill. Day after day the Viet artillery pounded the hill, and with every hour the ring tightened around the defenders. Bloody slaughter occurred when a relief effort was launched to free the hill, which could only be supplied by air, if at all.

On 12 April, Sgt Zurell noticed a small parachute hanging in the barbed wire. Attached to it was a small, well-wrapped parcel which aroused the sergeant's curiosity; despite continuous explosions, he crawled out to recover it. One may well imagine his surprise when he found that it contained a carton of Lucky Strike, two bottles of Rémy Martin cognac – and a general's star. It was marked for the personal attention of *Gen.* de Castries. And that was how the 4th Company, 1st BEP found out about the promotion of their colonel to general. They celebrated the event with two bottles of twelve-year-old cognac and a well-deserved smoke. As for the general's stars, they buried them so deep that they would never fall into the hands of the foe.

On 12 April, Gen. Giap launched his final assault. It began with a blistering bombardment from 150 cannon before his hordes rolled in as one man, yelling: '*Doc Lâp! Doc Lâp!* Independence! Independence! A thousand years for Uncle Ho!' The first wave had covered the better part of the distance between jungle and barbed wire when the last remaining strongpoints began to spit fire and destruction. Many of the attackers ran into the mortar explosions and were torn to pieces; others stopped just in time to receive the full impact of the next salvo. Scythed by the merciless hail of slugs from chattering machineguns, thousands toppled like skittles. But like a human avalanche, the next wave cascaded onward, shooting, stabbing, slashing at anything in their way . . .

Those in the trenches on other hills knew that the end was near. The valiant defenders of Diên Biên Phu had survived 170 days of 'hell in a small place'. Gen. de Castries tried to bolster the morale of his men when he went down into the dugouts to distribute medals. Everybody received a medal bereft of ribbons. He assured them: 'This is not going to end badly, something is going to happen.' But he didn't know what this 'something' could be, because as far as Hanoi and Paris were concerned, Diên Biên Phu was already written off.

The bombardment increased and the hill positions fell one after the other: Dominique and Anne-Marie, Claudine, Françoise and Isabelle. Attacked, conquered by the enemy, reconquered with horrendous losses, and lost again. On Huguette, Col. Bizard was down to 180 men from his original thousand when he received a message from de Castries: 'The operation to come to your rescue has failed. I leave all further decisions to you.' Huguette 5 was now down to twenty-five legionnaires, including the cognac-swigging Zurell and one young sub-lieutenant, Boisbouvier, who had been wounded so many times he had stopped counting. The tiny group suffered fire from eight 105mm cannon and the bombs from two companies of 120mm mortars. A steam hammer to smash a fly. In face of the valiant twenty-five were three *bo-dois* regiments, the 36th dug in on the northern slope, the 102nd in the west and the 88th in reserve. Still, the French held out until the night of 1 May, when Lt Boisbouvier was ambushed by a number of Viet and dragged away. His body was never found. At 3.30 that night, Cpl Novak sent a final message: 'I am holding with two men.' Then his radio went silent.

A message came through from Hanoi to the effect that

every man in the garrison had been cited for the Croix de Guerre. 'They thought in any case we would all die in combat so they might as well decorate us,' said Col. Bigeard. At that moment a loudspeaker from the Viet trenches played the famous World War II French Resistance song with its haunting line: '*Ami entends-tu le vol noir des corbeaux sur la plaine* . . . Friend, can you hear the black flight of ravens over the plain . . .'. Nobody could tell afterwards who started it, but every single French soldier in the trenches stood up and, in a clear, loud voice, joined in a rousing chorus of '*La Marseillaise*'.

6 May 1954, 0600 hours. Diên Biên Phu prepared for its last stand. Only one bastion still held out, Strongpoint Eliane, with Bigeard's tough Paras on top. They heard a roar and a whistle. Only the old legionnaires, survivors of Stalingrad, knew that this was the sound of the feared Katyushas. Each launcher simultaneously fired twelve rockets. A deluge of fire came down on the ridges of Eliane and buried its defenders under earth and rubble. Bigeard and Langlais made a decision – a daring one, but for them the only possible choice. They would take their men and break out towards Laos. Bigeard gave the operation a fitting name: '*Percée de sang* . . . Bloody Breakout'. De Castries offered to stay behind to take care of the many thousands of wounded.

'We gathered the last surviving chiefs around us and told them we would go for a breakout. And you know what they replied? "No, it's not worth it, we might as well die here, our men couldn't make it a hundred metres without passing out." So de Castries called Hanoi. "It's over," he said, and Navarre replied, "If it comes to it, do not raise the white flag, just stop fighting." That was it then.'[15]

The battle began in a heavy downpour. In a modern re-enactment of the medieval joust at Agincourt, men fought with

[15] Reported by Col. Bigeard.

bayonets and knives, sliding around and dying in the mud. The artillery fired point blank into their midst, mowing down friend and foe without making a distinction. The noise reached infernal proportions; thousands of rounds exploded, rimming the sky with red. The air became unbreathable; cordite fumes went into lungs and eyes. Apocalypse . . . *Götterdämmerung*. Fresh regiments of Viet Minh were thrown into the fray. Groups of Paras hung on; they fought the screaming masses with the desperation of the condemned, knowing only too well that this battle allowed neither defeat nor surrender. They didn't give an inch except when dead.[16]

'*Si tu es dans la merde jusqu'au cou, il faut qu'à chanter* . . . If you're up to your neck in shit, all you can do is sing . . .' The last stand was conducted by men who looked not remotely military: those whose legs had been amputated, with blood from stumps seeping through bandages, those half blinded by explosions, those with smashed bones in plaster casts, or those shivering with high fever. All had volunteered to take up a gun and '*crever avec les copains* . . . fight and die with their comrades'.

At 1700 hours on 7 May, Col. 'Bruno' Bigeard scribbled four short phrases on a page torn from his notebook: '*Cessez-le-feu à 17h 30* . . . Ceasefire at 1730 hours. Don't fire. No white flag. Till soon. Bruno.'

And below he wrote: '*Pauvre 6! Pauvres paras!* . . . Poor 6th! Poor Paras!'

Lt Allaire, the last surviving officer on Eliane 3, was asked by one of his men: '*C'est fini.?* . . . Is it over?' Through the powder smoke, Lt Allaire looked out over a valley where so much suffering had taken place – at the pathos, the brutalisation, the sheer savage meaningless of it all, impressions that could never be wiped from a man's mind. There were tears in his eyes. A tough Legion parachutist was crying.

'*C'est fini.*'

[16] Only about one hundred French managed to get away, and after weeks of suffering, disease and hunger, ended up at the last French base in Laos.

The facts

The politicians who had caused the defeat managed to put the blame on the military. A secret report issued by a commission investigating the disaster stated that 'the government neither intervened in the decision to occupy Diên Biên Phu, nor in the battle itself . . . it has been established that General Navarre took the initiative entirely on his own with his decision of 3 December 1953 to accept battle without previous consultation or approbation by Paris . . .' The committee did, however, make a comment which was quite significant: '. . . however, it had been pointed out to the government [on 24 July 1953], upon their request for a defence of Laos, the dangers which such an obligation engendered . . .' The report ended its apology with a phrase taken straight from Napoleon's textbook: '. . . considering that the battle for Diên Biên Phu had become the principal battle, priority for maximum support should have been accorded over all other operations.'

It was a poor epitaph and did not honour those who suffered the most. It was only an apology for the blind and deceitful arrogance of political and military leaders which had caused the ravaging of a distant land and wasted the lives of so many of its young citizens: 11,721 French and allied soldiers went into captivity; only 3,290 returned home. As to the fate of the others, nothing is known.

A few weeks after the end of the battle, two colonels met in the stately halls of France's Defence Ministry. One had just come from a meeting with his minister, where the implications of the recently signed Treaty of Geneva had been discussed.

'So, what does the minister think?'

'He thinks that because of what took place there it can never happen again.'

'What do you think?'

'We can always hope . . .'

Six months later, the Algerian War of Independence erupted.

The war for the liberation of Vietnam[17] was the longest conflict of the twentieth century. It lasted 10,360 days. It involved French, Chinese, Americans and Russians, and brought the world to the brink of disaster.

Did the Americans seriously consider dropping the 'big one' on Giap at Diên Biên Phu? Inconceivable given that they had already dropped two on Asia, at Hiroshima and Nagasaki. At the height of the Cold War, and with an unstable global situation, such action was politically unthinkable. The United States would have been chastised as an imperialist usurper and chased from the Asian continent. President Eisenhower's decision was the correct one.

It is a curious fact that, even after the fall of Diên Biên Phu, Ho Chi Minh always gave the impression that he would have much preferred collaboration with France to being sucked into the communist-orientated Chinese orbit.[18] In a private conversation, which took place during the World Congress of Communists in Moscow in the spring of 1959, Chairman Ho Chi Minh revealed to French communist leader Jacques Duclos: 'The greatest remorse of my political life is that I have not been able to arrive at an entente with France, a country which I have always loved and still respect dearly.'

Had Navarre's strategy worked and Diên Biên Phu been turned into a French victory, then Ho Chi Minh would

[17] The name is actually Chinese. In 207 BC, a Chinese warlord conquered the country and called it Nam Viet.

[18] J. Sainteny, *Histoire d'une paix manquée*, Paris/Amsterdam 1954. Mr Sainteny was French governor of Tonkin and knew Ho very well.

have been forced to the conference table, France would have followed General Léchères' original proposal, hung on another three years and then left through the diplomatic back door. Indochina would have become Vietnam, and Vietnam would have been a united country with Chairman Ho as head of state. A suitable arrangement would have been achieved with the Western powers and the war in Vietnam would never have taken place. Because, long before, there had been another significant encounter which so clearly pointed to Ho's nationalistic aims. It took place between Ho Chi Minh, Pham Van Dong[19] and an American emissary at the end of the war in Korea. The American diplomat asked if Ho Chi Minh wished the United States to mediate in order to arrive at a settlement between Ho's liberation movement and France. For a long time the Vietnamese revolutionary remained silent before he replied with a slight smile: 'If you can take care of the Chinese for us, we'll take care of the French ourselves.'

Yes, every country has its perennial enemy, and in the case of Vietnam its historic enemy was not some temporal colonial power. The arch-enemy of Vietnam was always, as it always will be, its giant neighbour looming to the north: China.

The French got it all wrong, and after them the Americans.

It was sheer arrogance on the part of French generals who underestimated their barefoot foe, this army of human ants that didn't need modern transport and resupplies but carried artillery into battle on their backs and on their bicycles. French General Bigeard paid them homage. 'These enduring little men, capable of covering fifty kilometres in the night on the strength of a bowl of rice, with running shoes, and then singing their way into battle, turned out to be exceptional fighting men and managed to defeat us.' And another thing: Diên Biên Phu was undoubtedly a vital strategic position.

19 This story was related to the author by Prime Minister Pham Van Dong during an interview in 1977.

The enemy had to pass through it to attack the coastal strips. By holding Diên Biên Phu the French could control the region, provided they held both the valley and the heights commanding it, and were able to get supplies through by road under any and all weather conditions. The French failed to do both. They were beaten at their own game.

For the French soldier the Indochina War carried either no meaning at all or a very different meaning from usual: that nothing had been lost – except lives. 'We'll show the people of France what their neglect, their incredible indifference, their illusions, their dirty little politics have led us to. How best may we show them? By dying, so that at least *l'honneur* may be saved. Our dead of Diên Biên Phu died in the name of another France, one for which they had respect. The only victory that remains is the victory of our honour.'[20]

A visitor today will still find twisted pieces of artillery around trenches collapsed under the impact not of shells but of monsoon rains. The command post is as it was that distant day on the plains of Diên Biên Phu. Only a small bronze plaque has been added. It records simply the moment of the end: '1750 hours, 7 May 1954'.

The Hinge of Battle at Diên Biên Phu was one phrase uttered by a politician who wanted to retain the pink indicating the French colonial empire. He turned it into 'a mousetrap that caught the cat'.

Diên Biên Phu spelled the beginning of the end for French colonialism.

20 Robert Guillain in *Le Monde*.

10

The War Office Regrets to Inform You . . .

13 January 1842 – Afghanistan

When you're wounded and left on Afghanistan's plains,
And the women come out to cut up your remains,
Just roll to your rifle and blow out your brains,
And go to your Gawd like a soldier.

Rudyard Kipling

In the spring of 1842, a letter arrived at the Islington home of Mrs Mary McCormick. It had been written by her twenty-nine-year-old son Jeffrey: 'It is a hell of a place, shooting at ghosts hiding behind rocks on a hill. Some of us will surely die, but don't worry about me, I'll be alright . . .' At the same time, a military courier delivered another note: *'The War Office regrets to inform you . . .'*

With the exception of the immortal stand by Leonidas and his three hundred Spartans at Thermopylae (490 BC), there are few examples of an entire force being annihilated. It was left to hill tribes, descendants of Genghis Khan, to wipe out a modern European army to its last man.

The era following the battles of Trafalgar and Waterloo, with their supreme victories over the most powerful army in Europe, was a time of high and noble values. Nelson had established Britain's command over the oceans of the world.

Britain's gunboat policy dictated its *Pax Britannica*. The laurel wreath of greatness, rightfully bestowed on Nelson and Wellington, was mainly undeserved by those who followed in their footsteps. Many pretended toughness as a cloak for their weakness. Some were just weak and didn't even pretend otherwise.

An outstanding example of pretension and incompetence was that of Major-General Sir William G.K. Elphinstone. He left no permanent impression on history, except perhaps that he managed to have his entire army massacred by barbarian tribesmen. Indecision and outright stupidity on the part of a military commander were the underlying cause of the disaster. Yet it would be unfair to put the full blame for the tragedy on the weakness of Elphinstone. He was as much the victim of political ignorance as a military failure. Also deserving of reproach is the Governor-General of India, Lord Auckland, a man preoccupied with the dreaded thought that the Russians were out to take over India, and that the Northwest Frontier had to be safeguarded at all costs. From this paranoid policy followed a blueprint for disaster. Auckland pushed Elphinstone into taking on the job, subject to Her Majesty's Government's approval of course, and ageing 'Elphy Bey' accepted without hesitation. For a sexagenarian with a nondescript military career, the challenge of Afghanistan was an opportunity not to be missed. When it was confirmed, he approached his task with trepidation. His orders, upon departure, were as militarily insane as they were politically impractical.

Afghanistan was in a state of permanent anarchy. For centuries, the 'top of the world' had been locked in perpetual strife between ethnic factions. Its overall ruler had to be a fox. In the 1830s, he was Emir Dost Mohammed. He nimbly manipulated one tribe against another, just as he played one colonial power against the next. The Persians (with the connivance of the Russians) claimed the province and town of Herat. At the other end of the country, Peshawar had been forcefully annexed by the Sikh ruler, the one-eyed Ranjit Singh, a close ally of England. The country was a hotbed of conspiracy, with Tsarist Russia and England bidding furiously for its support. The Tsar was anxious to stake his claim on Afghanistan before the British established themselves there. Agents of the Tsar were offering the Emir of Afghanistan a mixture of tempting bribes and menacing pressure.

The Anglo-Russian crisis over Afghanistan was set off by sheer accident. A young emissary from the British Foreign Office, Henry Rawlinson, riding along the Khyber Pass border to visit the Shah of Persia, whose invasion army was lying in siege before Herat, ran into a group of riders who turned out to be Russians. Their leader introduced himself as Baron Vitkevitch, bearing gifts from his Tsar to Emir Dost Mohammed. For the English agent, this set alarm bells ringing – Russians in Afghanistan! As Rawlinson spoke neither Russian nor Turkomani, a great confusion arose. The Englishman turned smartly and dashed back to raise the alarm. Storm bells began to jangle from London to Calcutta.

When Baron Vitkevitch arrived in Kabul on the eve of Christmas 1837, he was met to his great surprise not by the Emir, but by a senior British diplomat, who invited him to his house for Christmas dinner. This senior official of the India Office, Sir Alexander Burnes, had been hurried from Calcutta to Kabul by Lord Auckland. The situation Burnes was told to handle was highly delicate: keep Russia out of Afghanistan. Burnes had been quick off the mark and things were going quite well with Emir Dost Mohammed when Lord Auckland committed the unpardonable sin of writing a stinging letter to the Afghan ruler, demanding in no uncertain terms that he give up his claim on Peshawar to England's ally and stop seeing the Russian envoy. As a result of the note, Burnes was told to leave Kabul. When Britain's Foreign Secretary, Lord Palmerston, put pressure on St Petersburg, backed up by landing a regiment of troops on Kharg Island in the Persian Gulf, the Shah lifted the siege of Herat and Russia recalled Vitkevitch. The Russian envoy couldn't take the shame and shot himself in his room in Kabul, though evil tongues claimed that the British had had him assassinated.

With Emir Dost Mohammed greatly weakened, Lord Auckland sensed a political opening and opted to dispose of the Northwest Frontier problem once and for all. He took the advice of his political officer, William Macnaghten, who came up with a complicated scheme. Macnaghten's pawn was Shah Shujah, an Afghan despot who had been kicked out by his own people in favour of Dost Mohammed. Macnaghten suggested that they depose Dost and put Shujah, who would immediately renounce Afghanistan's claim to Peshawar in favour of England's ally, the Sikh monarch, on the throne. On 1 October 1838, Lord Auckland grossly meddled in the affairs of a sovereign country when he signed the 'Simla Manifesto'. At the stroke of a pen he deposed Dost Mohammed for England's puppet, Shujah. To back up his decree, he called into being a combined British and Indian force of 9,500, supported by 6,000 tribesmen of uncertain loyalty. This force, called the Army of Indus, was put under the command of the seasoned Gen. Sir John Keane, with Sir Alexander Burnes as his political adviser. For Britain, it was the beginning of a humiliating disaster.

The Afghans were a rough lot then – as they are still to this day.[1] They proudly claim as their ancestor none other than Genghis Khan, and, watching them handle their mountain ponies, this is entirely credible. They are born in a saddle, live in the saddle, and their main entertainment is the world's roughest sport, also practised from the saddle. It is called *Buskashi*, and consists of a mad horde dragging a goatskin filled with straw from one village to the neighbouring one,

[1] Main tribes: Pathans (Pashtus), Tajik, Uzbek, Turkmen, Hazara, Nuristani and Baluch. All are Moslems. During the Soviet invasion in the 1980s, I spent eight weeks as war correspondent/observer in Afghanistan.

while the opposing force can use any and all means to stop them from reaching their goal. Many have been killed during this entertainment. Their other favourite pastime is to shoot at anything that is foreign, be it English, Russian or Eskimo, should they ever dare to come to the country.

In this, Afghan tribes are greatly helped by the mountainous terrain of the Hindu Kush, with average heights of over 20,000 feet (highest elevation, Mount Istoro Nal, 7,455 metres/24,590 feet). The control of key corridors and mountain passes is of vital tactical importance. All traffic in and out of the country must pass through the narrow gorges, perfectly suited for an ambush. This in turn makes it necessary to secure adjacent uplands and mountains. The recurring principle is that rugged mountain terrain often provides good advantage to even an inadequately trained and undisciplined but well-positioned defensive force. Nowhere is this better illustrated than in Afghanistan, where only the sturdiest can survive, and where formidable mountain ranges have always served as the effective buffer for competing nations. Any invading force is well advised to listen to the wise words of Monsieur le Maréchal Maurice de Saxe: 'Those who wage war in mountains should never pass through defiles without first making themselves masters of the heights.' Many invaders have learned this bitter lesson.

The Army of the Indus set off in a holiday atmosphere. They took along all the necessary implements for grouse shooting, tiger hunts, polo and cricket – the lot. Not forgetting their cigars. For such a vital component of war one regiment allotted two camels just to carry their colonel's tobacco, while the commanding officer was supplied with sixty camels to carry his personal belongings. The officers took along their mistresses and their coolies; they had servants to shine their shoes, wash clothes and polish brass buttons. Including movable tent-brothels, the camp following was made up of close to forty thousand non-combatants. Their first target was

Kandahar. Burnes paid the local Baluchi chiefs handsomely to behave in a friendly manner during the long column's march through the Bolan Pass, and General Keane's army entered undefended Kandahar on 25 April 1839.

Next on the agenda was the walled fortress of Ghuznee. Keane had left his heavy siege guns behind, and it was left to the officer commanding the Bengal Engineers, Lt Henry Durand, to steal up to the locked gates, install powder charges and blow them up. His men tried four times with no positive results, while taking casualties. Until a Kashmiri, Mohan Lal, destined to play a major role in the invasion, informed Durand that most gates had been heavily walled up from the inside, all but the Kabul Gate. A diversionary attack was launched from the opposite side to draw off the defenders while Lt Durand placed his explosive charges at the Kabul Gate. This took place on the stormy night of 21 July 1839. The strong wind kept blowing out the fuses, before they finally ignited and blew the Kabul Gate off its hinges. Through the hole stormed units of the 4th Hussars, 16th Lancers, Somerset Light Infantry, Royal Leicestershire and Royal Munster Fusiliers. While the troops piled in without facing the slightest opposition, a regimental bugler got his signals mixed up, and instead of sounding 'attack' he sounded 'retreat', which had everyone turning around and racing back through the hole in the wall. By which time the Afghanis had organised some sort of defence; on the follow-up attack, the British units took seventeen casualties, while five hundred Afghanis died.

After a brief rest in Ghuznee, Keane's army marched on Kabul without meeting further resistance. On 7 August 1839, the puppet ruler installed courtesy of Lord Auckland, Shah Shujah, entered triumphantly through the deserted streets of the bazaar, leaving it up to Burnes, Her Majesty's Government's gold and the British soldier's steel to keep him on the throne. Thus, at the cost of only a few dozen casualties, the Russian threat had been stopped and Britain had established its domain over Afghanistan. War exhibits ascending and descending phases – here and now Britain was at its zenith.

After a brief stay, General Keane and half of his effectives departed back to India. Their new commander was General Cotton, a 'spit and polish' man. It was his choice to move the remaining occupation forces from the cramped but secure compound inside the Bala Hissar citadel to an open cantonment about a mile from the city, placed in the worst strategic position imaginable, a swamp surrounded by high hills, all of which were occupied by Afghan hill tribes. The camp's outer perimeter was quite extensive, two miles in circumference and only sparsely guarded. His confidence was such that he listened to no one. Cotton sneered at the mere suggestion that earthworks were needed against such illiterates as the Afghans. As long as his men drilled and marched and the band played, the good General Cotton was happy. The summit of his idiocy was to put the commissariat building, containing the entire stores for his army, a full four hundred yards *outside* the camp's perimeter, without giving the slightest thought to its protection in case of a surprise attack. So strong was the cocksure belief of Cotton that the Afghans would never dare go against British bayonets that, when the Commissariat Officer dared to remonstrate against the placing of his stores outside the camp, Cotton cut him off: 'I cannot waste my time on fruitless discussion about the location of sundry store buildings whilst I am erecting barracks for my troops.'

In the balmy autumn weather, the officers and their families or mistresses went on picnics, played polo and cricket. The food was provided by the *bazaaris*, the love life by dark-eyed beauties who willingly cheated on their husbands. The cuckolded men, mainly the super-rich *bazaari* traders, bore a rightful grudge, and their outraged honour was to play a decisive role in the months to come. Because *bazaaris* not only controlled trade but commerce, they also paid a 'road tax' to strategically located tribes and exerted control over passage through the passes. One who indulged freely in extramarital sex was Sir Alexander Burnes, who had moved from camp into a mud palace in town, where he lavishly entertained a string of lovely local women. That all of them were married didn't bother him in the least. But it did bother their husbands, and he would be number one on their list, should the time come.

In 1840, General Cotton handed over his post to a newcomer: 'You will have nothing to do here, all is peace.' If Cotton had been bad, the new commanding general was the acme of incompetence. Enter Major-General Sir William G.K. Elphinstone, perhaps the worst commanding officer ever, a man of ill health and confused thinking. His opening remark was: 'If anything occurs, for God's sake quickly clear the passes of all Afghans that we can get away.' It did little to raise morale.

William G.K. Elphinstone was physically as well as mentally incapable of taking on a major command. The rugged climate of Afghanistan's high plateau, scorching hot in the summer and with deep frost in the winter, called for an iron constitution and robust health, but these he no longer possessed. He suffered from various ailments, so many that he would have presented a prime subject for study in a medical school – bronchitis, gout and rheumatism to the extent that his legs were crippled; he couldn't sit on a horse and had to be carried around on a litter. As the military arm, administrating Britain's foreign policy will, he showed little finesse in diplomatic and political intrigue. He had no time for the local Emir and his squabbling court, and he refused to emulate the political envoys of the Governor of India, seeking to dominate and dictate London's demands by clever diplomatic moves. He loathed Afghanistan, called it 'a filthy place, mud ankle-deep in all the lanes', and regarded its inhabitants as 'treacherous heathens'. As he never came into contact with the locals, he never got to see the misery of the populace, nor did he care. He shied away from contact with his troops and hated every moment of his job as general commanding the backward place that was Kabul, and an army that some dice of fate had rolled together. His second-in-command, Brigadier John Shelton, the type of soldier with much courage but no brains, yet vain enough to claim all the credit for the achievement of the expedition, had no understanding whatsoever of his superior, and referred to him ironically as 'Elphy Bey'. He disliked Elphinstone as much as Elphinstone feared Shelton.

Elphinstone's council-of-war meetings were a farce. At every meeting, Brigadier Shelton had his servant prepare a camp bed inside the council room, where he then pretended to sleep, blissfully snoring to show his utter contempt for his weak superior. Elphinstone proved helpless; once he begged Shelton to stop this performance in front of junior officers, at which Shelton spat at him: 'I sneer at you!' After which Elphinstone sent off a dispatch: 'I regret to be obliged to disclose that I did not receive from Brigadier Shelton that cordial cooperation and advice I had a right to expect. On the contrary, he invariably found fault with all that was done and canvassed and condemned all orders.'

Emir Dost Mohammed, who had fled at the arrival of Keane's army, finally surrendered to the second political officer, Sir William Macnaghten. Savouring his triumph, Macnaghten dispatched a telegram: 'All is quiet from Dan to Beersheba.' He couldn't have been more wrong. Henry Rawlinson, from Kandahar, and Eldred Pottinger from the region north of Kabul, reported troubles brewing early in 1841, but their reports were discounted. Burnes warned Elphinstone to strengthen the cantonment's perimeter, but the general was too lethargic 'due to the weather' and did nothing.

With winter rapidly approaching, and more daily outrages to the Kabulis' honour, the Kashmiri Mohan Lal kept Burnes

Afghanistan
13 January 1842

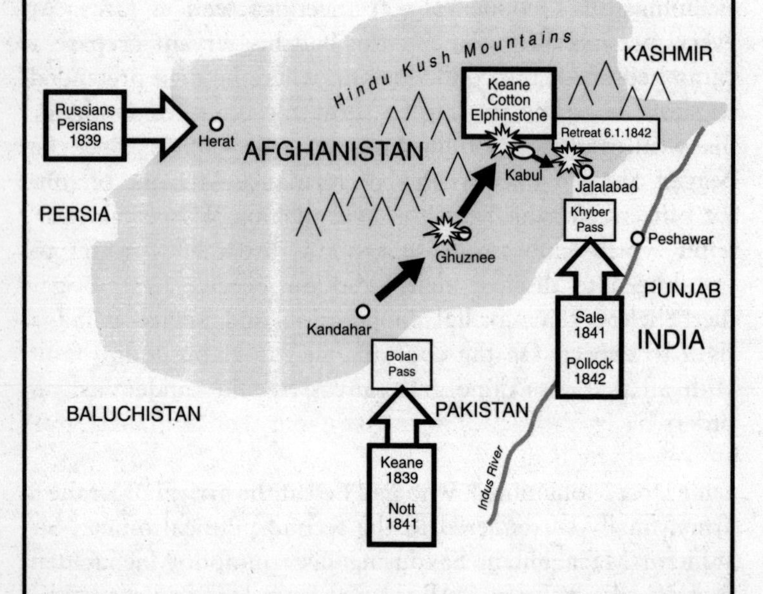

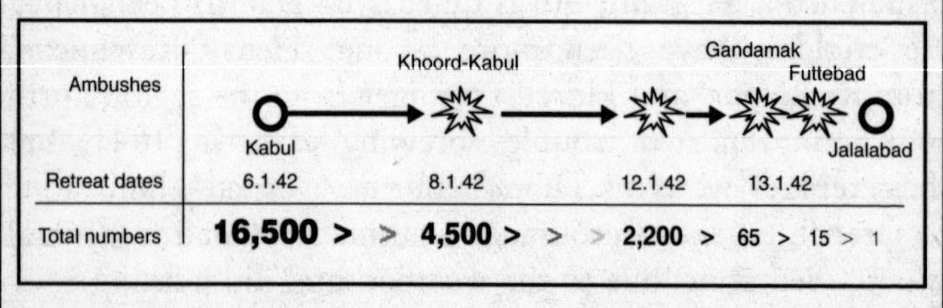

informed of events in the bazaar. The mood was getting ugly. Soon the passes would be clogged by snow. On 1 November, Lal came rushing into Burnes's office and begged him to move instantly into the cantonment, as the city had begun to seethe with shouting people. Burnes hesitated, and then it was too late – a mob had gathered outside his house. The rapacious rabble had been told by the *bazaaris* that the governor's palace contained a hoard of English gold. Burnes stepped outside his gate and told the crowd to go home, which they wouldn't. He then offered them money, which helped convince them of the existence of treasure. When all else failed, and the crowd belted him with stones, he ordered his sepoy detachment to fire into the crowd. That did it. The handful of sepoys were hacked to death while Burnes fled back through the door. His young aide, Broadfoot, pulled out his pistol, but before he was able to fire it he was killed. Burnes was caught in the courtyard by some of the cuckolded husbands and cruelly done to death. The firing could clearly be heard in camp, and soldiers were on the alert, yet inexplicably Elphinstone failed to rush to his governor's assistance. And that despite the fact that Mohan Lal, who had managed to make good his escape over a back wall and run to the camp, had implored him for immediate help.

One who did react was not a soldier but the political commissar, Macnaghten. Realising that the situation was quickly getting out of hand, he telegraphed for immediate military assistance to Calcutta. Lord Auckland was greatly alarmed by Macnaghten's panicky message. Having sent British soldiers to Kabul, 'it seems to me that it is our bound duty, both as a matter of humanity and policy, not to abandon them now'. He dispatched two forces, one under General Sale across the Khyber towards Jalalabad, the other under General Nott through Kandahar. This would instill hope in Elphinstone and his troop, and the mere advance of two armies would go a long way to ensure the Kabul garrison's safety by keeping the rebellious tribes off its back. For a while it did, but then Lord Auckland's expectations for the relief expedition's progress were to prove dangerously over-optimistic. As soon as both forces crossed into the mountainous regions, they were mauled by Afghans and had to take shelter, General Sale in Jalalabad and Nott in Kandahar. That left Elphinstone and his Kabul garrison on their own. The news, that no relief could be under way before spring, was deeply distressing, and left Elphinstone more depressed than ever.

While the troops demanded action to avenge Burnes's murder and uphold the Empire's flag, Elphinstone's indecision added to their discontent and frustration. The troops almost mutinied when their commander-in-chief refused to retaliate. Unpunished murder, dysentery and high-altitude fever sapped their morale. And this while Kabul was bereft of any kind of defence; the hill tribes had decamped, fearing a retaliation by British guns. The Kabul mob had disappeared from the muddy lanes and crept into hiding. One forceful sortie of battalion size could have altered the entire situation. Nothing of the kind happened – the 4,500 soldiers of the British garrison were left cowering inside their camp, and this greatly encouraged the Afghans. Elphinstone couldn't shoulder responsibility, even when not surrounded by hostiles. For the whole of his stay he scarcely left the encampment, and thereby had little or no cognisance of the situation. *Bazaari* gold brought the tribesmen back, and no sooner were they back on the hills than the entire population turned upon the invader. A considerable number of British soldiers fell victim to weeks of crazy savagery. They were shot in camp from the surrounding hills, ambushed in country lanes, their throats were slashed on patrol, and visiting the town to do their shopping became tantamount to a death sentence.

As the weeks slipped by, Macnaghten felt that Elphinstone's caution was disproportionate to the importance of his task.

More than that, the general had gone completely off his head. He kept pestering Macnaghten to arrange surrender terms, since 'my men are running out of ammunition'. The fact was that the garrison had enough powder and shot to sustain a twelve-month siege. Macnaghten cabled General Sale in Jalalabad to take over the Kabul command; but Sale's army was already encircled and he couldn't reach Kabul without risking his own forces.

The days were getting shorter and frost began to cover the ground. Soon, snow in the outlying regions would make travelling through the passes impossible. The troops' morale dropped below zero; one day the soldiers had to look on helplessly as the street rabble pilfered their commissariat storehouse and made off with food, their rum ration and, worst of all, their winter woollies. And Elphinstone did nothing to stop it. Meanwhile, the subzero cold was about to set in and they were still standing guard in their tropical cottons.

For weeks now the hill tribes had taken a heavy toll of British sentries with well-aimed pot shots. It was twenty-three days after Burnes's murder when Brigadier Shelton finally decided to take some action. Leading a battalion force from the 44th Regiment, he attacked a nearby hill overlooking the British camp which was crawling with insurgents. His sortie from camp was an ill-conceived operation. At the outset, they managed to clear a large portion of the hill with his cannon, and the counter-fire became more and more sporadic as the men behind the muskets were shredded by grapeshot. Gunfire was obviously highly effective against hill tribes. But he was never able to explain why he had taken only a single cannon on the operation. Within minutes, the gun overheated and stopped firing. It left the redcoats standing in an open field, with Afghan horsemen milling about. Shelton ordered his men to form squares. Such a tactic would have worked against Napoleon's battalions on the fields of Europe, but not against wild Afghan tribes sitting behind rocks on a hill. In fact, massed squares presented an ideal target, and the Afghans peppered the tightly compressed British formation with a hail of bullets from their long-barrelled *jezails*. Even after two years of incessant fighting, British officers had still failed to understand the killing potential of the long-barrelled Afghan muskets, carrying over a much longer range than anything the British had to counter them with. Also, the Afghans were expert marksmen, trained from early boyhood, and every bullet struck its man. The 44th Foot suffered a frightful toll, leaving over three hundred dead on the field. Shelton, struck by fragments from five bullets, would also have died, had he not been carried off in the rush of his 44ers, scurrying hell-bent back into camp. When Elphinstone lamented the many casualties, Shelton replied testily, referring pointedly to his general's inactivity: 'We showed them!' Showed them what? If the British were surprised by the well-organised resistance, they had another surprise coming in the person of Emir Dost Mohammed's son, Akbar.

Mohammed Akbar, a charismatic, fanatical zealot who counted on the tribes' religious fervour in tackling the infidels, arrived on the scene in the company of six thousand members of his fierce warrior tribe. He was brave and wily, and his speciality was lying in wait to strike from a strong ambush position. Instead of attacking into the mouths of Elphinstone's cannon, Akbar offered Macnaghten a ceasefire, his sole condition the immediate removal of Shah Shujah, a deal which the India Office representative foolishly refused, and that despite the fact that Mohan Lal had informed him that Akbar commanded at least thirty thousand well-armed tribesmen. Macnaghten set out to do what had always worked for England throughout the ages: divide and rule. He would split the various ethnic factions. With this in mind, he sent out his man for all seasons, Mohan Lal, to spread rumour among tribal leaders. In the meantime, he would stall Akbar with a horse trade. He proposed to leave Shah Shujah in nominal power, but assign Mohammed Akbar as his Grand Vizier. To sweeten his proposal, he offered the peaceful departure of the British Assistance Force by the spring of 1842. His offers came too late. However, Akbar accepted to discuss them during a talk with Macnaghten. A personal meeting was arranged. Macnaghten was under no illusion as to the difficulty of putting an end to the fighting. His orders had come from on high, but how could the high-minded politicians in London and Calcutta know anything about the problems he had to face? They still indulged in dangerously wishful thinking regarding the prospects for a peaceful settlement. 'The British Government cannot enforce its will without militarily occupying the whole country, towns *and mountains*,' was to be Macnaghten's final message to Calcutta.

On 23 December 1841, Macnaghten climbed on his horse and, together with three of his secretaries, rode through the snow to the banks of the Kabul river to meet with Akbar Khan. They sat down on carpets spread out on freshly fallen snow and were offered the customary sweet tea. 'Will you accept our demand?' asked Akbar Khan. Macnaghten understood that Akbar was referring to the removal of Shah Shujah. 'Why not?' he replied. Akbar nodded, not in acceptance but as a signal. The political officer was grabbed, tied up, tossed across a saddle and brought into town, while his three assistants were hacked to pieces by Akbar's men. In an ultimate insult, Macnaghten was shot and killed with pistols he himself had presented as the governor's gift to Akbar's father, Emir Dost Mohammed. After the killing, Macnaghten's head was cut off, stuck on a pike and paraded through Kabul, while his headless corpse was hoisted on to a pole in the bazaar before it was dragged through the streets behind a galloping horse. The troops had to watch the horrid procession from the cantonment, and Elphinstone was so shocked by the gratuitous bloodshed that once again he failed to act.

The general's conscience was sorely trying him, but he still blamed his blunders on everyone but himself. 'All the elements have combined to thwart me in my task.' It is true that internal friction among his command increased his handicap, and the strain was all the more severe because it fell on troops already under pressure. But, as in any army at war, it is the leader who matters. His personal problems were aggravated by a 'lucky shot' from the hill. While being carried around on his litter, a bullet struck him in the buttock. And so he was carried about lying on his belly, and his soldiers quickly renamed him 'hole-in-the-arse Elphy'.

For the once proud Army of the Indus, Christmas 1841 was a cold and sad affair. The troops were freezing in their summer cottons and their rations had been cut to a minimum. After the loss of their food stores and other provisions, starvation was rampant. The noose was tightening around them. Shelton tried one final sortie. At 8 a.m. on the day after Christmas, the platoon officers' whistles began to blow along the British line. Four hundred British and Indian troops advanced towards the nearest hill in broad view, shoulder to shoulder. The Afghans opened fire and began to sweep the approaching troops aside like leaves. Instead of ordering a halt to their advance, Shelton doubled the effort, thinking the sheer mass of bodies would carry the line of hills. His thought must have been that, in order to overwhelm the snipers, he would send an infinite number of targets against them. Quite amazingly, two companies, under courageous and able commanders, gained success. With planted bayonets, they dealt a blow to Akbar's men when they forced them to abandon a choice position and flee into the rabbit-warren of narrow lanes in the city. But once the companies set off in pursuit, they were caught in an ambush on the bank of the Kabul river and cut to pieces by a horde of shrieking tribesmen. After that setback, even Shelton felt a premonition of the looming disaster.

Worried that Akbar Khan was up to his old tricks, Macnaghten's replacement for the murdered political officer, Eldred Pottinger, suggested that the garrison be moved behind the walls of the Bala Hissar fortress to await spring and the arrival of a relief army. Both Elphinstone and Shelton overruled his suggestion. 'If we cannot achieve a peaceful retreat, then we shall shoot our way out.' One tribesman, hostile to Akbar, had tried to warn the British that they were walking into a trap, that Akbar was in no mood to keep his word, and that none of them would come out of Afghanistan alive. This warning only made Brigadier Shelton more determined to see things through.

Indeed, they had to force God's hand and make a break for it while there were still some healthy troops to walk, because holding out in Kabul meant certain death. With their powerful artillery they stood a good chance of blasting their way out of the trap. Had Shelton acted forcefully, overriding the utter neglect of his superior and taking over the command, they probably could have made it. But Shelton was an officer steeped in the best of British tradition, and hierarchy still counted for him. And so, owing to the inbred duty to follow the chain of command, as laid down in the Duke of Wellington's rules, this final opportunity was relinquished. With a paralysed British general on one side, and the Napoleon of Afghanistan on the other, the eventual outcome was predictable. In what in actual fact amounted to surrender, Pottinger rode out in search of Akbar to work out a deal for safe passage. It was 5 January 1842.

Mohammed Akbar's undisciplined warriors had been keeping up withering fire for months and were running dangerously short of ball and powder. To continue the harassment, they desperately had to get hold of the British gunpowder; but that was kept stored inside the cantonment and defended by dug-in cannon. Akbar knew only too well that his men could be stampeded by the effect of cannon fire. It was the roar of the big guns which panicked them. Also, his riders could handle infantry musket fire, but they had no defence against the terrible grapeshot. Akbar was just as anxious to reach a deal as were the British. Only he knew it –

and they didn't. It came as no surprise when guards led Pottinger into his presence. Hoping that with brashness he could bluff his way through, Pottinger huffed: 'I come on a mission of peace, not as your prisoner.' Akbar smiled, offered his profuse apologies and sent off the armed guards. A long haggling session took place. Pottinger had a feeling that he was coming out ahead when, out of the blue, Akbar said: 'We will grant your men safe conduct, we will provide them with provisions and an armed escort, but you must leave all your artillery and powder stores behind.' Pottinger was shocked; he could not possibly accept such an outrageous demand without reference to the military commander, he said. Akbar had to allow the Englishman a way to save face, and he quickly added that he would give permission for the departing forces to take with them three mule guns and six smaller field pieces; but in exchange they had to leave behind some married officers and their families as hostages to guarantee their good faith.

When Akbar's condition became known, a furious row erupted. Both Pottinger and Shelton pointed out the folly in giving up their heavy mountain batteries. 'General, it is my considered opinion that giving up the guns would lead to disaster,' offered Pottinger. Elphinstone frowned but said nothing.

'We have good artillery and plenty of it. So let's use it,' snarled Shelton. 'On a break-out, they will have to come at us and that puts them in a bad position. They will break.'

'We must accept.' Elphinstone had lost all control; exhaustion dulled his eyes.

'Sir, I don't think so.' Pottinger felt icy despair. He made a final effort to change the general's mind. 'I fear Akbar is up to no good.'

Elphinstone felt a great weight upon him, and his stomach was troubling him. But there was nothing else for it. He turned to Shelton: 'Brigadier, I want you to bring the guns to the depot and get the men ready to move out.'

Shelton's face was aflame. He was breathing hard, a bewildered look on his face. 'Given a bit of luck, we can lure him down out of those damned bloody rocks. And when he is extended, we'll chop him off with our cannons.'

Elphinstone drew his head in like a turtle. 'We can't. No matter how much I wish. Or trust in God.'

'Then God will not help us without our guns.'

'Thus began the most disastrous retreat in British military history that was to end in awful completeness.'[2] The exodus from Kabul – with only three of their precious guns and without the promised tribal escort – began on the dark winter morning of 6 January 1842. From that moment on 16,500 men, soldiers, servants and camp followers marched to their death. All were exhausted and worn out before they set off on their long trek for Jalalabad. General Elphinstone's world was compressed into the chaos of what he could see lying before him, which wasn't very much in the gloom of a winter morning. And Shelton's eyes told him, as he led his tired, starving units out of the cantonment, that his boys would begin falling around him damn soon. His memory of Waterloo was bad, but this was worse. No sooner had the last soldier left camp than the long column was subjected to fire from the heights. At the same time, hordes of Kabulis invaded their abandoned camp to strip it bare.

Seen from the mountaintops, the snow-covered plain became a frieze covered with moving black dots. A column that could no longer be called an army, 700 British and 3,800 Indian soldiers, accompanied by an endless stream of camp followers, was headed for the garrison of Jalalabad, which they expected to reach in one week. The vanguard was made up of the last 400 men of the 44th Foot, plus 100 Indian cavalry leading their near-famished horses by the bridle. Next came the families; only small children were allowed

[2] Historian John Kaye.

to ride in great wicker baskets, slung over the backs of the few available camels. The rest struggled on foot through the snow, getting wet during the day and freezing their feet during the chill of the night in the high altitude. There was one happy creature, a baby, pressed close to its mother's breast. The haggard-looking woman was sitting by the side of the road. Her little one was at the stage when a child utters its first words, and it never stopped babbling as the stream of refugees passed. But hunger hardened people against the fate of others, even if it was the fate of their own kith and kin. And so the starving mother was left behind to die.

Already the first day proved an agonising march, through snow, over precipitous mountain tracks, more suitable for goats than an army, continuously under attack from thousands of tribesmen shooting down from cracks and peaks. Riders dashed up to the undefended part of the long column, killing women and unarmed civil servants and driving off pack mules with vital provisions. They even drove off one of the camels with tiny tots screaming from the wicker baskets (miraculously, most of the children survived). In the afternoon, the sky darkened, the heavens opened and a violent storm blew dark masses of snow over the land. The temperature dropped to twenty below zero. It was so cold so suddenly that entire ranks fell and others had to climb over them. In the attempt to get away, the track was lined with broken and capsized carts, their loads scattered on the snow. The exhausted and starved horses fell dead or foundered in their harness. When night fell, the column had covered a mere five miles; 2,500 died, or were left behind, during the first day. For the remaining 14,000, only one tent was saved from the day's attacks. The mass of people was now out in the open, in the bitter cold, without provisions, stuck in a treeless landscape without even a shred of hope of gathering wood for fires to warm their frozen limbs. Some just lay down to die; others, unable to bear the terror of their situation, walked into the freezing night, never to be seen again. Of those who survived that terrible first night, many woke up with frostbitten fingers and toes.

The second day was a repeat of the first, only worse. The wind swept horizontally over the ground. The soldiers' breath formed a hard crust of ice on their collars. And those were the lucky ones, who could walk. Many had no more strength in their frozen feet; they dragged themselves along but couldn't keep up with the rest and were immediately done to death by Afghan women following in the wake of the misery. One attack followed the next, and during one of these the Afghans captured two of the three British cannon and all the powder.

They had now reached the rugged part of the country, a solid mountain barrier, skirted by precipitous cliffs and seamed with steep gullies. In the midst of this mountain, as if split by God's fist, lay a narrow gorge, the four-kilometre-long Khoord-Kabul Pass, the only passable track from Kabul to Jalalabad. In the early afternoon of the second day, a group of riders appeared. Their leader was Akbar Khan. He cursed the English for having left Kabul before his escort had been gathered, and told them that they had to wait until he had negotiated their safe passage through the gorge with the tribes. Eldred Pottinger tried to alert Elphinstone that this was but another ruse by the wily Afghan to delay them. In vain. Elphinstone was now so weak that reasoning was beyond him. The general ordered a rest, while Akbar rode ahead, not to arrange safe passage but to place his thousands of marksmen on the cliffs overlooking the narrow *mullah* (gorge) of the pass.

'I have obtained your safe passage,' he promised on his return that evening. It lifted the mood of the British somewhat. On 8 January, led by some of Akbar's men, the column moved towards the pass narrows. No sooner had they entered the track in between the sheer cliffs than Akbar's men whipped their horses, dashed ahead and disappeared. Up on the cliffs there was a sudden flash of fire. Report and echo came together. They had run into a well-prepared death trap. The depths of the gorge and the whole country around them roared. A terrible grinding process was taking place. Bullets swept through them, and many tumbled into the snow and stained it with their blood. For a moment some found shelter under an overhang, before their sergeants whistled to make them dash along the track. There they fell in heaps. Despite the heavy losses, the men struggled forward. Shelton, gallantly exposing himself, was wounded. By the time the survivors made it to the exit from the gorge, Elphinstone's men had been whittled down to 450 soldiers and some 4,000 camp followers. But because the fire had stopped it set up a false hope in the men. 'By God – we're going to make it!'

A regimental medical officer, Surgeon-Major Dr William Brydon, marvelled at the spirit of self-sacrifice that, over the past two days, had propelled the men forward in response to the simple shrill sound of a subaltern's whistle. Their willingness to die almost shamed him. All had one thing in common – they wouldn't surrender their lives. Brydon heard one particularly outspoken sergeant, Jeffrey McCormick of the 44th, who put it even more succinctly: 'I prefer to die covered in blood than to die in bed covered in piss!'

Morning, noon and night, the gorge had been filled with the snarling sounds of ricochets, tearing down the last curtain between the Afghans and hell. And still Elphinstone placed trust in the explanations of Akbar, who claimed that he had been unable to restrain the wild war tribes, not loyal to him, from attacking in the Khoord-Kabul pass. He kept assuring Elphinstone of his devoted friendship and asked the general to trust him – and the old fool did. He then offered to take care of the women and children. Only nine families accepted, and though they had to endure some ghastly months as Akbar's captives, they lived through the ordeal to tell their story.

For the next few days, the attacks continued unabated. A stream of soldiers and followers fell by the wayside; first the horses failed, and then the men. One British soldier had a black, swollen foot, an Indian had shins covered by open ulcers. It was bloody agony where the thin trousers stuck to the flesh. Some used their muskets as crutches. They dragged themselves onward because any straggler was immediately killed by the tribal hags and their offspring. Like ghouls, they wouldn't leave the dead in repose, but looted the corpses of shirts and boots. By 12 January, Elphinstone was left with 200 soldiers and 2,000 civilians. The rest were lying in the bloodstained snow in heaps, like frozen sparrows.

It was at this juncture that General Elphinstone turned into a hero. Painfully, his men hoisted him on to a horse. In the company of only one aide, he made his way into Akbar's camp to try to negotiate safe passage by giving up all of his weapons. Akbar was in no mood to negotiate further. The general was taken prisoner, but still he managed to send out his aide to tell Shelton not to wait for his return but to continue before the Afghans were given a chance to assemble for an ambush. The Afghans had constructed a barrier made of thorn bushes and placed it across the middle of the next gorge. Elphinstone's arrival at Akbar's camp had diverted their attention; they had abandoned their ambush position and, for once, a gorge was not manned. The redcoats had stolen up to the thorn-bush obstacle and were almost across when the cry of a baby betrayed their position. In no time the Afghans were back, and vigorously attacked from above and from the rear. In the face of the snorting, stamping, sabre-swinging tribal riders, the British and Indians proved helpless; they fell where they stood, shot from above or slashed by swords. It would have been the end; however, the thorn-bush barrier stopped the riders and provided a certain amount of shelter. One of the few who managed to climb over the thorn bushes was Dr William Brydon. Once clear, he came upon an Indian cavalry *subadhar*, bleeding from an open chest wound. Brydon bent down to hold the dying man's head. 'Doctor, take my horse and God send you may get to Jalalabad in safety.' As Brydon rode off, he could hear the cries of the wounded and the death rattle of the dying. The blackness of night was more merciful than the tribesmen, for they took no prisoners.

Only two small groups remained – forty-five soldiers and twenty officers, all of them desperately tired from a night of continuous fighting, who had managed to make their way past the thorn barrier. They were all from the 44th Foot. On 13 January 1842, they reached the village of Gandamak, thirty miles from Jalalabad. Across the wide plain they could see the smoke from the campfires of General Sale's forces. Only one more day's march and they would reach safety. But before they could set out on the last leg of their escape, they found themselves confronted by a seething mass of wild faces. There was not a stick of cover anywhere. At first, the Afghans made no attempt to approach the bayonets. Then the tribesmen fired. Their volley crashed into the lined-up soldiers from a distance of twenty yards. Three soldiers fell dead, four more fell sixty seconds later. Their captain was hit in the left arm and hip. Already bleeding profusely, he attacked with bare steel. Then he fell down, but got to his feet again to continue his lonesome charge, staggering like a drunken man, leaving a thin trail of blood behind him. He was dying fast. The rest, mercilessly exposed as they were, never had a chance. Another volley laid low another swath of 44ers. There was a combined chorus of ferocious English curses and Afghan yells as the pent-up fury of the long-suffering 44ers was unleashed on their hated tormentors. Now the bayonet came into its own. Yelling at the tops of their voices, they stumbled forward after their captain. They left a mounting trail of Afghan bodies in their wake. Those of the Afghans who tried to cut through the ring of steel were speared. As the massacre raged on, countless more tribesmen hurled themselves up the battered slope.

A bullet plucked at Sergeant McCormick's coat. He looked down and saw the gash. But he was not hit. A tall tribes-man was coming uphill at him, waving a curved sword.

McCormick ran towards him and fired. The swordsman's face dissolved. And right behind the warrior came another, holding a musket. McCormick stumbled downhill with his fixed bayonet, unable to stop, seeing only the black hole of the Afghan's musket yards away . . . rushing with a giant yell towards the black hole . . .

Then it was over. The valiant stand by the 44th had lasted ten minutes. Sixty-one were killed, four taken prisoner and decapitated minutes later by the enraged Afghans. Quiet settled over the bloody hill and the corpse-littered slope. The stillness after seven days of continued battle stunned the senses.

Another action took place on the same day. William Brydon had joined the other group of survivors, fifteen riders in all. Pushing their horses to the limit, they found themselves a mere fifteen miles from Jalalabad when their horses could go no farther without a rest. They had just come over a series of hills when, in the distance, they spotted the walls of Jalalabad. So near, yet so far. The last fifteen of an army of 4,500 climbed from their saddles in the hamlet of Futtebad. For once, the villagers proved extremely hospitable, offering them food and drink. The men were so relieved to be out of the fighting that they gave themselves over to their first meal in a week without a second thought. It was the final trick the Afghans played on the last of the British. While the hungry soldiers had their fill, and afterwards took a rest, a villager rode out to fetch the armed tribesmen. The British, drowsy and half asleep after eating so well, were surprised by a crescendo of whooping and firing. Ten soldiers died immediately; five jumped on their horses to make good their getaway. Their tired horses were no match for the fresh ponies of the Afghans. Four were chased down and cut from their saddles. Only one managed to hide out until nightfall, although severely bleeding from a bullet wound.

Early next morning, a lookout on the walls of Jalalabad saw a lone horse stumbling across the snowy plain, its rider hanging on to its neck. A patrol was sent out. They brought back the only survivor of the Army of the Indus.

Surgeon-Major Dr William Brydon.

For days General Sale's men were kept on the lookout for more survivors. None came. There was one more soldier who reached Jalalabad. Months passed before Major-General Sir William G.K. Elphinstone's body arrived, rolled up in a carpet, courtesy of Akbar Khan.

Her Majesty the Queen was shocked. England was shocked. The old Duke of Wellington was shocked, and he was what mattered. He insisted on restoring Britain's reputation. Two armies were mustered, one under General Nott, the other under General Pollock. They took Jalalabad on 16 April 1842, then swept everything before them until they arrived before Ghuznee. There the Afghans came on like a swarm of flies and were killed like flies. They seemed determined to die. The Gurkhas fired no shots; they fought only with knives and fists. The Indians, having had to look at the thousands of skeletons by the side of the road, the mutilated bodies of their comrades-in-arms, took no prisoners and killed all they could lay their hands on.

The road to Kabul was open. The newly constituted Army of the Indus arrived there on the morning of 15 September 1842. They looked across the water to the old town walls and the high, slender minarets rising above the foaming Kabul river. The soldiers stood there, feeling the defeat suffered by those who had been there before them more bitterly still – as if they were being judged before the tribunal of history.

Abandoned by his tribal chieftains, Akbar Khan fled to Bamyian. He had taken with him a number of hostages, including Eldred Pottinger. General Pollock dispatched Captain Sir Richmond Shakespear with six hundred cavalry to liberate the captives. This he accomplished in a tearful reunion.

Ranjit Singh died soon afterwards. Shah Shujah was murdered by Akbar. Akbar Khan disappeared and old Dost Mohammed was brought back from exile in India to recover his throne. For Her Majesty's Government, this seemed the best solution among a series of bad options. It wasn't, because Dost allied himself with the Sikhs, and together they fought the British but were defeated at Gujrat in February 1849, and Peshawar was annexed by Britain.

There were arguments *ad nauseam* about the incompetence of Elphinstone's command and his panicking at critical turns in the disastrous retreat. For such senseless waste of life, whether brought about by ignorance or want of moral courage, a commander must be held accountable to his nation as well as before history. But what also deserved consideration was the bungling by Britain's India Office and its highest official. It is imperative that every military campaign have clearly defined political objectives. In the beginning, England had one – preventing the Russian takeover of India. But once this problem had been resolved, the strategic objective was lacking, as were the political principles that should have been applied across the chessboard of Afghanistan and India. Instead, England launched itself into a modern war between two civilisations which quickly turned into a combat between two cultures and religions. A superpower fought against a society that still believed in the life of a thousand years ago.

Lord Auckland was relieved of his position as Governor of India. Punitive expeditions to the Khyber Pass and beyond into Afghanistan were to mark the next hundred years of British rule in India. The war never ended, it just became harder as a new secret dimension was added to it – the unseen danger of fanatical fighters appearing like shadows to strike at invading infidel armies. Western 'enlightened thinking' fought a utopian religious fundamentalism, which proved incapable of formulating a modern conception of politics and government. In the nineteenth century, most people were shut out of world events. As a result, the issues and even the countries involved were largely unfamiliar to them. The Anglo-Afghan war was certainly one of these issues.

On a bright October day in 1842, General Sir George Pollock ordered the destruction of Kabul's thousand-year-old Great Bazaar. Since the fall of the town, its shutters had been closed, and the silence was uncanny. Radiant sunshine lay over everything, and its minarets were bathed in light. It took British engineers two days to wire up the entire town centre. An immense explosion shattered the air. In a great flash the architectural monument of early Islamic culture was blown to smithereens. The minarets' slender towers collapsed in a dense cloud of smoke and greyish-brown dust. The great cloud of choking grime covered the city of Kabul for days – almost 159 years to the day before a cloud of similar magnitude would cover the city of New York.

On 11 October 1842, the British Army pulled out of Kabul. It had achieved nothing and left behind only bad memories. The day the last of the British armies marched away from Afghanistan, they left the frontier open – and it has stayed open behind them.

The facts

The British disaster in Afghanistan is the story of one man. General Elphinstone was the wrong man, in the wrong place, assigned to the wrong task. He became one of the most tragic and compelling figures in British history. His inertia and its effects are outstanding proof that in war it is the single man and not the great mass which counts, and that one man can be more decisive, or, in this case, destructive, than ten thousand. To give the order to leave Kabul in the middle of winter, crossing enemy-infested country in subzero temperatures, was foolishness. But to abandon the cannon was downright insane and sealed a British army's fate.

Epilogue

Is This the End?

'I cannot believe that God plays dice with the cosmos.'
Albert Einstein, 5 April 1953

The Gulf War had almost ended. A defeated Iraqi army was fleeing along the four-lane highway from Kuwait City when two points appeared over the horizon. Moments later, with an ear-shattering roar, two giant bombers of the US Air Force lumbered low over the massed men and vehicles. Suddenly, both whipped skyward and oblong cylinders dropped from both planes. They hung in the air, suspended under great ballooning parachutes, and floated towards the ground. At an altitude of three hundred metres the silvery cigars disintegrated in a blinding flash that could be seen for many miles. Beneath a gigantic ball of fire, everything was instantly transformed into molten metal, burnt rubber and calcinated corpses.

'God is on the side of the big battalions,' stressed the French Marshal Turenne, and then Napoleon went on to prove it. His type of warfare was predominant until a mushroom cloud spelled an end to the kind of bludgeoning, cutting and shooting warfare humanity had suffered for thousands of years. The atomic bomb was a weapon of such horrific mass destruction that world opinion turned against those who had it – and who were prepared to use it. Especially the Americans; not only did they have it, but they were the only nation ever to have dropped it on a target. In the face of a wave of protests from abroad, and peace marchers in their own country, their specialists went back to the drawing board and devised something just as potent, but non-nuclear.

The first such device was called the FAE bomb, for fuel-air-explosive – a revolutionary new liquid fuel that no longer depended on an oxidiser but greedily sucked available oxygen from the atmosphere before it ignited. Its explosion created a shock wave of tremendous pressure, which blew out eardrums and turned brains to mush. It killed people but it didn't destroy their equipment, which could then be recovered and reused against those who had built it. With the greatest of ease, a force could move into battle with nothing more than a bucket of paint, removing the dead bodies from a tank and, with a few strokes of the brush, changing a red-star into a white-star insignia, thereby altering its nationality. To make sure that this bomb functioned, they put a bunch of chimpanzees on wooden poles at the US weapons testing ground at China Lake, and then dropped an FAE bomb on them. It worked. This kind of exercise was greatly frowned upon by animal protection groups, especially once they got hold of a copy of the film, produced by and for the US forces, entitled *The Monkey Movie*, whose stars dropped off their poles as if struck by lightning.

The inventive minds with their fingers on the proverbial trigger worked hard to come up with something even better. They found it with BLU 82, which used a huge amount of PBXN-type explosive similar to that in use in modern torpedo warheads. They created a true monster, weighing 7.5 tons, so big that it could only be delivered by a special cradle on rollers and dropped from an aircraft with an open cargo bay. Over the target area, the aircraft suddenly pulled up to stand on its tail, allowing the bomb to slide out, like a letter from a mailbox. Suspended on giant parachutes, it floated slowly towards the ground. Its effect was similar to that of an atomic weapon – only it was a clean bomb. There was no radiation – and that allowed the aggressor to move into the stricken area within minutes of the firestorm. It was the ideal weapon against massed enemy formations, such as the conventional forces of China. It should be stated that it is not only the US which possesses this terrible weapon – the Russians have it too. Just in case.

The first time the US Air Force and its specialists tried out their super-bomb was over a stretch of desert sand in a Nevada proving ground. They found that it worked to perfection. The next time they used it was on a highway from Kuwait to hell. British forward scouts, who had not been let in on the secret, saw the flash and the subsequent cloud and thought that the Americans had nuked Kuwait with a cluster of atomic bombs. American pilots, looking down on a fire scar of scorched earth[1] where nothing had survived, quickly baptised their super-weapon Hades – as in hell. And hell it was, signalling once and for all the end of the big battalions.

That was the world that was for thousands of years. Suddenly a new danger developed. Not armies versus armies, one superpower against another, but terrorism engendered by religious fanaticism. They humbled an empire by aiming at its cathedrals. The very symbols of might and faith crumbled. For that, no one was prepared.

During the Cold War, strategic capabilities were synonymous with nuclear capabilities, and all superpower strategic planning focused on nuclear deterrence and response against a single adversary (USA vs USSR). Today, potential enemies are developing simple capabilities to wage strategic warfare by implicitly or explicitly threatening high-value political,

[1] Approximately one kilometre in diameter.

military or economic targets with unsophisticated but equally powerful weapons of destruction (hijacked airplanes) and disruption (anthrax).

In an altered relationship between the major powers, the strategic environment facing the modern world has changed radically in the past decade. There are no longer fixed battle lines *à la* Stalingrad; more and more, huge powers with their sophisticated arsenals find themselves going up against an invisible enemy in a rocky moonscape where crude weapons can inflict great damage. The Afghan way of fighting an intruder depends on exacting the maximum casualties to make his invasion unprofitable. Most important, they put their survival into the hands of Allah with their fighting philosophy directed towards sacrifice for a belief. Our security over the next several decades will depend increasingly on our ability to deter and respond effectively to strategic regional conflicts with significant potential to escalate to the highest levels of violence.

During the Cold War, planning for strategic warfare became synonymous with planning for US–Soviet nuclear warfare for the simple reason that it was difficult to envision large-scale, conventional warfare between the two superpowers that would not quickly escalate to the use of nuclear weapons. However, regional conflicts played out within the context of the broader ideological and strategic conflict between the two superpowers (Korea, Vietnam) tamped down pressures for escalation and proliferation for fear that conflict would spiral out of control. This is no longer the case. Now the possibility looms that smaller rogue states, or even independent terror groups, might try to involve the rest of the world in a general conflict. By evoking financial or religious issues, a regional pariah may hope to prevent these powers building coalitions with their potential allies (an Islamic alliance refusing to fight an Islamic terrorist).

In this changing environment, any great power must transform its thinking about deterring and defeating such threats. The goal of deterrence is to prevent aggression by ensuring that, in the mind of a potential assailant, the risks of aggression outweigh the gains. In a future security environment, the powers that regulate a harmonious existence will need to broaden their conception of deterrence to include defensive means designed to persuade any gambler that the likelihood of success is too low to make an attack worth the price of certain retaliation against his own highly valued assets.

Indeed, over the next ten to twenty years, at least one major world power (the USA) will be able to choose from a larger, more flexible menu of offensive and defensive military options to shape an adversary's calculations of risk and gain. This range of strategic capabilities could include not only nuclear weapons but also defences against missiles and other means of delivering weapons of mass destruction, precision-guided conventional weapons, offensive and defensive information warfare, air defence, passive defence, special operations, space operations, non-kinetic weapons such as lasers, and intelligence, surveillance and reconnaissance capabilities. These capabilities could be combined in any number of ways to deter potential aggressors from threatening or using strategic warfare. If deterrence fails, many of these tools could also be employed to manage the escalatory process so as to preserve military objectives at the lowest possible level of conflict.

Likewise, one of the most serious challenges is developing credible responses to chemical and biological weapon attacks. A biological attack against a major city could well evoke a nuclear response. But what about a biological attack that destroys the agricultural sector of a region, or one that kills scores of troops?

The conduct of strategic warfare by regional adversaries will become an important feature of the new international environment. The world powers will only be able to realise their full potential in this latest military mission by rigorously reviewing their requirements, addressing their shortcomings, and adapting their plans and capabilities to meet the challenge of future strategic regional conflicts.

The first battle on record was Armageddon in 1469 BC. As a matter of dry statistics, of the 3,470 years of recorded history only 268 years have been without a war! To understand history one must understand war, and its consequences.

War has been with us since cavemen beat each other to death with stone clubs. Man's first mortal combat was over a morsel of meat and the possession of fire. The ages refined the method of killing but not that of death itself. The dawn of mankind was followed by the rise of great empires, which imposed the will of one upon the rest. Then, as it still happens today, the world was largely dominated by military autocracies, and the course of history depended on the intellectual clarity and decisions of comparatively few. It brought on the era of kings and Caesars. War became their means for imperial expansion. Their weapons, from club to mace, had hardly improved from primitive times. In the circumstances the lessons learned about human combat were not of any great importance to any of the participants concerned. Sheer muscle and numerical superiority were all. Those who had fared less badly than their enemy cashed in on what glory was going – from taking over the cave to occupying a castle, a nation, a continent.

'If the various campaigns and uprisings which have taken place [in Italy] have given the appearance that military ability has become extinct, the true reason is that the old methods of warfare were not good and no one has been able to find new ones. A man newly risen to power cannot acquire greater reputation than by discovering new rules and methods.' Niccolò Machiavelli wrote these lines in his famous *Il Principe* five hundred years ago. His philosophy found its justification in the Age of Gunpowder. It was considered the end of ends.

* * *

The world refuses to stand still.

'Today the world's a safer place,' some experts tell us. The Nuclear Age has stopped conflict and combat being dependent on the roll of a dice. No longer is there a call for massive armies to conquer or deter. Everything has changed with the present formula, which has simplified the old equation of 'God is on the side of the big battalions' and replaced it with 'One man – one plane – one bomb'.

Once again, we ask ourselves: is this the end? I doubt it – there is no limit to the ingenuity of man when it comes to devising new means to dispense with his fellow man.

The many wars of history shook the world, but didn't quite destroy it.

Let us leave it that way.

Bibliography

Chapter 1

Bibliothèque Nationale, Paris

Gregoire de Tours, Bishop of Tours, *Histoire des Francs*, *c.* AD 538–594

Jordanes (an autodidact Christian Goth) *De originae actibusque Getarum* or *The Origins and Deeds of the Goths*, *c.* AD 551

Deguignes, M. *Histoire Générale des Huns, etc . . .* Paris 1756

Dévignes, G. *Ici le monde changea le maître*, Paris 1953

Gibbon, E. *Die Germanen im Römischen Westreich*, Olten 1935

Gordon, C.D. *The Age of Attila*, Michigan 1960

Grousset, R. *Histoire d'Asie*, Paris 1950

Guizot, F. *L'histoire de la civilisation*, Paris 1856

Hambis, L. *Attila et les Huns*. Paris 1972

Hodgkin, T. *Italy and Her Invaders*, London 1880

Homan, B. *Geschichte des Nibelungenliedes*, Berlin 1924

Homeyer, H. *Attila der Hunnenkönig von seine Zeitgenossen dargestellt*, Berlin 1951

McGovern, W.M. *The Early Empires of Central Asia, a study of the Huns*, Chapel Hill 1939

Maenchen-Helfen, O. *The World of the Huns*, Berkeley 1973

Mierow, C.C. *The Gothic History of Jordanes*, London 1915

Thierry, A. *L'histoire d'Attila*, Paris 1856

Thompson, E.A. *A History of Attila and the Huns*, Oxford 1948

Chapter 2

Barbaro, N. *Giornale dell' assedia di Constantinopoli*, (repr.) Venice 1856
Finlay, G. *A History of Greece*, London 1877
Ganem, H. *Les Sultans Ottomans*, Paris 1902
Gfrörer, A.F. *Byzantinische Geschichten*, Frankfurt 1872
Gibbon, E. *The Decline and Fall of the Roman Empire*, Dent, 1960–2
Mijatovich, C. *Constantine, the Last Emperor of the Greeks*, London 1892
Pears, E. *The Destruction of the Greek Empire and the Story of the Capture of Constantinople, London 1903*
Schlumberger, G. *Le Siège, la Prise et le Sac de Constantinople par les Turcs en 1453*, Paris 1914
Vlasto, E.A. *Les Derniers Jours de Constantinople*, Paris 1883

Chapter 3

Archives Nationales, Paris
Revue de l'Institut Napoléon, Paris
Bainville, J. *Napoléon*, Paris 1931
Bibl, V. *François II, beau-père de Napoléon*, Paris 1936
Duff-Cooper, A. *Talleyrand*, London 1932
Fisher, H.L.A. *Napoleonic Statesmanship: Germany*, Oxford 1903
Fesser, G. *Die Schlacht bei Auerstedt und Iena*, Berlin 1986
Fournier, A. *Napoleon I*, Leipzig 1886
Frèche, L. *Dans le sillage de Napoléon, sergent du 24 Reg d'infantrie*, (repr.) Levallois 1994
Kircheisen, F. *Bibliographie Napoléonienne*, Paris 1912
Lefebvre, G. *Napoleon*, Paris 1953
Markham, F.M.H. *Napoleon*, New York 1966

Masséna (Maréchal), *Mémoires*, Paris 1848
Schlosser, F. *Geschichte des 18 Jhdts bis zur Schlacht von Austerlitz*, Heidelberg 1864
Vandal, A. *Napoléon et Alexandre*, Paris 1891

Chapter 4

Ambrose, S.E. *Crazy Horse and Custer, Two American Warriors*, New York 1975
De Water, V.F. *Glory-Hunter: A Life of General Custer*, New York 1934
Frost, L.A. *The Custer Album*, Seattle 1964
Godfrey, E.S. *Custer's Last Battle*, Cent. Ill. Monthly Magazine, vol. XLIII, 1892
Kuhlman, C. *Legend into History: The Custer Mystery*, Harrisburg 1951
Marshall, S.A. *Crimsoned Prairie*, New York 1972
Utley, R. *Custer and the Great Controversy*, Los Angeles 1962

Chapter 5

Document section, British Library, London
Colenso, F.E. *History of the Zulu War and its Origin*, London 1880
Furneaux, R. *The Zulu War: Isandhlwana and Rorke's Drift*, Philadelphia 1963
Lloyd, A. *The Zulu War*, London 1973
Morris, D.R. *The Washing of the Spears*, New York, 1965
Smith-Dorrien, H.L. *My Forty-Eight Years in the Service*, London 1925
Wood, Sir E. *From Midshipman to Field Marshal*, London 1906

Chapter 6

I am indebted to those who, during my many visits to the

Irish Republic and Ulster as a correspondent, helped me understand and showed me the sights. My special thanks go to Robert Kee, author and former colleague.

Contemporary newspaper and magazine articles
Document section, British Library, London
Catholic Bulletin, *Easter Week and After, eye-witness accounts*, 1916
Caulfield, Max, *The Easter Rebellion*, London 1964
McHugh, Roger, *Dublin 1916*, London 1966
O'Casey, Sean, *Autobiography*, London 1971–3
O'Malley, Ernie, *On Another Man's Wound*, London 1936
Ryan, Desmond, *James Connolly*, Dublin/London 1924
Irish Times, *Sinn Fein Rebellion Handbook*, 1917

Chapter 7

Akten zur Deutschen Auswärtigen Politik, Serie D
Archives Nationales, Paris
Blue Book of the British Government, Basel 1939
Deutsches Historisches Institut, Paris
Izvestia, 27 August 1939
Livre Jaune Français, Paris 1939
White Book of Polish Government, Basel 1940

Abshagen, K.H. *Canaris*, Stuttgart 1949
Borejsza, J.W. *Antyslawizm Adolfa Hitlera*, Warsaw 1988
Dahlerus, B. *Der Letzte Versuch*, Munich 1948
Dahms, H.G. *Geschichte des 2. Weltkrieges*, Tübingen 1965
Deutscher Generalstaab des Heeres, *Feldzug in Polen 1939*, Berlin 1941
Dubiel, P. *Wrzesien 1939*, Katowice 1960
Göldner, P. *Der Feldzug in Polen 1939*, Berlin 1939
Graml, H. *Europas Weg in den Krieg*, Munich 1990
Groscurth, H. *Tagebuch eines Abwehroffiziers*, Stuttgart 1970

Heiber, H. *Hitlers Lagebesprechungen*, 1942–1945, Stuttgart 1962
Henderson, N. *Failure of a Mission*, London 1940
Heusinger, A. *Befehl im Widerstreit*, Stuttgart 1950
Hillgruber, A. *Die Zerstörung Europas*, Berlin 1988
Hoyt, E.P. *The Death of the U-boats*, New York 1988
Jurga, T. *Bzura 1939*, Warsaw 1984
Klessmann, C. *September 1939*, Göttingen 1989
Peis, G. *The Man Who Started the War*, London 1960
Potjomkin, W. *Geschichte der Diplomatie* (Germ. transl.), Moscow 1947
Schmidt, Paul, *Statist auf der diplomatischen Bühne*, Bonn 1949
Schönlein, P./Wollenberg, J./Wyrozumski, J./Ajnenkiel, A. *Menetkel: Das Gesicht des Zweiten Weltkrieges*, Cracow 1991
Vormann, Nikolaus von, *Der Feldzug 1939 in Polen*, Weissenburg 1958

Chapter 8

My father was on the Eastern Front, wounded and evacuated. Some details come from stories told to his young son. I visited the Stalingrad battlefield and I am grateful to many of the military and civilian participants from both sides of this dramatic confrontation who added their own stories to this account. The account of the secret armies of Stalin was first revealed to me in Stalingrad in the mid-eighties; I then came upon recently released Russian files and also found confirmation in the brilliant account by Walter Kerr, who was a correspondent in Moscow.

Adam, W. *Der schwere Entschluss*, Berlin 1965
Carrel, P. *Unternehmen Barbarossa*, Berlin 1963
Churchill, W. *The Second World War*, vol. IV: *The Hinge of Fate*, London 1951

Deutsche Aussenpolitik, vol. 10, Berlin 1961

Doerr, H. *Der Feldzug nach Stalingrad; Versuch eines Operativen Überblickes*, Darmstadt 1955

Drechsler, K. *Vom Überfall auf die Sowjet Union*, Berlin 1983

Dupuy, E. and T.N. *Military History*, New York 1986

Feis, H. *Churchill, Roosevelt, Stalin. The War They Waged*, Princeton 1957

Gehlen, R. *The Service. The Memoirs of General Reinhard Gehlen* (transl. D. Irving), New York 1972

Gerlach, H. *The Forsaken Army* (transl. Richard Graves), London 1958

Gilbert, F. *Hitler Directs His War*, New York 1950

Goebbels, J. *The Goebbels Diaries* (transl. L. Lochner), New York 1948

Goerlitz, W. *Paulus and Stalingrad. A life of Field-marshal Paulus* (transl. Col. R.H. Stevens), London 1963

Grossman, V. *Vie et destin*, Paris 1984

Halder, F. *Generaloberst Halder, Kriegstagebuch*, Stuttgart 1964

—— *Der Russlandfeldzug bis zum Marsch auf Stalingrad*, Stuttgart 1962

Harriman, A. *Special Envoy to Churchill and Stalin*, New York 1975

Heiber, H. *Hitlers Lagebesprechungen, 1942–1945*, Stuttgart 1962

Hillgruber, A. *Kriegstagebuch des OKW 1940–1945, Der Zenit des 2. Weltkrieges*, Mainz 1977

Hoxha, E. *With Stalin*, Tirana 1984

Kehring, M. *Stalingrad – Analyse einer Schlacht*, Stuttgart 1974

Kerr, W. *The Secret of Stalingrad*, London 1979

—— *The Russian Army. Its men, its leaders, its battles*, New York 1944

Krushchev, N. *Krushchev remembers: the last testiment*, Boston 1974

Loewenheim, F.L./Langley, H.D./Jones, M. *Roosevelt and*

Churchill, New York 1975
Medwedew, R. *Das Urteil der Geschichte – Stalin*, Berlin 1992
Schröter, Heinz, *Stalingrad – bis zur letzten Patrone*, Klagenfurt 1955
Seth, R. *Stalingrad: Point of Return*, London 1959
Shtemenko, S. *Gen. Shtemenko Notes from Stavka*, Ministry of Defence Papers, Moscow 1968
Telpuchovski, B. *Die Sowjetische Geschichte des Grossen Vaterland. Krieges*, Frankfurt 1961
Werth, A. *The Year of Stalingrad*, New York 1947

Chapter 9

I am greatly indebted to French General Pierre Gallois, a geostrategist and author of many books, for his detailed outline of the battle, and the political implications. I would also like to thank Gen. Giap, the late Prime Minister Pham Van Dong and Dr Duong Quynh Hoa of HCMC pediatric hospital for their narratives in Hanoi and Saigon during my various visits to Vietnam.

Bibliographie de la guerre d'Indochine, Librairie de l'Armée, Paris
Bergot, E. *Les 170 Jours de Diên Biên Phu*, Paris 1979
Fall, B. *Un coin d'enfer*, Paris 1966
Gallois, P. *Le Sablier du siècle*, Lausanne 1999
Gras, Y. *Deux revers du CEF en Indochine*, Ecole supérieure de guerre, 1971
Grauwin, Cdt. *J'étais médecin à Diên Biên Phu*, Paris 1955
Nguyen Van Thong, *Retour à Diên Biên Phu*, Hanoi 1961
Roy, J. *La Bataille de Diên Biên Phu*, Paris 1963
Sainteny, J. *Histoire d'une paix manquée*, Paris/Amsterdam 1954
Tournoux, J.R. *Secrets d'Etat*, Paris 1960

Index